FLY ME TO THE MOON

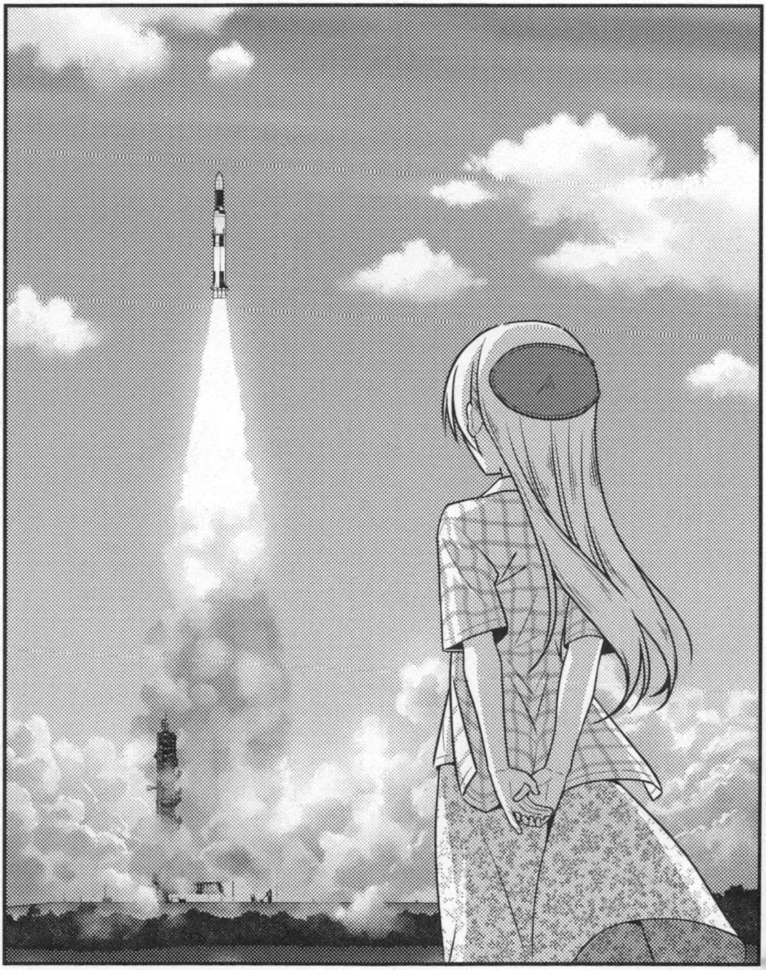

VOLUME 11

KENJIRO HATA

FLY ME TO THE MOON

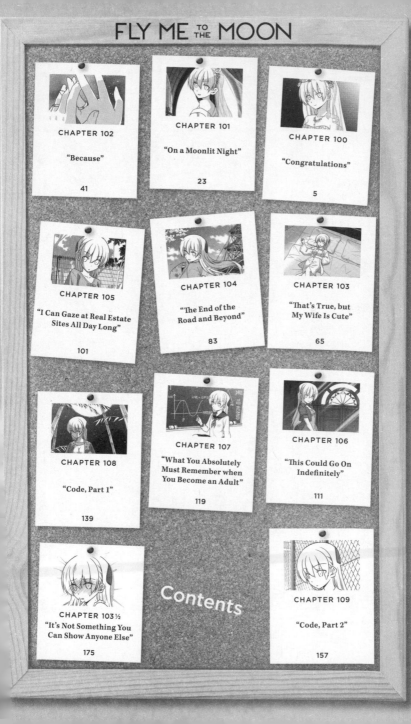

Contents

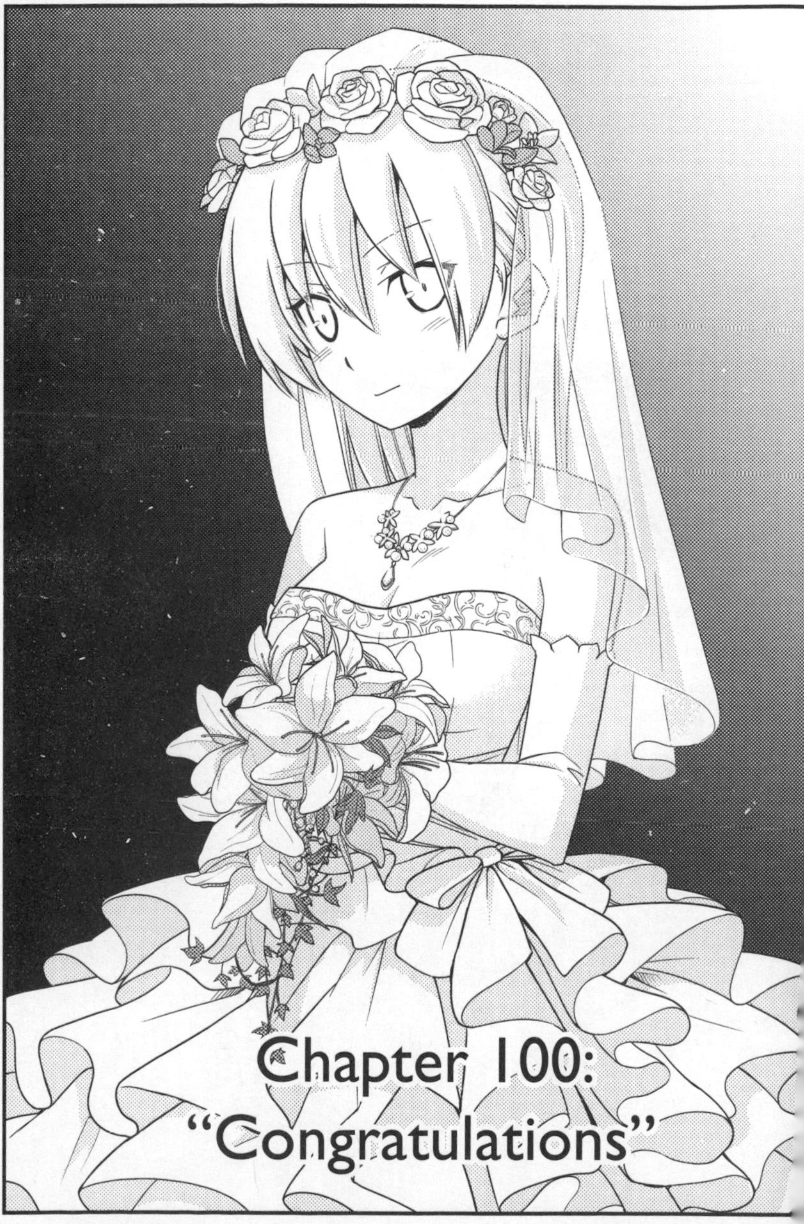
Chapter 100:
"Congratulations"

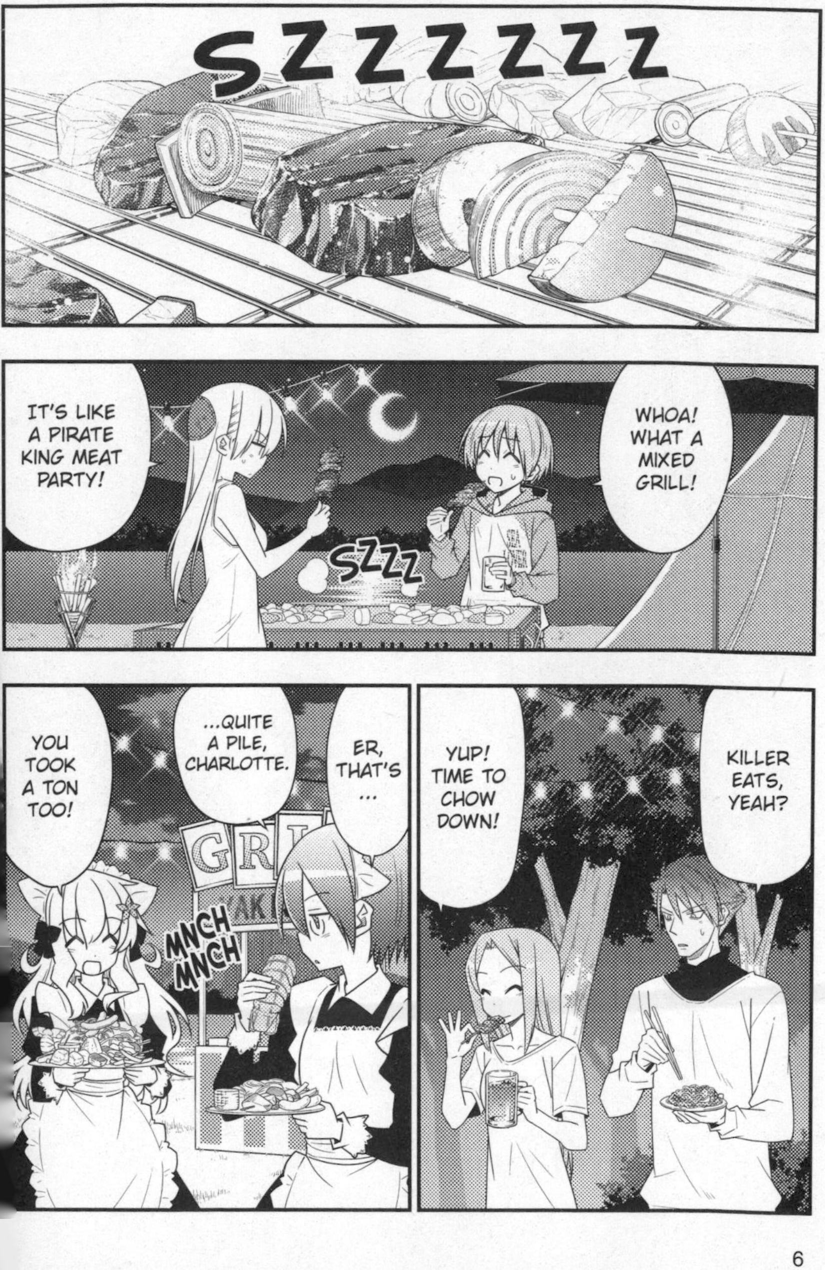
SZZZZZZ
WHOA! WHAT A MIXED GRILL!
IT'S LIKE A PIRATE KING MEAT PARTY!
SZZZ
KILLER EATS, YEAH?
YUP! TIME TO CHOW DOWN!
ER, THAT'S ...
...QUITE A PILE, CHARLOTTE.
YOU TOOK A TON TOO!
MNCH MNCH

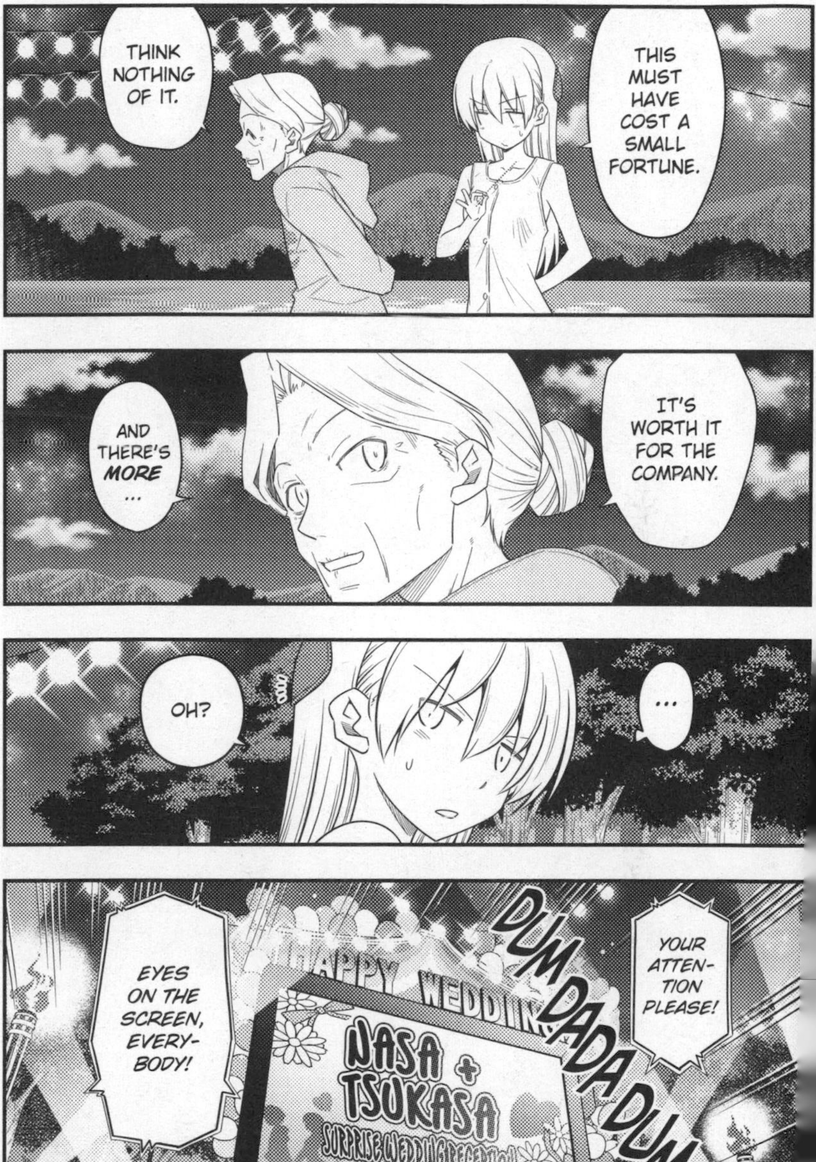
THIS MUST HAVE COST A SMALL FORTUNE.
THINK NOTHING OF IT.
IT'S WORTH IT FOR THE COMPANY.
AND THERE'S MORE ...
...
OH?
YOUR ATTENTION PLEASE!
DUM DADA DUM
HAPPY WEDDING
NASA + TSUKASA
SURPRISE WEDDING RECEPTION
EYES ON THE SCREEN, EVERYBODY!

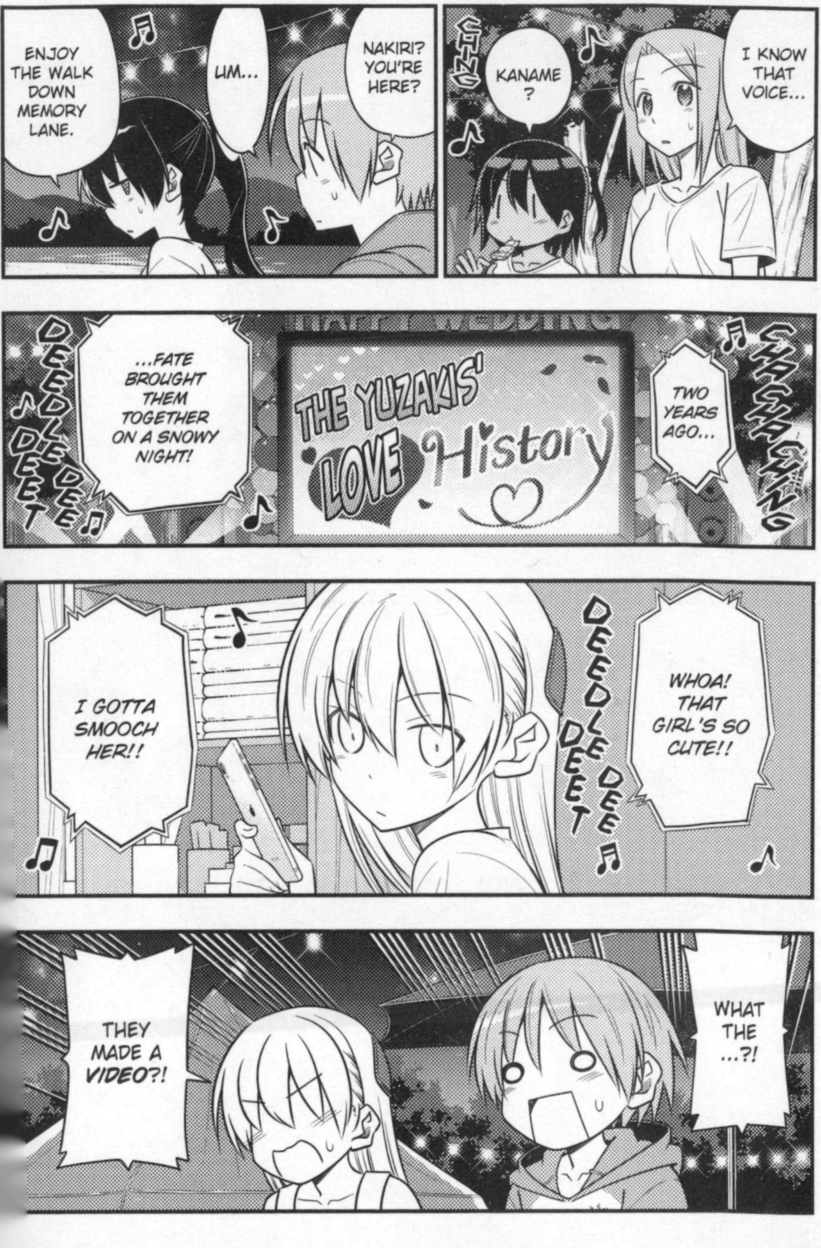
I KNOW THAT VOICE...
KANAME ?
CHING
NAKIRI? YOU'RE HERE?
UM...
ENJOY THE WALK DOWN MEMORY LANE.
CHACHACHING
TWO YEARS AGO...
THE YUZAKIS' LOVE History
...FATE BROUGHT THEM TOGETHER ON A SNOWY NIGHT!
DEEDLE DEE DEET
DEEDLE DEE DEET
WHOA! THAT GIRL'S SO CUTE!!
I GOTTA SMOOCH HER!!
WHAT THE ...?!
THEY MADE A VIDEO?!

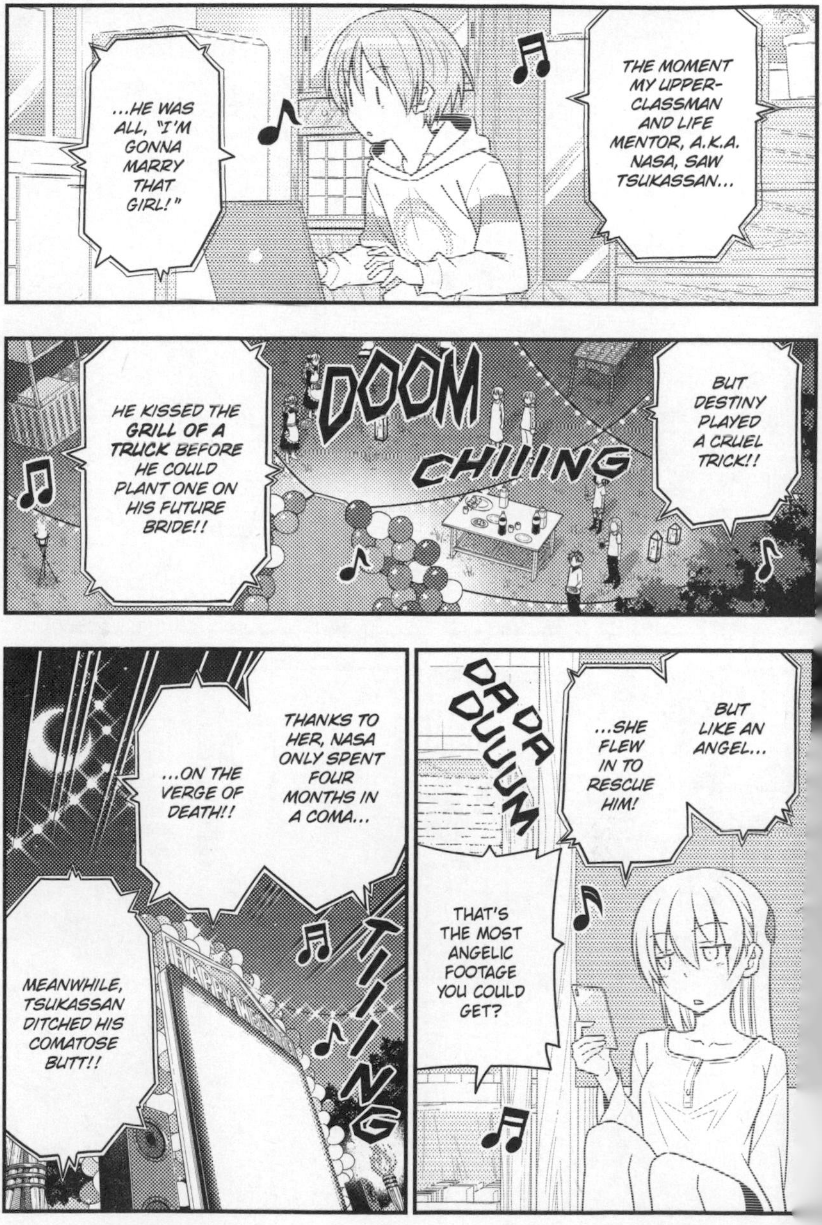
THE MOMENT MY UPPER-CLASSMAN AND LIFE MENTOR, A.K.A. NASA, SAW TSUKASSAN...
...HE WAS ALL, "I'M GONNA MARRY THAT GIRL!"
BUT DESTINY PLAYED A CRUEL TRICK!!
DOOM
CHIIING
HE KISSED THE GRILL OF A TRUCK BEFORE HE COULD PLANT ONE ON HIS FUTURE BRIDE!!
BUT LIKE AN ANGEL...
...SHE FLEW IN TO RESCUE HIM!
DA DA DUUUM
THAT'S THE MOST ANGELIC FOOTAGE YOU COULD GET?
THANKS TO HER, NASA ONLY SPENT FOUR MONTHS IN A COMA...
...ON THE VERGE OF DEATH!!
MEANWHILE, TSUKASSAN DITCHED HIS COMATOSE BUTT!!
TIIIING

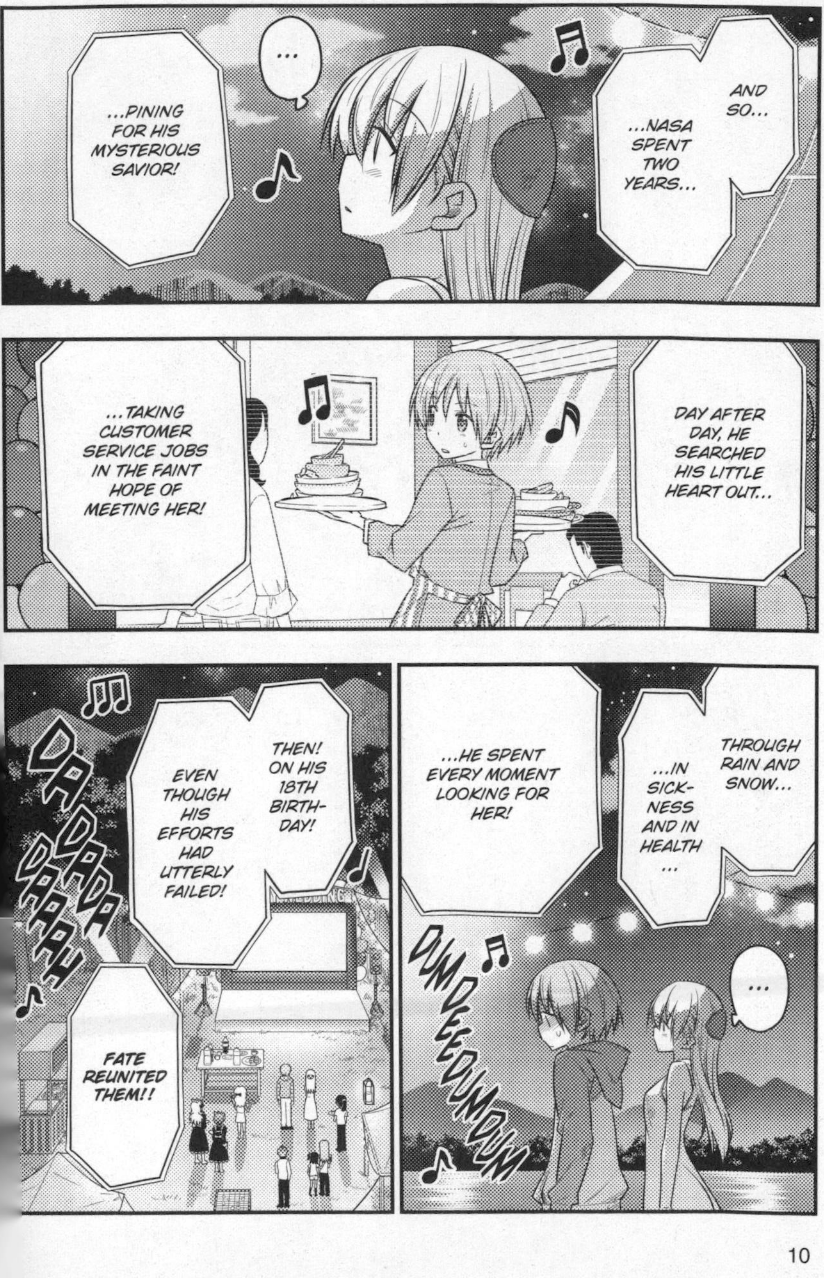
AND SO...
...NASA SPENT TWO YEARS...
...
...PINING FOR HIS MYSTERIOUS SAVIOR!
DAY AFTER DAY, HE SEARCHED HIS LITTLE HEART OUT...
...TAKING CUSTOMER SERVICE JOBS IN THE FAINT HOPE OF MEETING HER!
THROUGH RAIN AND SNOW...
...IN SICKNESS AND IN HEALTH...
...HE SPENT EVERY MOMENT LOOKING FOR HER!
DUMDEEDUMDUM
...
THEN! ON HIS 18TH BIRTHDAY!
EVEN THOUGH HIS EFFORTS HAD UTTERLY FAILED!
DA DADA DAAAH
FATE REUNITED THEM!!

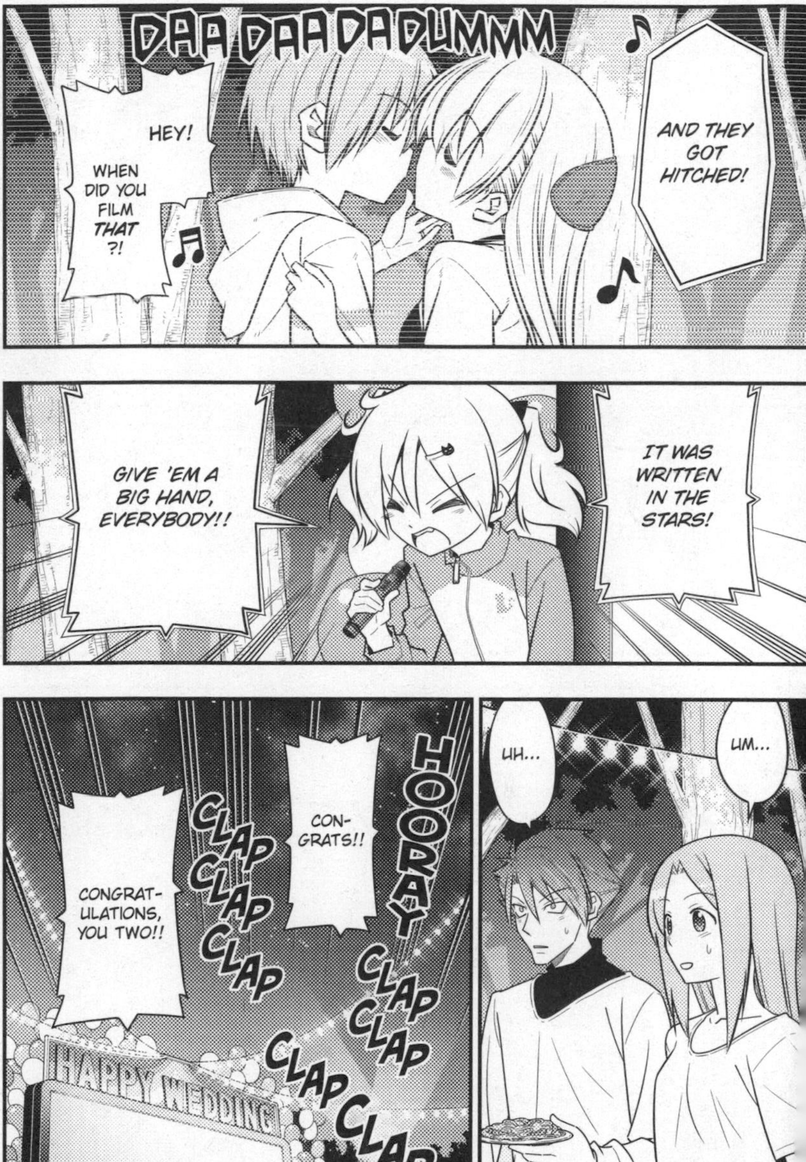
DAA DAA DA DUMMM
AND THEY GOT HITCHED!
HEY!
WHEN DID YOU FILM *THAT*?!
IT WAS WRITTEN IN THE STARS!
GIVE 'EM A BIG HAND, EVERYBODY!!
UM...
UH...
HOORAY
CLAP CLAP
CLAP CLAP
CON-GRATS!!
CLAP CLAP CLAP CLAP
CONGRAT-ULATIONS, YOU TWO!!
HAPPY WEDDING

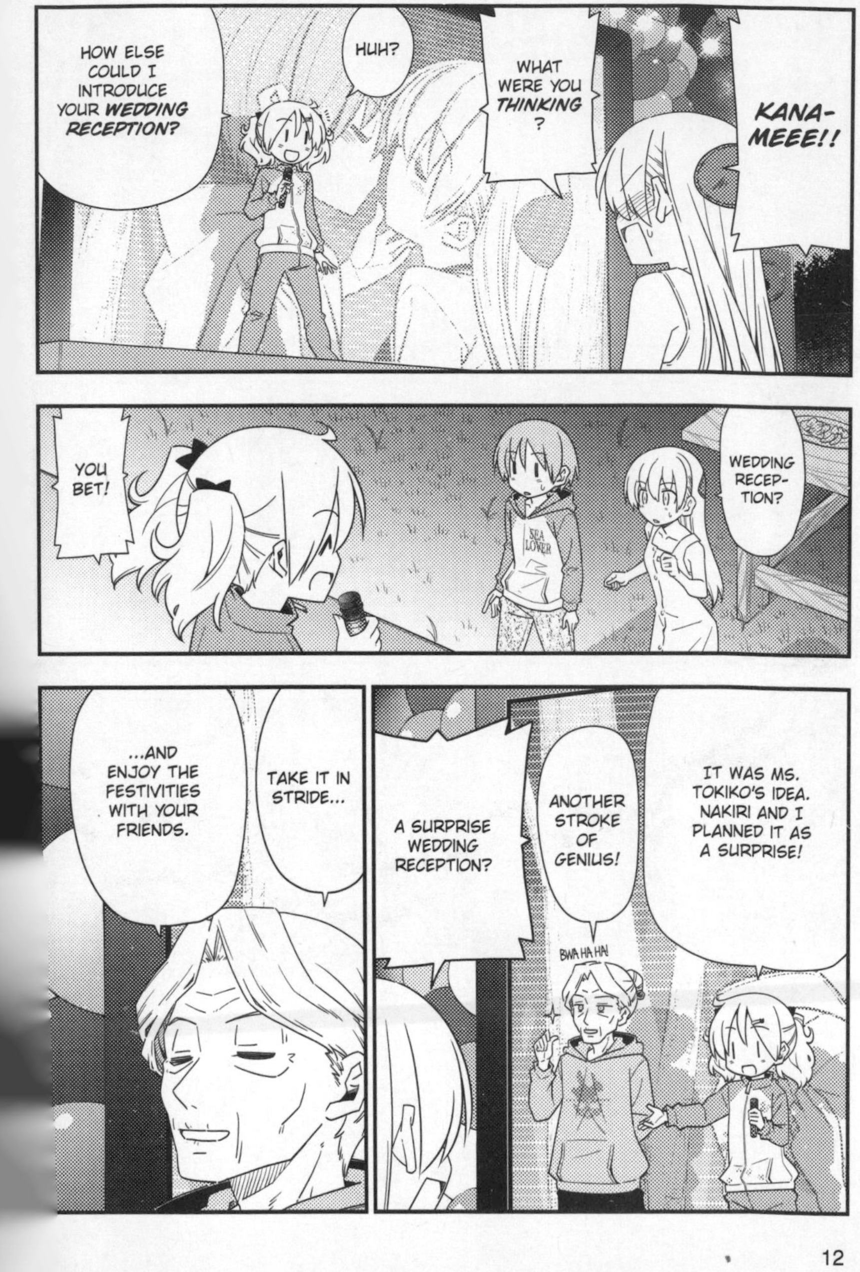
KANA-MEEE!!
WHAT WERE YOU THINKING?
HUH?
HOW ELSE COULD I INTRODUCE YOUR WEDDING RECEPTION?
WEDDING RECEP-TION?
YOU BET!
IT WAS MS. TOKIKO'S IDEA. NAKIRI AND I PLANNED IT AS A SURPRISE!
ANOTHER STROKE OF GENIUS!
BWA HA HA!
A SURPRISE WEDDING RECEPTION?
TAKE IT IN STRIDE...
...AND ENJOY THE FESTIVITIES WITH YOUR FRIENDS.

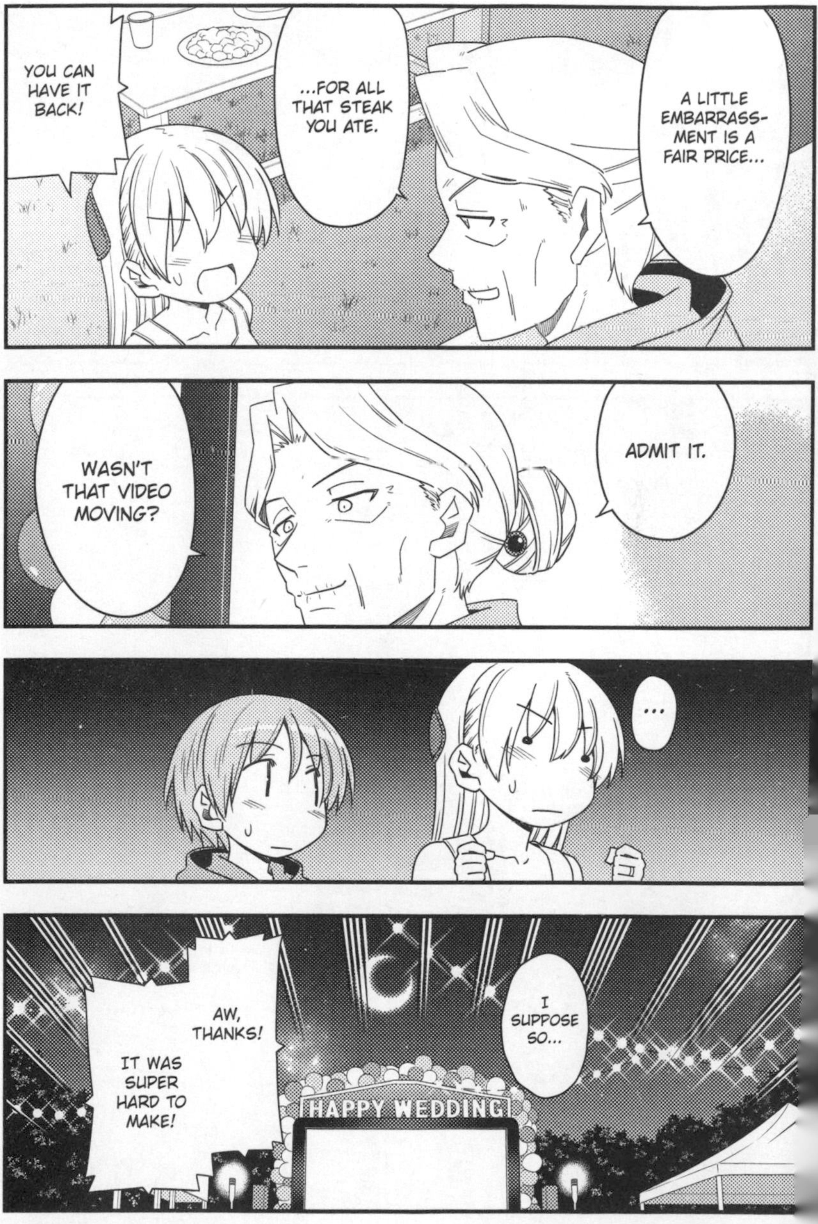
A LITTLE EMBARRASS-MENT IS A FAIR PRICE...
...FOR ALL THAT STEAK YOU ATE.
YOU CAN HAVE IT BACK!
ADMIT IT.
WASN'T THAT VIDEO MOVING?
...
I SUPPOSE SO...
AW, THANKS!
IT WAS SUPER HARD TO MAKE!
HAPPY WEDDING

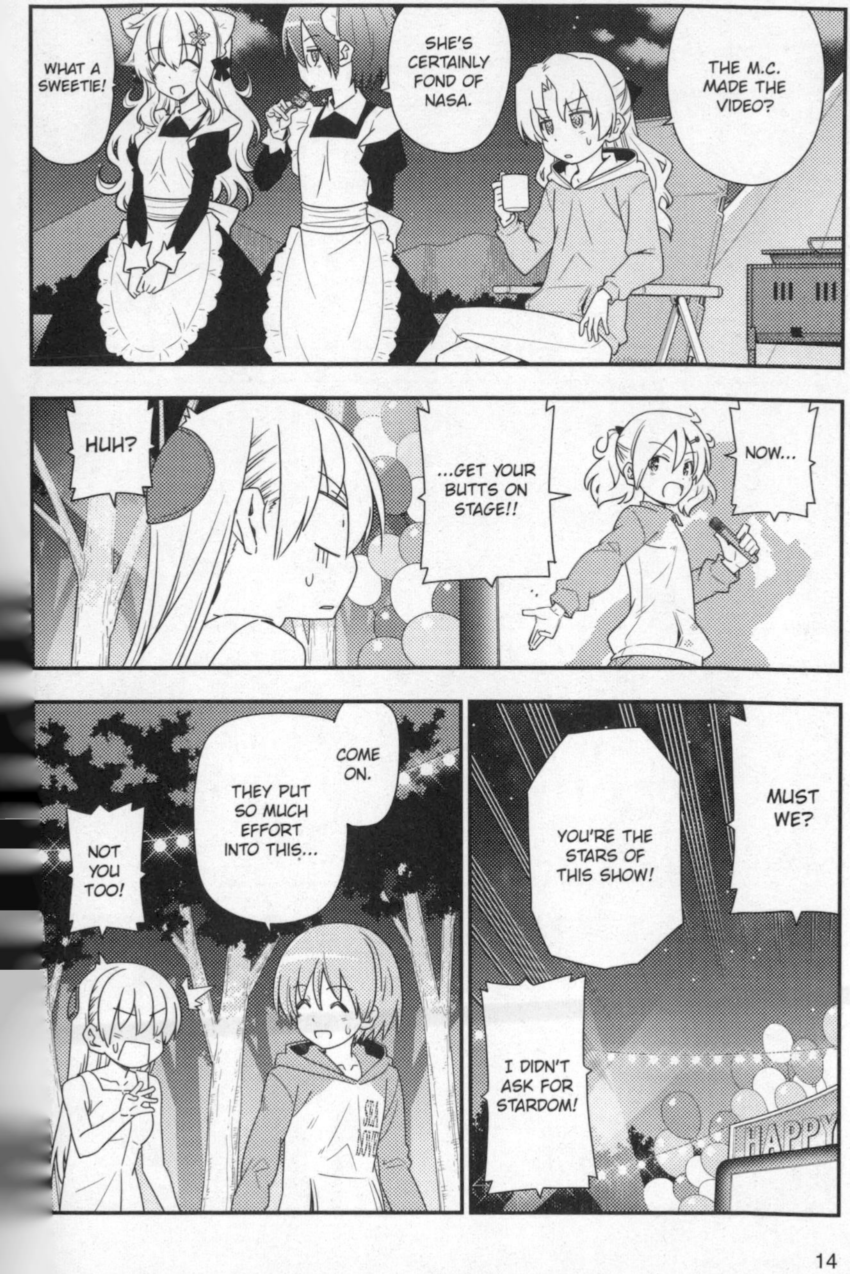
THE M.C. MADE THE VIDEO?
SHE'S CERTAINLY FOND OF NASA.
WHAT A SWEETIE!
NOW...
...GET YOUR BUTTS ON STAGE!!
HUH?
MUST WE?
YOU'RE THE STARS OF THIS SHOW!
I DIDN'T ASK FOR STARDOM!
HAPPY
COME ON.
THEY PUT SO MUCH EFFORT INTO THIS...
NOT YOU TOO!

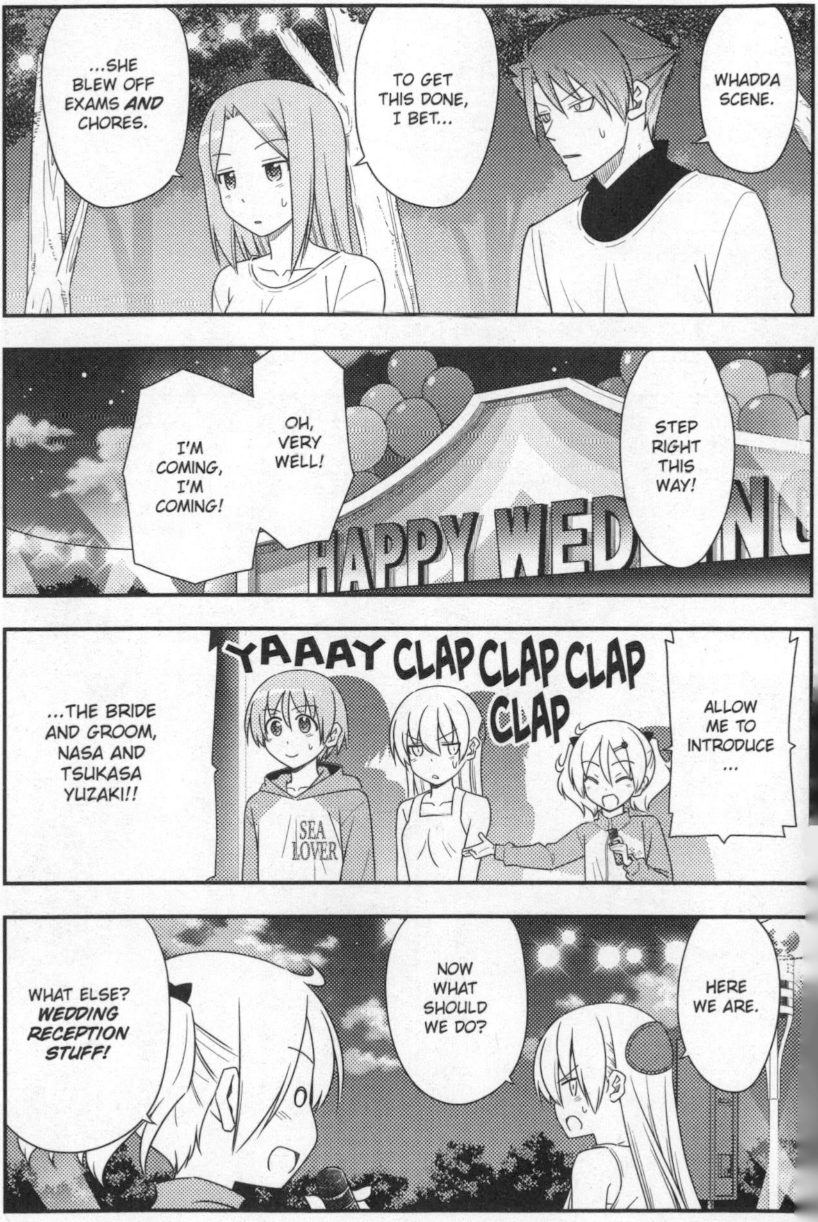
WHADDA SCENE.
TO GET THIS DONE, I BET...
...SHE BLEW OFF EXAMS *AND* CHORES.
STEP RIGHT THIS WAY!
OH, VERY WELL!
I'M COMING, I'M COMING!
HAPPY WED
ALLOW ME TO INTRODUCE...
YAAAY CLAP CLAP CLAP CLAP
...THE BRIDE AND GROOM, NASA AND TSUKASA YUZAKI!!
SEA LOVER
HERE WE ARE.
NOW WHAT SHOULD WE DO?
WHAT ELSE? ***WEDDING RECEPTION STUFF!***

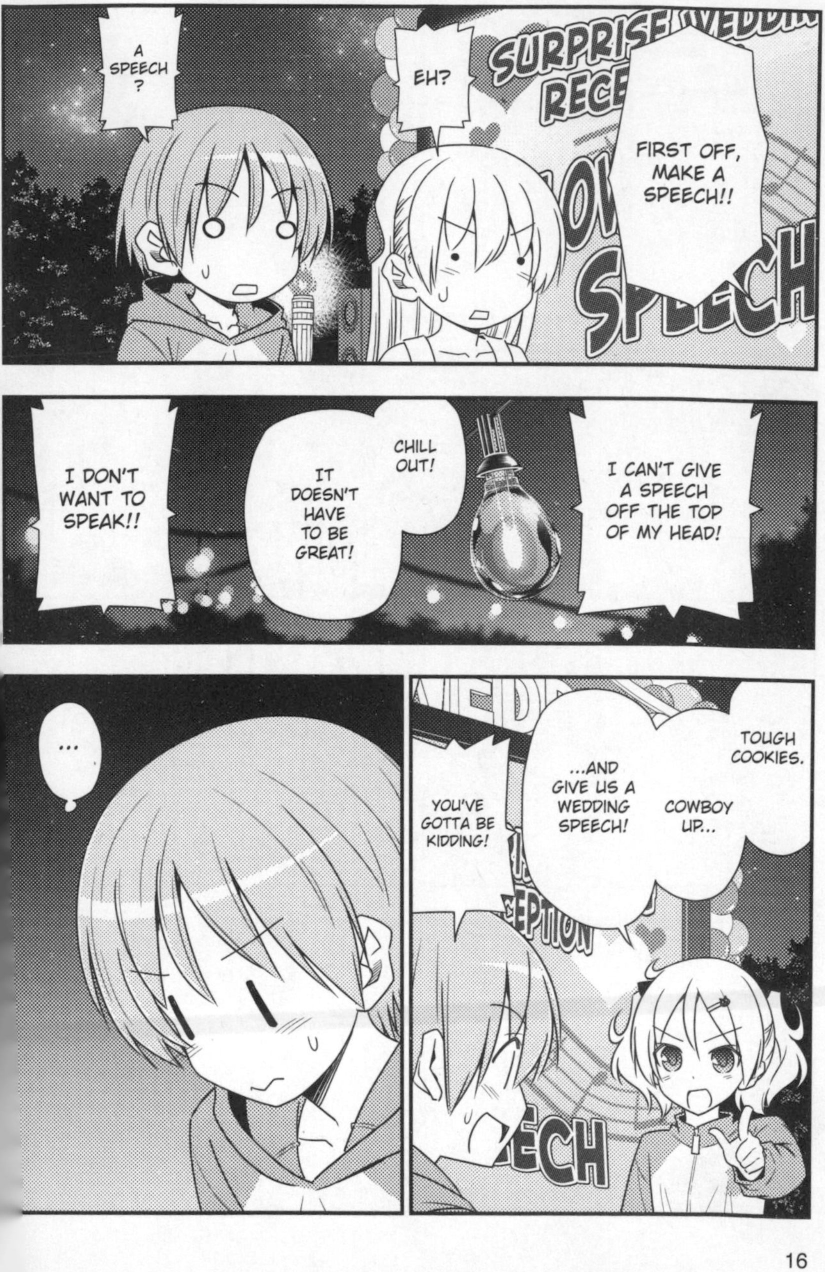
FIRST OFF, MAKE A SPEECH!!
SURPRISE
SPEECH
EH?
A SPEECH?
I CAN'T GIVE A SPEECH OFF THE TOP OF MY HEAD!
CHILL OUT!
IT DOESN'T HAVE TO BE GREAT!
I DON'T WANT TO SPEAK!!
TOUGH COOKIES.
COWBOY UP...
...AND GIVE US A WEDDING SPEECH!
YOU'VE GOTTA BE KIDDING!
...

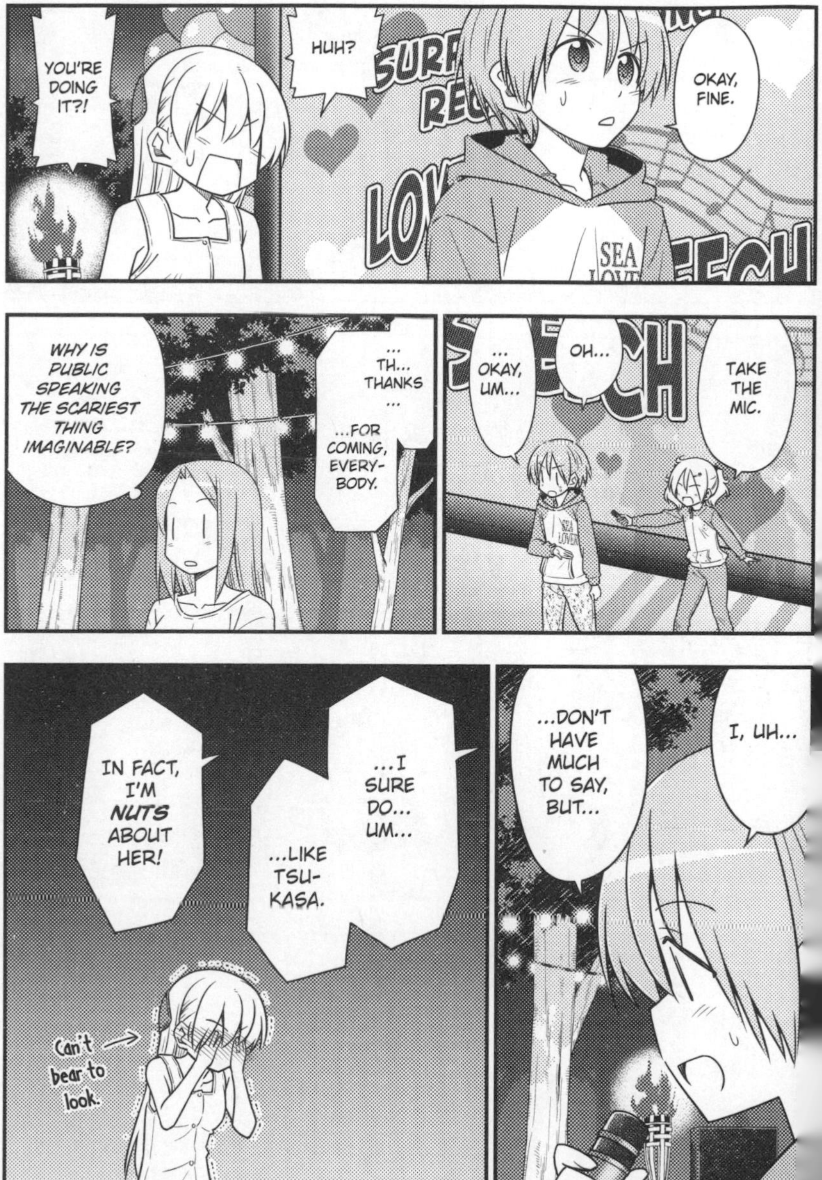
OKAY, FINE.
HUH?
YOU'RE DOING IT?!
TAKE THE MIC.
OH...
...OKAY, UM...
...TH... THANKS...
...FOR COMING, EVERYBODY.
WHY IS PUBLIC SPEAKING THE SCARIEST THING IMAGINABLE?
I, UH...
...DON'T HAVE MUCH TO SAY, BUT...
...I SURE DO... UM...
...LIKE TSUKASA.
IN FACT, I'M NUTS ABOUT HER!
Can't bear to look.

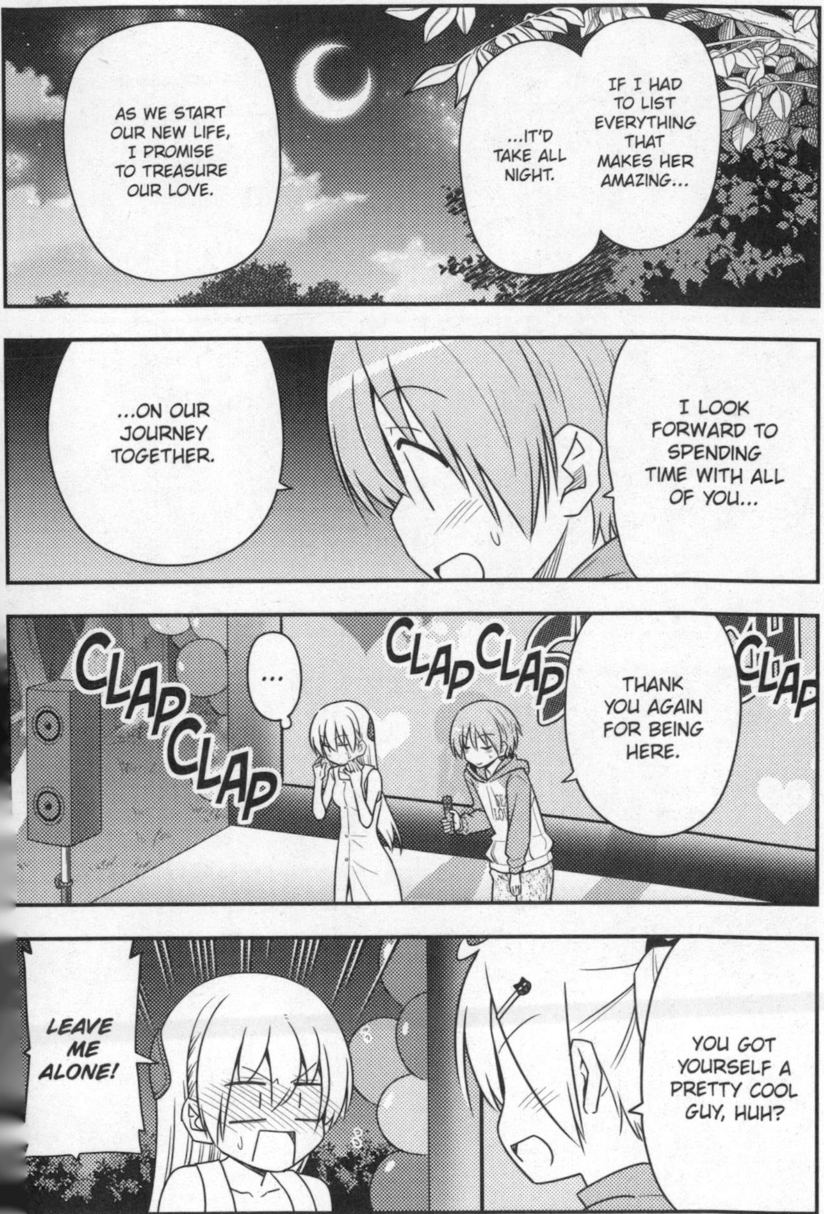
IF I HAD TO LIST EVERYTHING THAT MAKES HER AMAZING...
...IT'D TAKE ALL NIGHT.
AS WE START OUR NEW LIFE, I PROMISE TO TREASURE OUR LOVE.
I LOOK FORWARD TO SPENDING TIME WITH ALL OF YOU...
...ON OUR JOURNEY TOGETHER.
CLAP
THANK YOU AGAIN FOR BEING HERE.
CLAP CLAP
...
CLAP CLAP
YOU GOT YOURSELF A PRETTY COOL GUY, HUH?
LEAVE ME ALONE!

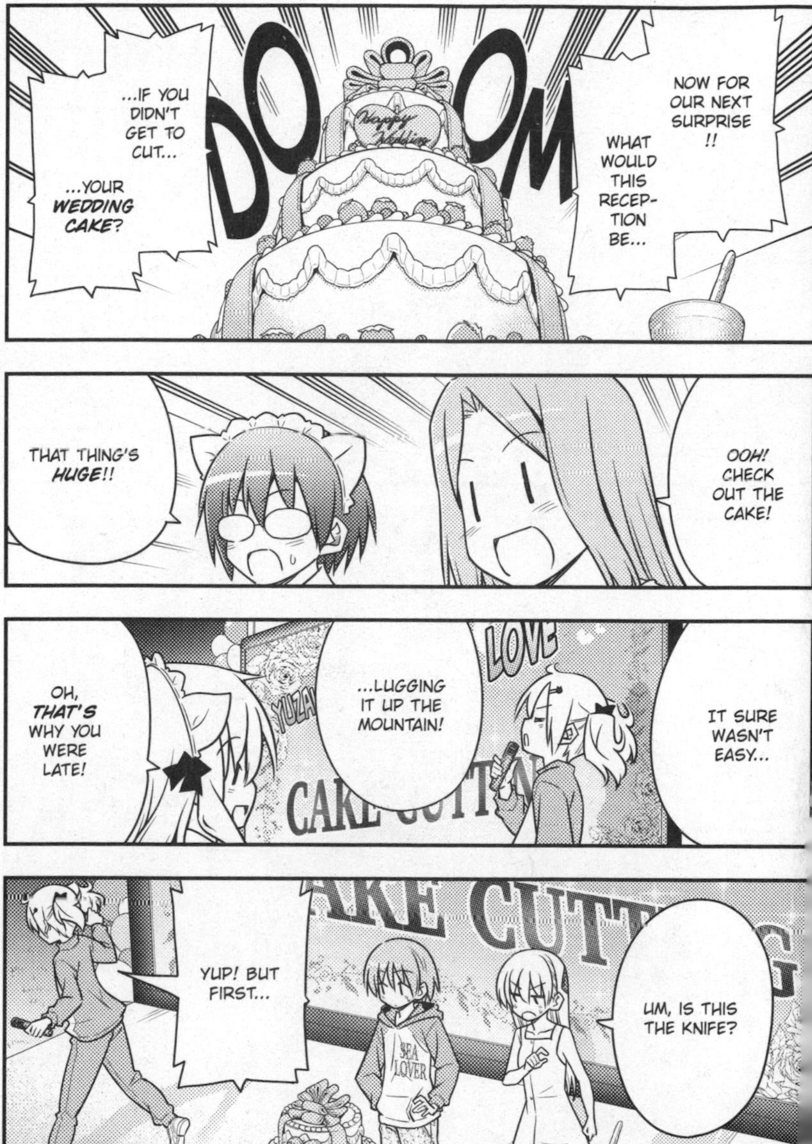
NOW FOR OUR NEXT SURPRISE!!
WHAT WOULD THIS RECEPTION BE...
DOOM
...IF YOU DIDN'T GET TO CUT...
...YOUR WEDDING CAKE?
OOH! CHECK OUT THE CAKE!
THAT THING'S HUGE!!
IT SURE WASN'T EASY...
LOVE
...LUGGING IT UP THE MOUNTAIN!
OH, THAT'S WHY YOU WERE LATE!
UM, IS THIS THE KNIFE?
SEA LOVER
YUP! BUT FIRST...

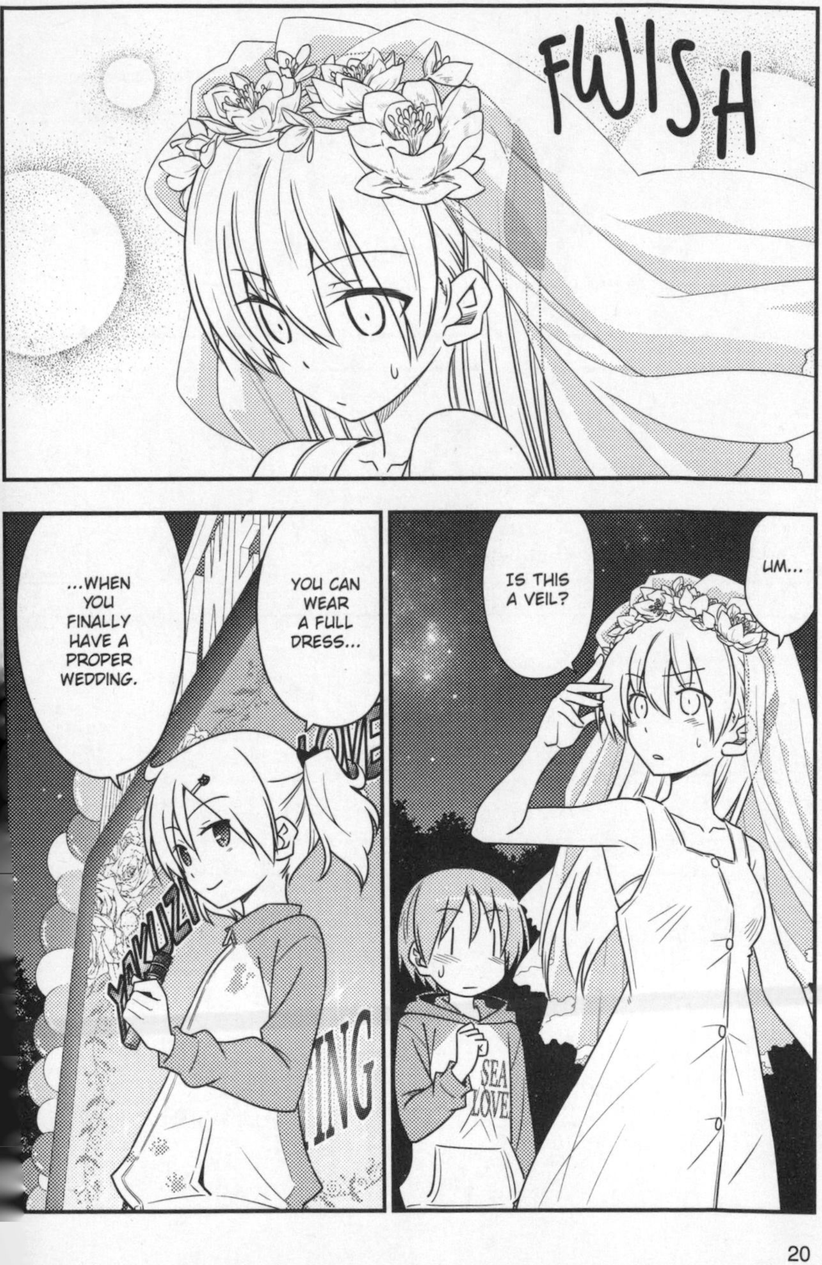
FWISH
UM...
IS THIS A VEIL?
SEA LOVE
YOU CAN WEAR A FULL DRESS...
...WHEN YOU FINALLY HAVE A PROPER WEDDING.

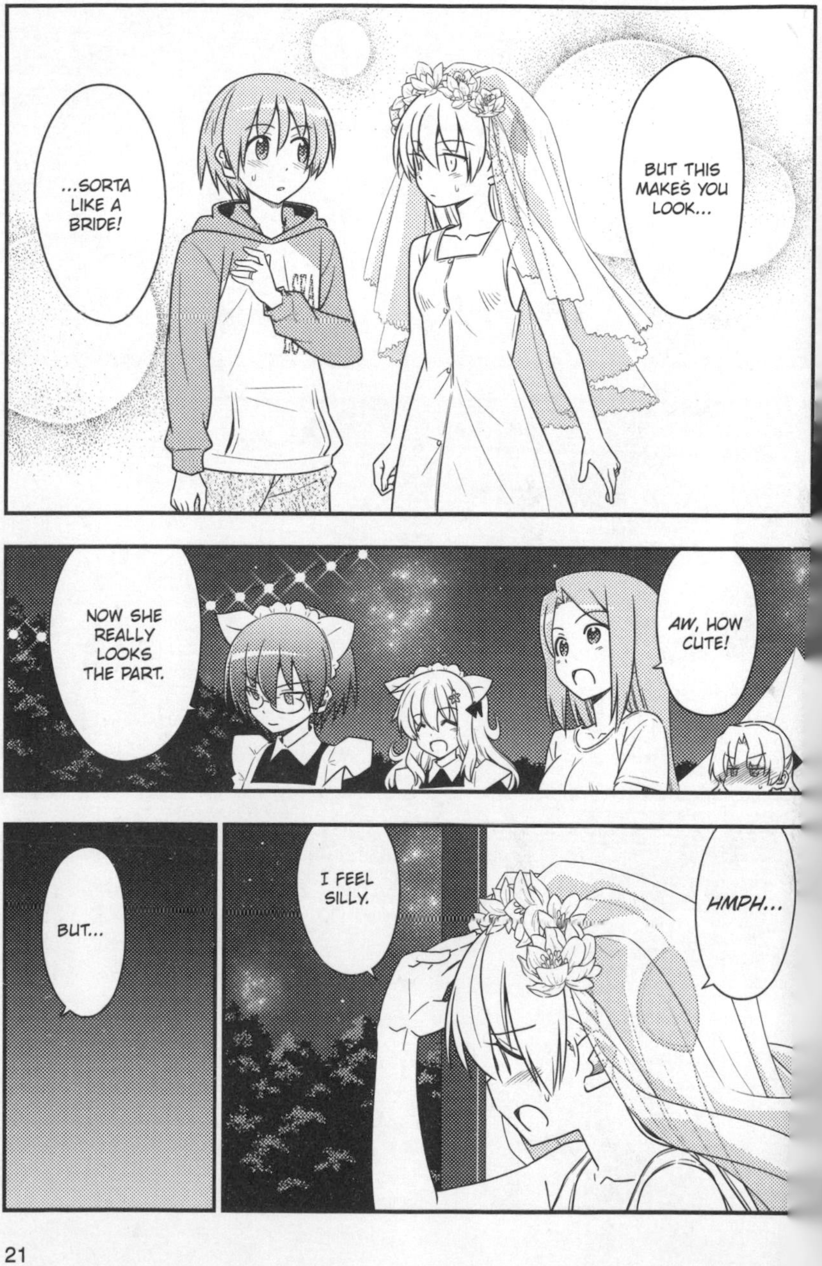
BUT THIS MAKES YOU LOOK...
...SORTA LIKE A BRIDE!
AW, HOW CUTE!
NOW SHE REALLY LOOKS THE PART.
HMPH...
I FEEL SILLY.
BUT...

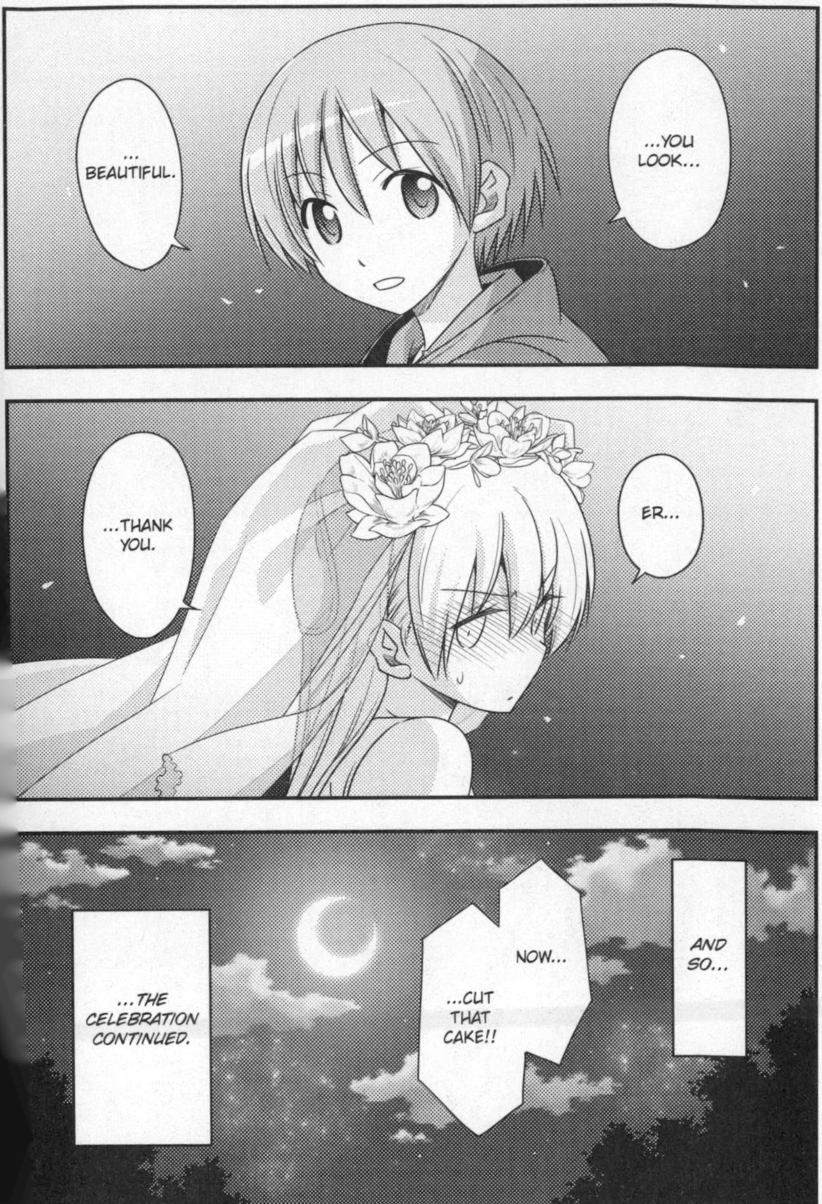
...YOU LOOK...
... BEAUTIFUL.
ER...
...THANK YOU.
AND SO...
NOW...
...CUT THAT CAKE!!
...THE CELEBRATION CONTINUED.

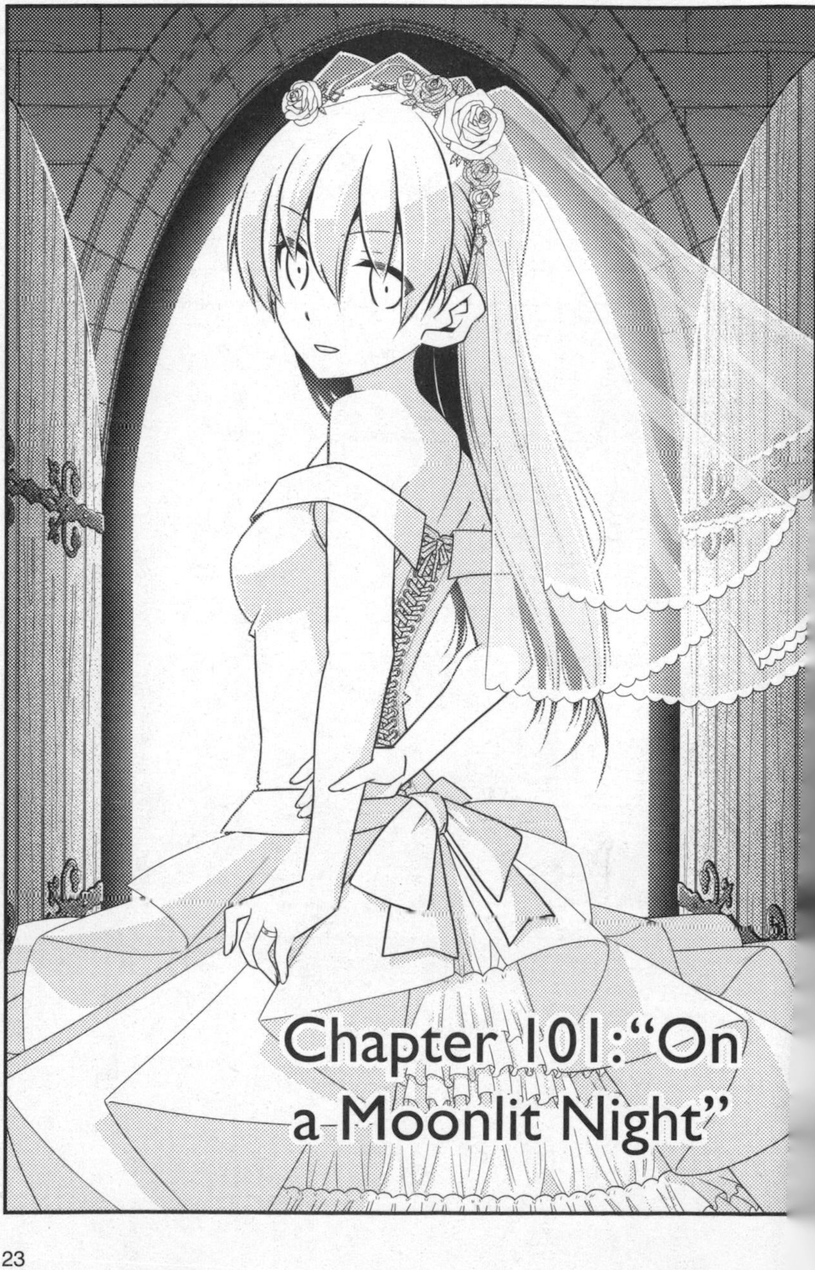
Chapter 101: "On a Moonlit Night"

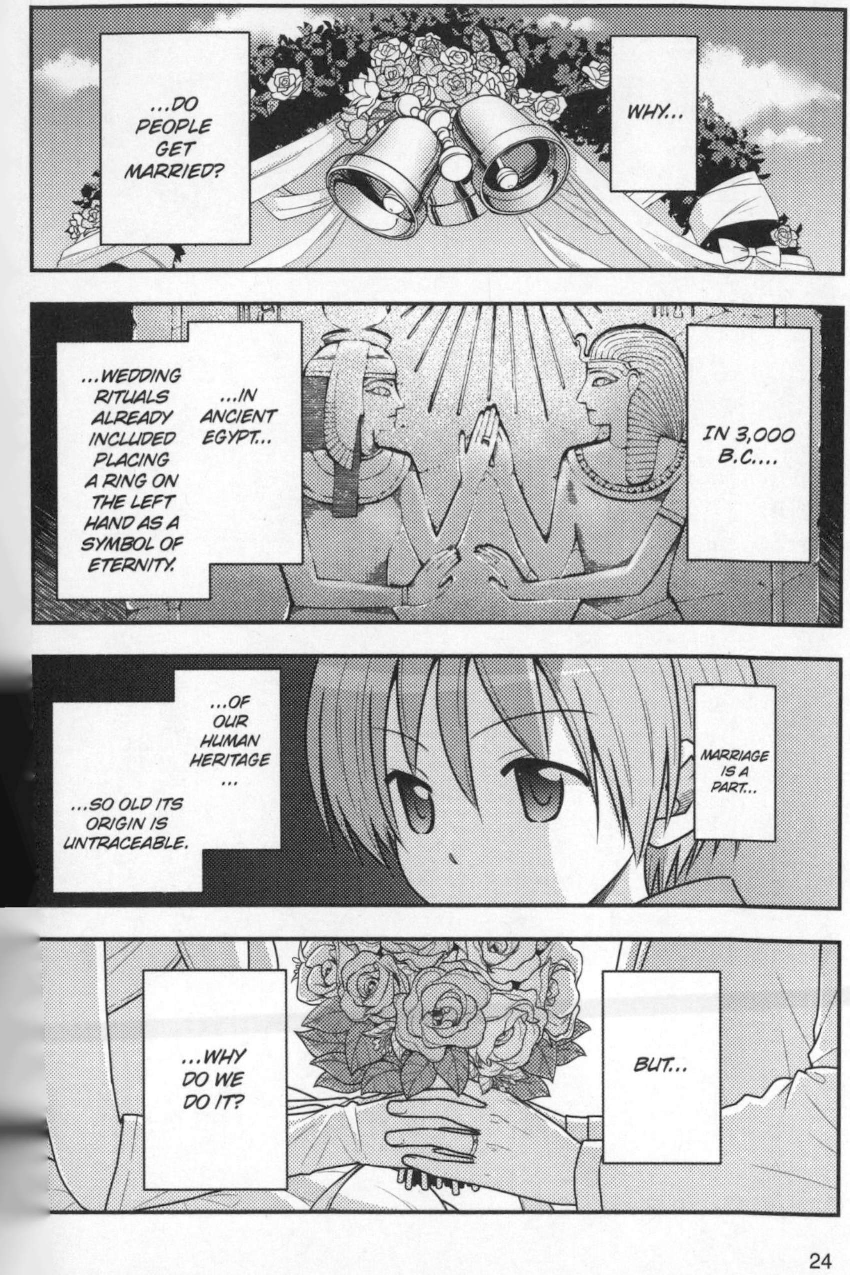
WHY...
...DO PEOPLE GET MARRIED?
IN 3,000 B.C....
...IN ANCIENT EGYPT...
...WEDDING RITUALS ALREADY INCLUDED PLACING A RING ON THE LEFT HAND AS A SYMBOL OF ETERNITY.
MARRIAGE IS A PART...
...OF OUR HUMAN HERITAGE ...
...SO OLD ITS ORIGIN IS UNTRACEABLE.
BUT...
...WHY DO WE DO IT?

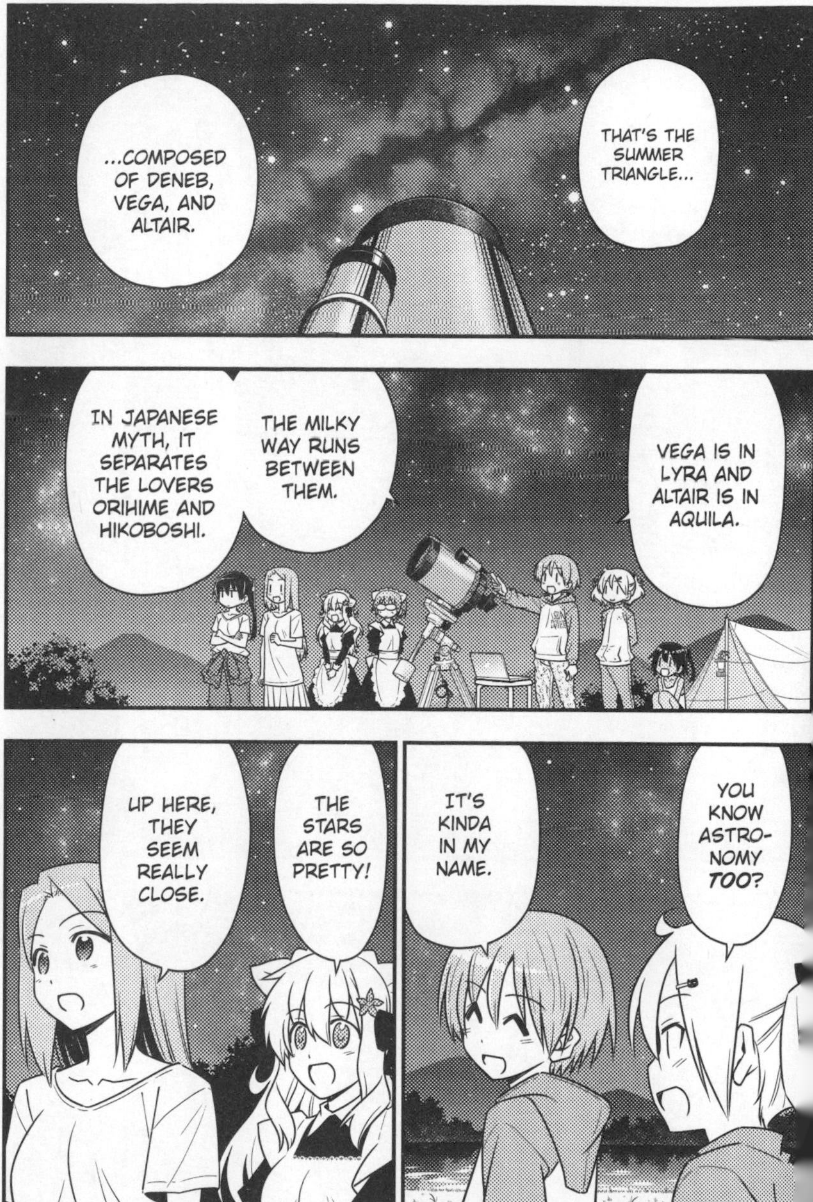
THAT'S THE SUMMER TRIANGLE...
...COMPOSED OF DENEB, VEGA, AND ALTAIR.
VEGA IS IN LYRA AND ALTAIR IS IN AQUILA.
THE MILKY WAY RUNS BETWEEN THEM.
IN JAPANESE MYTH, IT SEPARATES THE LOVERS ORIHIME AND HIKOBOSHI.
YOU KNOW ASTRO-NOMY *TOO*?
IT'S KINDA IN MY NAME.
THE STARS ARE SO PRETTY!
UP HERE, THEY SEEM REALLY CLOSE.

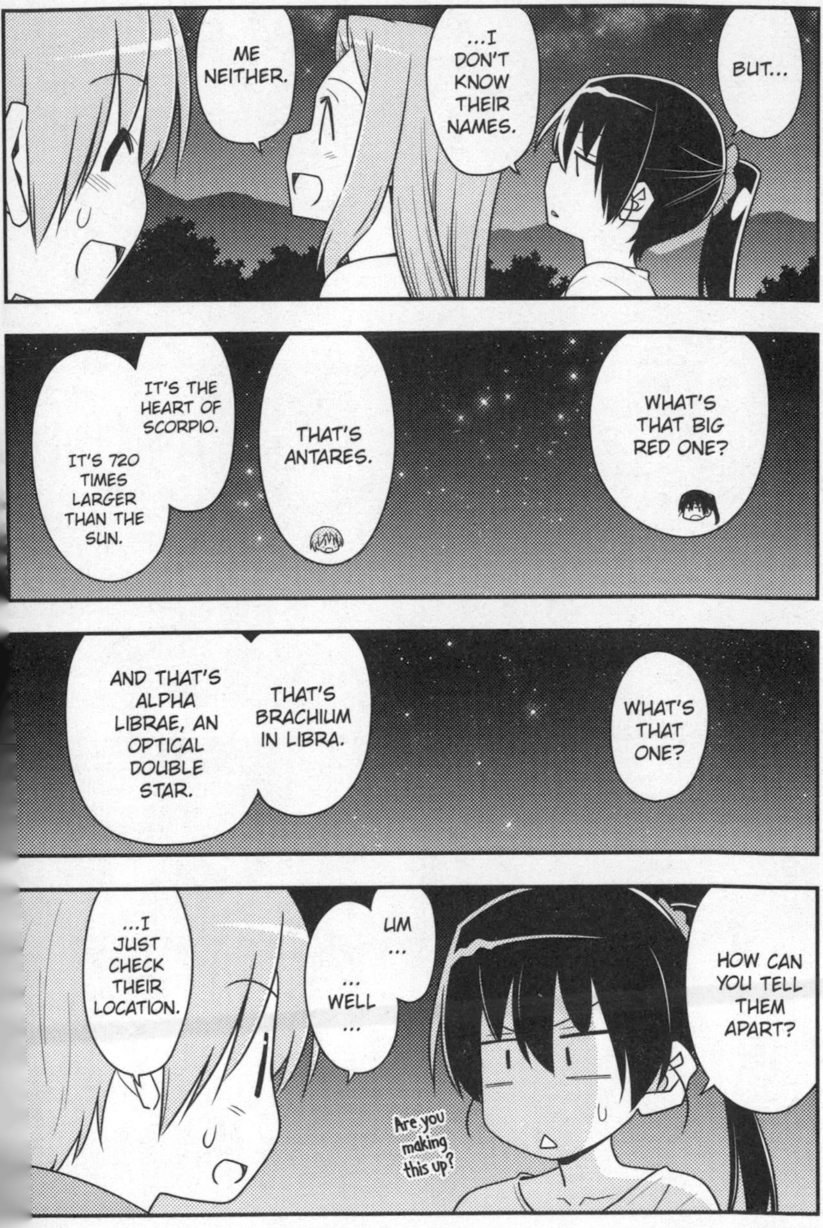
BUT...
...I DON'T KNOW THEIR NAMES.
ME NEITHER.
WHAT'S THAT BIG RED ONE?
THAT'S ANTARES.
IT'S THE HEART OF SCORPIO.
IT'S 720 TIMES LARGER THAN THE SUN.
WHAT'S THAT ONE?
THAT'S BRACHIUM IN LIBRA.
AND THAT'S ALPHA LIBRAE, AN OPTICAL DOUBLE STAR.
HOW CAN YOU TELL THEM APART?
UM... ...WELL...
...I JUST CHECK THEIR LOCATION.
Are you making this up?

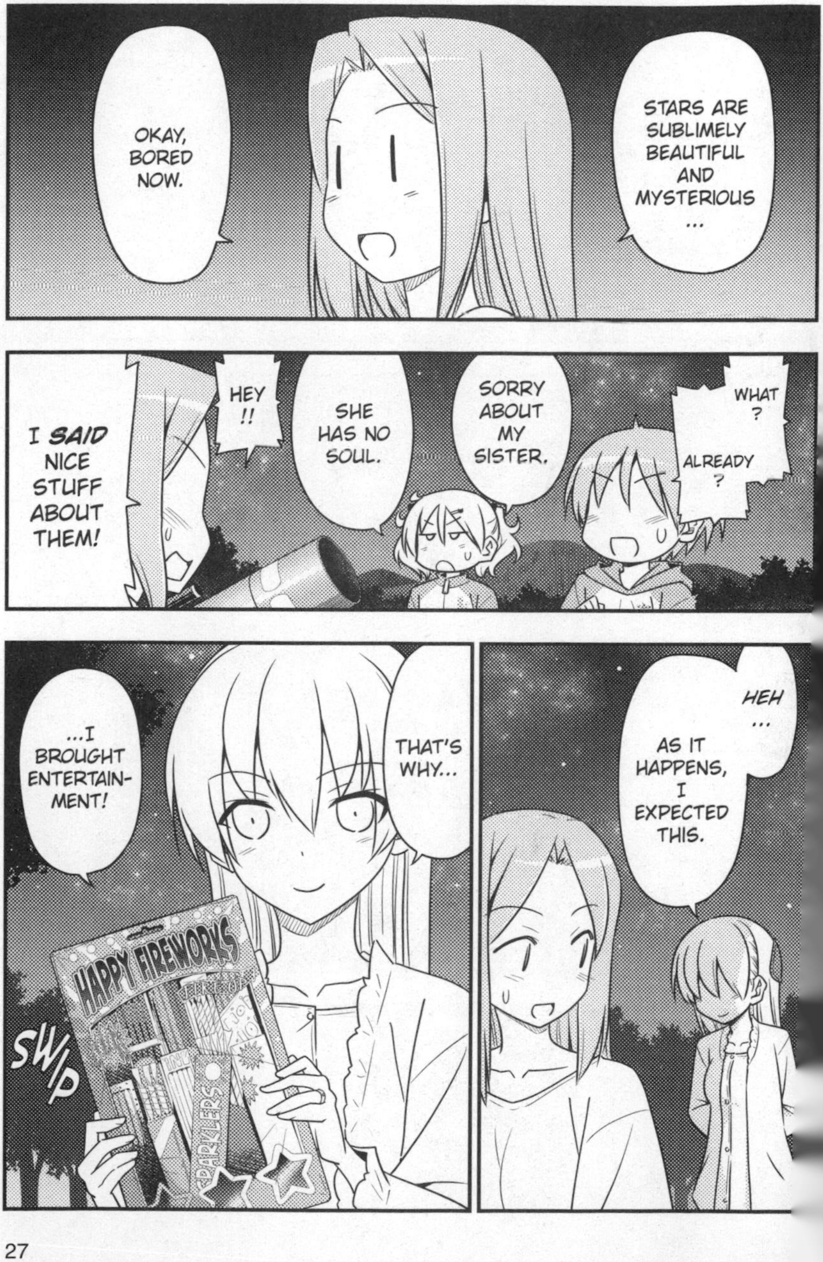
STARS ARE SUBLIMELY BEAUTIFUL AND MYSTERIOUS ...
OKAY, BORED NOW.
WHAT? ALREADY?
SORRY ABOUT MY SISTER.
SHE HAS NO SOUL.
HEY!!
I *SAID* NICE STUFF ABOUT THEM!
HEH... AS IT HAPPENS, I EXPECTED THIS.
THAT'S WHY...
...I BROUGHT ENTERTAINMENT!
HAPPY FIREWORKS
SWIP

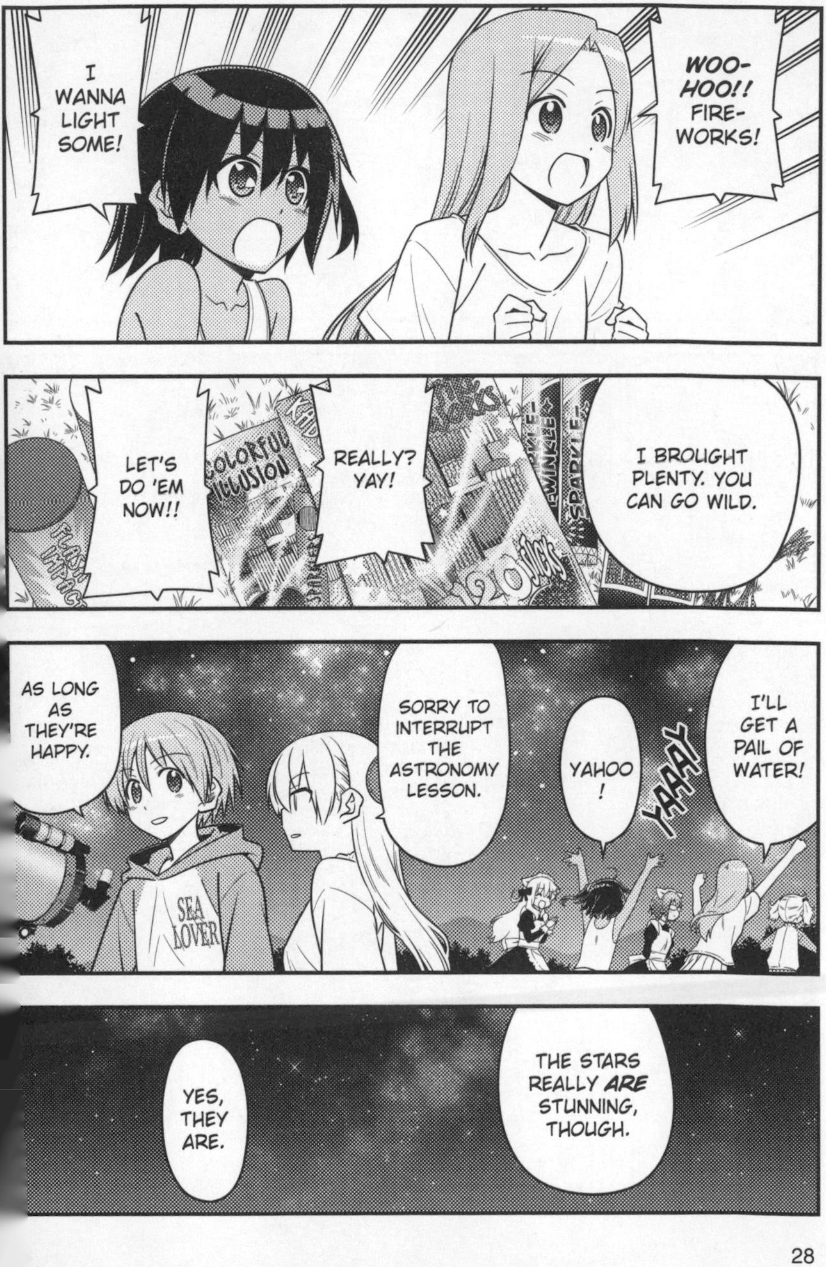
WOO-HOO!! FIRE-WORKS!
I WANNA LIGHT SOME!
I BROUGHT PLENTY. YOU CAN GO WILD.
REALLY? YAY!
COLORFUL ILLUSION
LET'S DO 'EM NOW!!
FLASH IMPACT
TWINKLE
SPARKLE
I'LL GET A PAIL OF WATER!
YAAAY
YAHOO!
SORRY TO INTERRUPT THE ASTRONOMY LESSON.
AS LONG AS THEY'RE HAPPY.
SEA LOVER
THE STARS REALLY ARE STUNNING, THOUGH.
YES, THEY ARE.

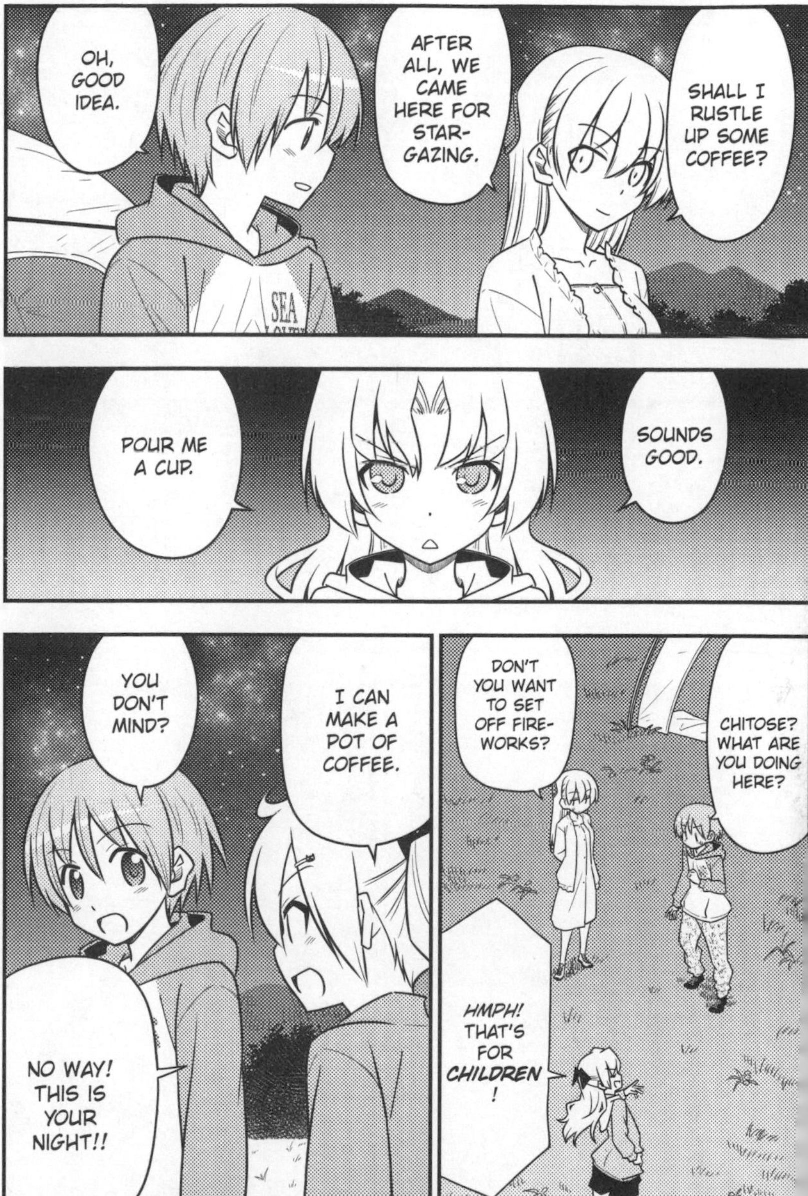
SHALL I RUSTLE UP SOME COFFEE?
AFTER ALL, WE CAME HERE FOR STAR-GAZING.
OH, GOOD IDEA.
SEA
SOUNDS GOOD.
POUR ME A CUP.
CHITOSE? WHAT ARE YOU DOING HERE?
DON'T YOU WANT TO SET OFF FIRE-WORKS?
HMPH! THAT'S FOR ***CHILDREN*** !
I CAN MAKE A POT OF COFFEE.
YOU DON'T MIND?
NO WAY! THIS IS YOUR NIGHT!!

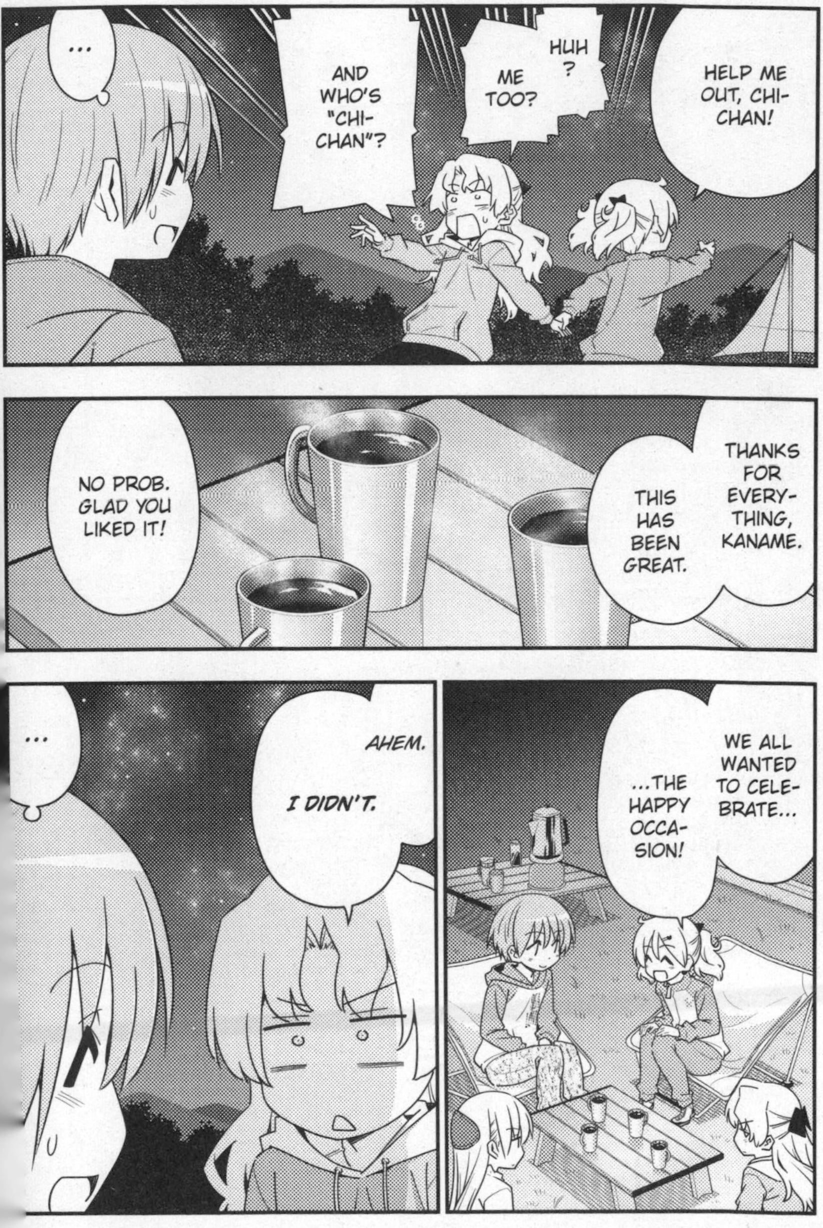
HELP ME OUT, CHI-CHAN!
HUH?
ME TOO?
AND WHO'S "CHI-CHAN"?
...
THANKS FOR EVERY-THING, KANAME.
THIS HAS BEEN GREAT.
NO PROB. GLAD YOU LIKED IT!
WE ALL WANTED TO CELE-BRATE...
...THE HAPPY OCCA-SION!
AHEM.
I DIDN'T.
...

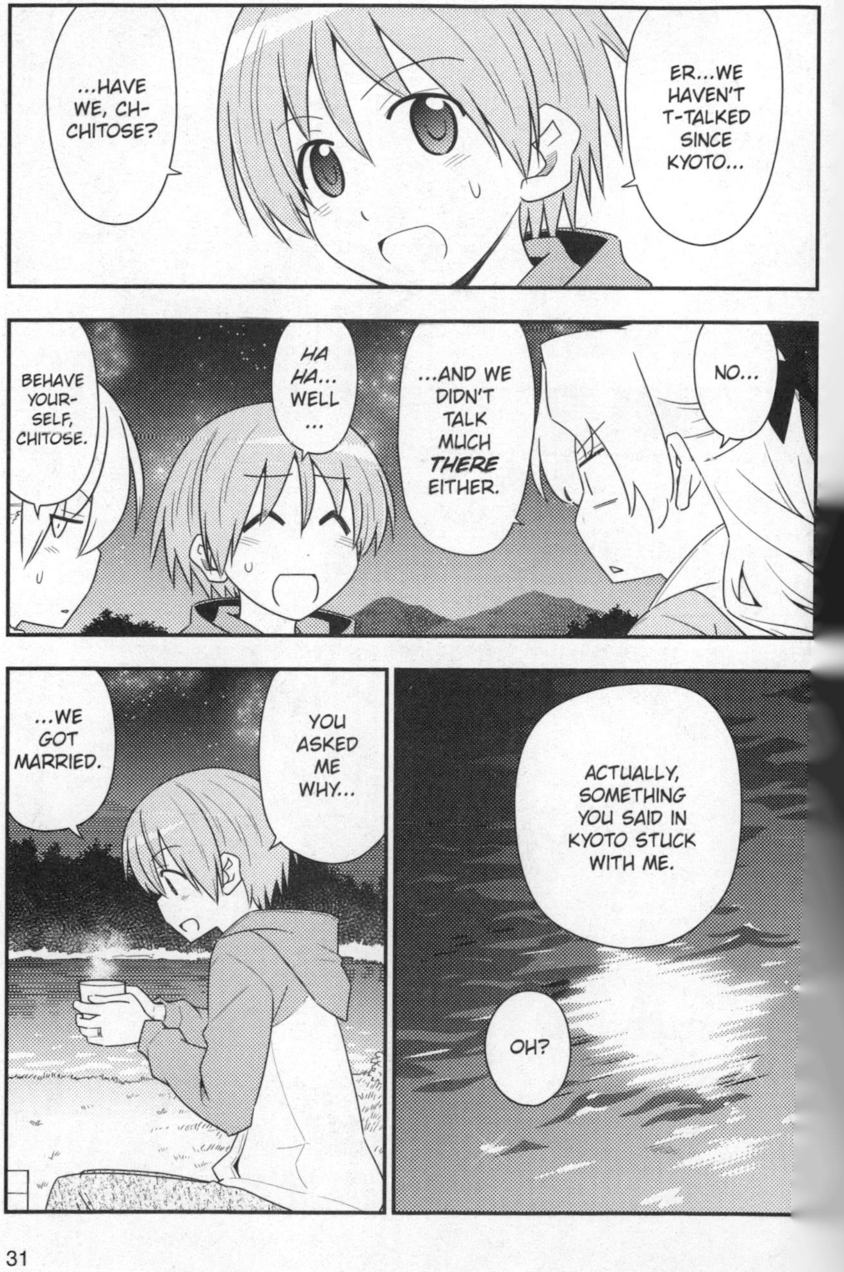
ER...WE HAVEN'T T-TALKED SINCE KYOTO...
...HAVE WE, CH-CHITOSE?
NO...
...AND WE DIDN'T TALK MUCH *THERE* EITHER.
HA HA... WELL ...
BEHAVE YOURSELF, CHITOSE.
ACTUALLY, SOMETHING YOU SAID IN KYOTO STUCK WITH ME.
OH?
YOU ASKED ME WHY...
...WE GOT MARRIED.

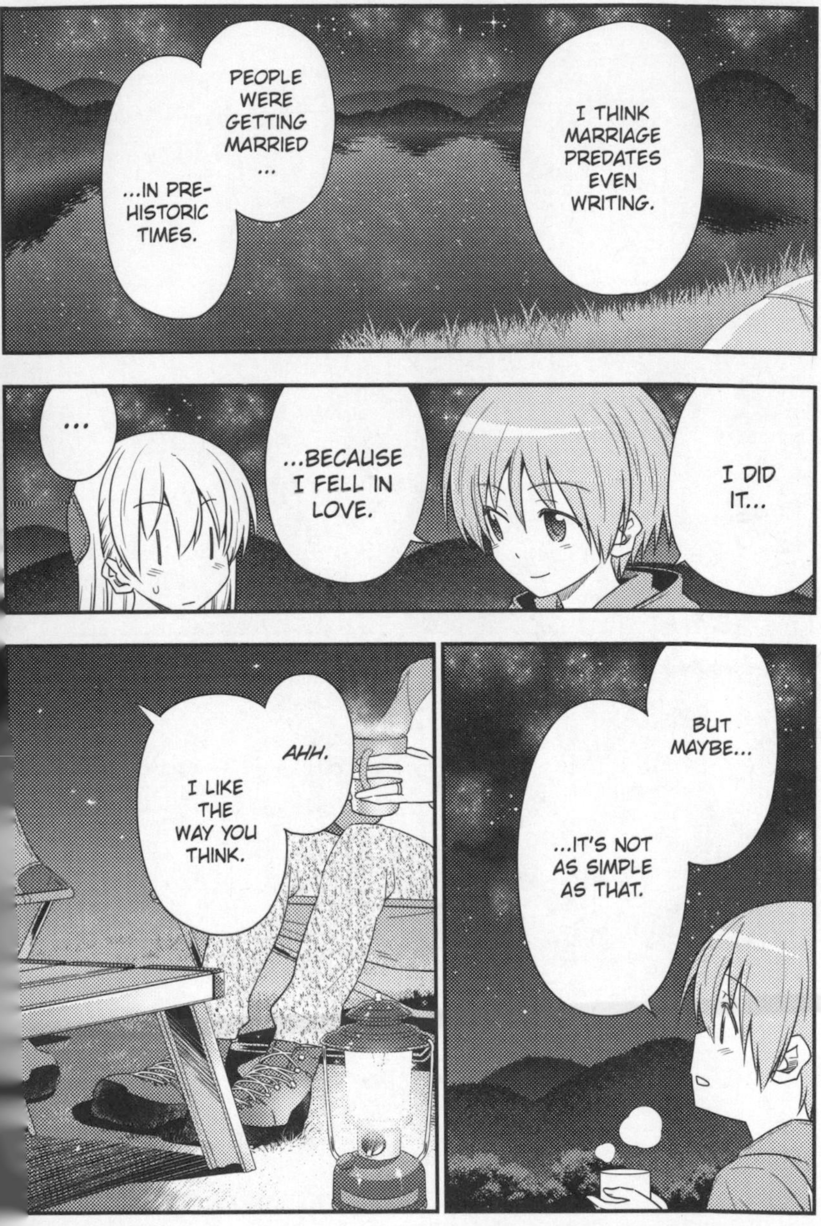
I THINK MARRIAGE PREDATES EVEN WRITING.
PEOPLE WERE GETTING MARRIED ...
...IN PRE-HISTORIC TIMES.
I DID IT...
...BECAUSE I FELL IN LOVE.
...
BUT MAYBE...
...IT'S NOT AS SIMPLE AS THAT.
AHH.
I LIKE THE WAY YOU THINK.

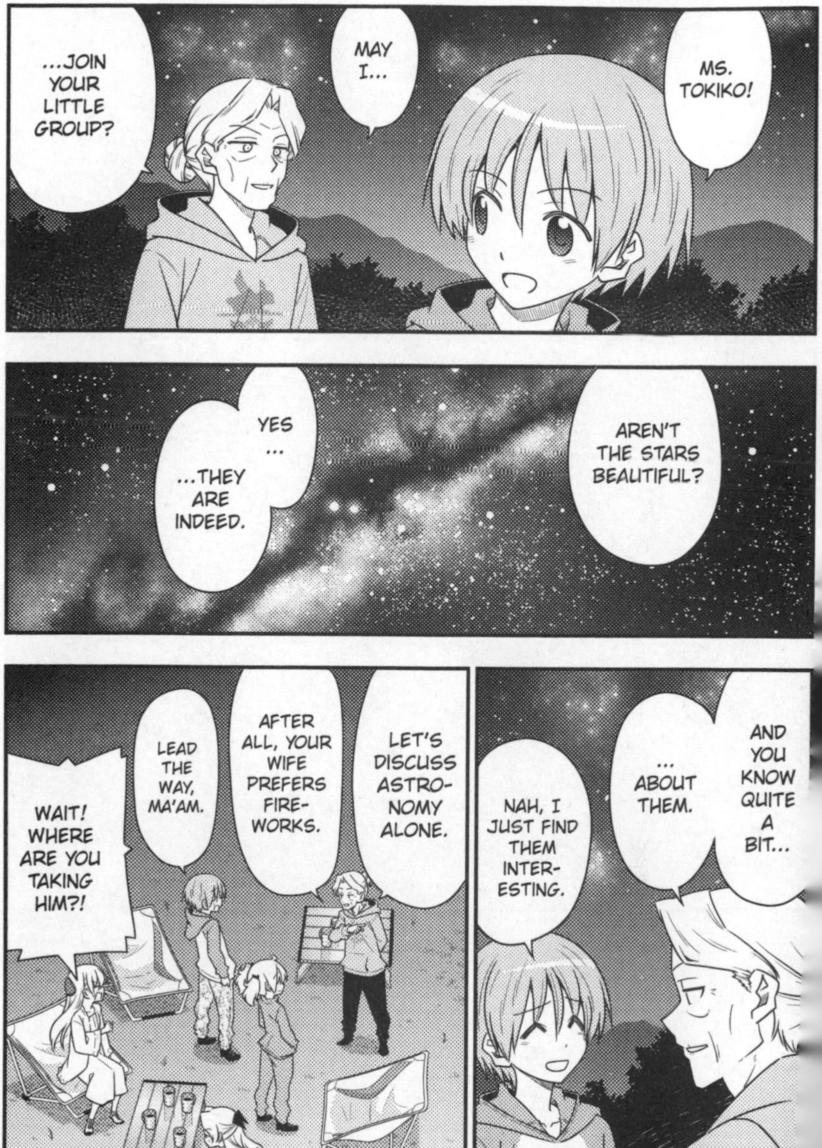
MS. TOKIKO!
MAY I...
...JOIN YOUR LITTLE GROUP?
AREN'T THE STARS BEAUTIFUL?
YES ...
...THEY ARE INDEED.
AND YOU KNOW QUITE A BIT...
... ABOUT THEM.
NAH, I JUST FIND THEM INTER-ESTING.
LET'S DISCUSS ASTRO-NOMY ALONE.
AFTER ALL, YOUR WIFE PREFERS FIRE-WORKS.
LEAD THE WAY, MA'AM.
WAIT! WHERE ARE YOU TAKING HIM?!

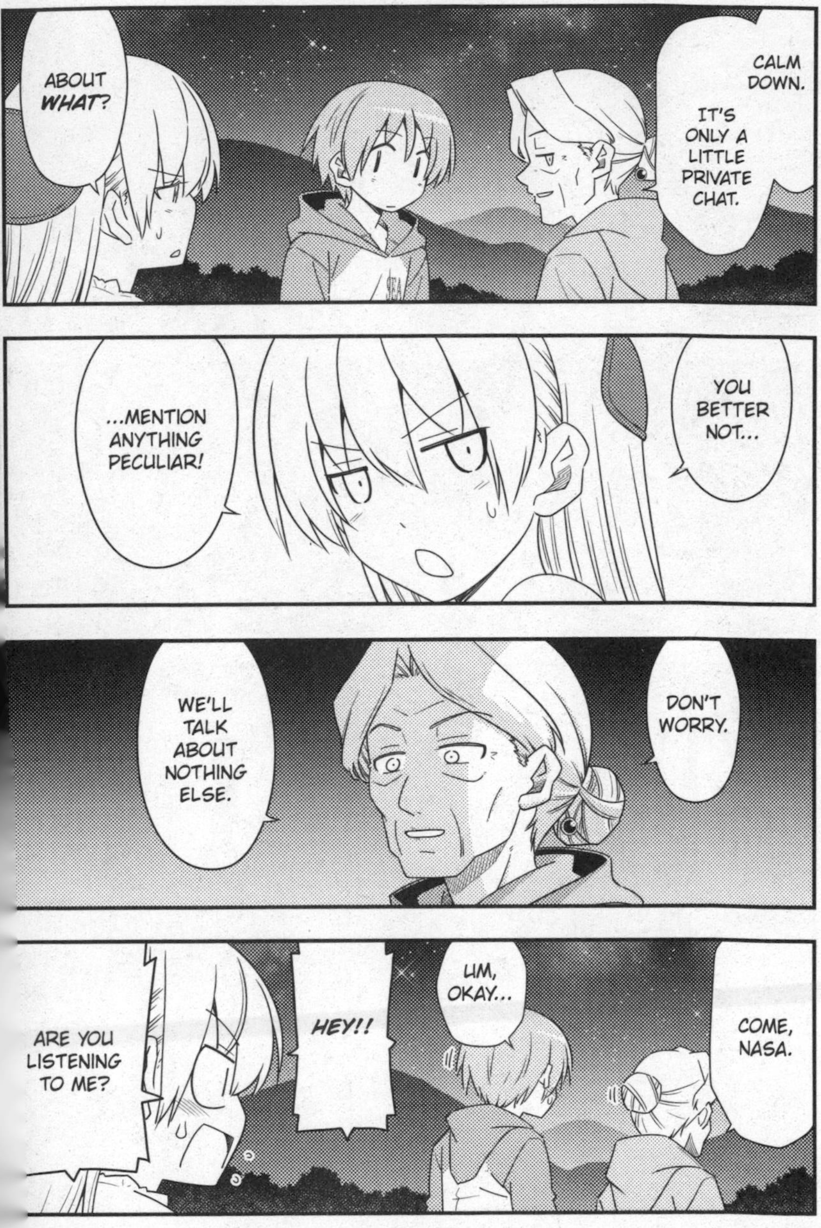
CALM DOWN.
IT'S ONLY A LITTLE PRIVATE CHAT.
ABOUT *WHAT*?
YOU BETTER NOT...
...MENTION ANYTHING PECULIAR!
DON'T WORRY.
WE'LL TALK ABOUT NOTHING ELSE.
COME, NASA.
UM, OKAY...
HEY!!
ARE YOU LISTENING TO ME?

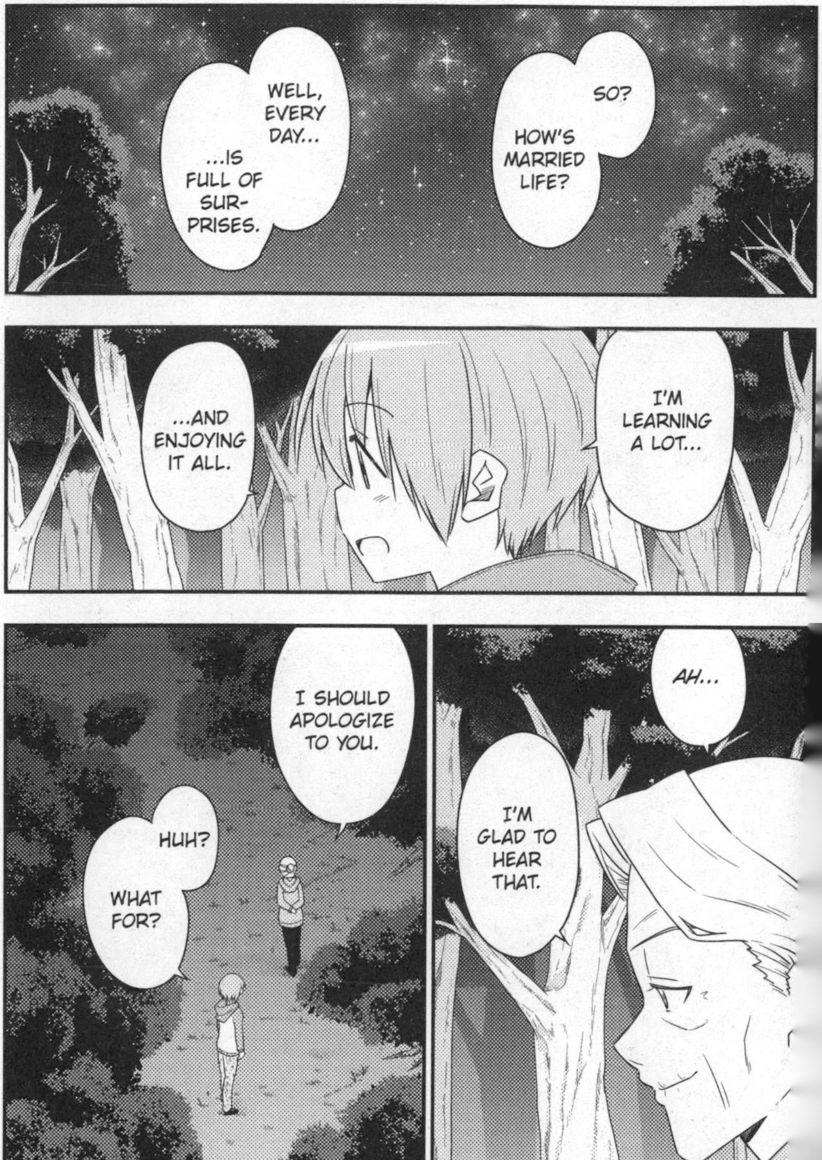
SO?
HOW'S MARRIED LIFE?
WELL, EVERY DAY...
...IS FULL OF SURPRISES.
I'M LEARNING A LOT...
...AND ENJOYING IT ALL.
AH...
I'M GLAD TO HEAR THAT.
I SHOULD APOLOGIZE TO YOU.
HUH?
WHAT FOR?

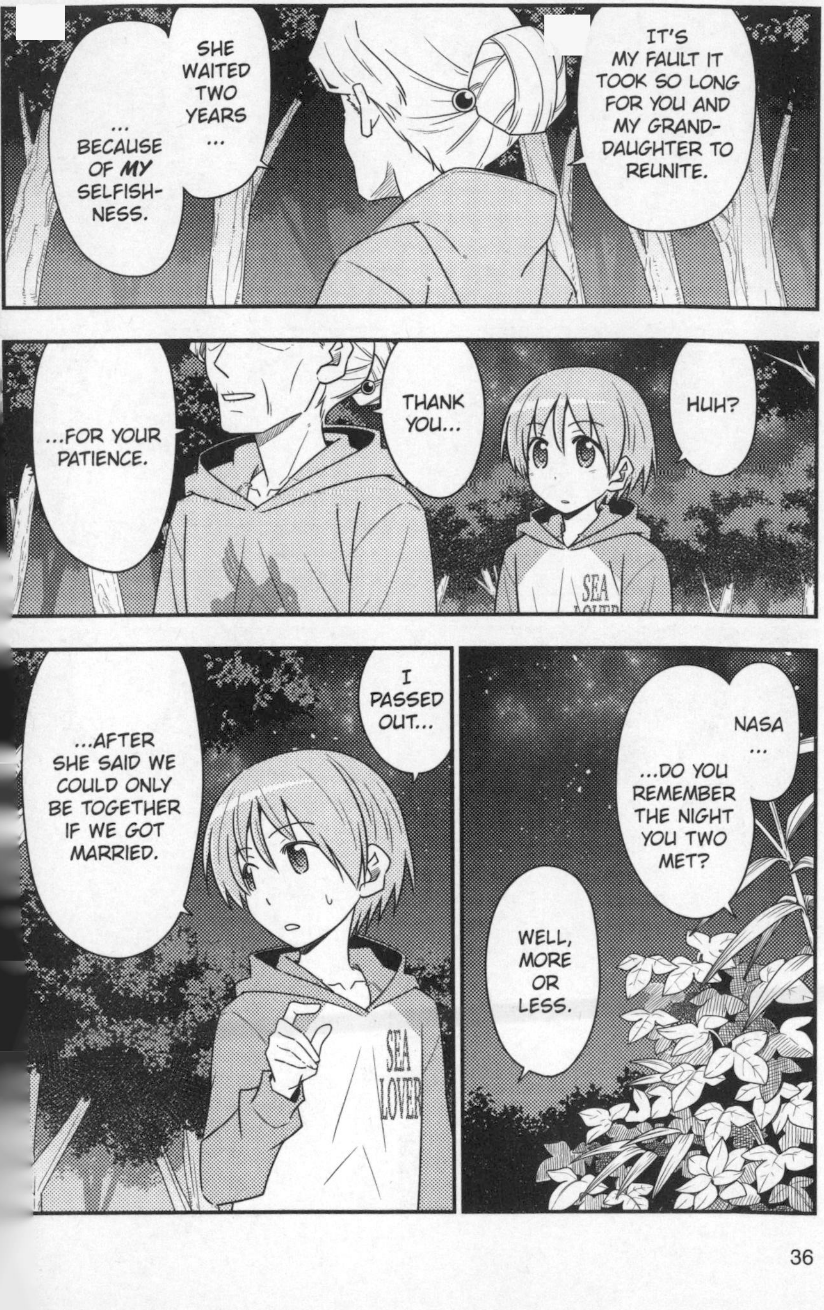
IT'S MY FAULT IT TOOK SO LONG FOR YOU AND MY GRAND-DAUGHTER TO REUNITE.
SHE WAITED TWO YEARS ... ... BECAUSE OF *MY* SELFISH-NESS.
HUH?
THANK YOU...
...FOR YOUR PATIENCE.
NASA ... ...DO YOU REMEMBER THE NIGHT YOU TWO MET?
WELL, MORE OR LESS.
I PASSED OUT...
...AFTER SHE SAID WE COULD ONLY BE TOGETHER IF WE GOT MARRIED.
SEA LOVER

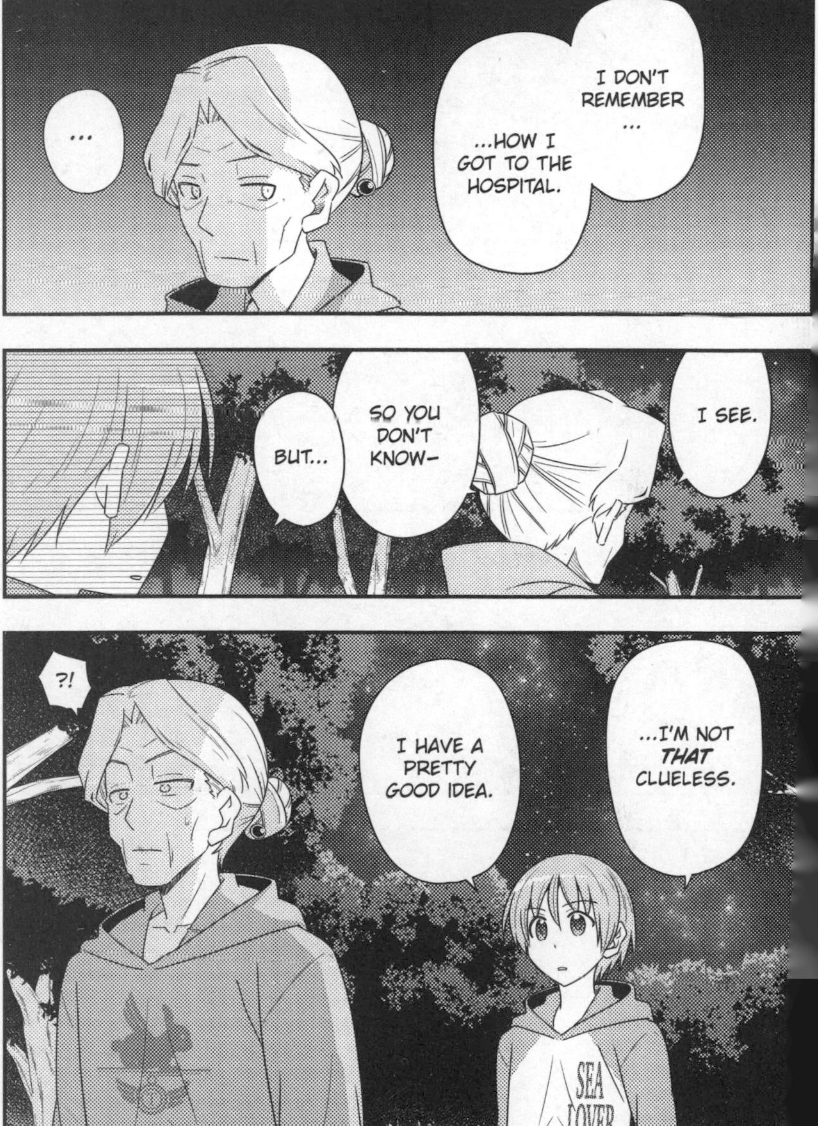
I DON'T REMEMBER ...
...HOW I GOT TO THE HOSPITAL.
...
I SEE.
SO YOU DON'T KNOW-
BUT...
...I'M NOT *THAT* CLUELESS.
I HAVE A PRETTY GOOD IDEA.
?!
SEA LOVER

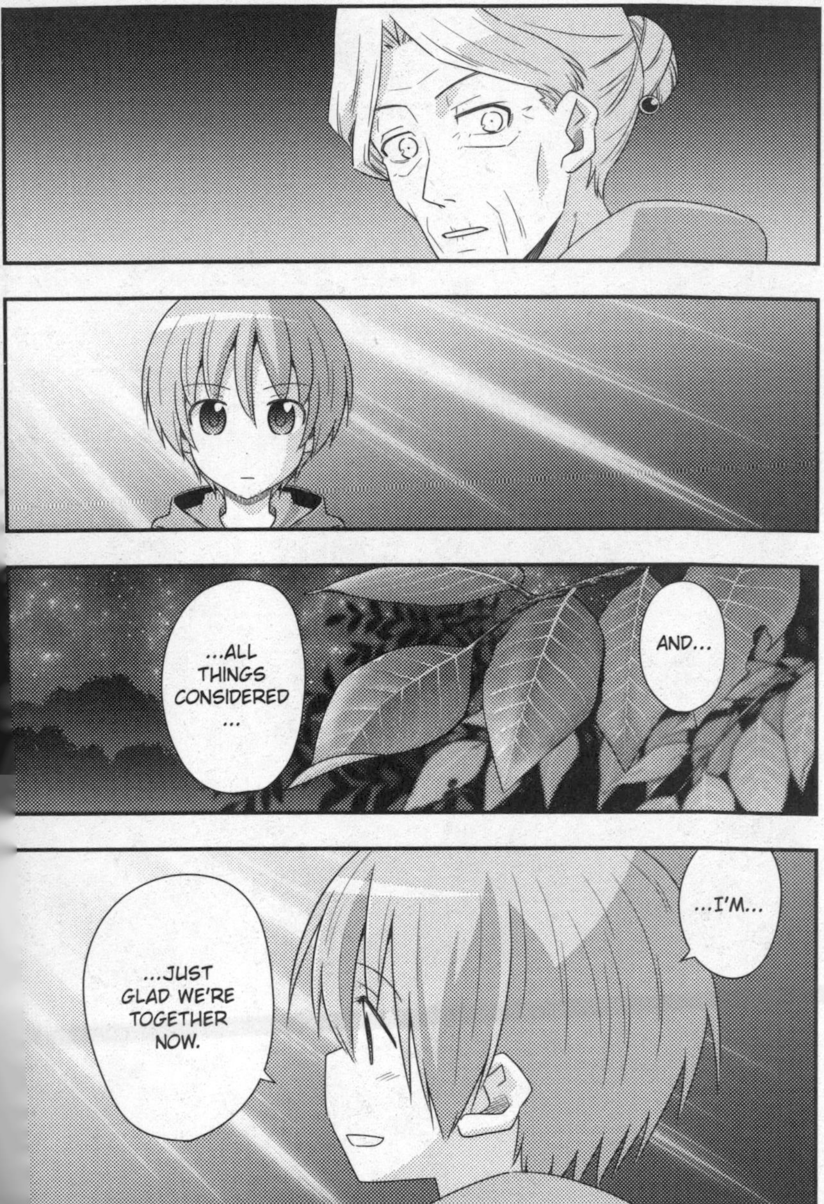
AND...
...ALL THINGS CONSIDERED ...
...I'M...
...JUST GLAD WE'RE TOGETHER NOW.

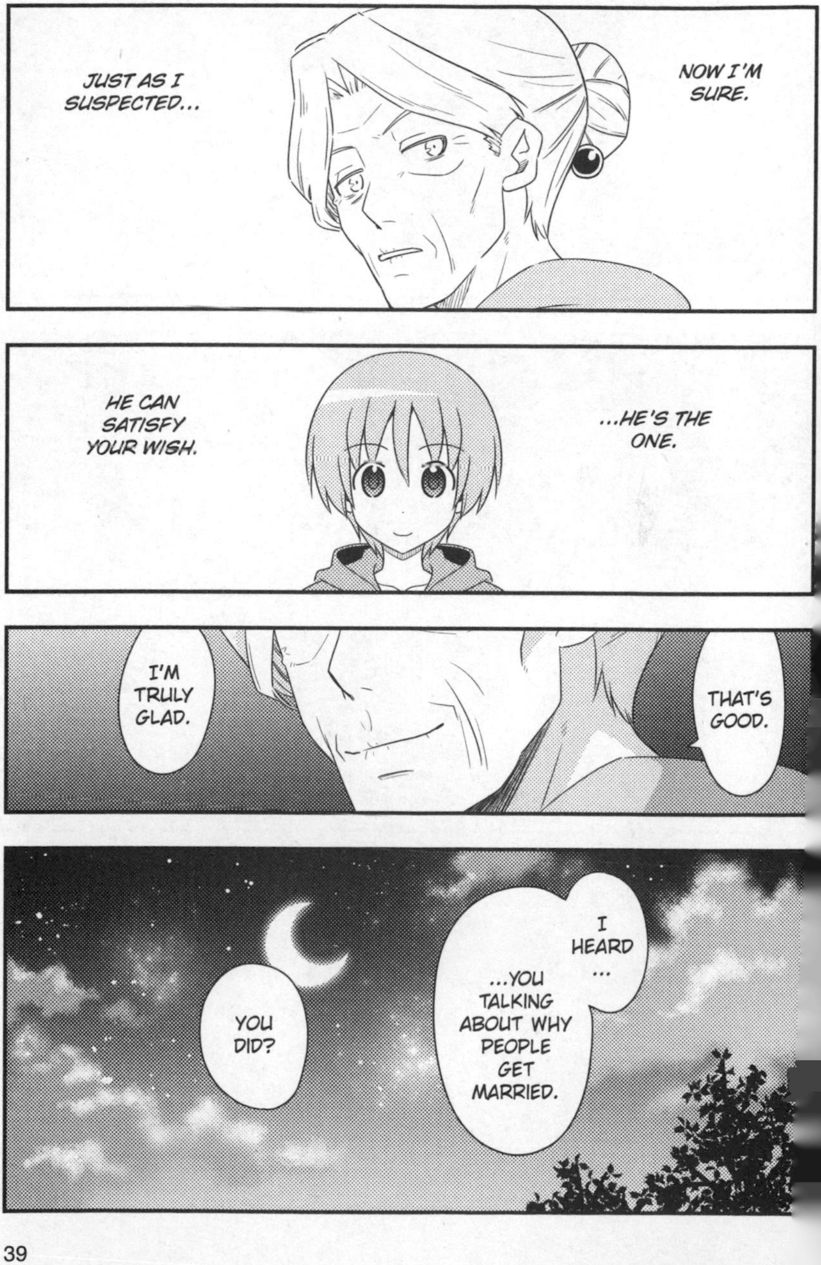
NOW I'M SURE.
JUST AS I SUSPECTED...
...HE'S THE ONE.
HE CAN SATISFY YOUR WISH.
THAT'S GOOD.
I'M TRULY GLAD.
I HEARD ...
...YOU TALKING ABOUT WHY PEOPLE GET MARRIED.
YOU DID?

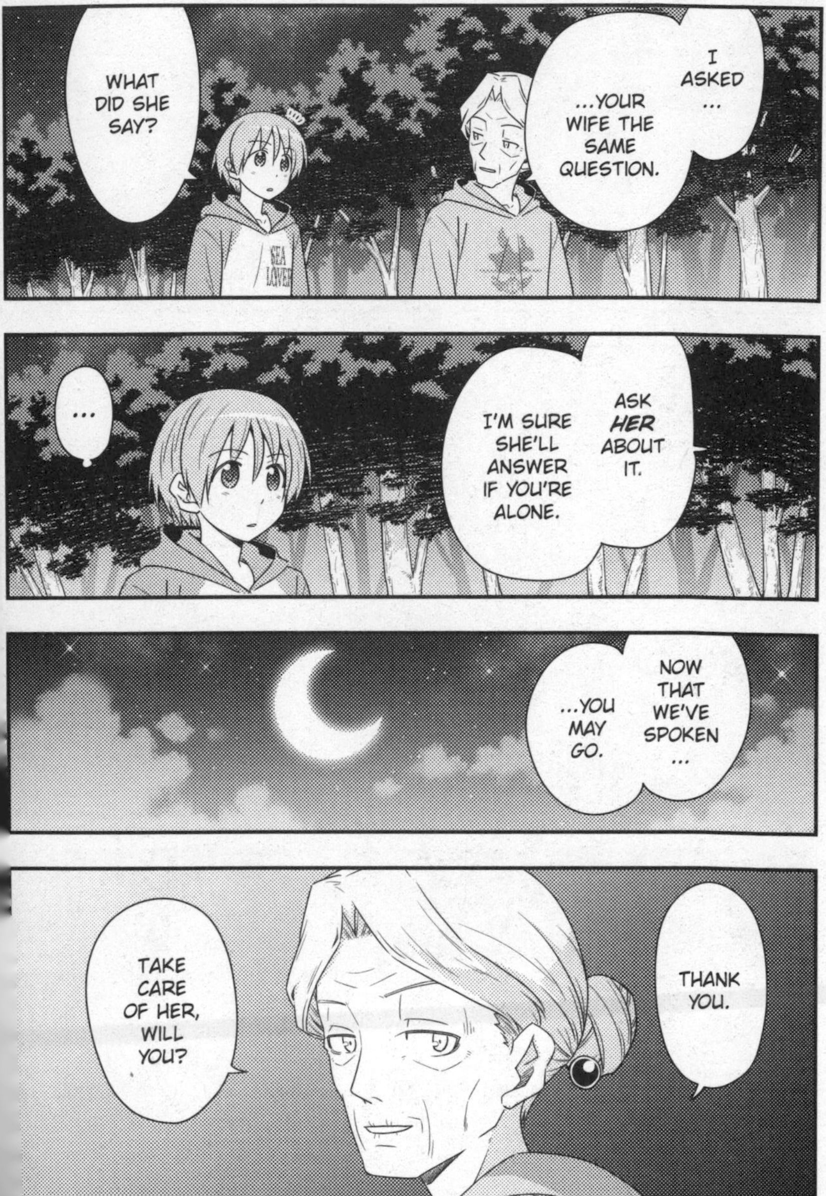
I ASKED ...
...YOUR WIFE THE SAME QUESTION.
WHAT DID SHE SAY?
ASK *HER* ABOUT IT.
I'M SURE SHE'LL ANSWER IF YOU'RE ALONE.
...
NOW THAT WE'VE SPOKEN ...
...YOU MAY GO.
THANK YOU.
TAKE CARE OF HER, WILL YOU?

Chapter 102: "Because"

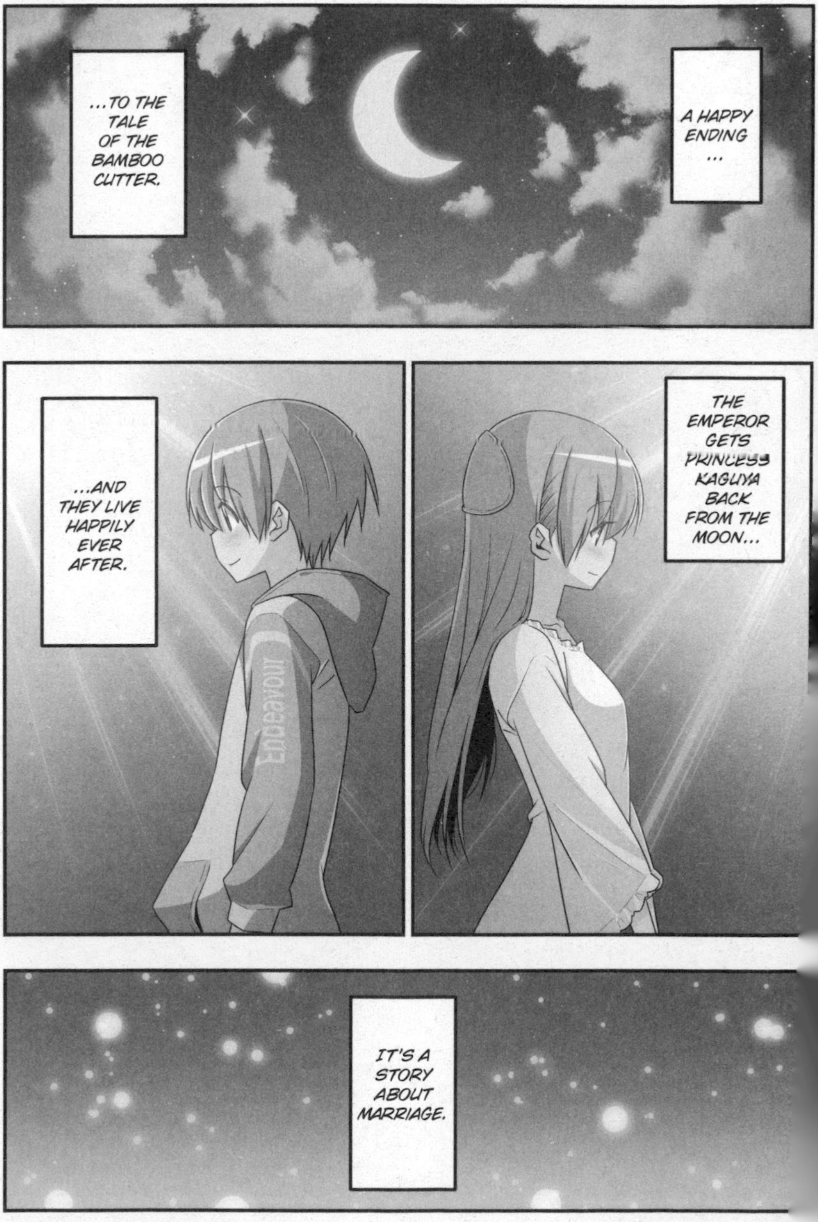

A HAPPY ENDING ...
...TO THE TALE OF THE BAMBOO CUTTER.
THE EMPEROR GETS PRINCESS KAGUYA BACK FROM THE MOON...
...AND THEY LIVE HAPPILY EVER AFTER.
IT'S A STORY ABOUT MARRIAGE.

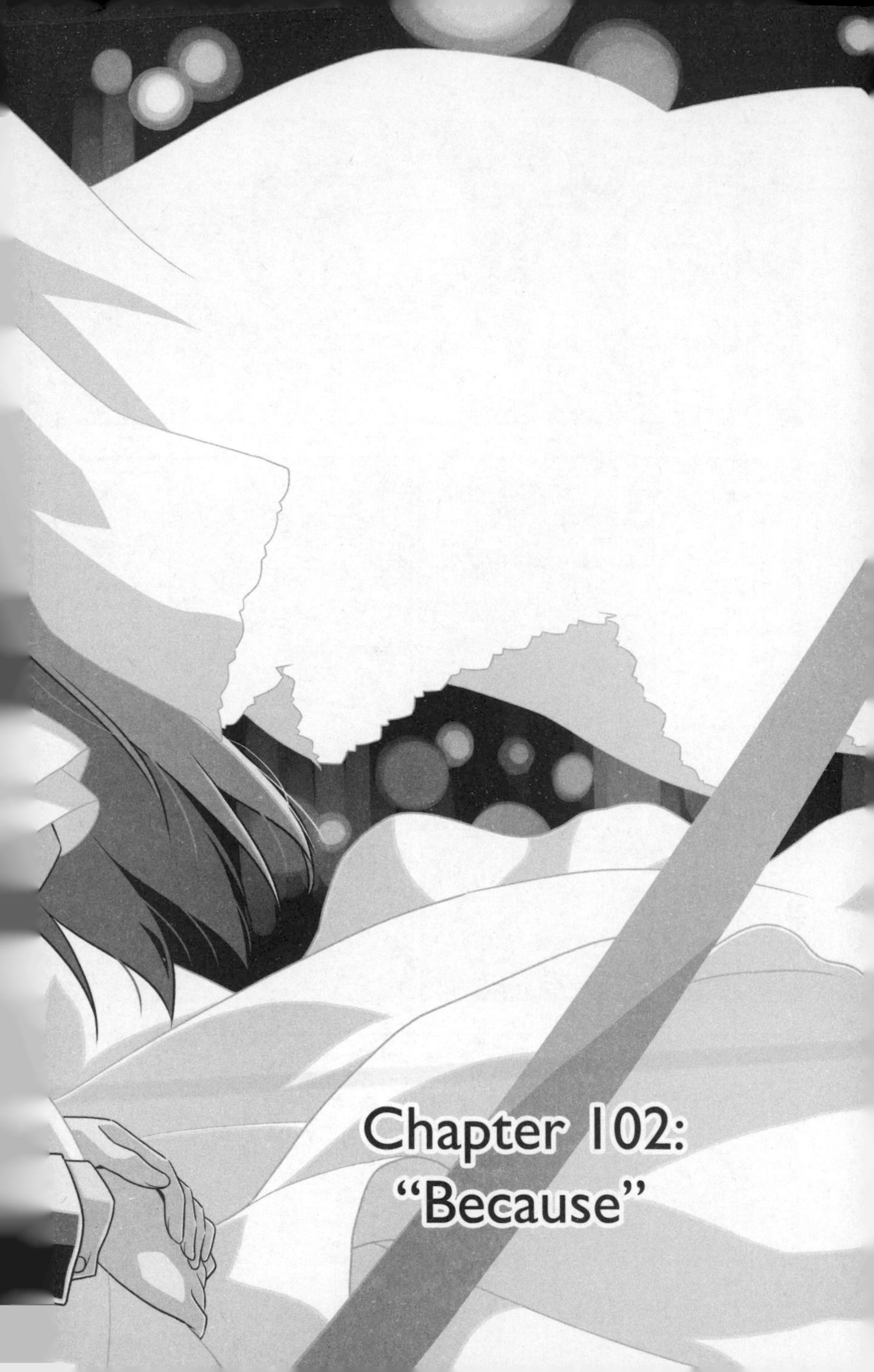
Chapter 102:
"Because"

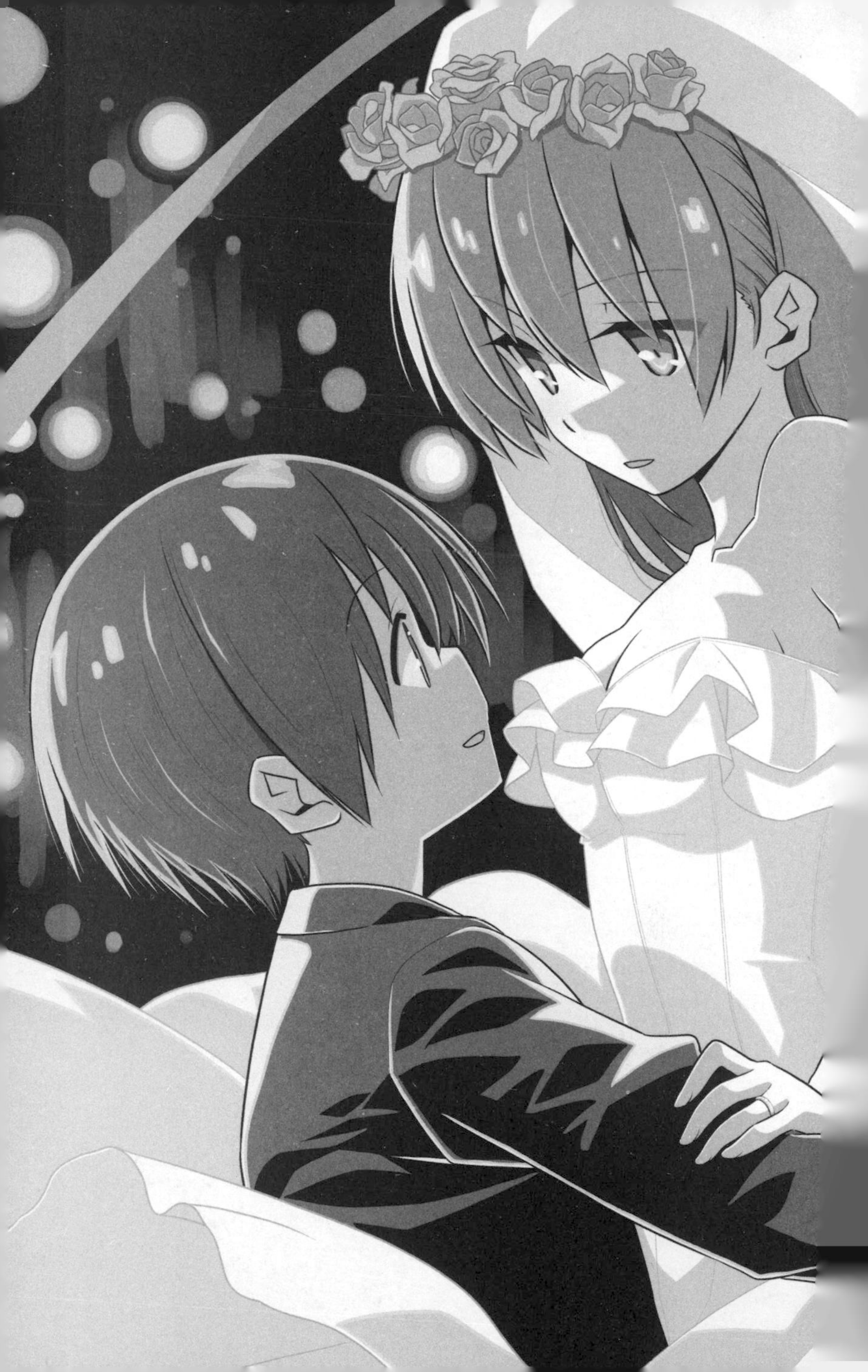

FLY ME ^{TO}_{THE} MOON

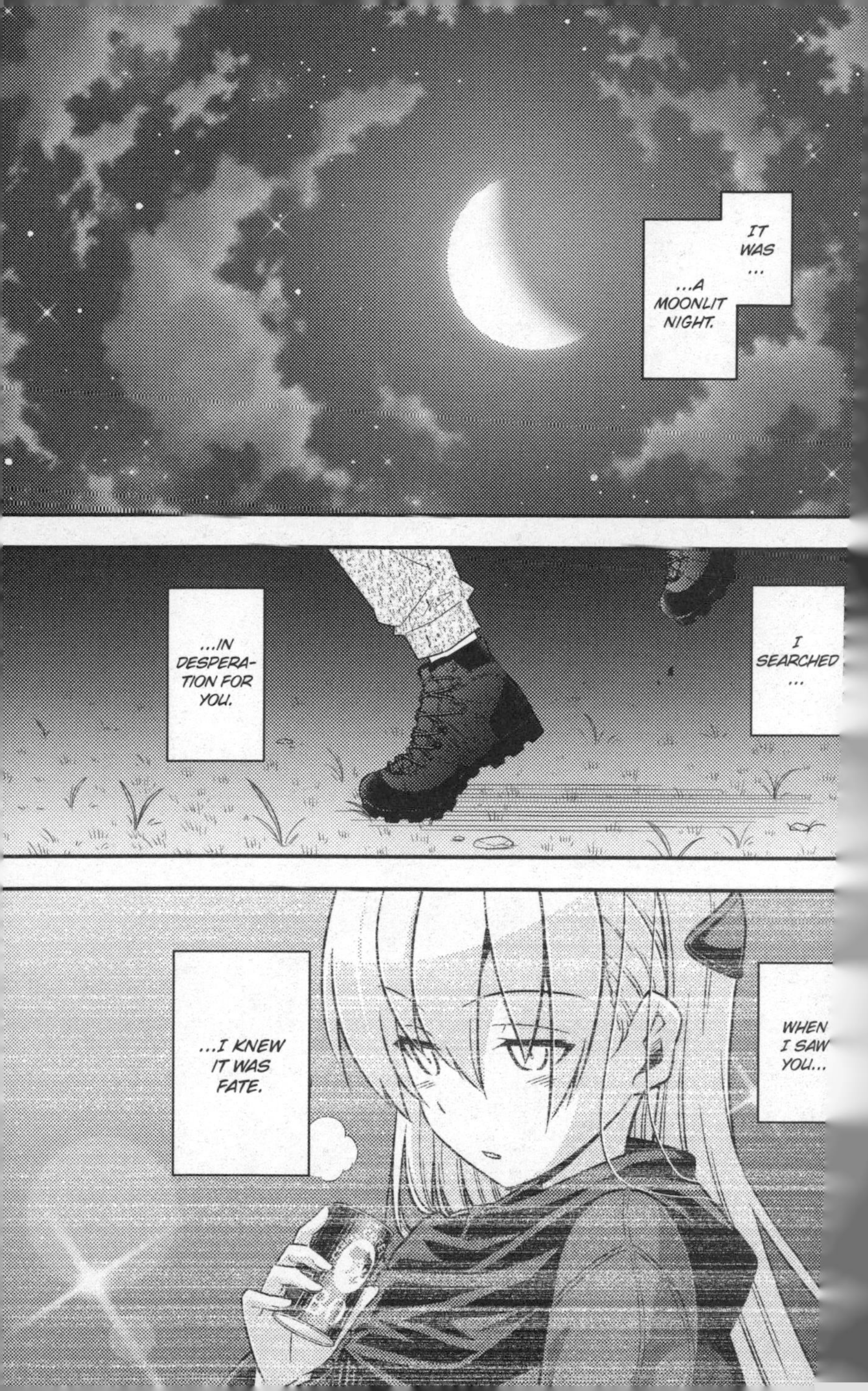
IT WAS ...
...A MOONLIT NIGHT.
I SEARCHED ...
...IN DESPERATION FOR YOU.
WHEN I SAW YOU...
...I KNEW IT WAS FATE.

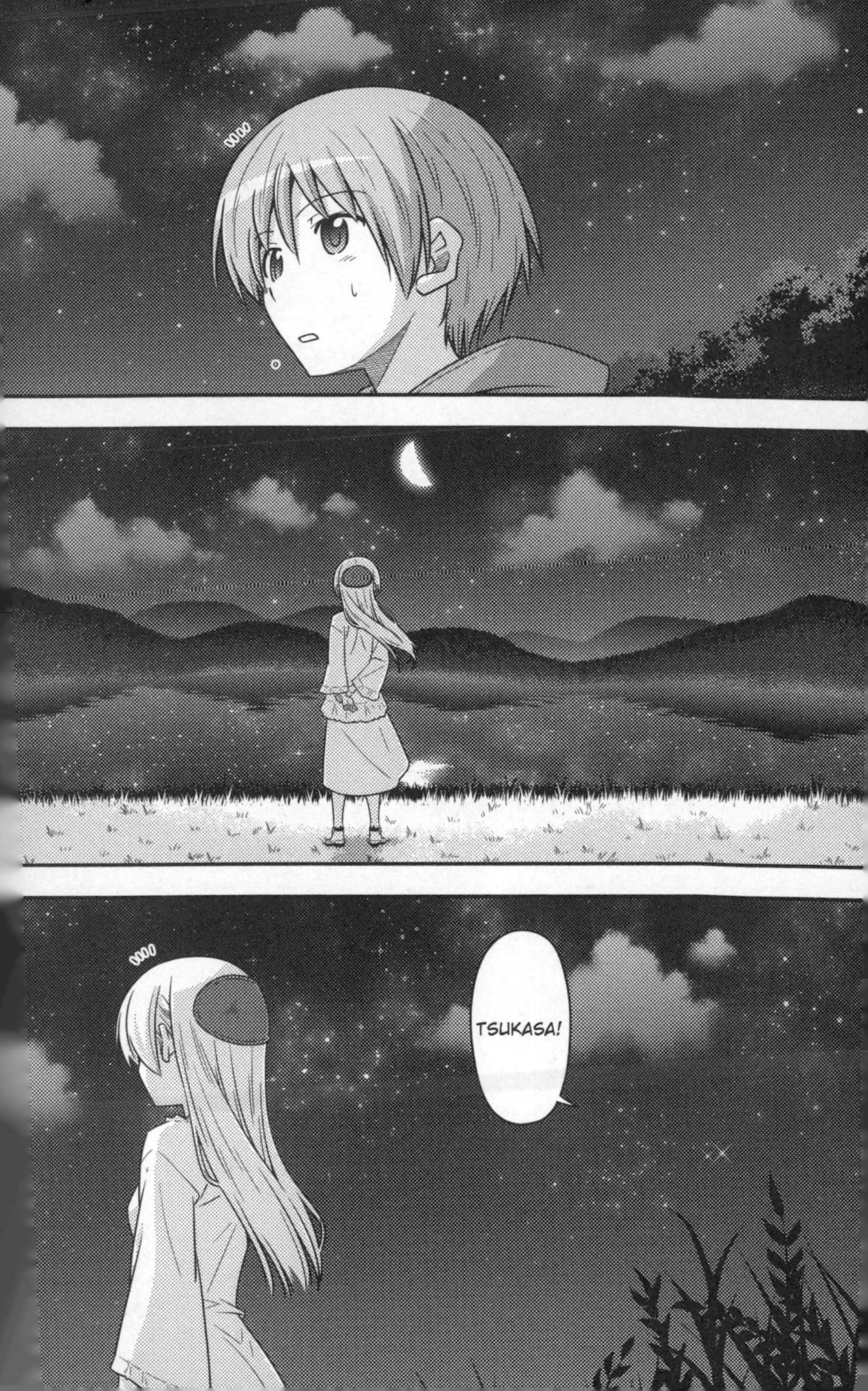
TSUKASA!

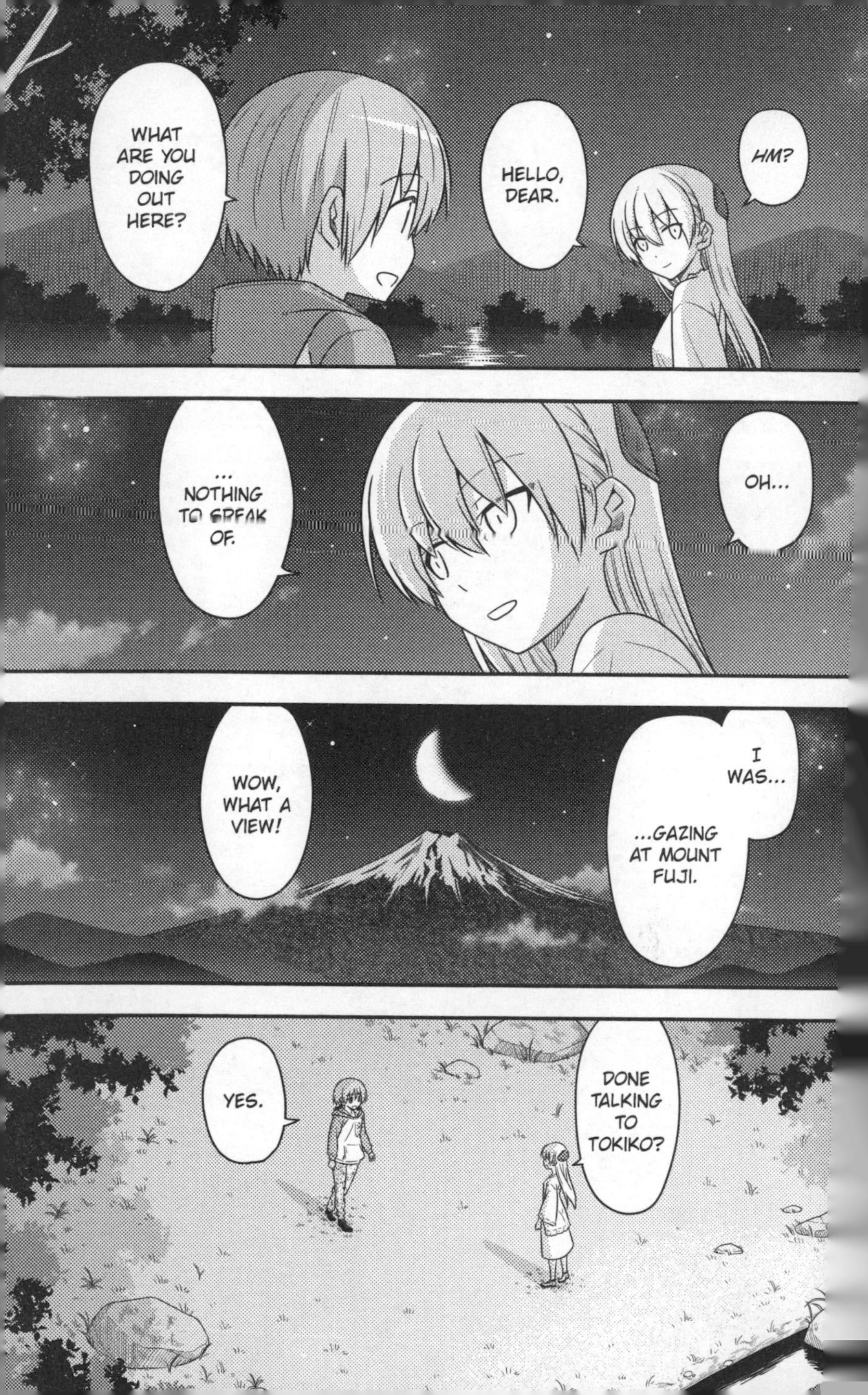
HM?
HELLO, DEAR.
WHAT ARE YOU DOING OUT HERE?
OH...
...NOTHING TO SPEAK OF.
I WAS...
...GAZING AT MOUNT FUJI.
WOW, WHAT A VIEW!
DONE TALKING TO TOKIKO?
YES.

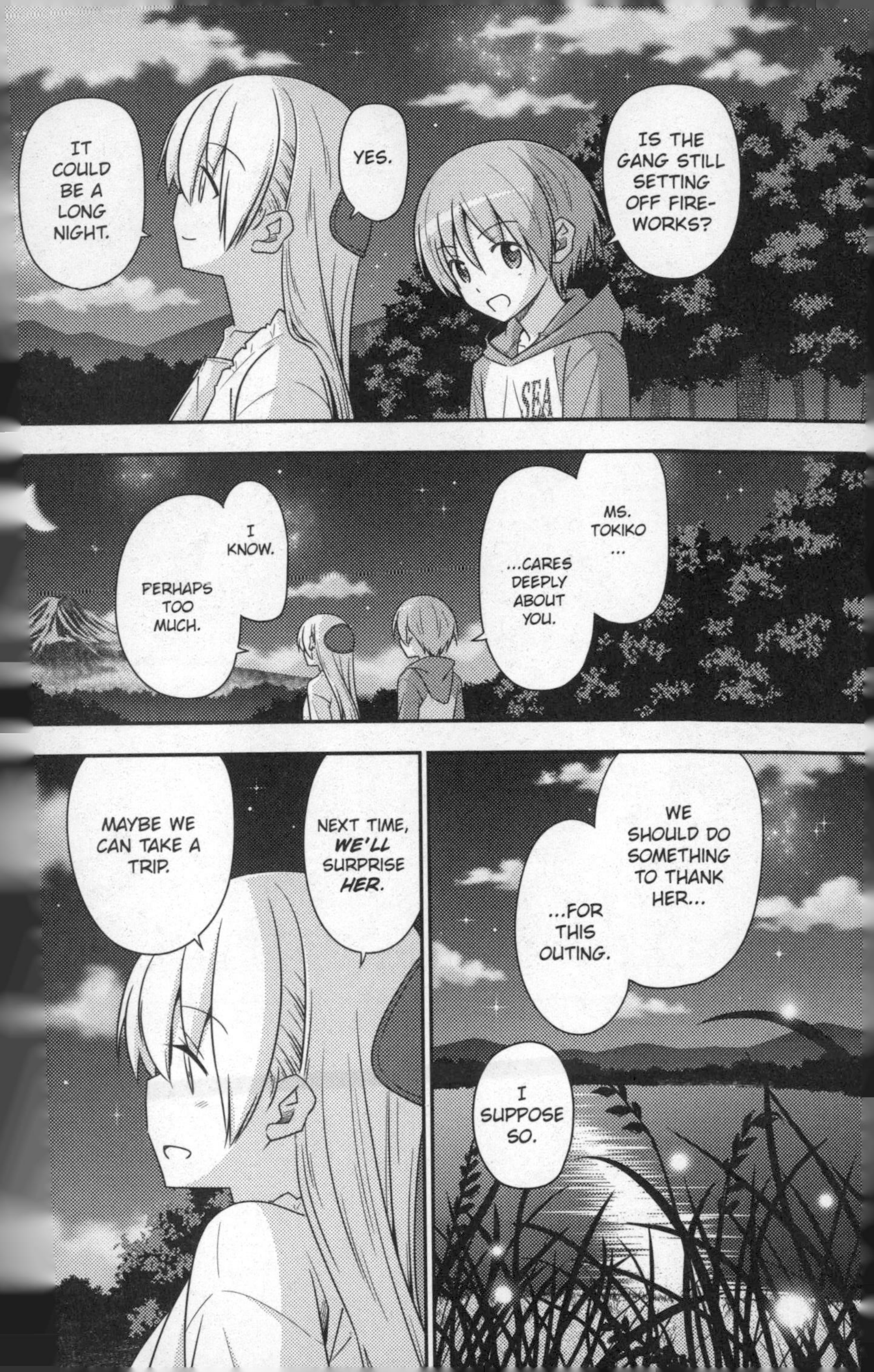
IS THE GANG STILL SETTING OFF FIRE-WORKS?
YES.
IT COULD BE A LONG NIGHT.
MS. TOKIKO ...
...CARES DEEPLY ABOUT YOU.
I KNOW.
PERHAPS TOO MUCH.
WE SHOULD DO SOMETHING TO THANK HER...
...FOR THIS OUTING.
I SUPPOSE SO.
NEXT TIME, *WE'LL* SURPRISE *HER*.
MAYBE WE CAN TAKE A TRIP.

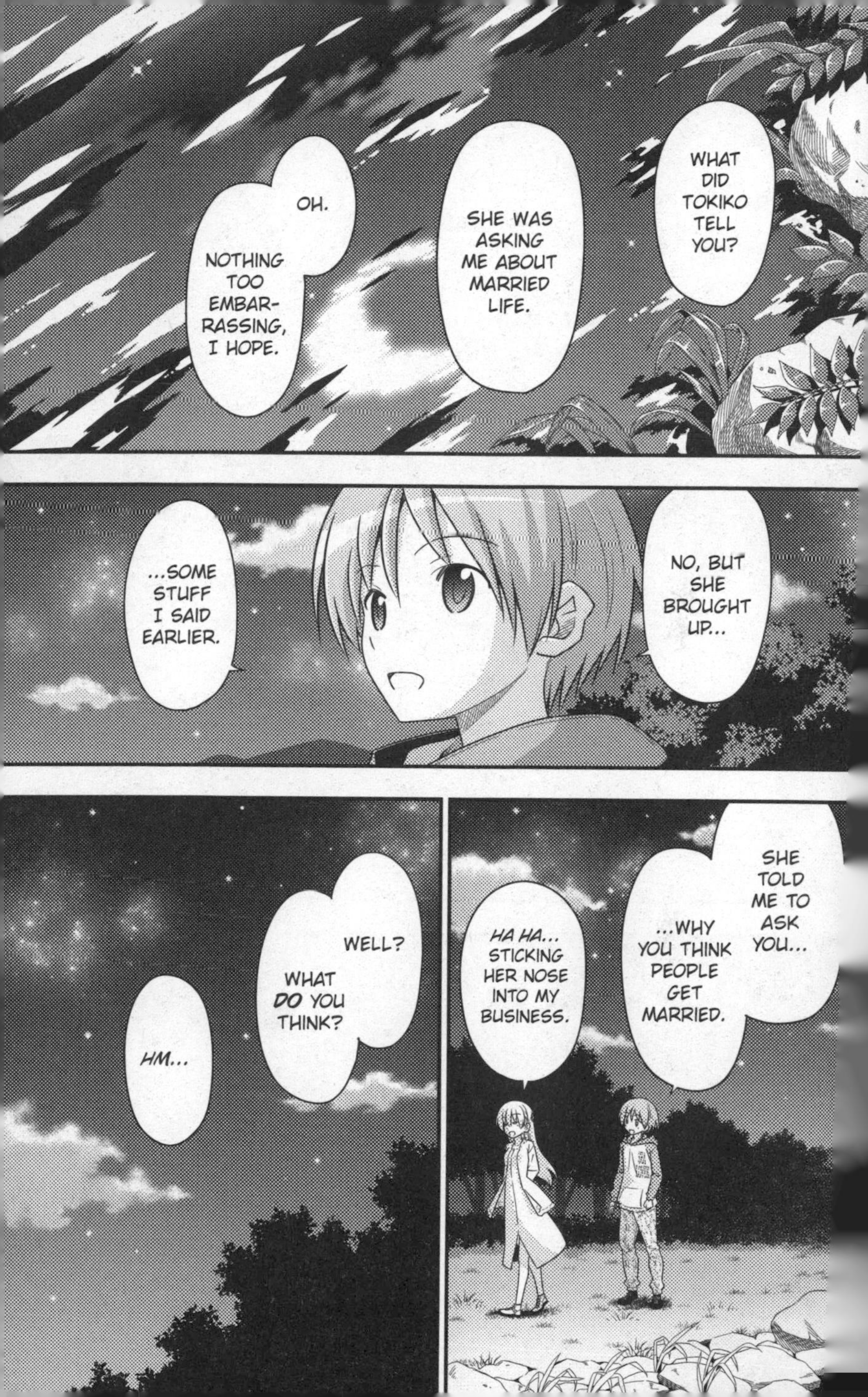
WHAT DID TOKIKO TELL YOU?
SHE WAS ASKING ME ABOUT MARRIED LIFE.
OH.
NOTHING TOO EMBARRASSING, I HOPE.
NO, BUT SHE BROUGHT UP...
...SOME STUFF I SAID EARLIER.
SHE TOLD ME TO ASK YOU...
...WHY YOU THINK PEOPLE GET MARRIED.
HA HA... STICKING HER NOSE INTO MY BUSINESS.
WELL?
WHAT *DO* YOU THINK?
HM...

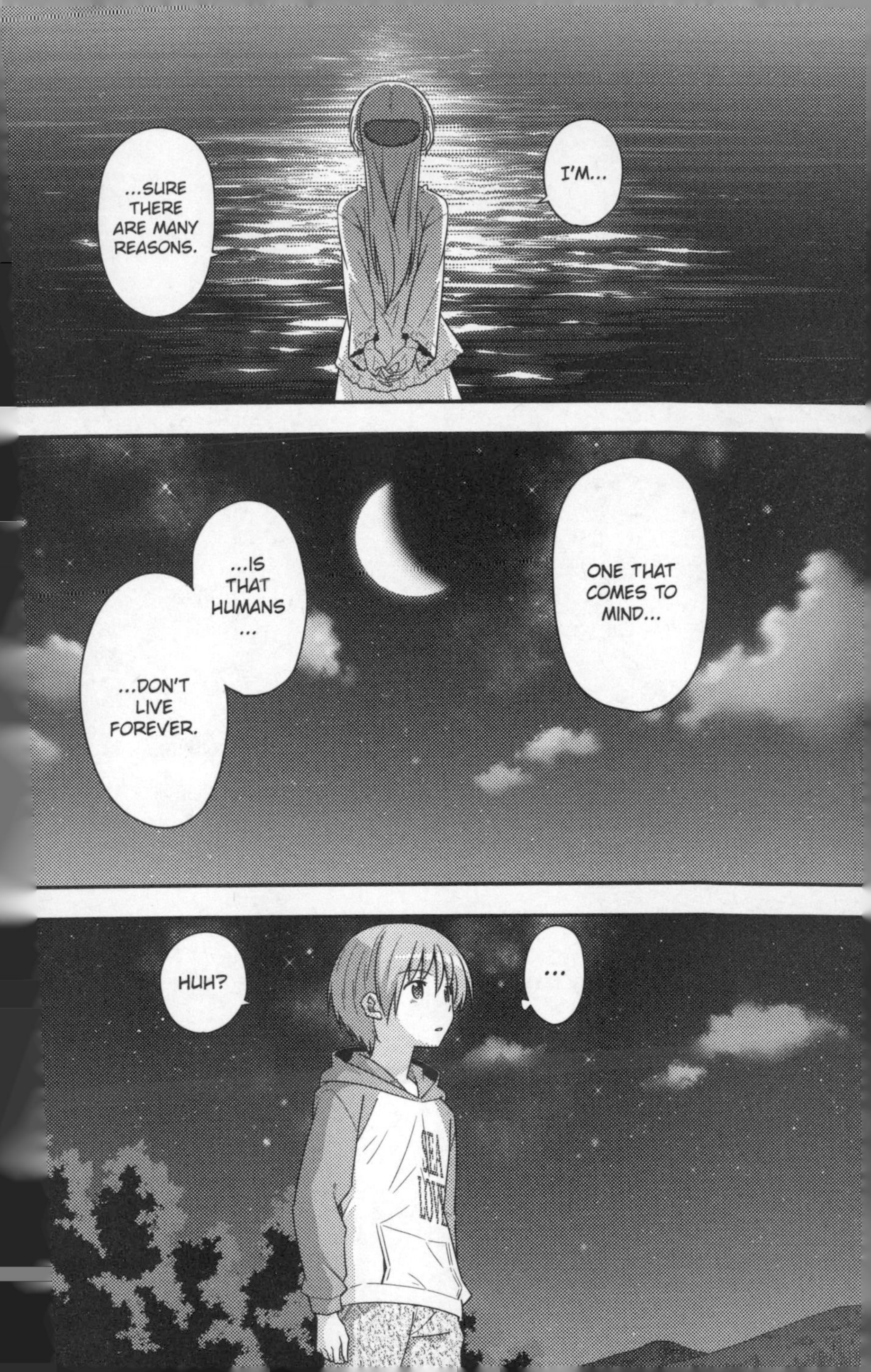
I'M...
...SURE THERE ARE MANY REASONS.
ONE THAT COMES TO MIND...
...IS THAT HUMANS...
...DON'T LIVE FOREVER.
...
HUH?

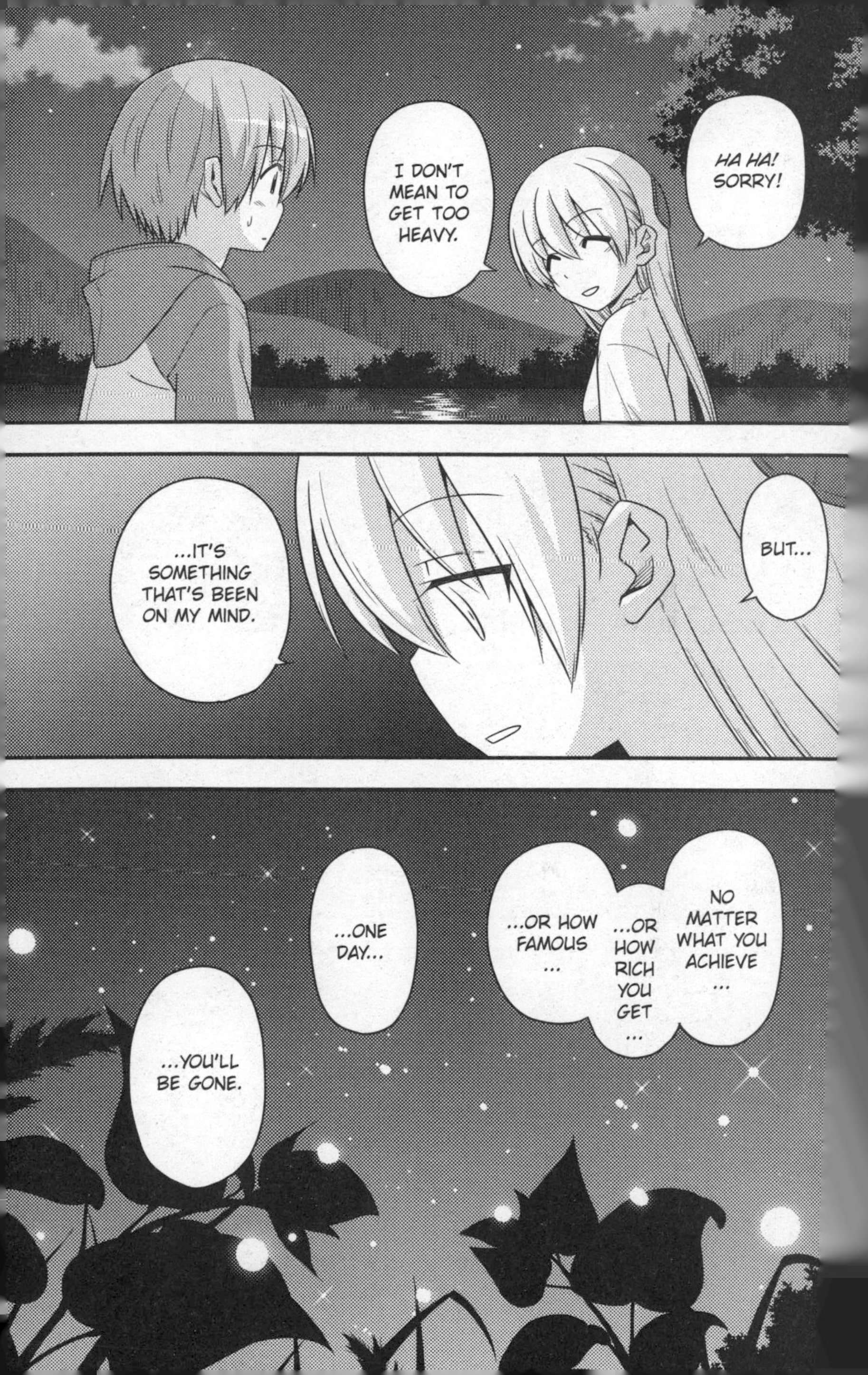
HA HA! SORRY!
I DON'T MEAN TO GET TOO HEAVY.
BUT...
...IT'S SOMETHING THAT'S BEEN ON MY MIND.
NO MATTER WHAT YOU ACHIEVE ...
...OR HOW RICH YOU GET ...
...OR HOW FAMOUS ...
...ONE DAY...
...YOU'LL BE GONE.

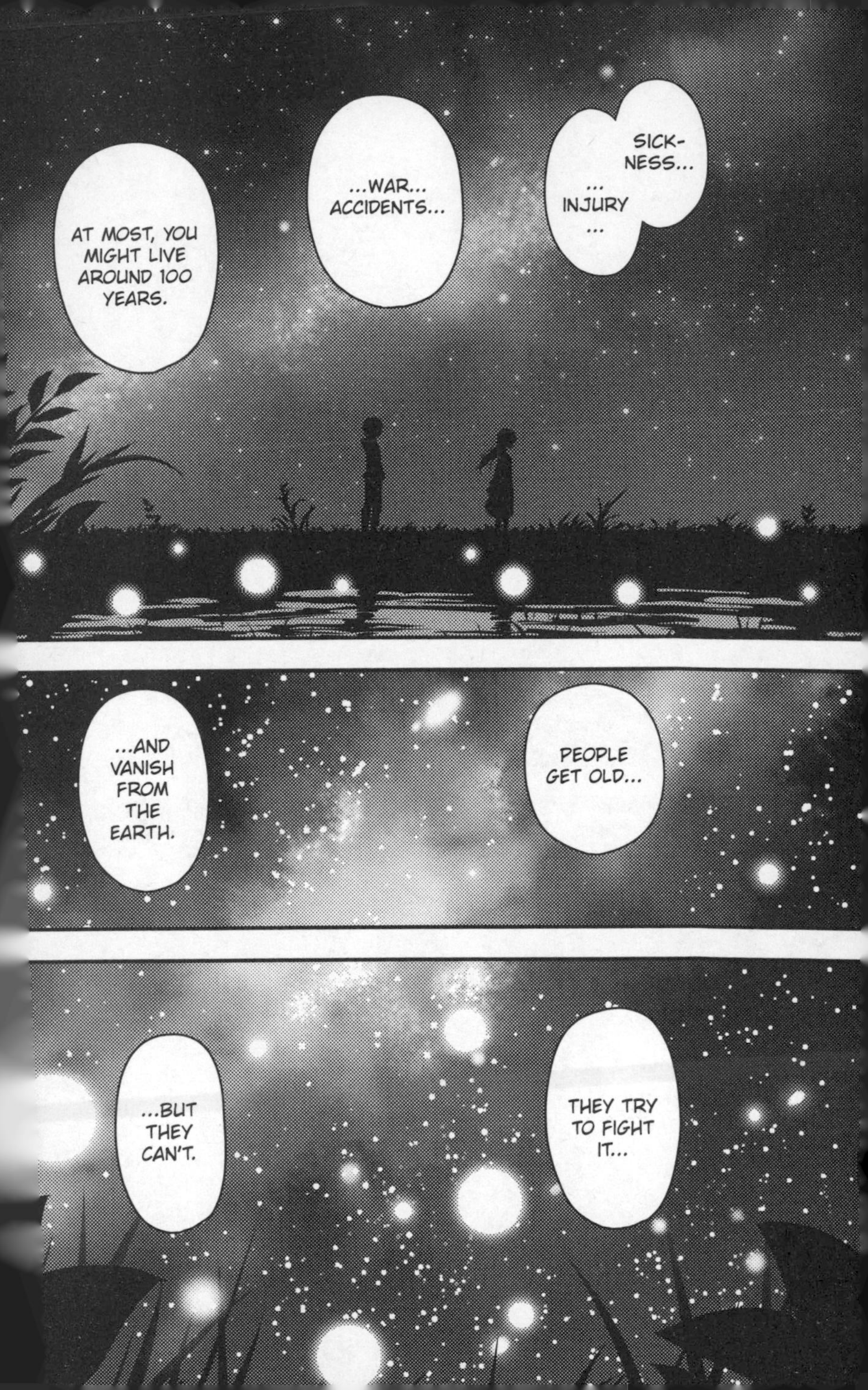
SICK- NESS... ... INJURY ...
...WAR... ACCIDENTS...
AT MOST, YOU MIGHT LIVE AROUND 100 YEARS.
PEOPLE GET OLD...
...AND VANISH FROM THE EARTH.
THEY TRY TO FIGHT IT...
...BUT THEY CAN'T.

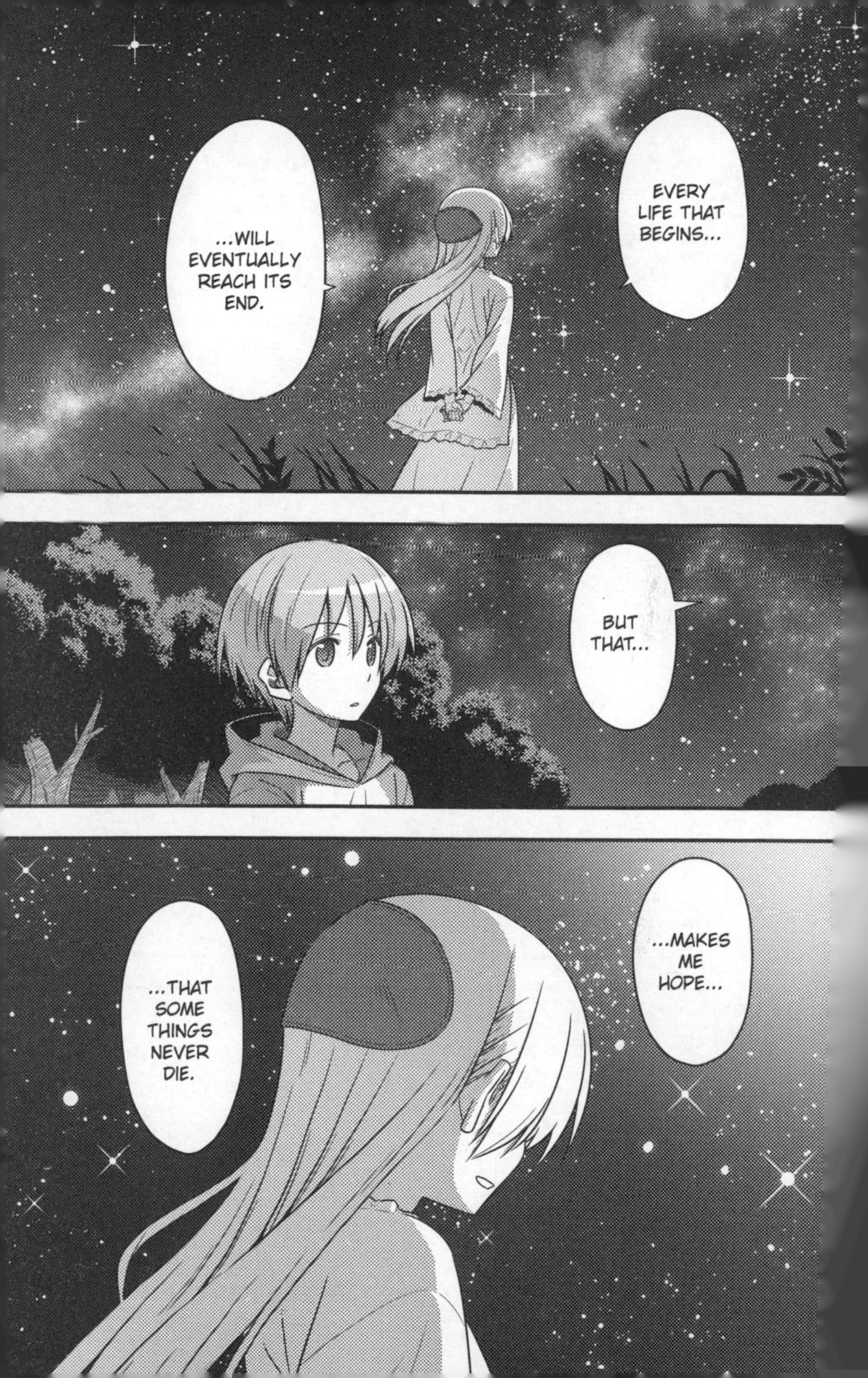
EVERY LIFE THAT BEGINS...
...WILL EVENTUALLY REACH ITS END.
BUT THAT...
...MAKES ME HOPE...
...THAT SOME THINGS NEVER DIE.

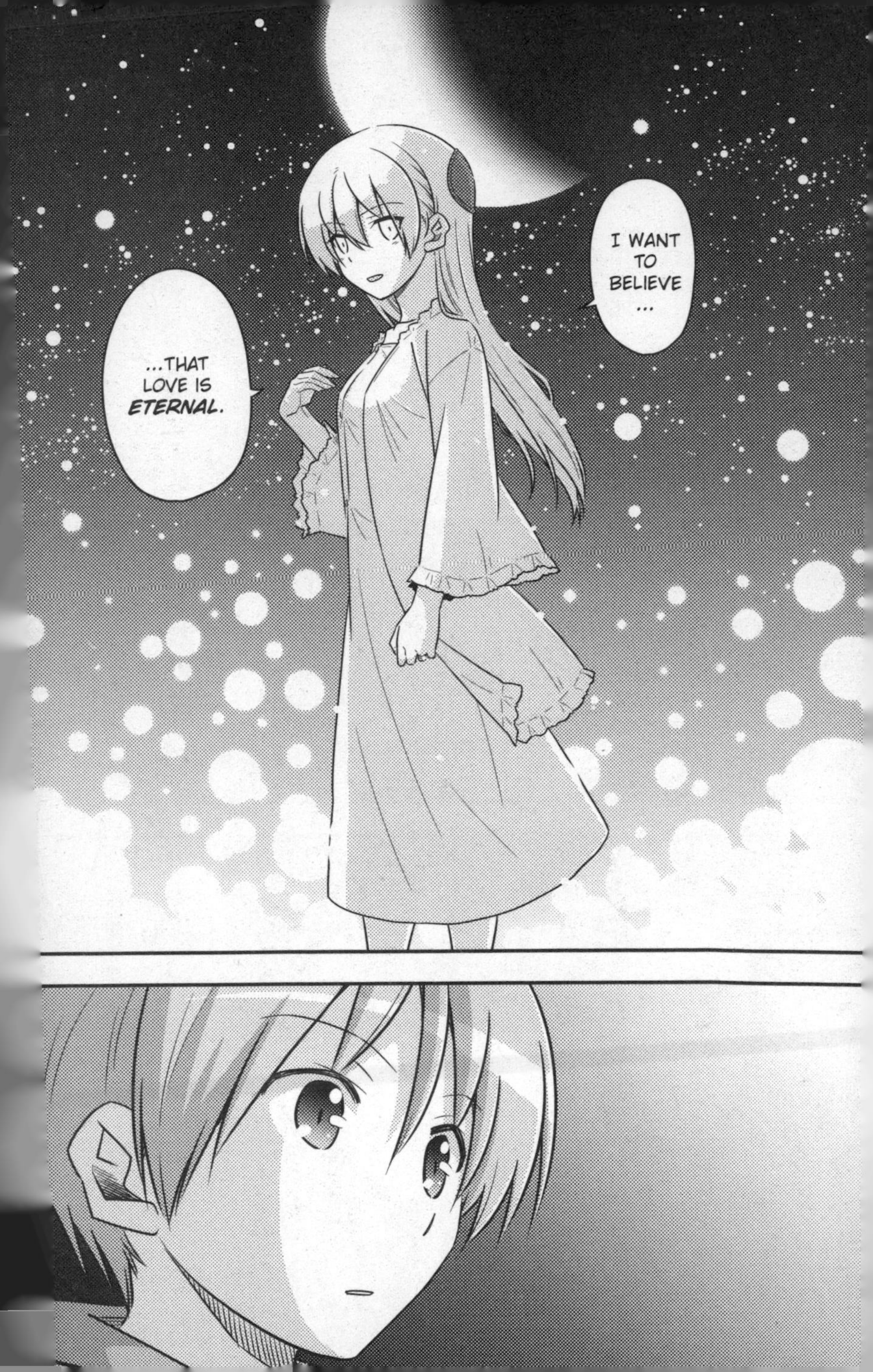
I WANT TO BELIEVE ...
...THAT LOVE IS ETERNAL.

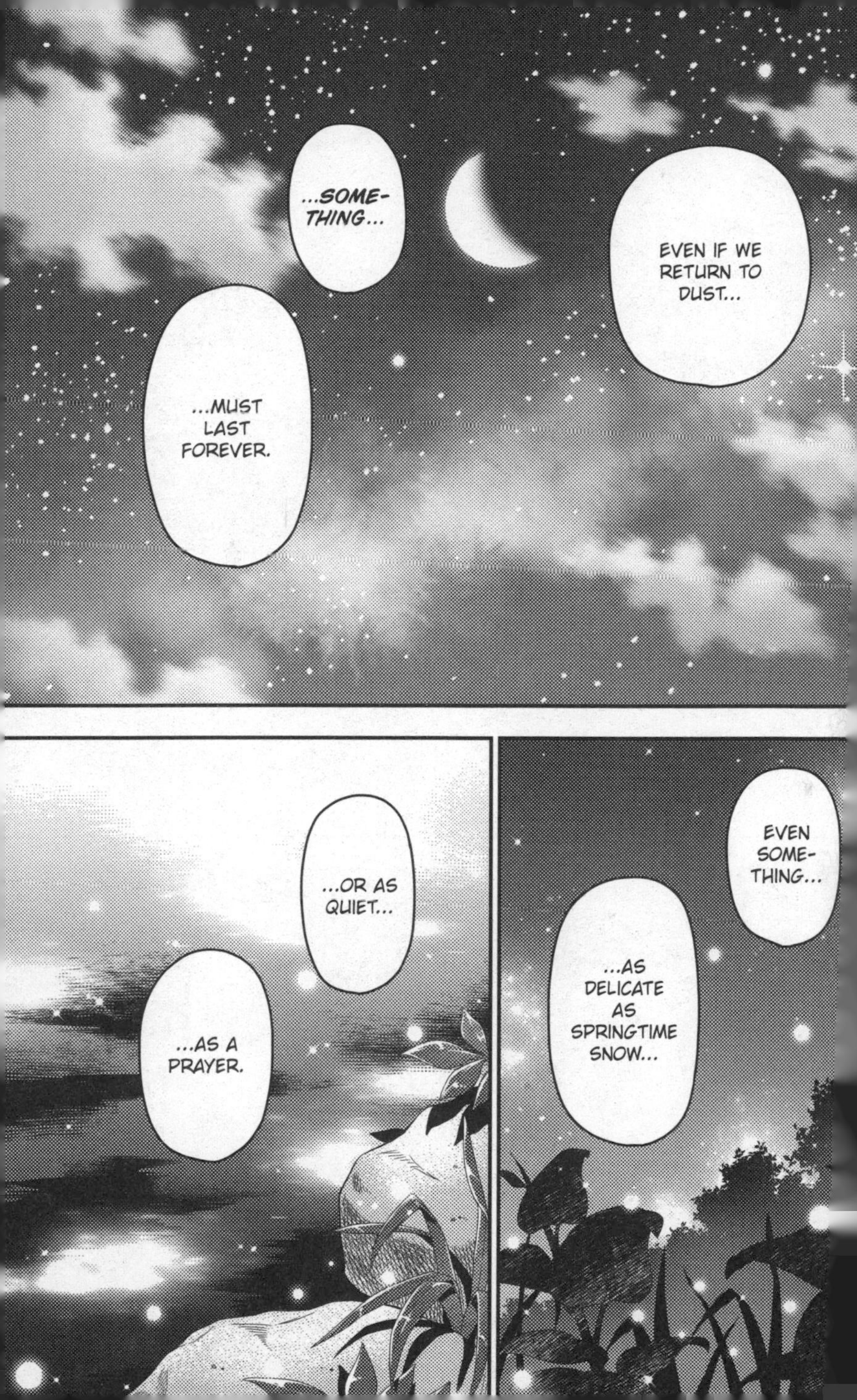
EVEN IF WE RETURN TO DUST...
...SOME-THING...
...MUST LAST FOREVER.
EVEN SOME-THING...
...AS DELICATE AS SPRINGTIME SNOW...
...OR AS QUIET...
...AS A PRAYER.

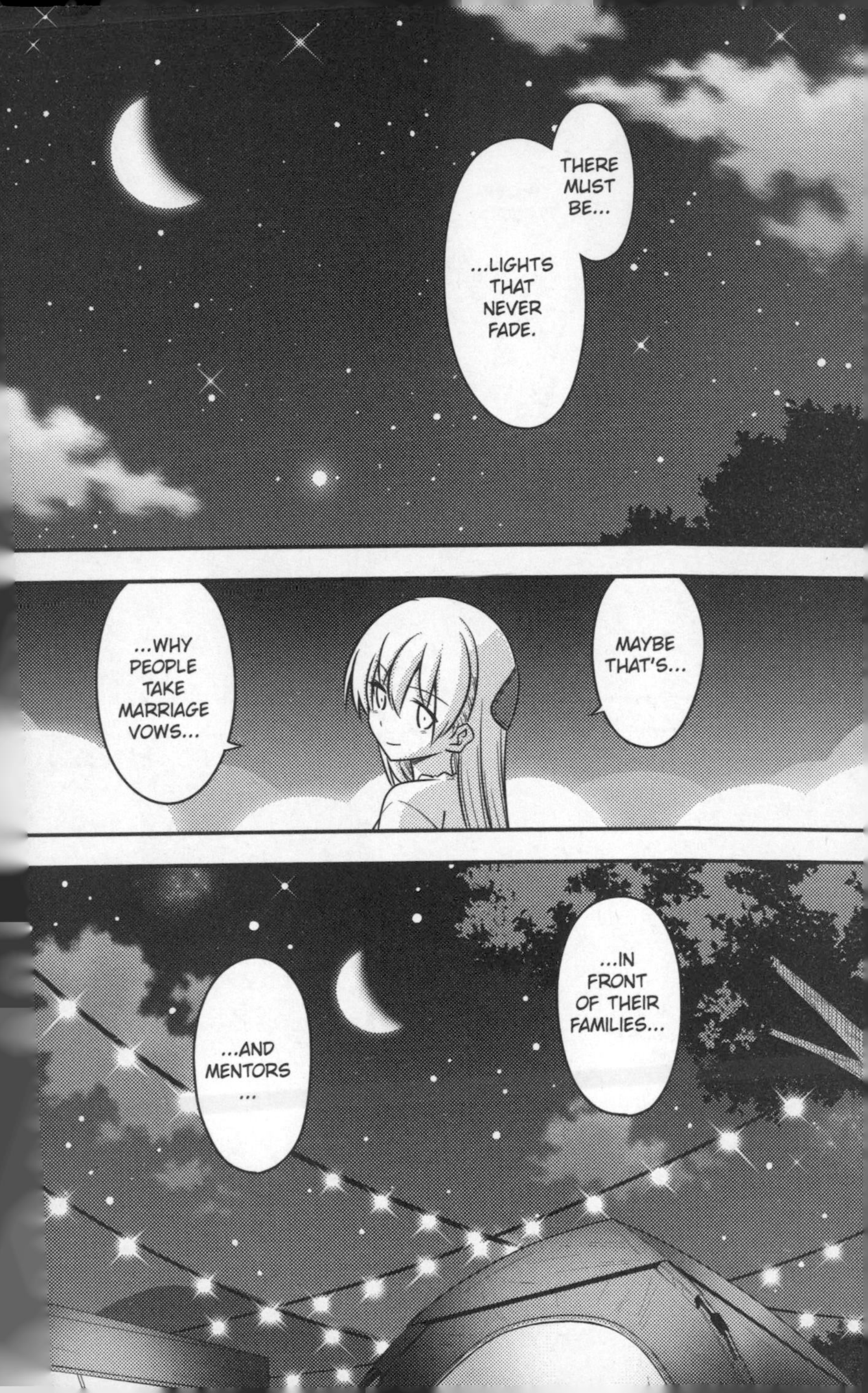
THERE MUST BE...
...LIGHTS THAT NEVER FADE.
MAYBE THAT'S...
...WHY PEOPLE TAKE MARRIAGE VOWS...
...IN FRONT OF THEIR FAMILIES...
...AND MENTORS ...

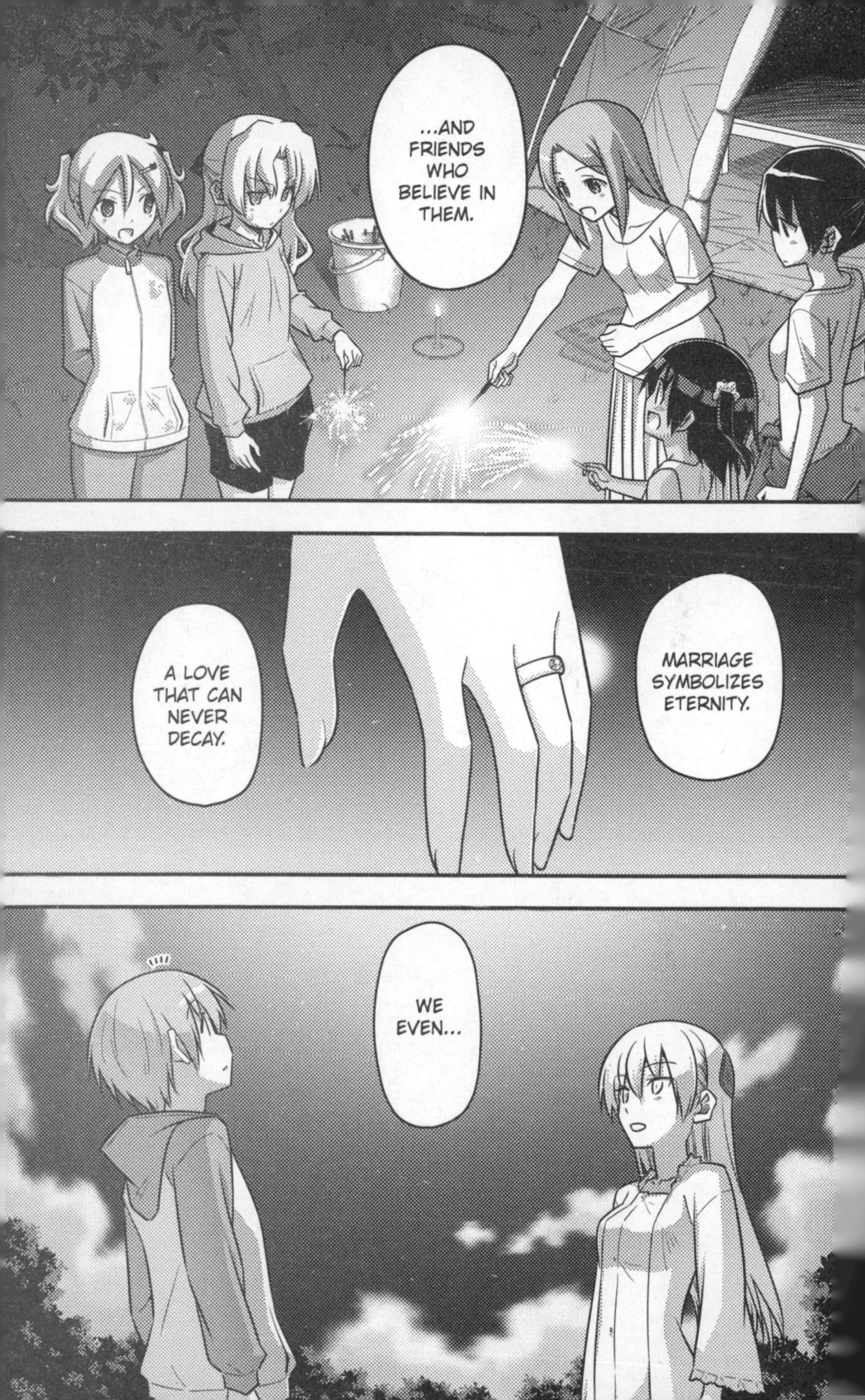
...AND FRIENDS WHO BELIEVE IN THEM.
MARRIAGE SYMBOLIZES ETERNITY.
A LOVE THAT CAN NEVER DECAY.
WE EVEN...

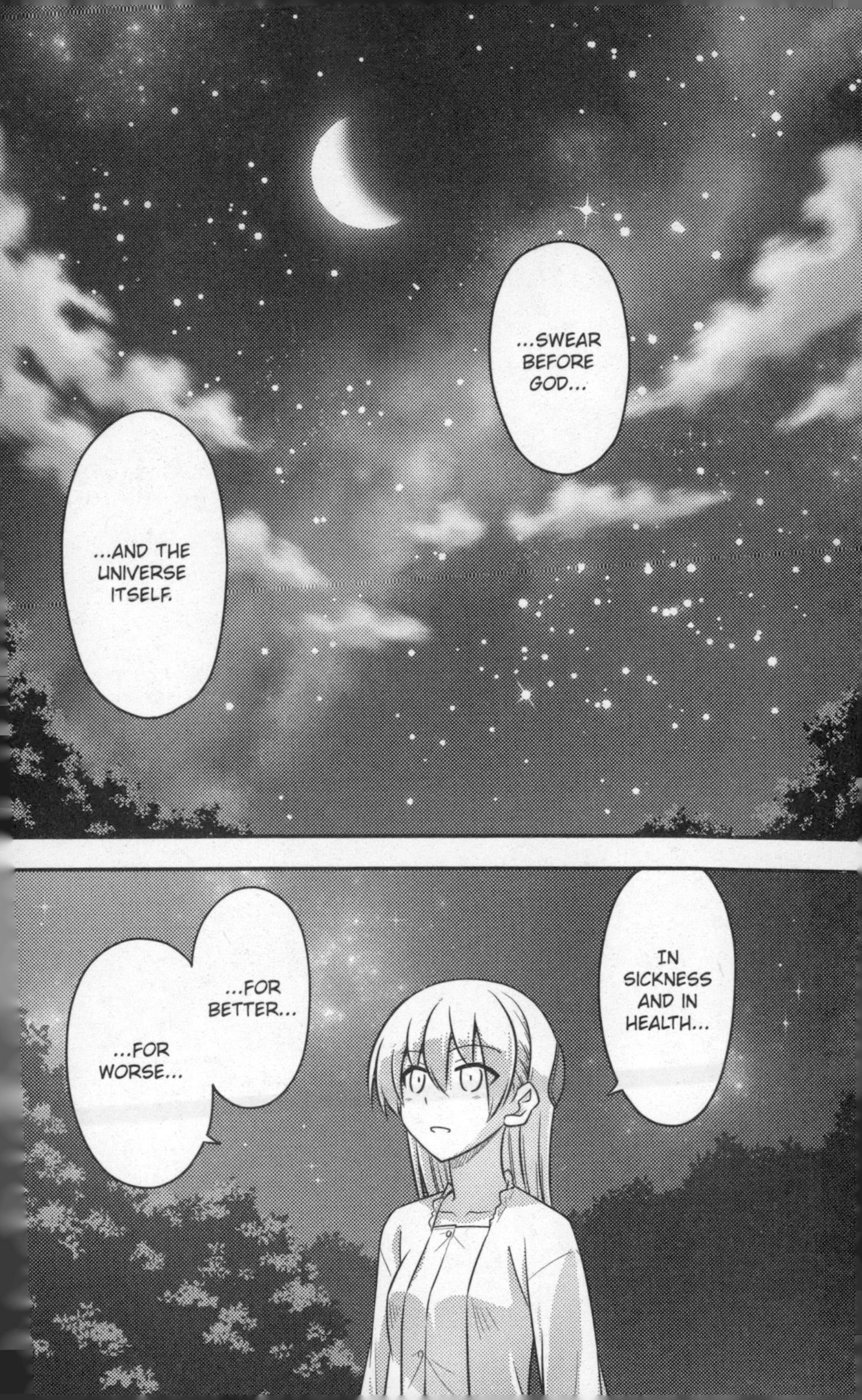
...SWEAR BEFORE GOD...
...AND THE UNIVERSE ITSELF.
IN SICKNESS AND IN HEALTH...
...FOR BETTER...
...FOR WORSE...

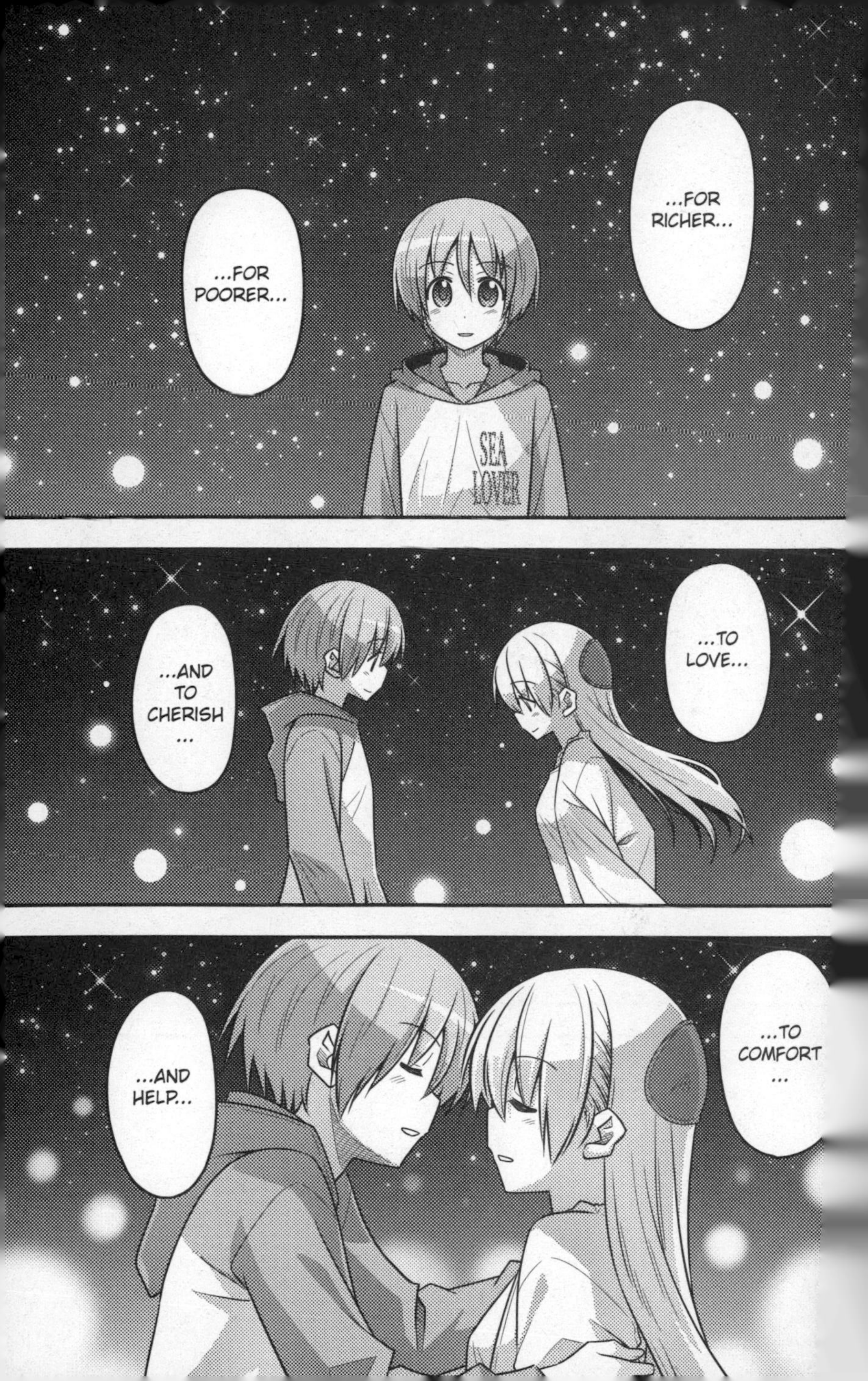
...FOR RICHER...
...FOR POORER...
SEA LOVER
...TO LOVE...
...AND TO CHERISH ...
...TO COMFORT ...
...AND HELP...

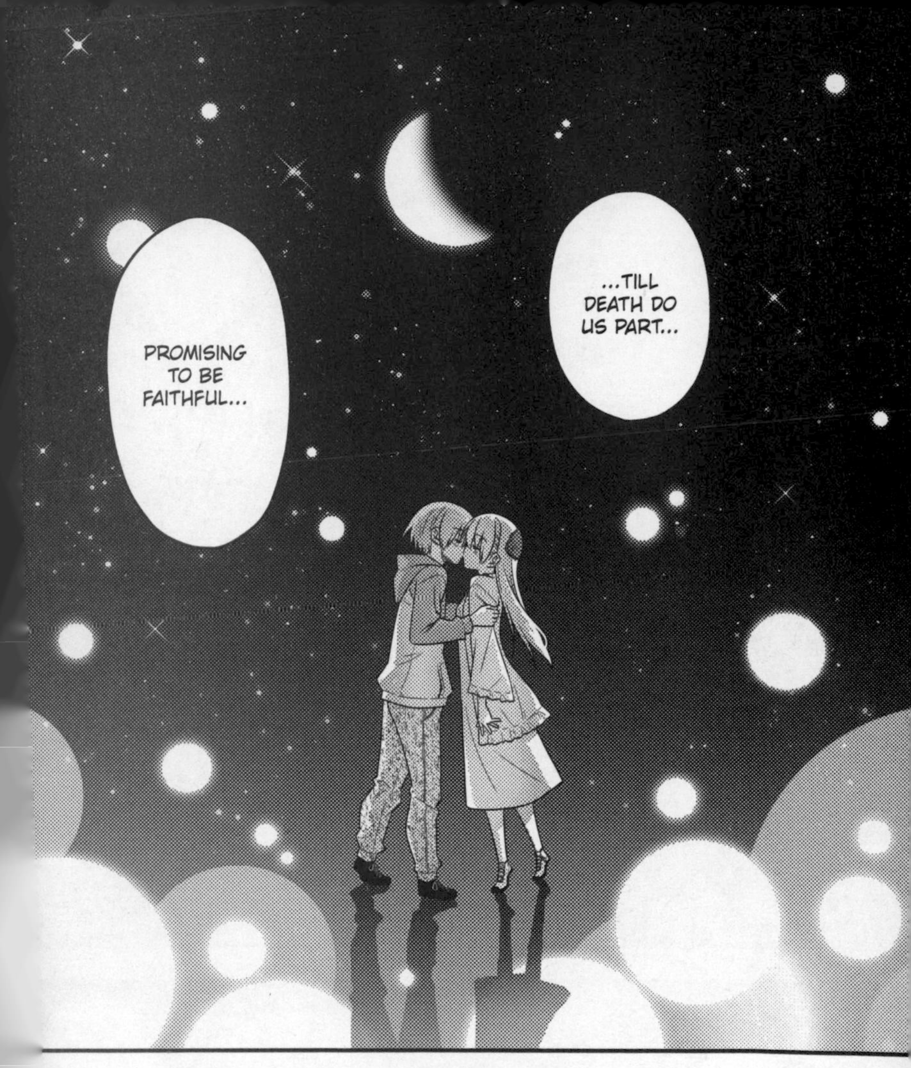
...TILL DEATH DO US PART...
PROMISING TO BE FAITHFUL...
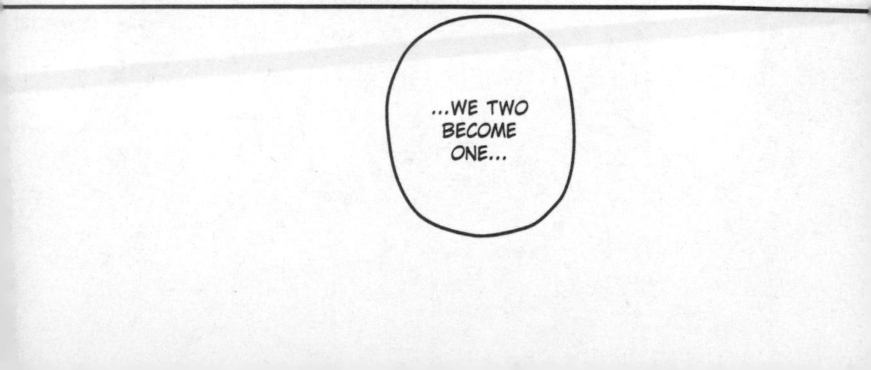
...WE TWO BECOME ONE...

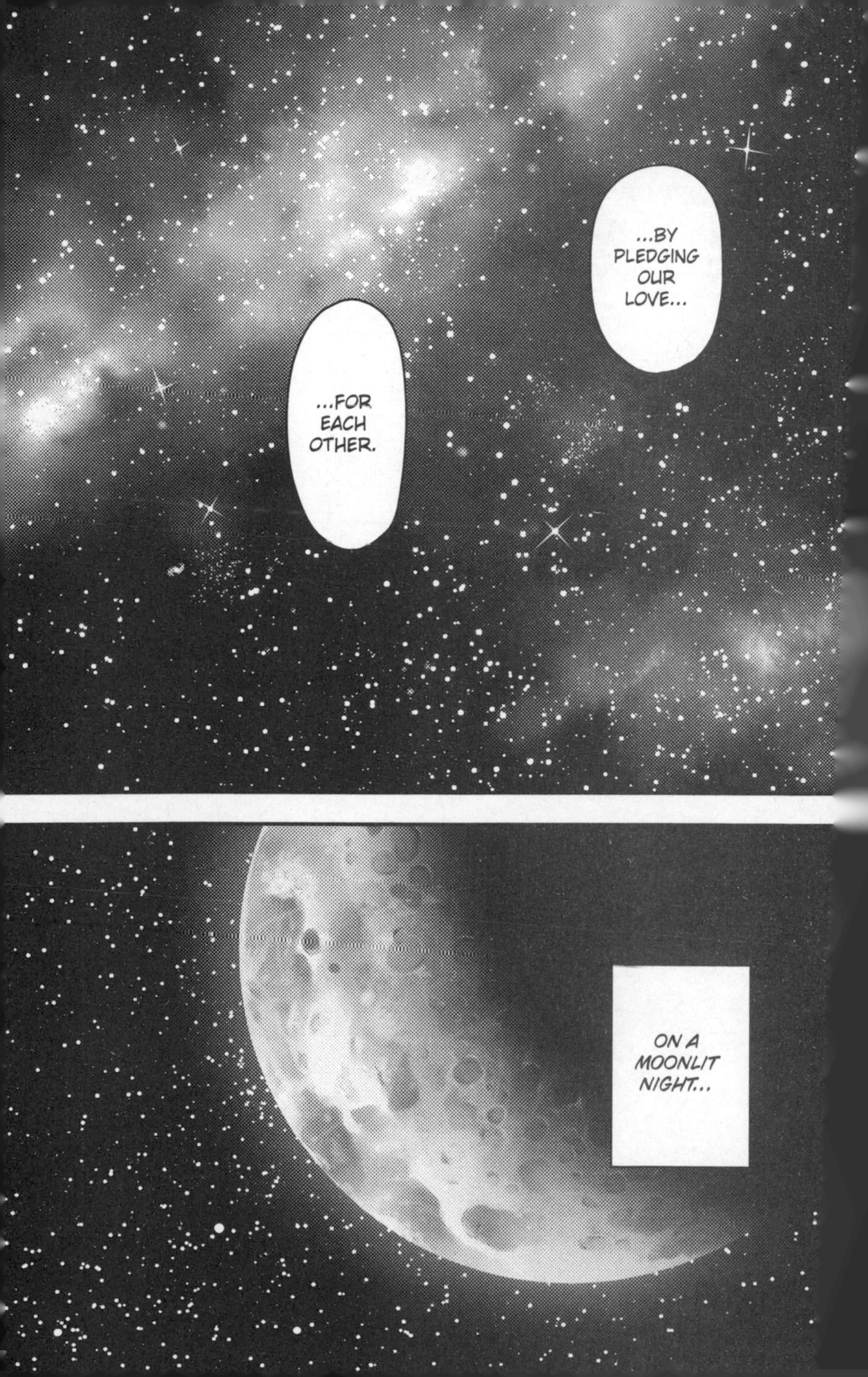
...BY PLEDGING OUR LOVE...
...FOR EACH OTHER.
ON A MOONLIT NIGHT...

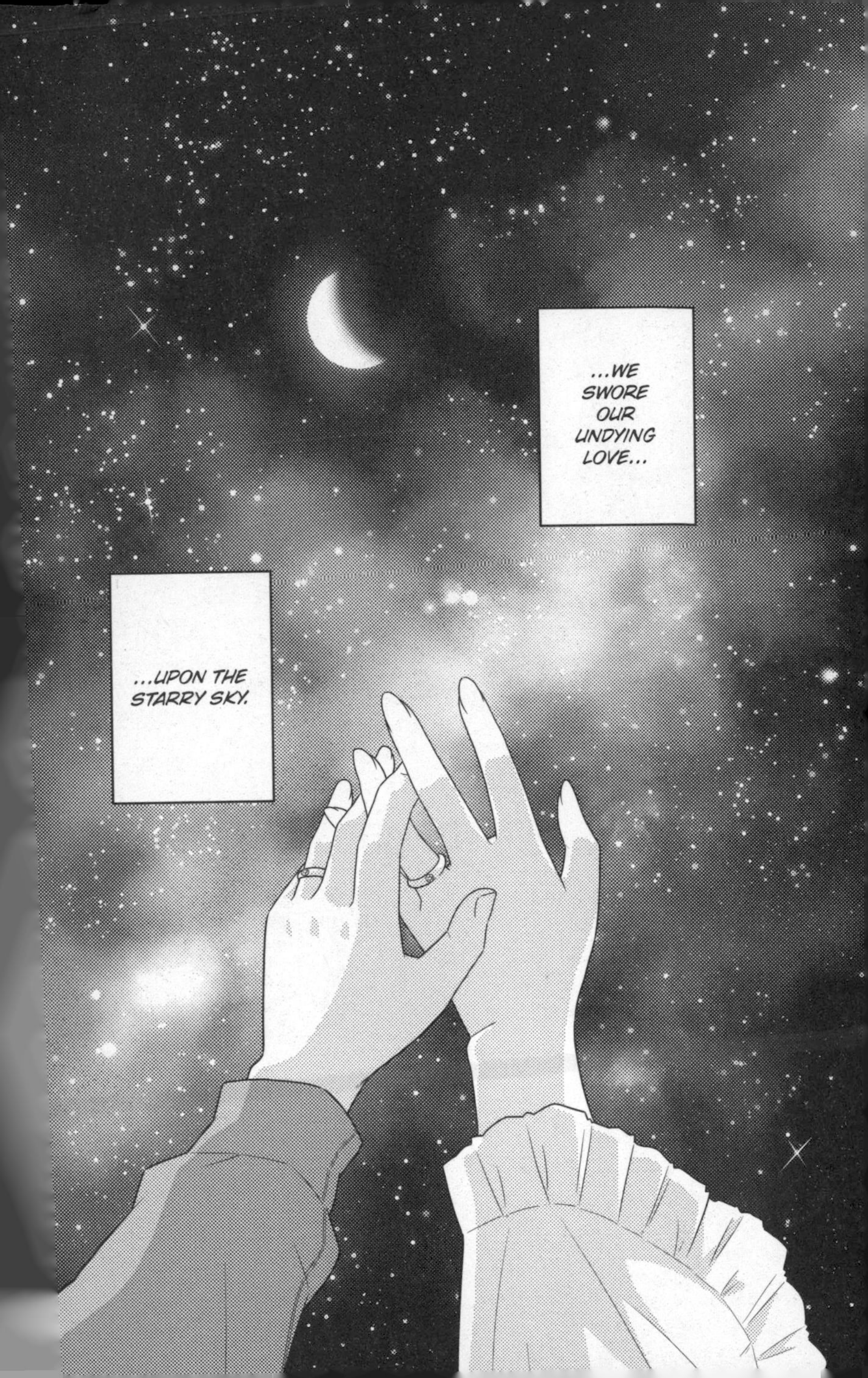
...WE SWORE OUR UNDYING LOVE...
...UPON THE STARRY SKY.

FLY ME TO THE MOON

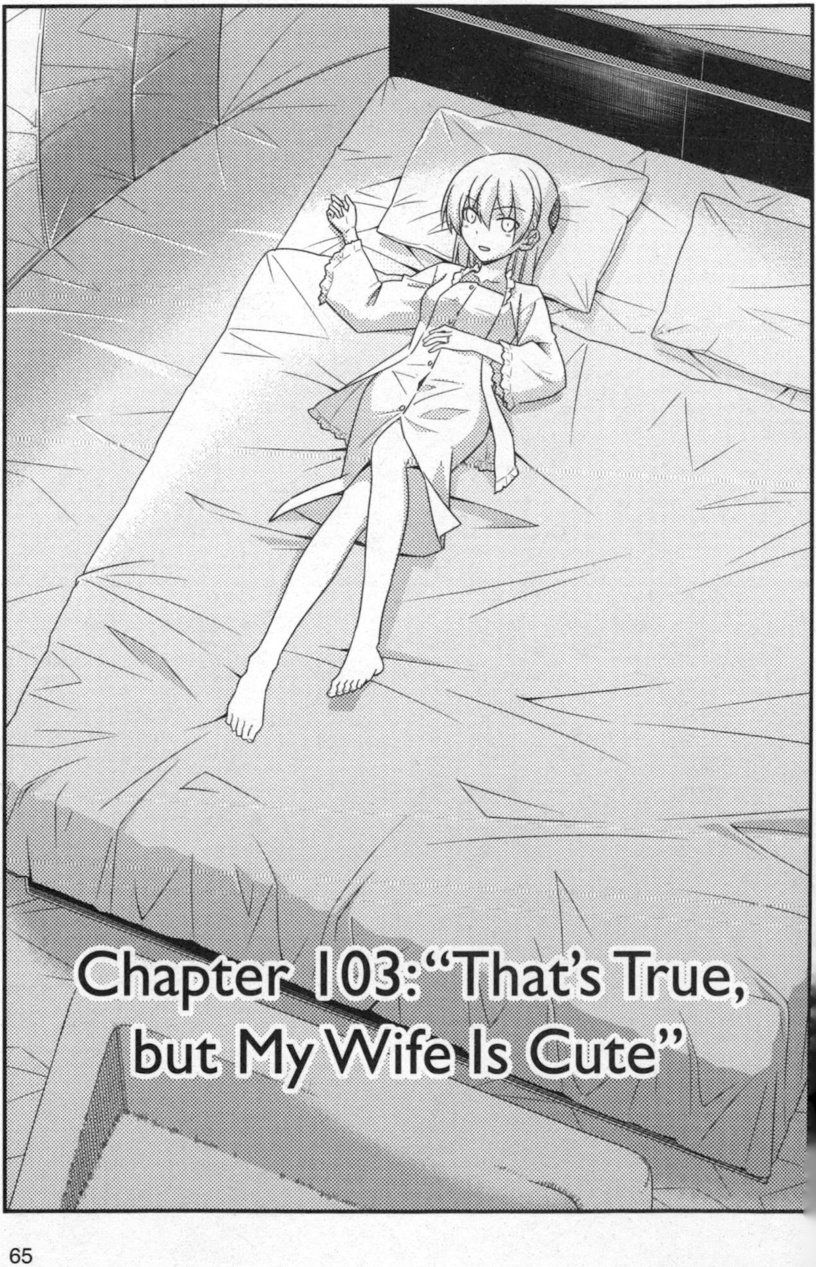
Chapter 103: "That's True, but My Wife Is Cute"

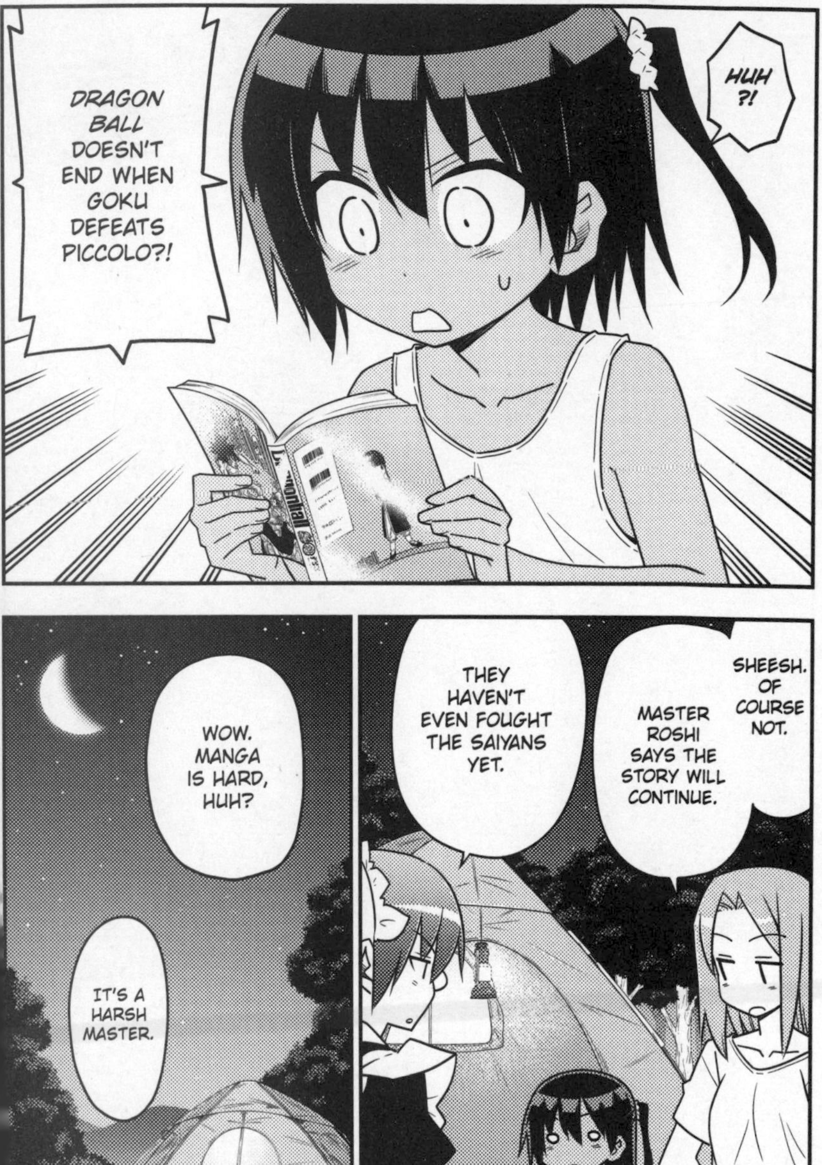
HUH ?!
DRAGON BALL DOESN'T END WHEN GOKU DEFEATS PICCOLO?!
SHEESH. OF COURSE NOT.
MASTER ROSHI SAYS THE STORY WILL CONTINUE.
THEY HAVEN'T EVEN FOUGHT THE SAIYANS YET.
WOW. MANGA IS HARD, HUH?
IT'S A HARSH MASTER.

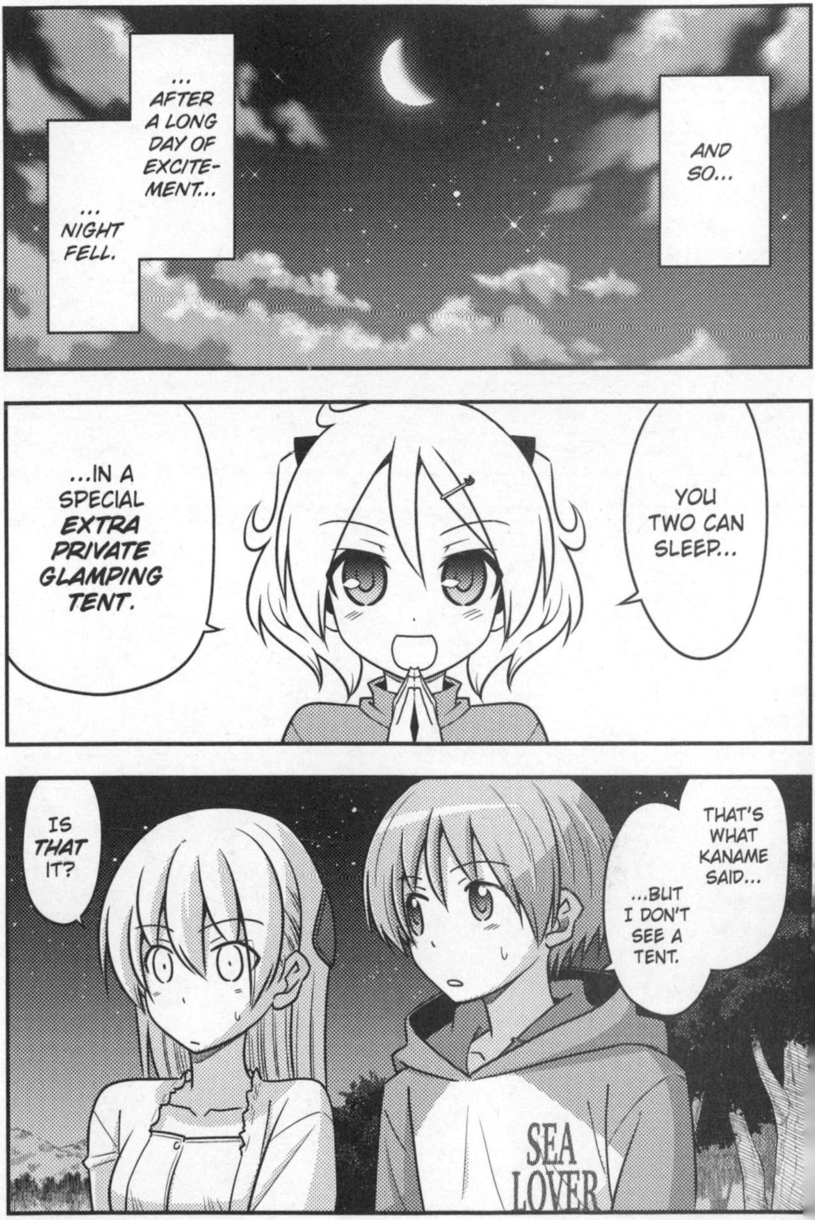
AND SO...
... AFTER A LONG DAY OF EXCITEMENT...
... NIGHT FELL.
YOU TWO CAN SLEEP...
...IN A SPECIAL EXTRA PRIVATE GLAMPING TENT.
THAT'S WHAT KANAME SAID...
...BUT I DON'T SEE A TENT.
IS THAT IT?
SEA LOVER

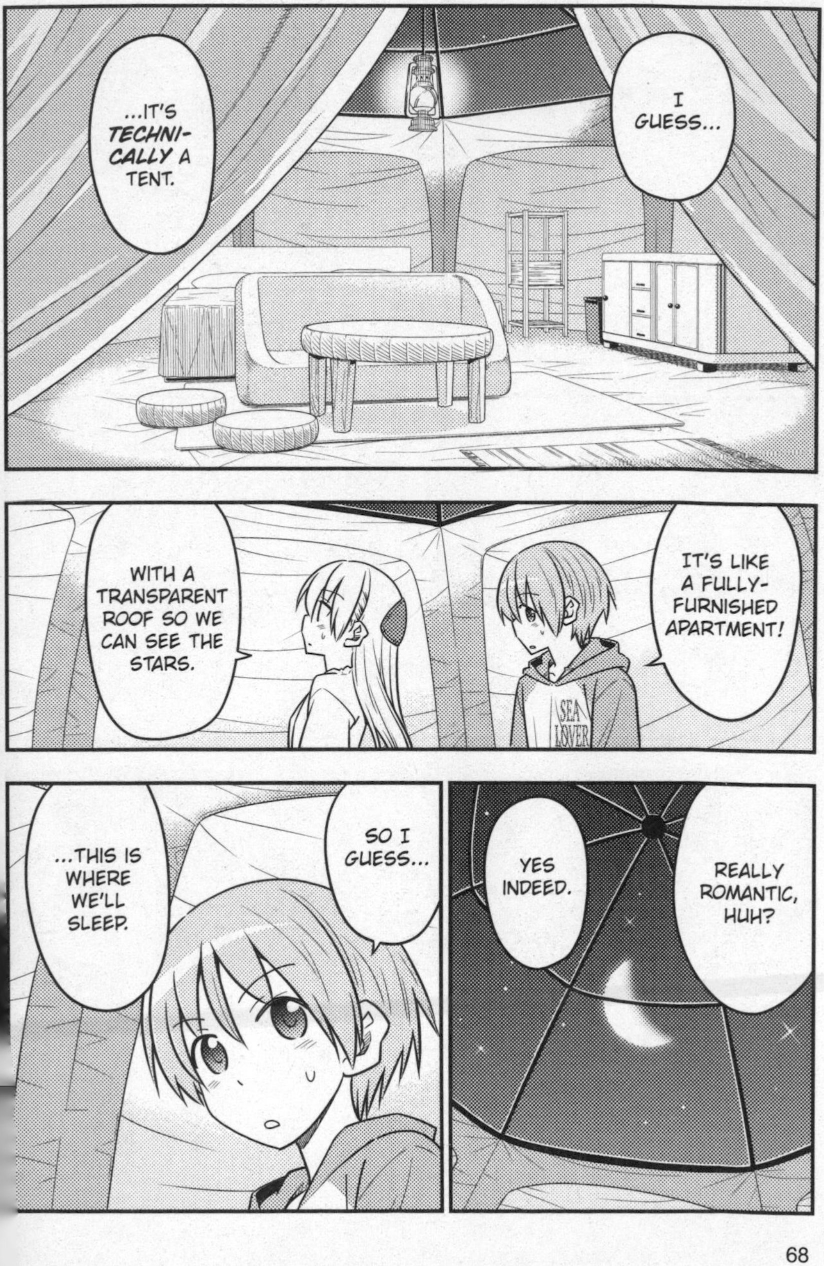
I GUESS...
...IT'S *TECHNICALLY* A TENT.
IT'S LIKE A FULLY-FURNISHED APARTMENT!
SEA LOVER
WITH A TRANSPARENT ROOF SO WE CAN SEE THE STARS.
REALLY ROMANTIC, HUH?
YES INDEED.
SO I GUESS...
...THIS IS WHERE WE'LL SLEEP.

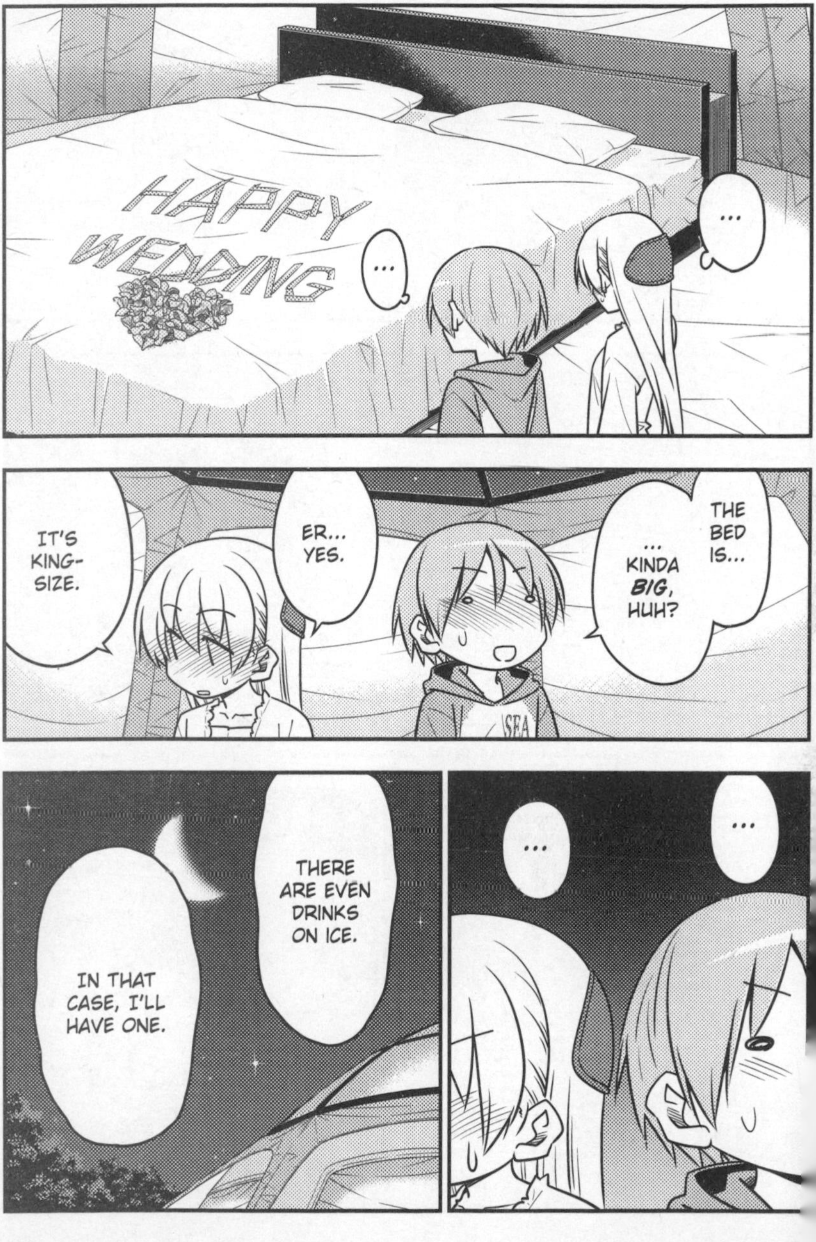
...
HAPPY WEDDING
...
THE BED IS... ...KINDA BIG, HUH?
ER... YES.
IT'S KING-SIZE.
...
...
THERE ARE EVEN DRINKS ON ICE.
IN THAT CASE, I'LL HAVE ONE.

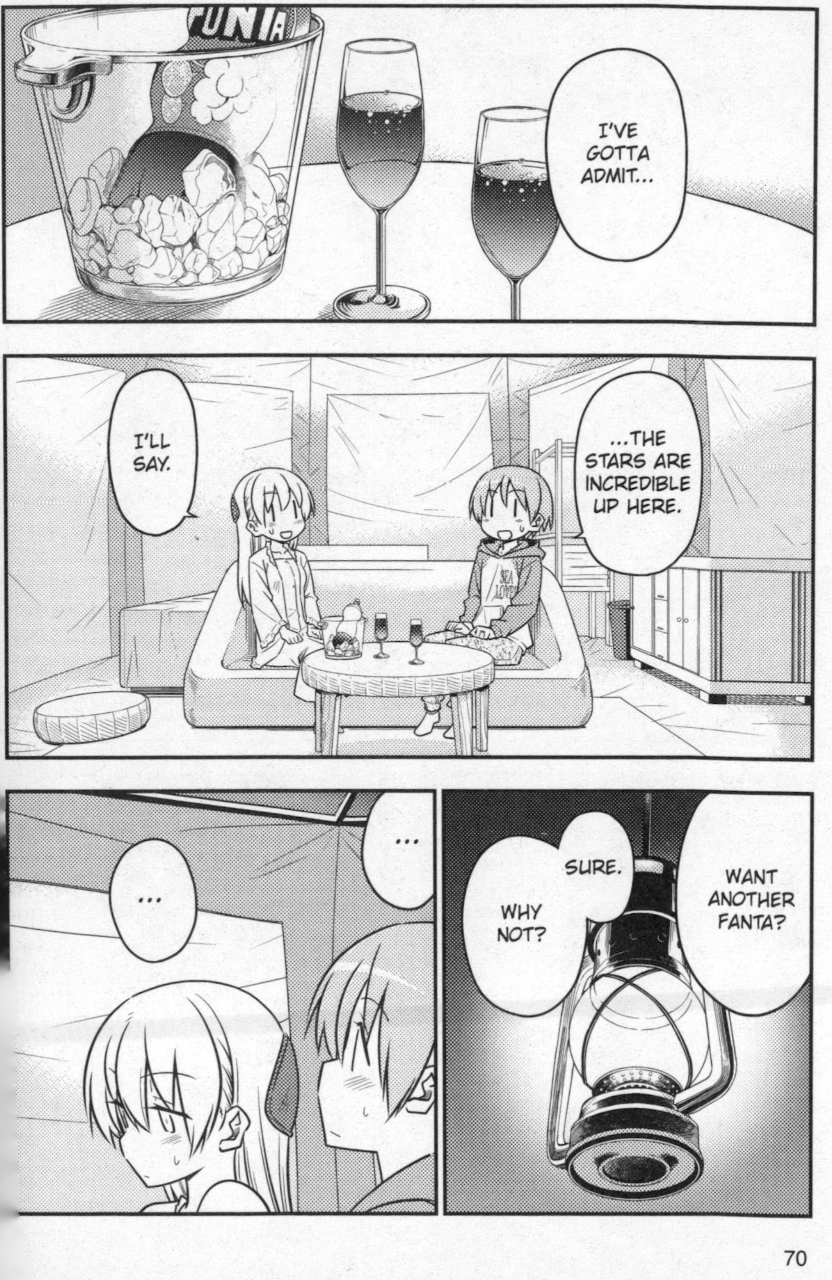
I'VE GOTTA ADMIT...
...THE STARS ARE INCREDIBLE UP HERE.
I'LL SAY.
WANT ANOTHER FANTA?
SURE.
WHY NOT?
...
...

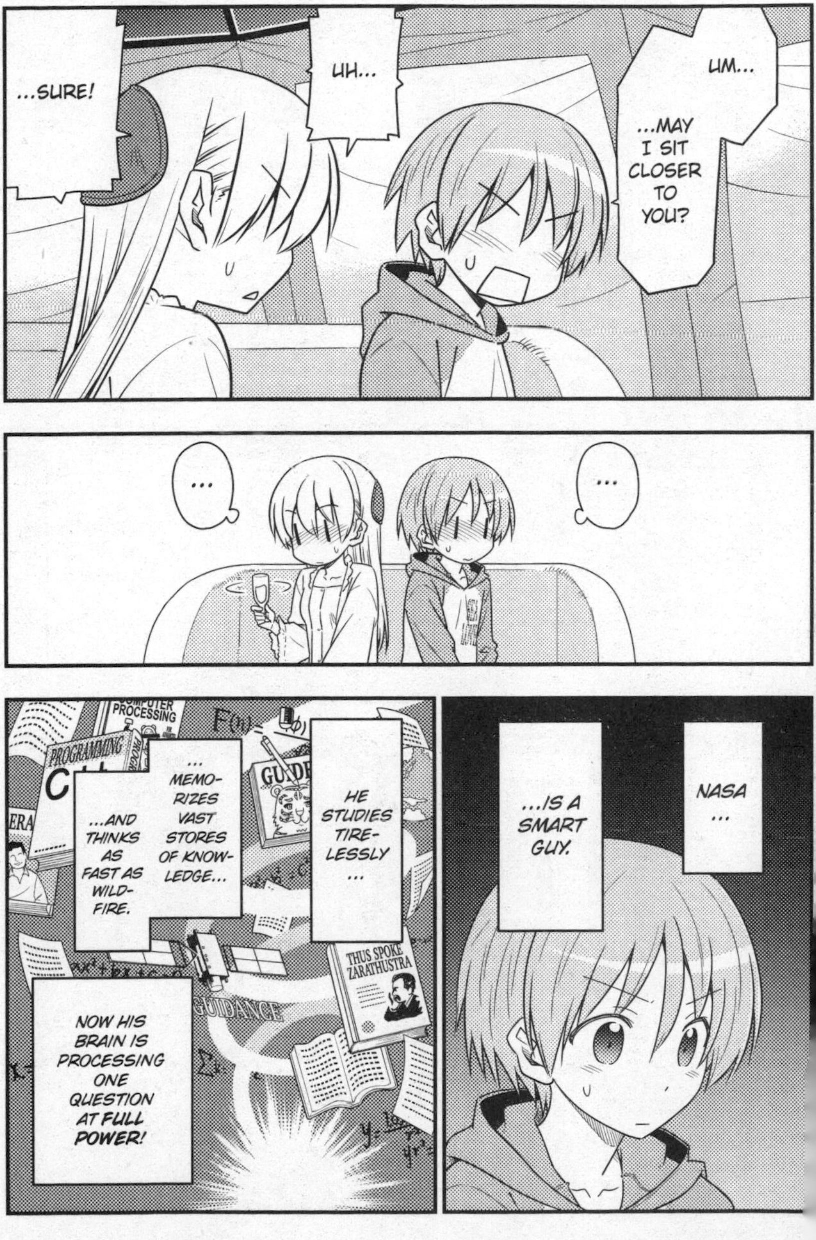
UM...
...MAY I SIT CLOSER TO YOU?
UH...
...SURE!
...
...
NASA...
...IS A SMART GUY.
HE STUDIES TIRELESSLY...
...MEMORIZES VAST STORES OF KNOWLEDGE...
...AND THINKS AS FAST AS WILDFIRE.
COMPUTER PROCESSING
PROGRAMMING
C
GUIDE
THUS SPOKE ZARATHUSTRA
GUIDANCE
NOW HIS BRAIN IS PROCESSING ONE QUESTION AT FULL POWER!

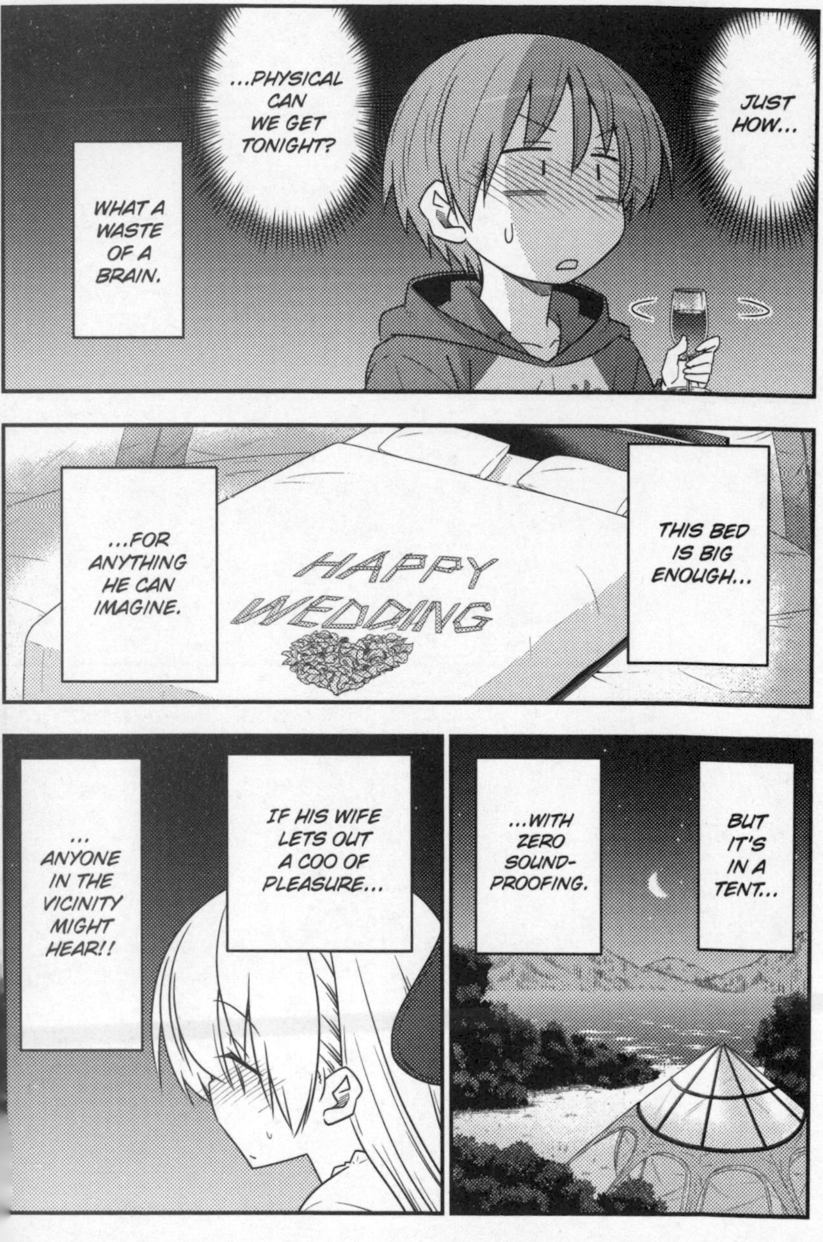
JUST HOW...
...PHYSICAL CAN WE GET TONIGHT?
WHAT A WASTE OF A BRAIN.
THIS BED IS BIG ENOUGH...
HAPPY WEDDING
...FOR ANYTHING HE CAN IMAGINE.
BUT IT'S IN A TENT...
...WITH ZERO SOUND-PROOFING.
IF HIS WIFE LETS OUT A COO OF PLEASURE...
... ANYONE IN THE VICINITY MIGHT HEAR!!

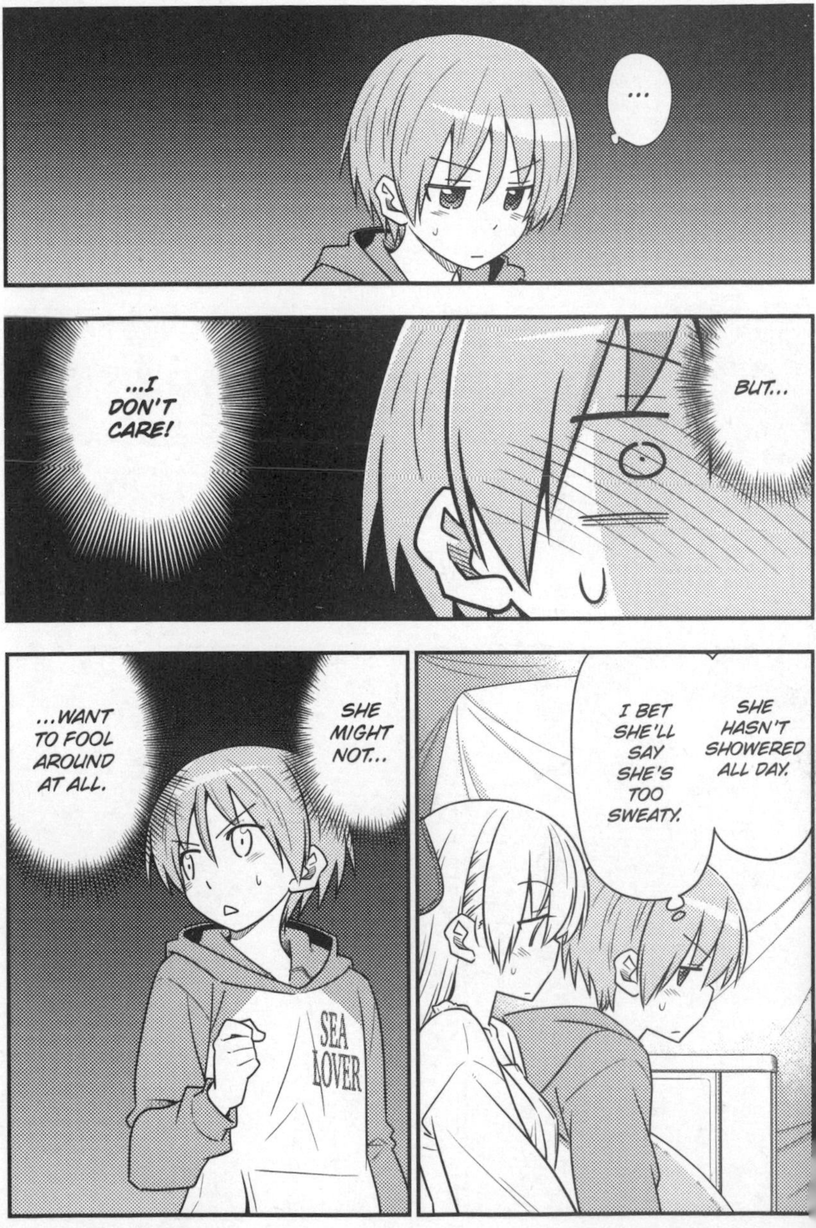
...
BUT...
...I DON'T CARE!
SHE HASN'T SHOWERED ALL DAY.
I BET SHE'LL SAY SHE'S TOO SWEATY.
SHE MIGHT NOT...
...WANT TO FOOL AROUND AT ALL.
SEA LOVER

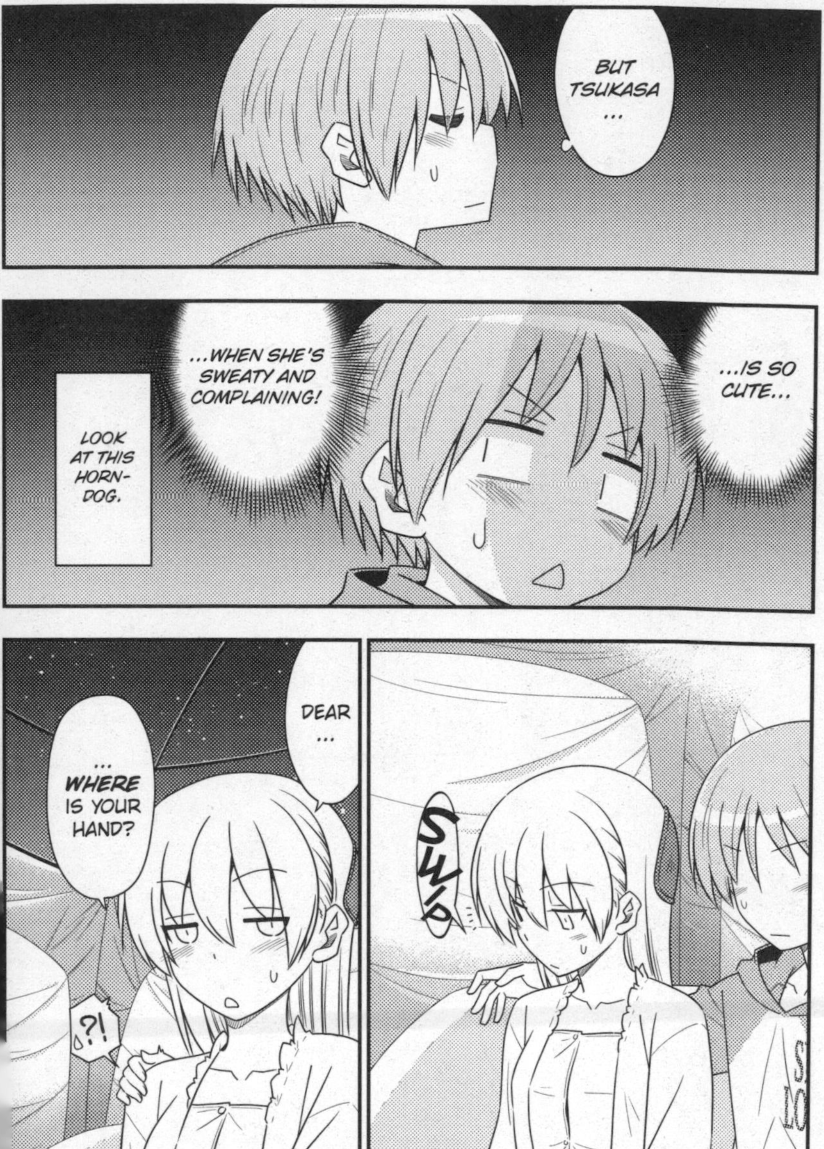
BUT TSUKASA ...
...IS SO CUTE...
...WHEN SHE'S SWEATY AND COMPLAINING!
LOOK AT THIS HORN-DOG.
SWIP
DEAR ...
... WHERE IS YOUR HAND?
?!

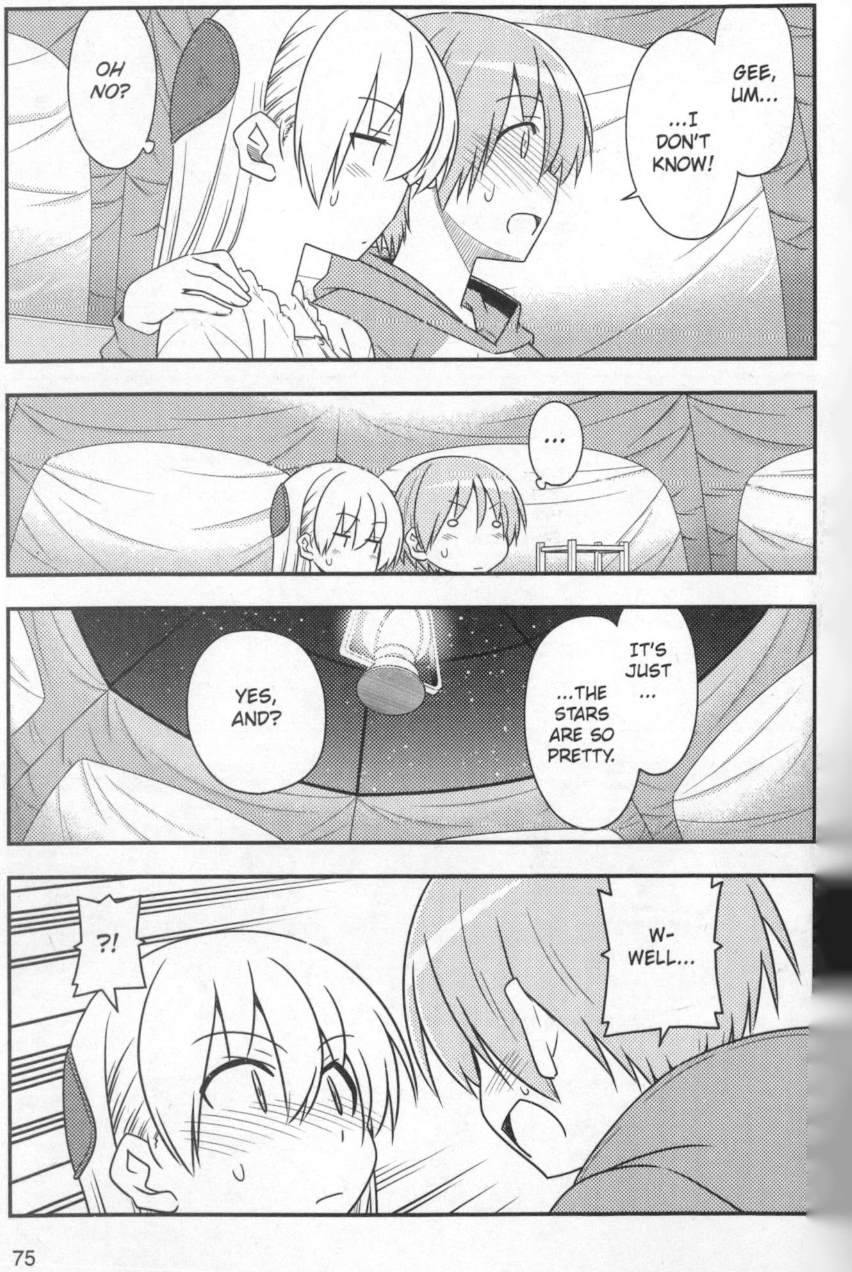
GEE, UM...
...I DON'T KNOW!
OH NO?
...
IT'S JUST ...
...THE STARS ARE SO PRETTY.
YES, AND?
W-WELL...
?!

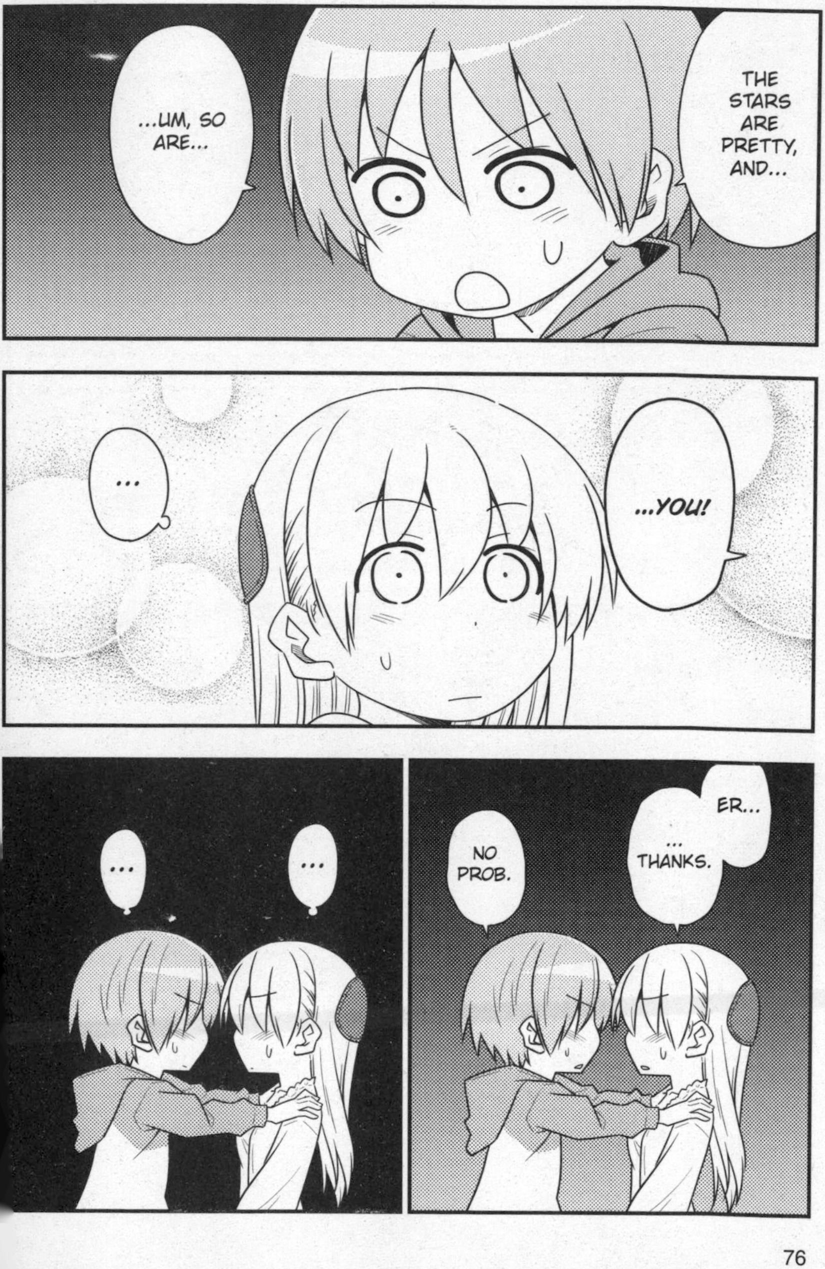
THE STARS ARE PRETTY, AND...
...UM, SO ARE...
...YOU!
...
ER... ... THANKS.
NO PROB.
...
...

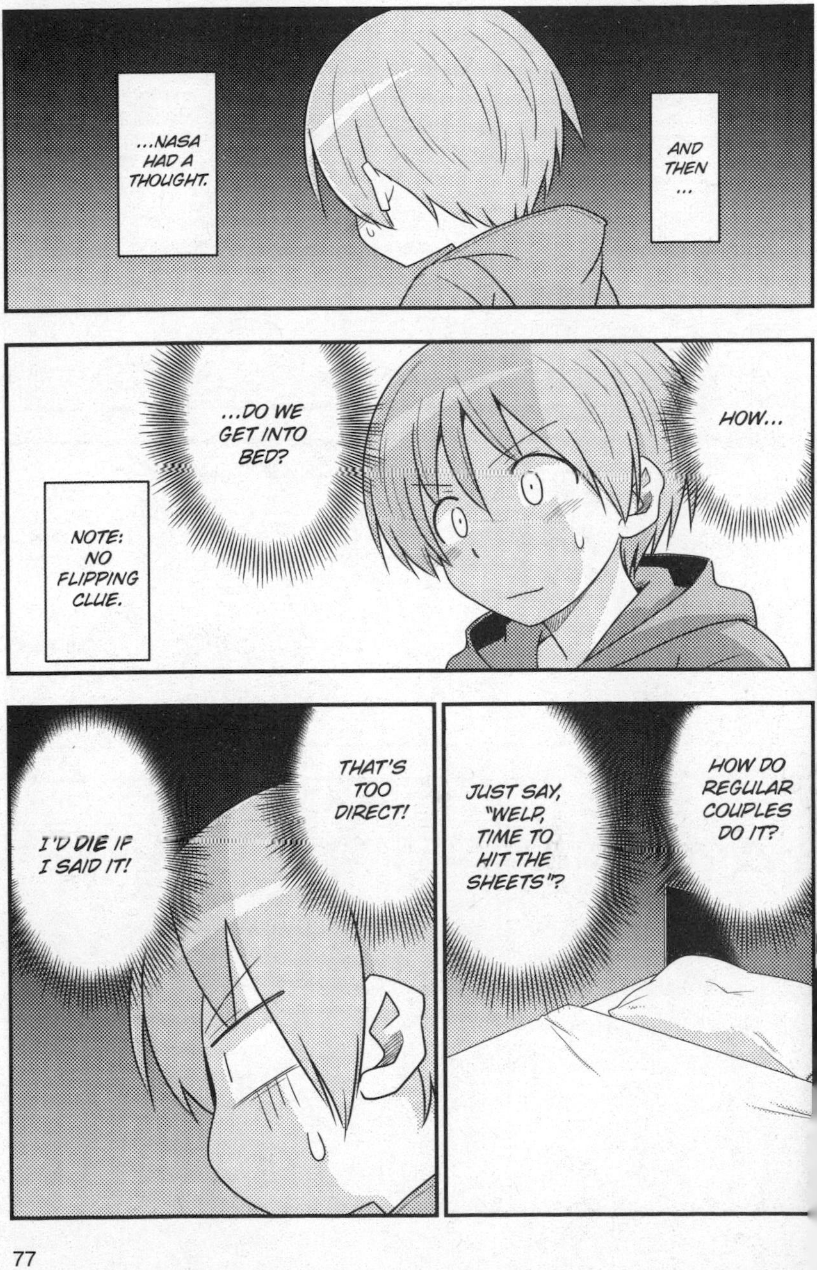
AND THEN ...
...NASA HAD A THOUGHT.
HOW...
...DO WE GET INTO BED?
NOTE: NO FLIPPING CLUE.
HOW DO REGULAR COUPLES DO IT?
JUST SAY, "WELP, TIME TO HIT THE SHEETS"?
THAT'S TOO DIRECT!
I'D DIE IF I SAID IT!

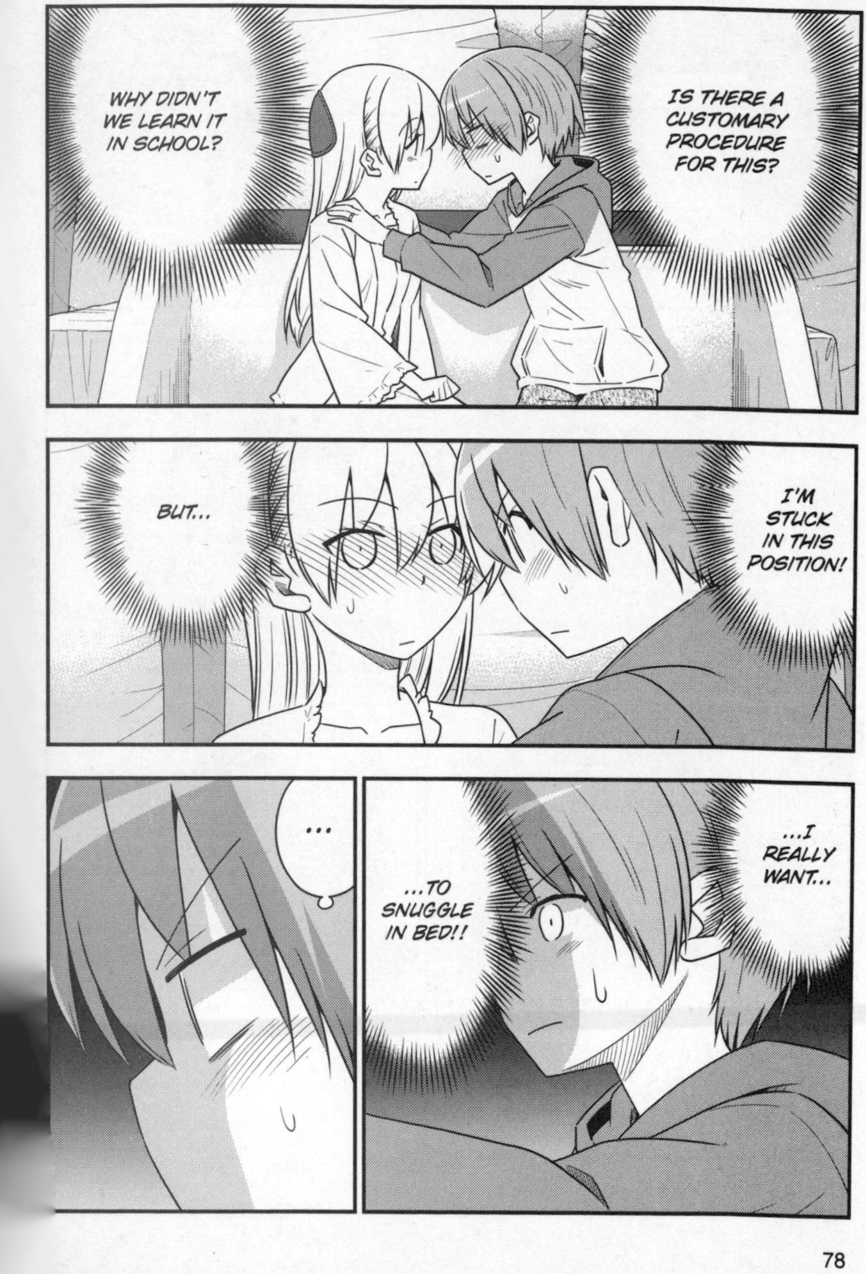
IS THERE A CUSTOMARY PROCEDURE FOR THIS?
WHY DIDN'T WE LEARN IT IN SCHOOL?
I'M STUCK IN THIS POSITION!
BUT...
...I REALLY WANT...
...TO SNUGGLE IN BED!!
...

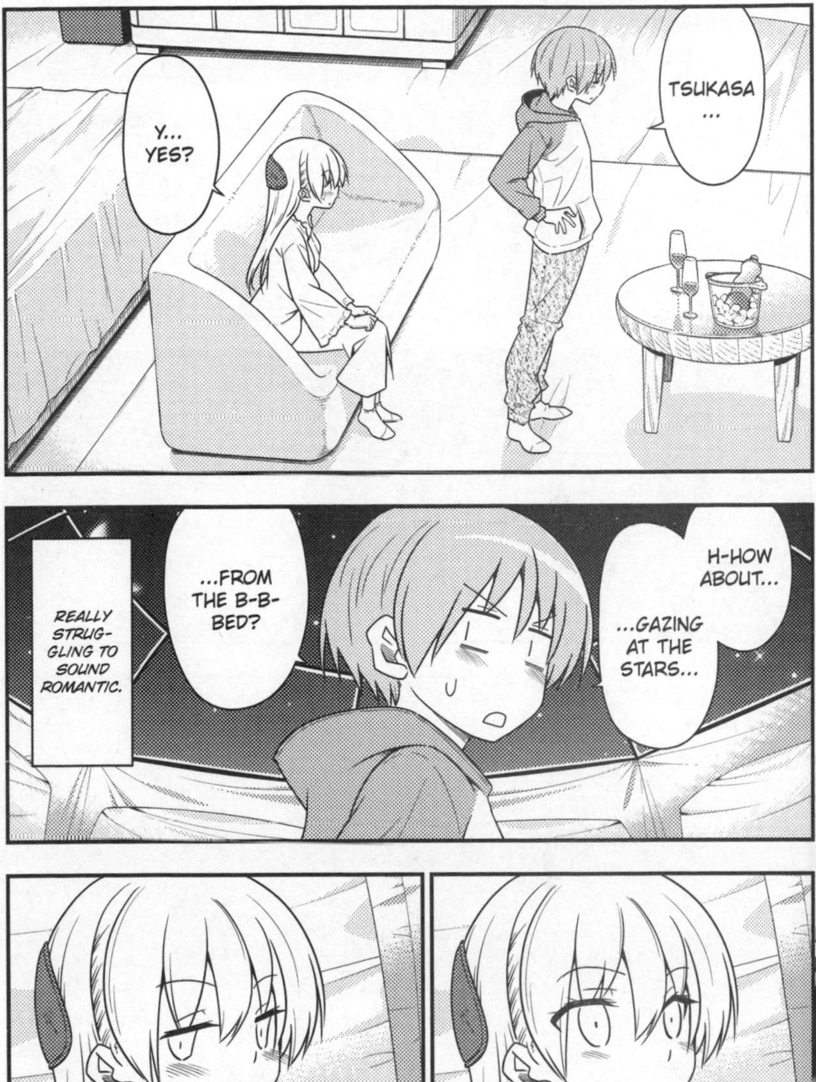
TSUKASA ...
Y... YES?
H-HOW ABOUT...
...GAZING AT THE STARS...
...FROM THE B-B-BED?
REALLY STRUGGLING TO SOUND ROMANTIC.

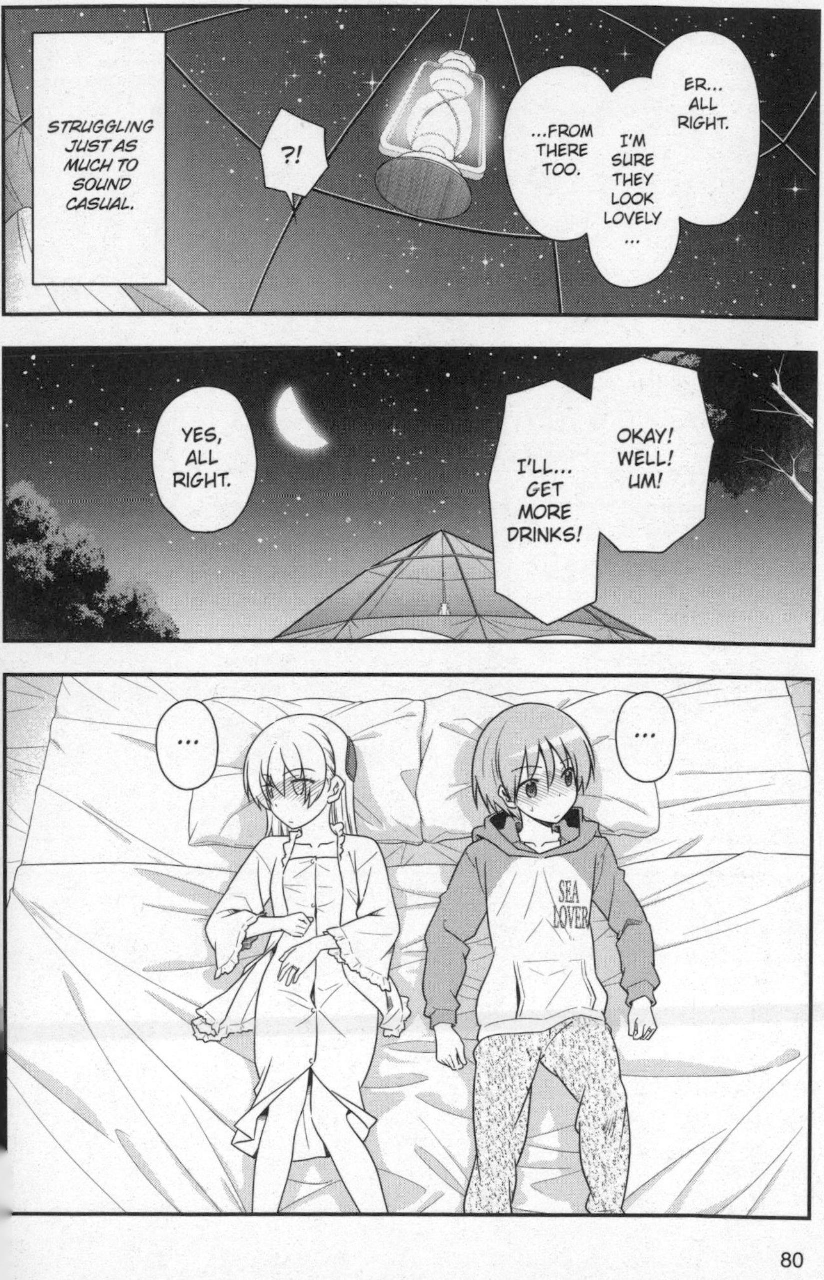
ER... ALL RIGHT.
I'M SURE THEY LOOK LOVELY ...
...FROM THERE TOO.
?!
STRUGGLING JUST AS MUCH TO SOUND CASUAL.
OKAY! WELL! UM!
I'LL... GET MORE DRINKS!
YES, ALL RIGHT.
...
SEA LOVER
...

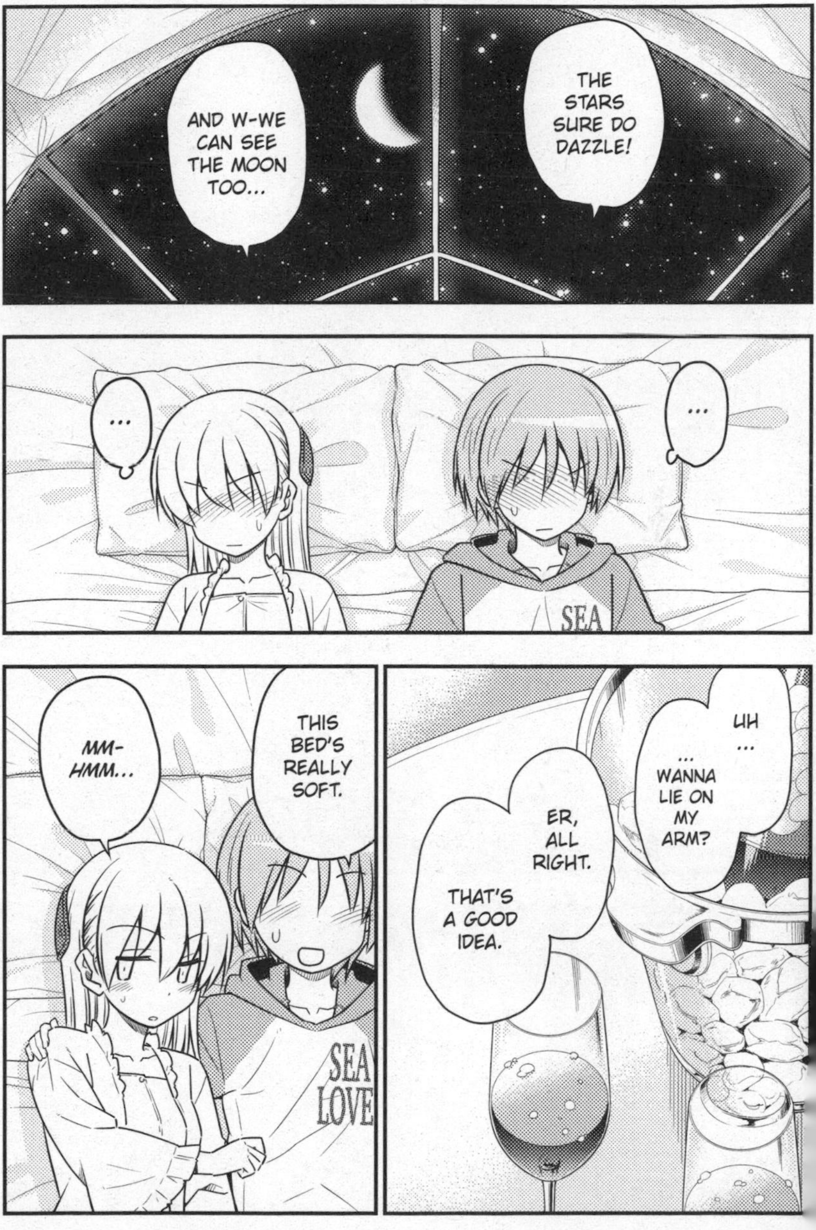
THE STARS SURE DO DAZZLE!
AND W-WE CAN SEE THE MOON TOO...
...
...
UH... ...WANNA LIE ON MY ARM?
ER, ALL RIGHT. THAT'S A GOOD IDEA.
THIS BED'S REALLY SOFT.
MM-HMM...
SEA
SEA LOVE

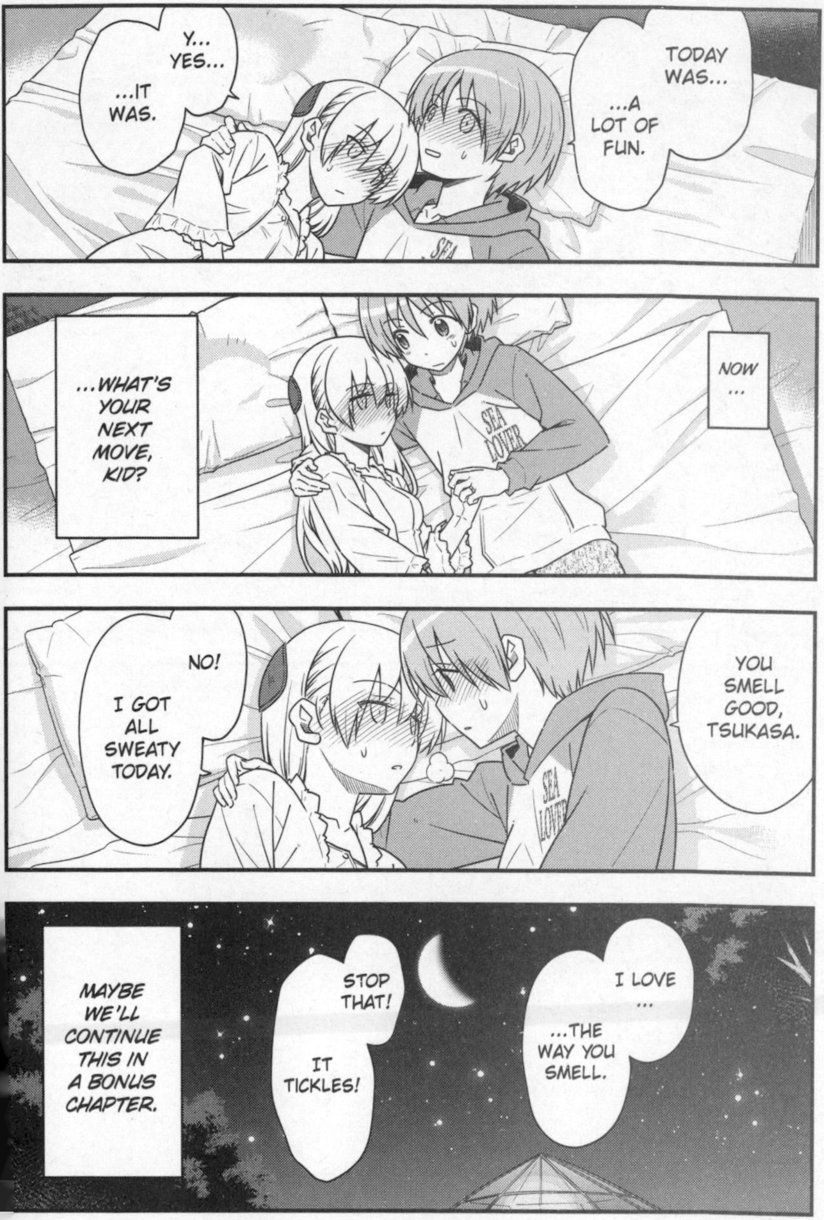
TODAY WAS... ...A LOT OF FUN.
Y... YES... ...IT WAS.
NOW...
...WHAT'S YOUR NEXT MOVE, KID?
YOU SMELL GOOD, TSUKASA.
NO! I GOT ALL SWEATY TODAY.
I LOVE... ...THE WAY YOU SMELL.
STOP THAT! IT TICKLES!
MAYBE WE'LL CONTINUE THIS IN A BONUS CHAPTER.

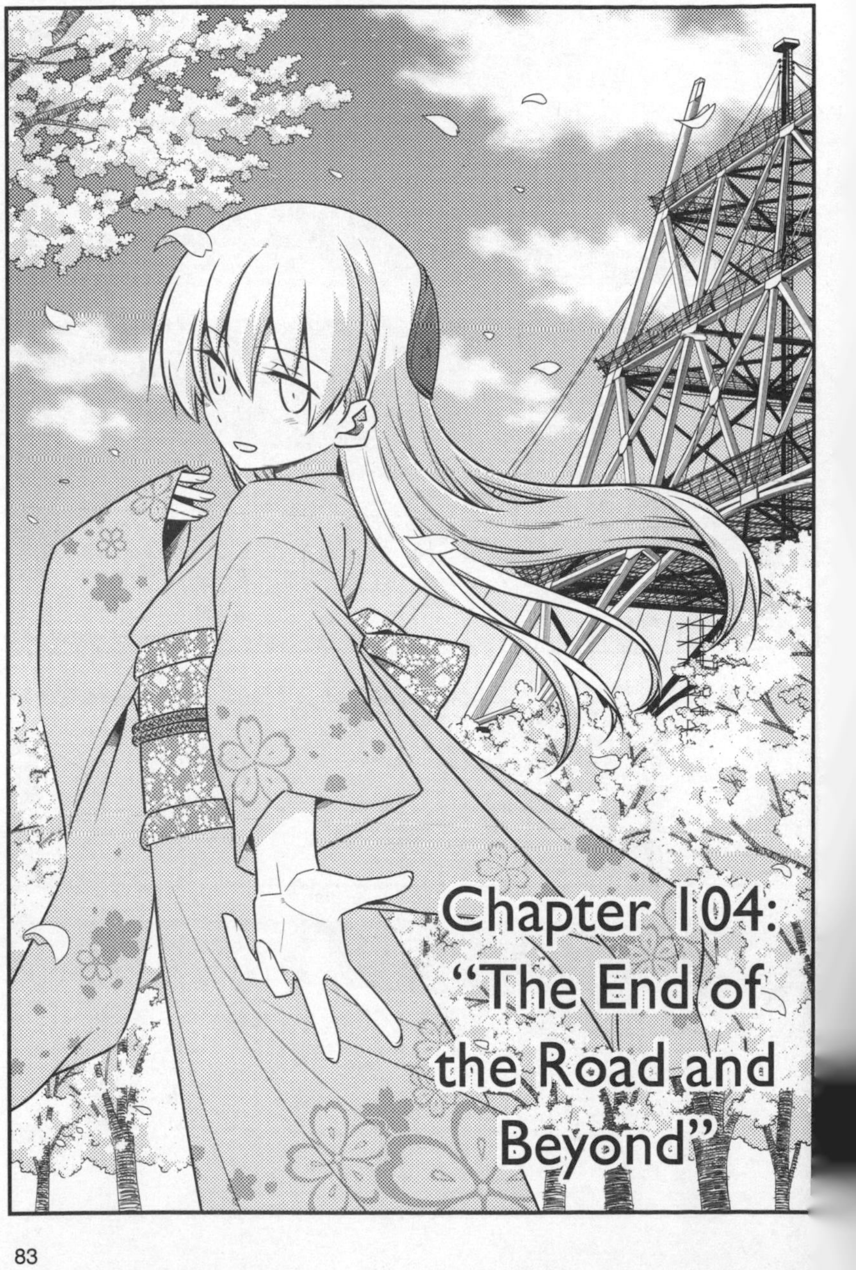
Chapter 104:
"The End of the Road and Beyond"

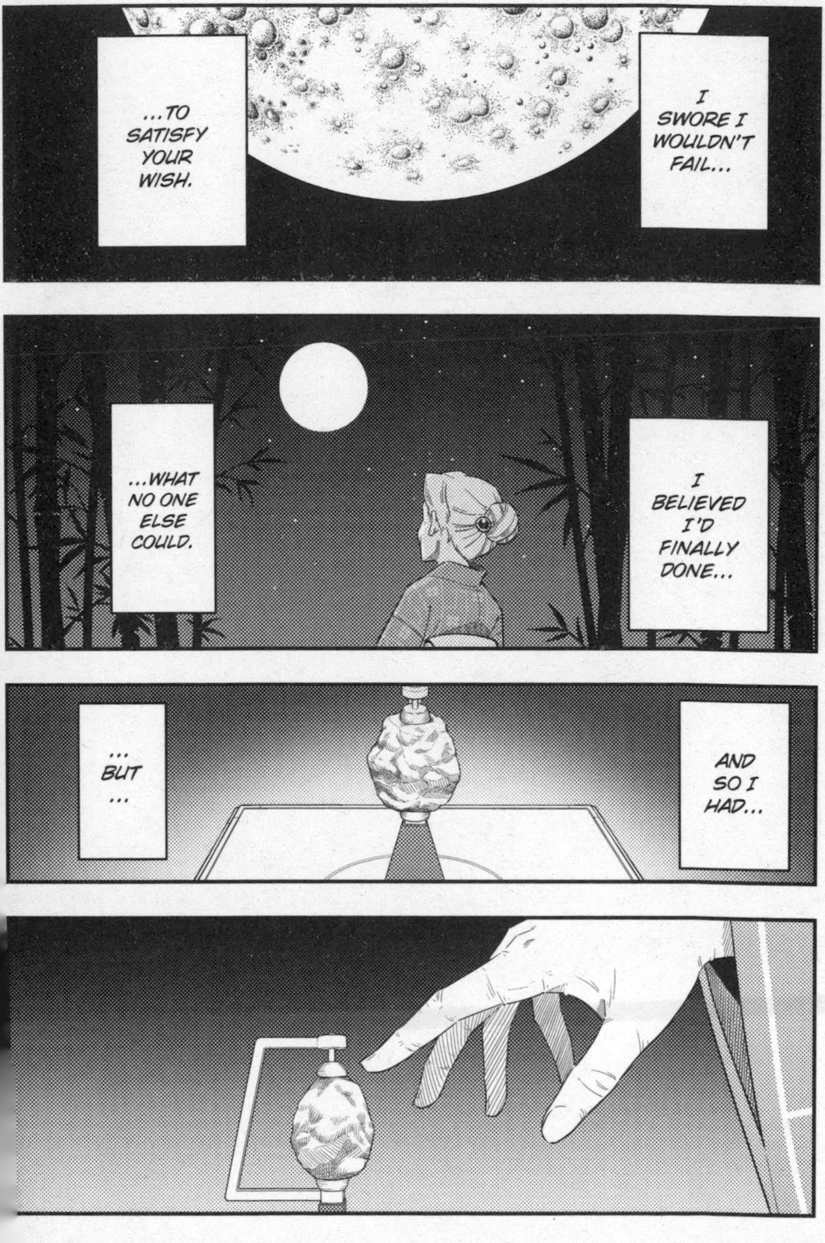
I SWORE I WOULDN'T FAIL...
...TO SATISFY YOUR WISH.
I BELIEVED I'D FINALLY DONE...
...WHAT NO ONE ELSE COULD.
AND SO I HAD...
... BUT ...

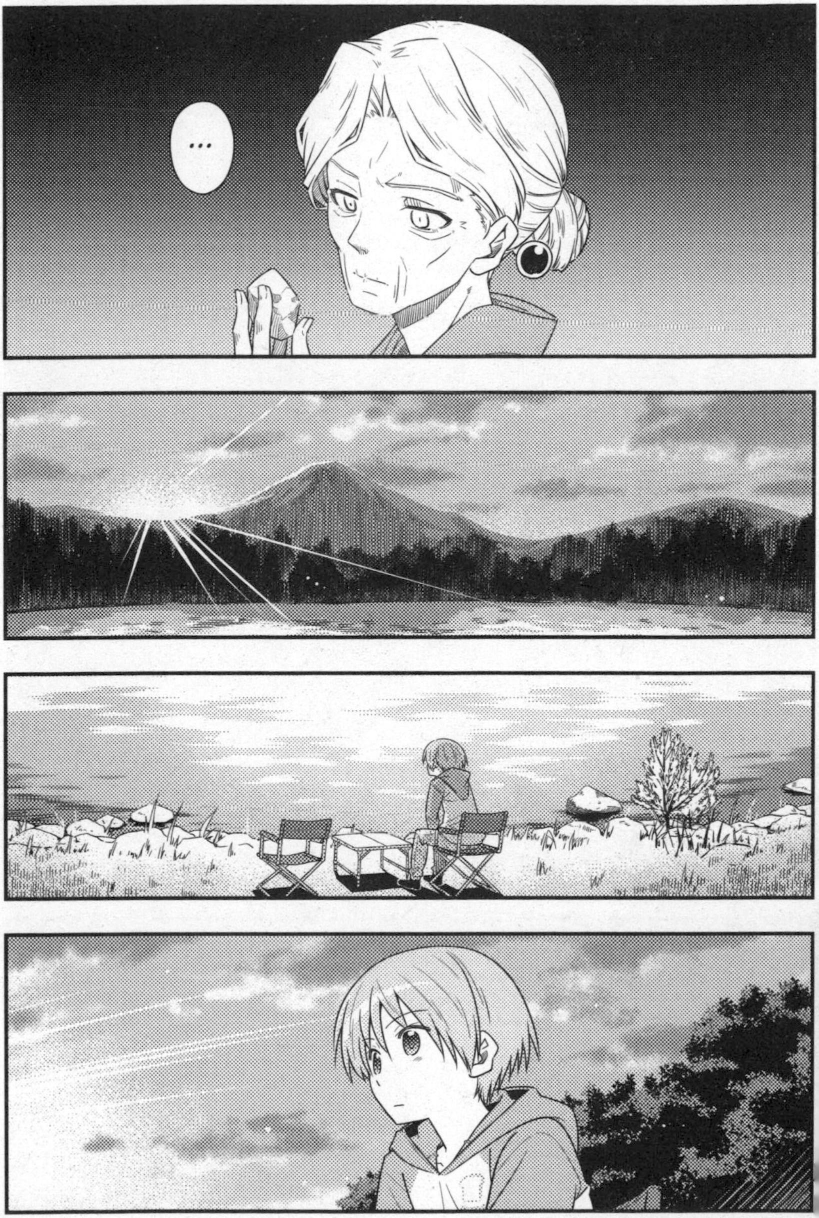
...

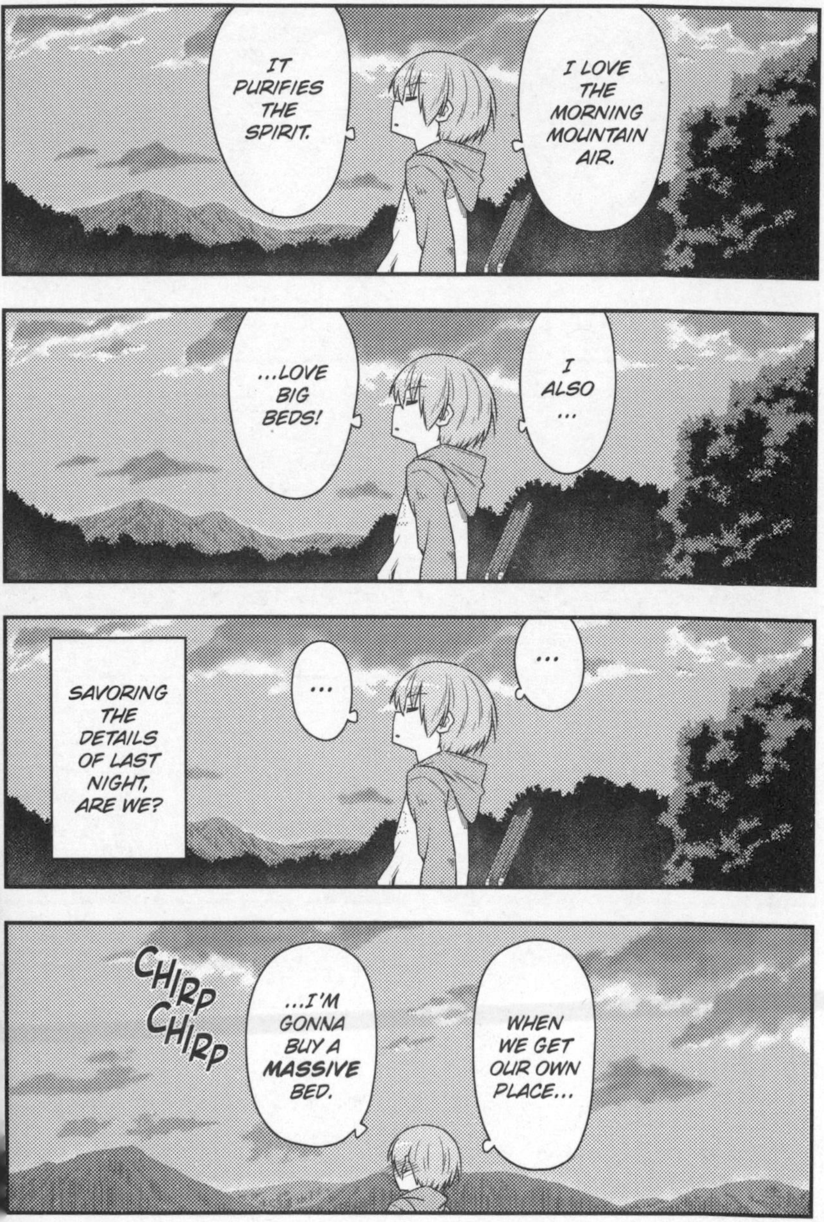
I LOVE THE MORNING MOUNTAIN AIR.
IT PURIFIES THE SPIRIT.
I ALSO ...
...LOVE BIG BEDS!
...
...
SAVORING THE DETAILS OF LAST NIGHT, ARE WE?
WHEN WE GET OUR OWN PLACE...
...I'M GONNA BUY A **MASSIVE** BED.
CHIRP CHIRP

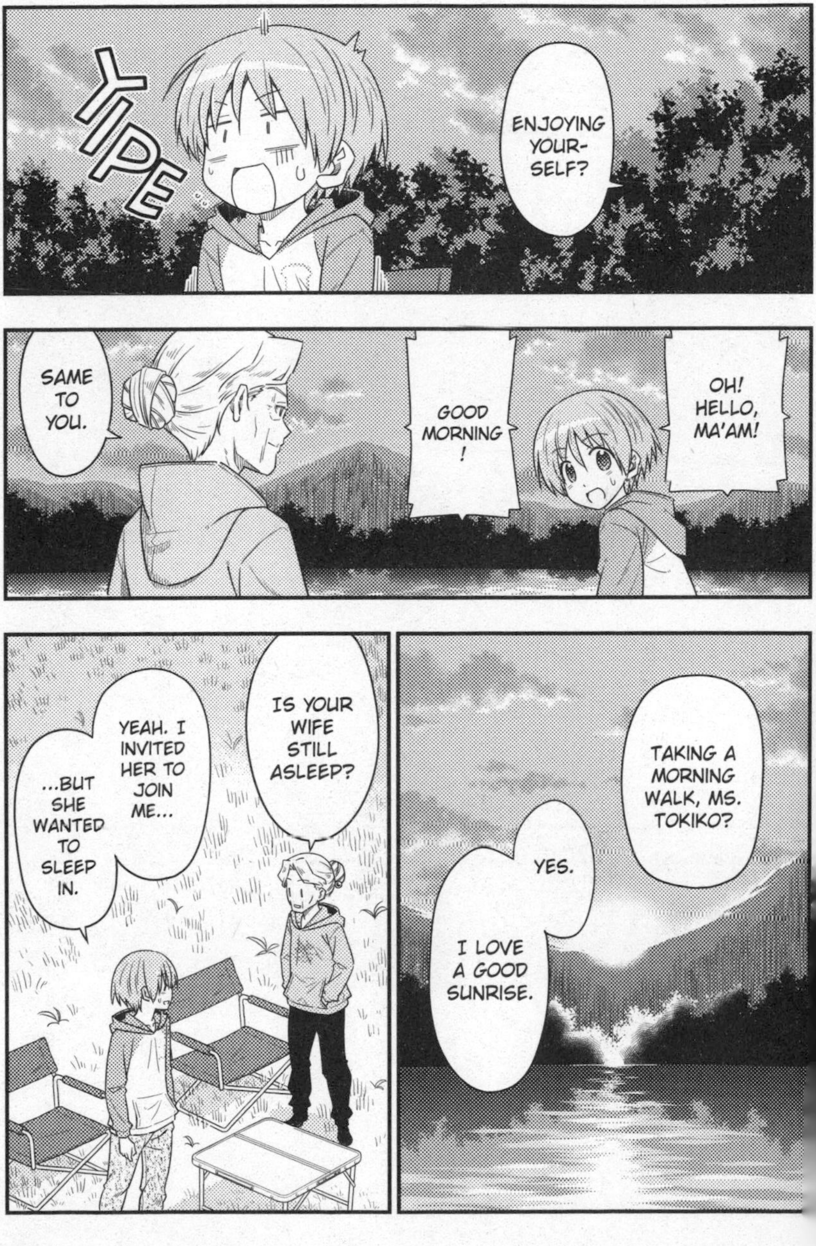
ENJOYING YOURSELF?
YIPE
OH! HELLO, MA'AM!
GOOD MORNING!
SAME TO YOU.
TAKING A MORNING WALK, MS. TOKIKO?
YES.
I LOVE A GOOD SUNRISE.
IS YOUR WIFE STILL ASLEEP?
YEAH. I INVITED HER TO JOIN ME...
...BUT SHE WANTED TO SLEEP IN.

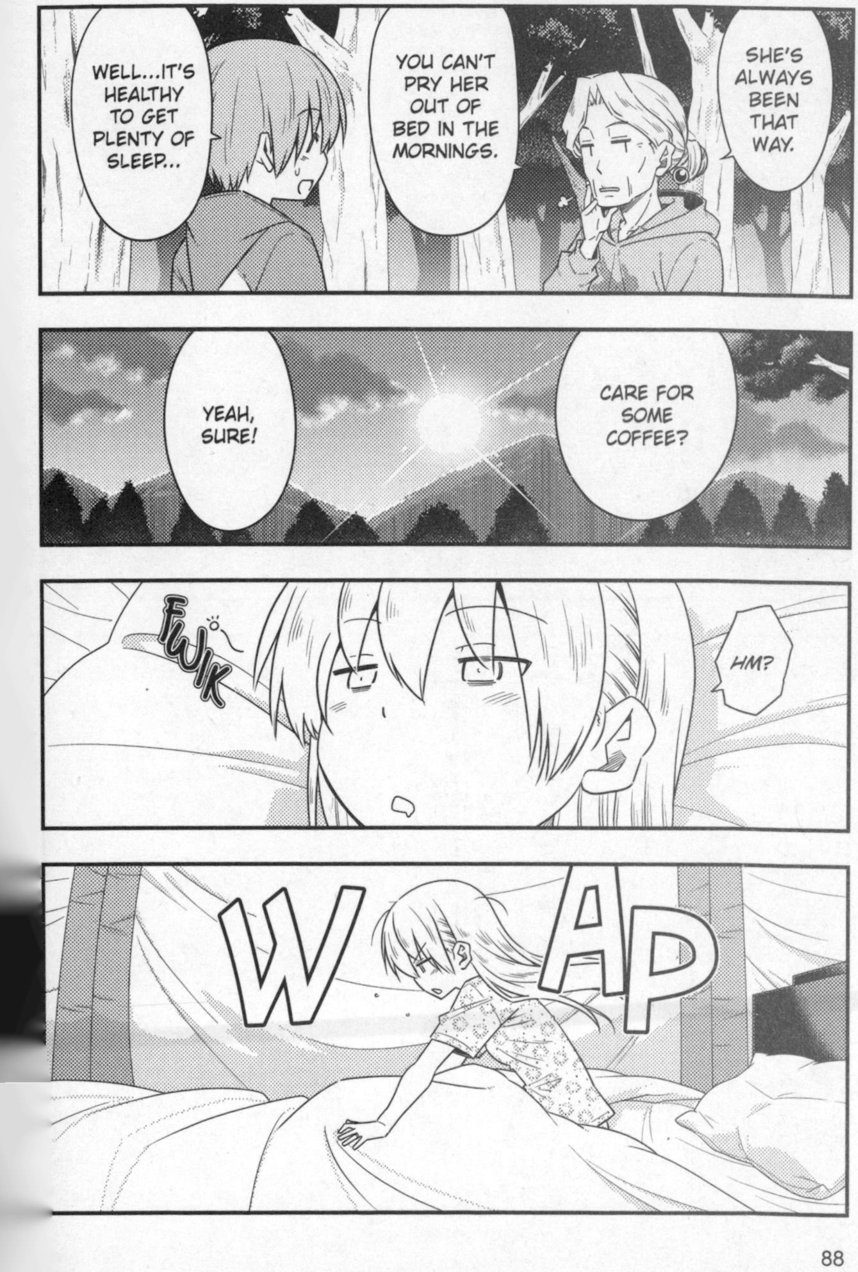
SHE'S ALWAYS BEEN THAT WAY.
YOU CAN'T PRY HER OUT OF BED IN THE MORNINGS.
WELL...IT'S HEALTHY TO GET PLENTY OF SLEEP...
CARE FOR SOME COFFEE?
YEAH, SURE!
HM?
FWIK
WAP

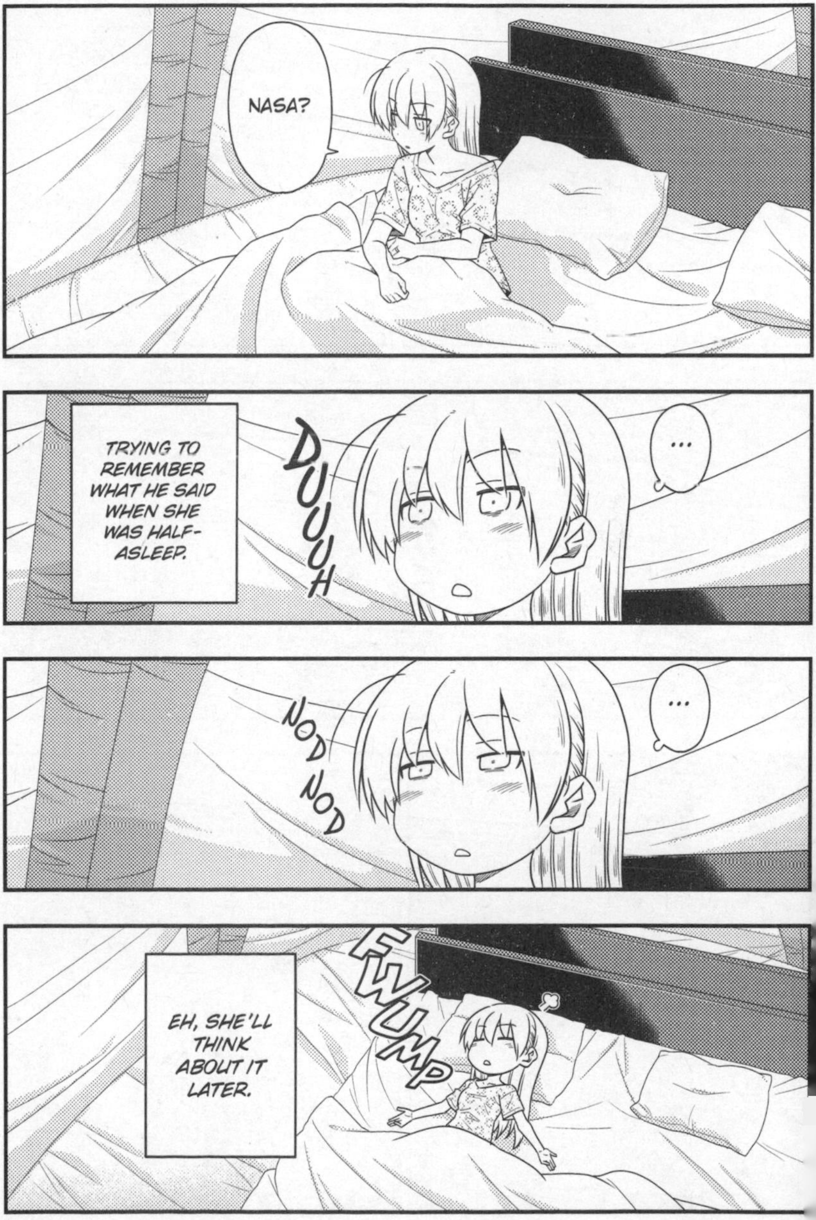
NASA?
TRYING TO REMEMBER WHAT HE SAID WHEN SHE WAS HALF-ASLEEP.
DUUUH
...
NOD NOD
...
EH, SHE'LL THINK ABOUT IT LATER.
FWUMP

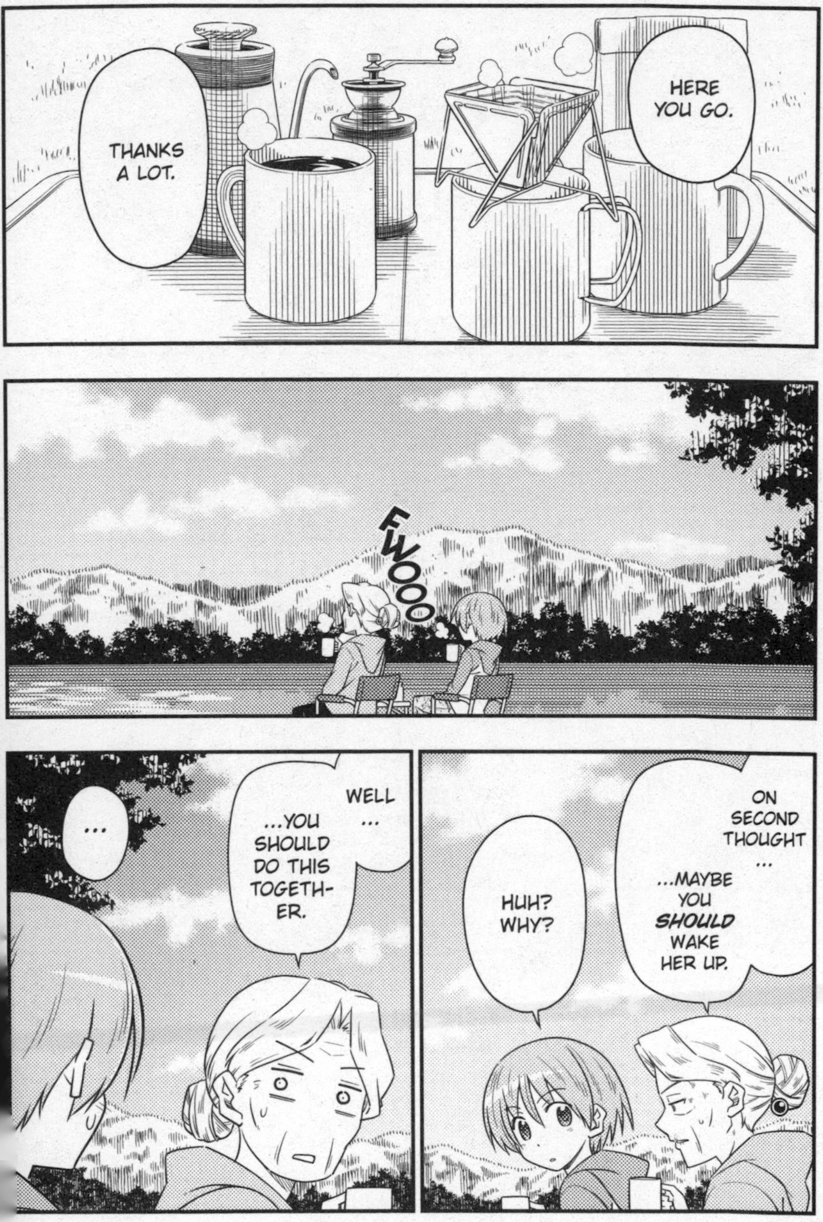
HERE YOU GO.
THANKS A LOT.
FWOOO
ON SECOND THOUGHT ... ...MAYBE YOU *SHOULD* WAKE HER UP.
HUH? WHY?
WELL ... ...YOU SHOULD DO THIS TOGETH-ER.
...

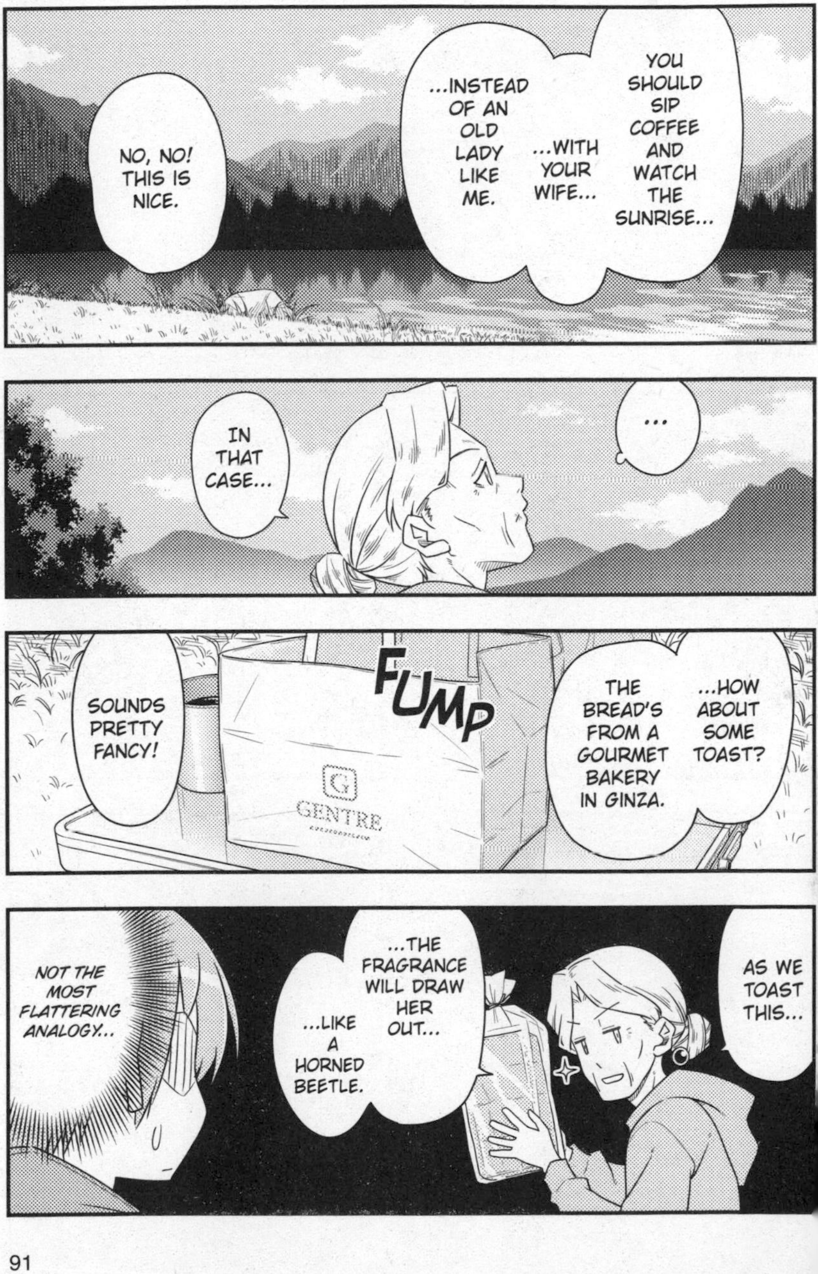
YOU SHOULD SIP COFFEE AND WATCH THE SUNRISE...
...WITH YOUR WIFE...
...INSTEAD OF AN OLD LADY LIKE ME.
NO, NO! THIS IS NICE.
...
IN THAT CASE...
...HOW ABOUT SOME TOAST?
THE BREAD'S FROM A GOURMET BAKERY IN GINZA.
FUMP
GENTRE
SOUNDS PRETTY FANCY!
AS WE TOAST THIS...
...THE FRAGRANCE WILL DRAW HER OUT...
...LIKE A HORNED BEETLE.
NOT THE MOST FLATTERING ANALOGY...

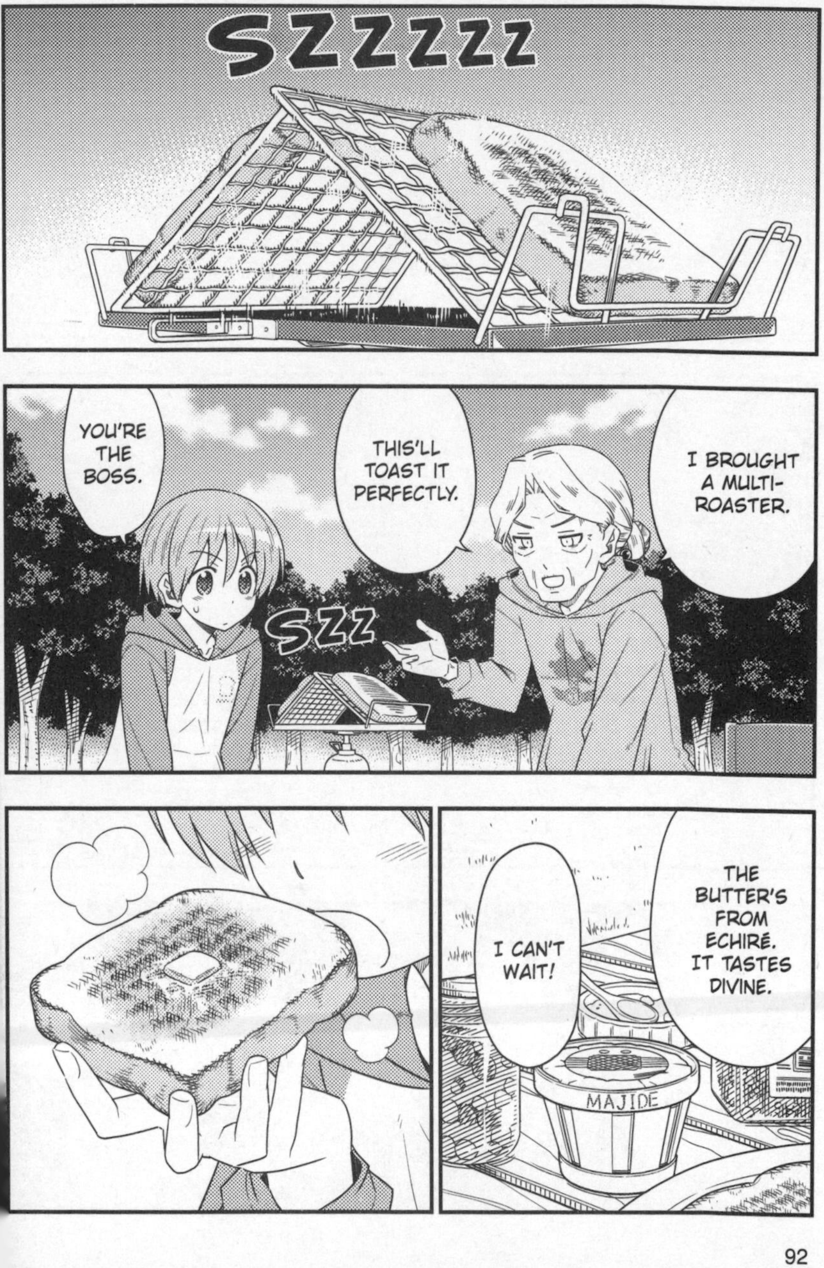
SZZZZZ
I BROUGHT A MULTI-ROASTER.
THIS'LL TOAST IT PERFECTLY.
SZZ
YOU'RE THE BOSS.
THE BUTTER'S FROM ECHIRÉ. IT TASTES DIVINE.
I CAN'T WAIT!
MAJIDE

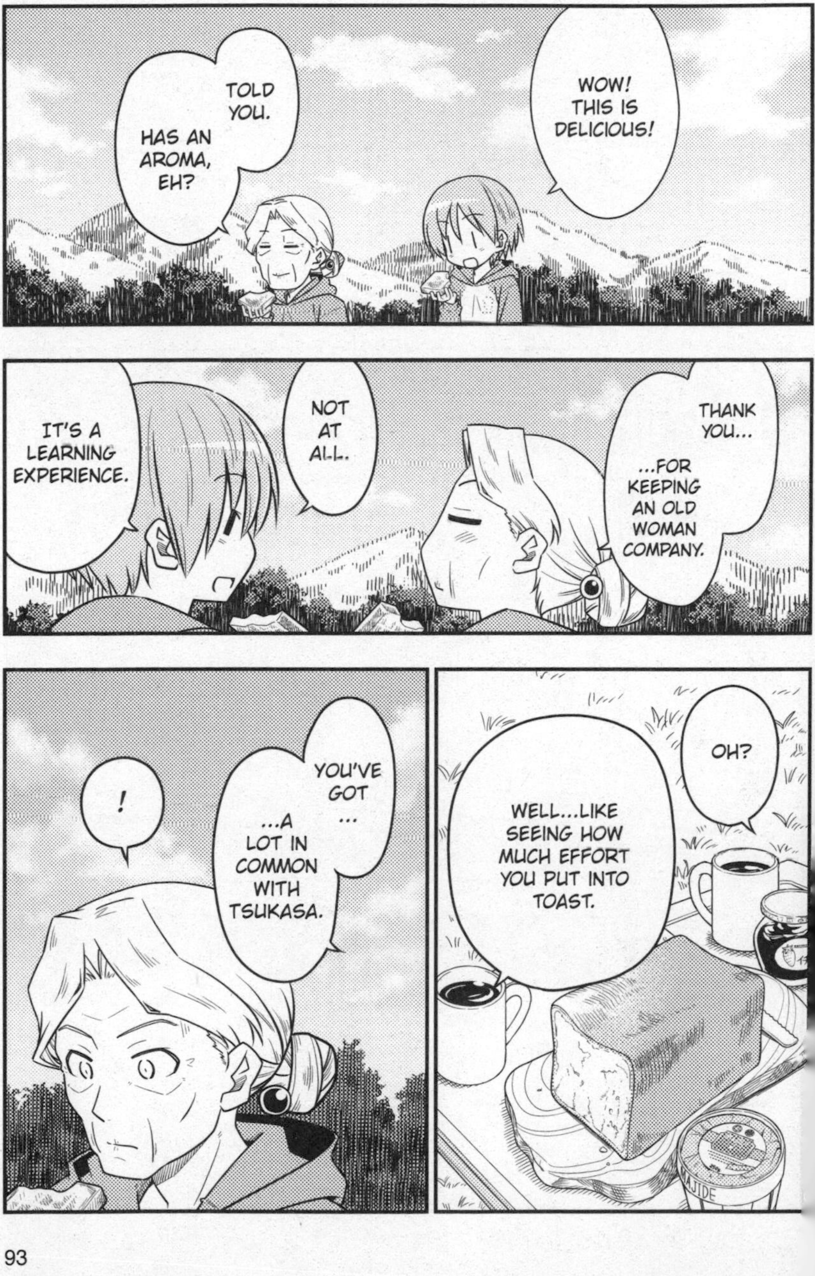
WOW! THIS IS DELICIOUS!
TOLD YOU. HAS AN AROMA, EH?
THANK YOU... ...FOR KEEPING AN OLD WOMAN COMPANY.
NOT AT ALL.
IT'S A LEARNING EXPERIENCE.
OH?
WELL...LIKE SEEING HOW MUCH EFFORT YOU PUT INTO TOAST.
MAJIDE
YOU'VE GOT ... ...A LOT IN COMMON WITH TSUKASA.
!

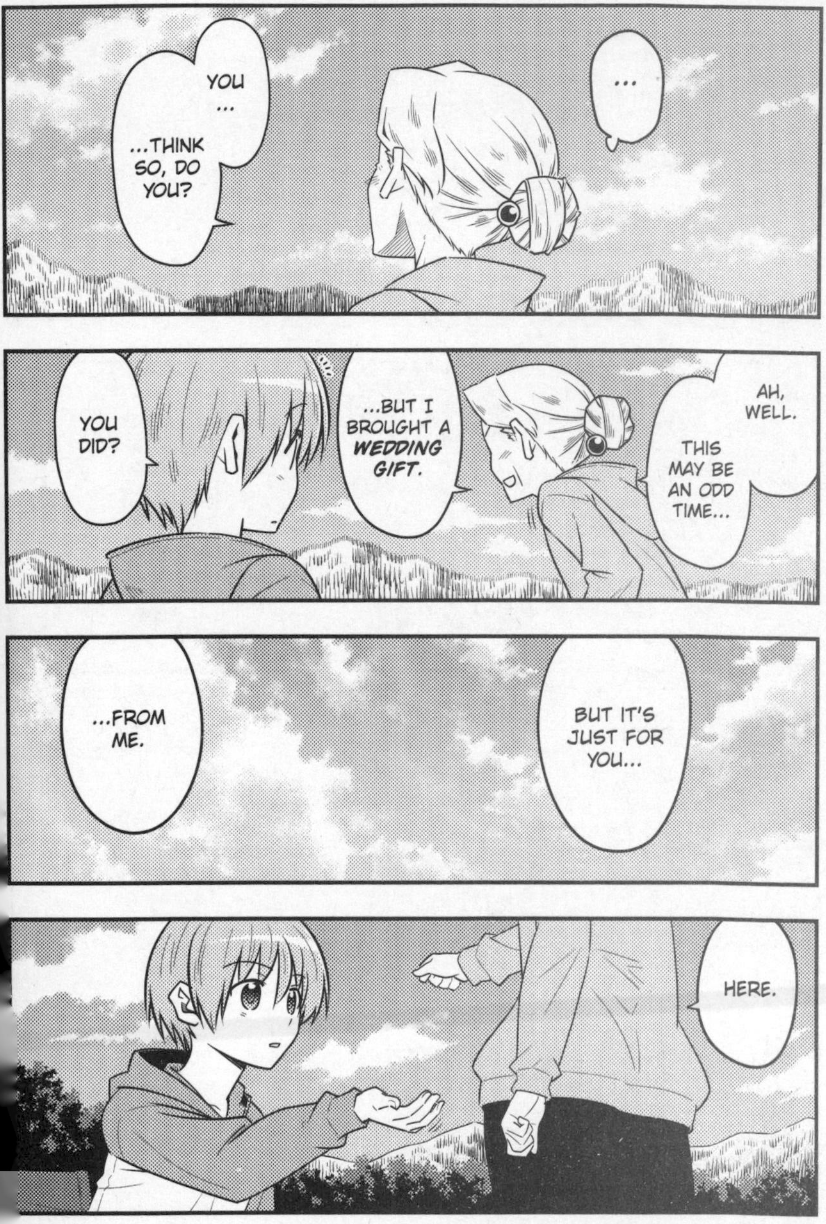
...
YOU ... ...THINK SO, DO YOU?
AH, WELL. THIS MAY BE AN ODD TIME...
...BUT I BROUGHT A *WEDDING GIFT*.
YOU DID?
BUT IT'S JUST FOR YOU...
...FROM ME.
HERE.

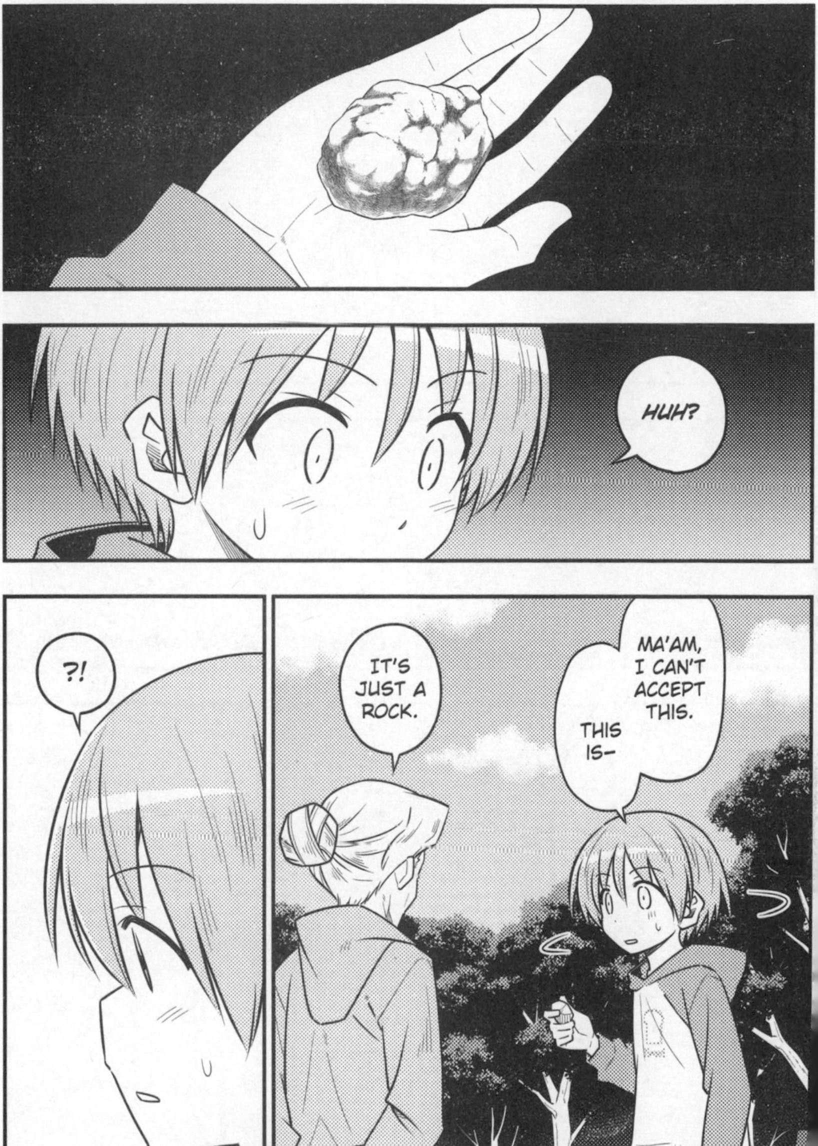
HUH?
MA'AM, I CAN'T ACCEPT THIS.
THIS IS–
IT'S JUST A ROCK.
?!

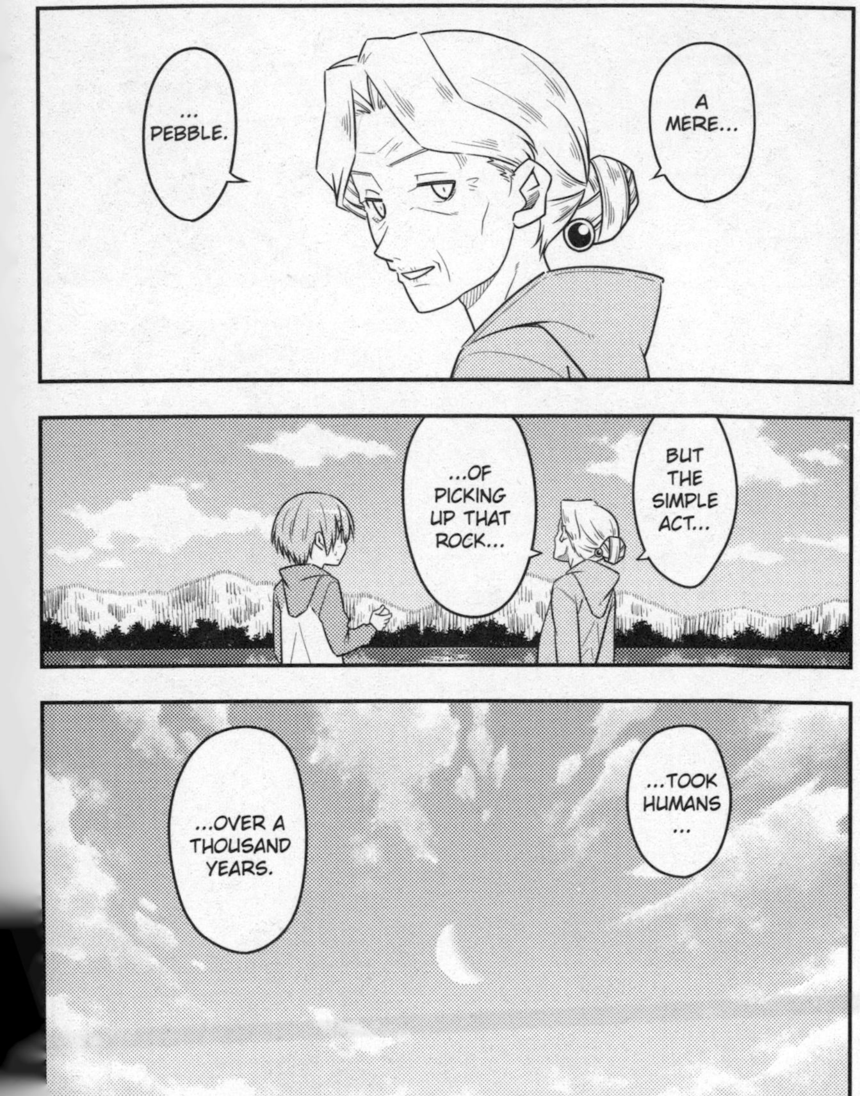
A MERE...
...PEBBLE.
BUT THE SIMPLE ACT...
...OF PICKING UP THAT ROCK...
...TOOK HUMANS ...
...OVER A THOUSAND YEARS.

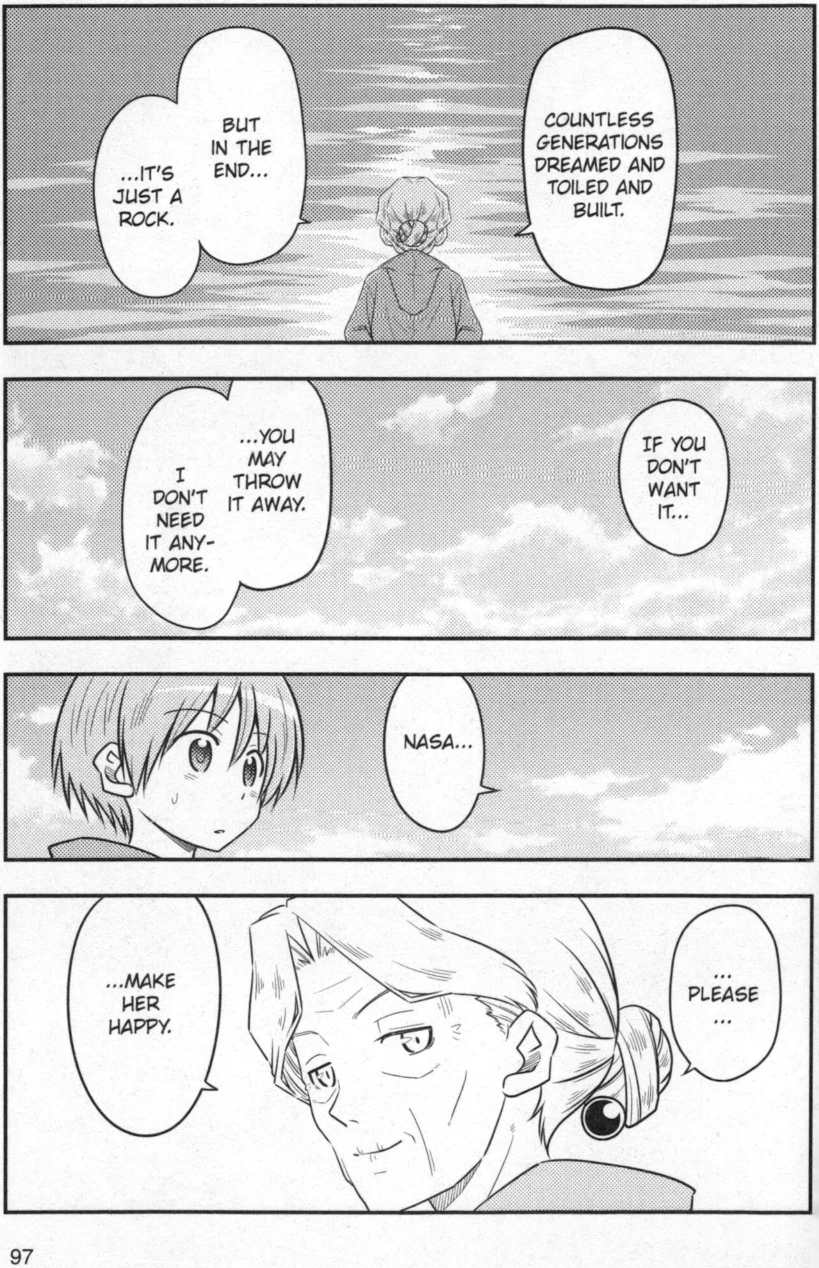
COUNTLESS GENERATIONS DREAMED AND TOILED AND BUILT.
BUT IN THE END...
...IT'S JUST A ROCK.
IF YOU DON'T WANT IT...
...YOU MAY THROW IT AWAY.
I DON'T NEED IT ANY-MORE.
NASA...
...PLEASE...
...MAKE HER HAPPY.

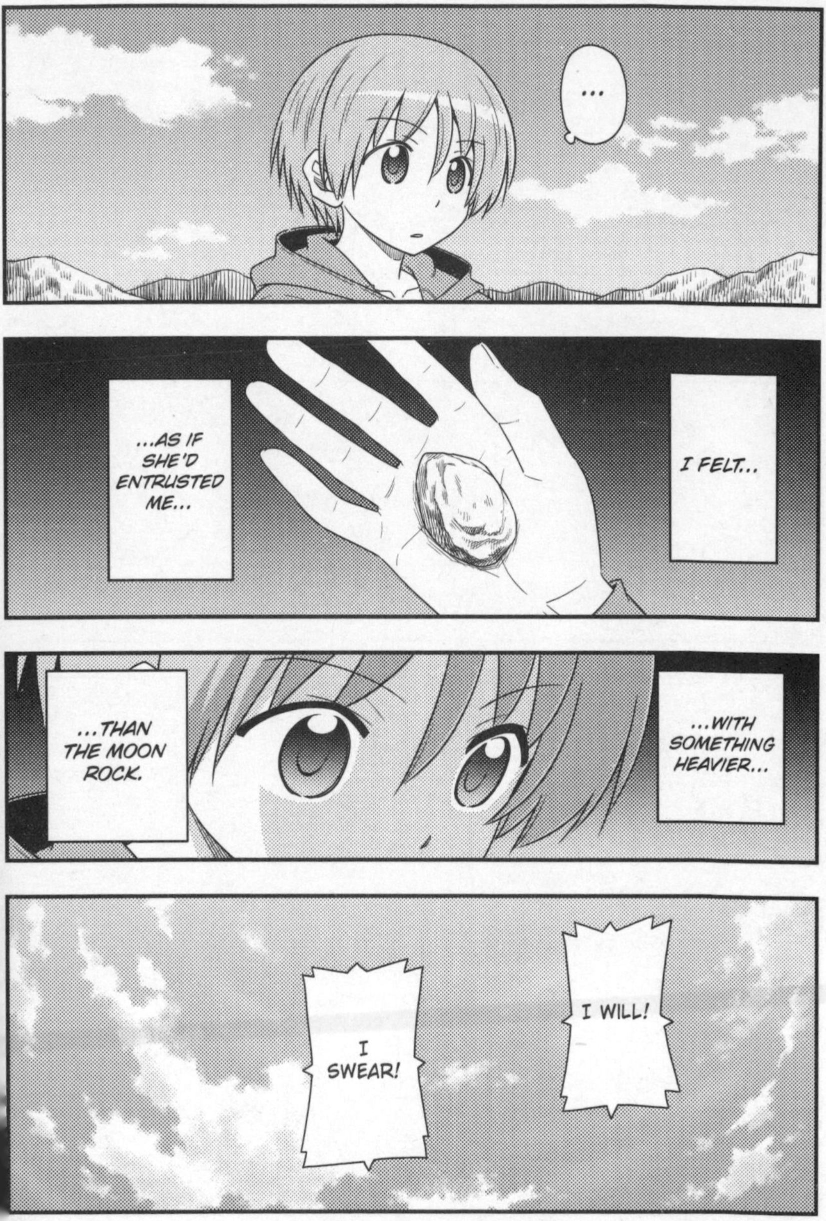
...
I FELT...
...AS IF SHE'D ENTRUSTED ME...
...WITH SOMETHING HEAVIER...
...THAN THE MOON ROCK.
I WILL!
I SWEAR!

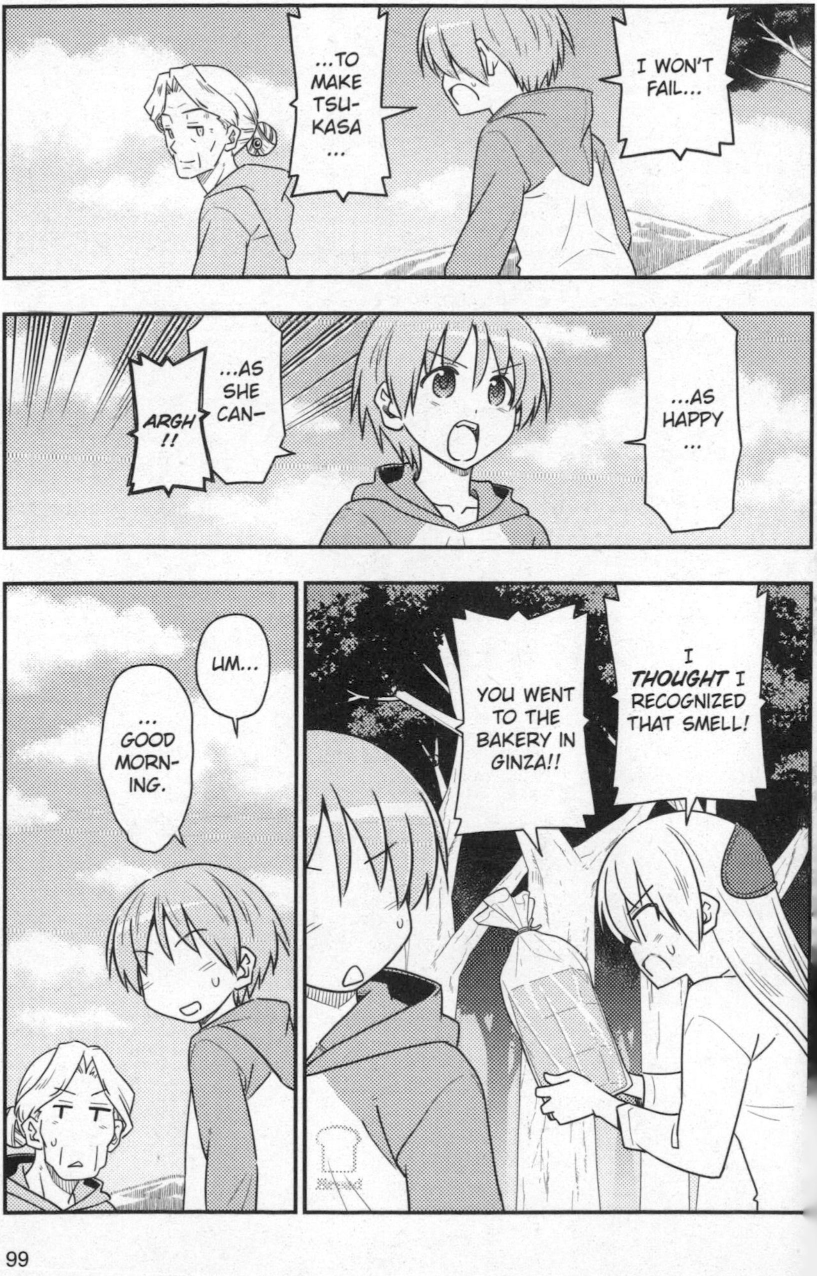
I WON'T FAIL...
...TO MAKE TSUKASA...
...AS HAPPY...
...AS SHE CAN–
ARGH!!
I *THOUGHT* I RECOGNIZED THAT SMELL!
YOU WENT TO THE BAKERY IN GINZA!!
UM...
...GOOD MORNING.

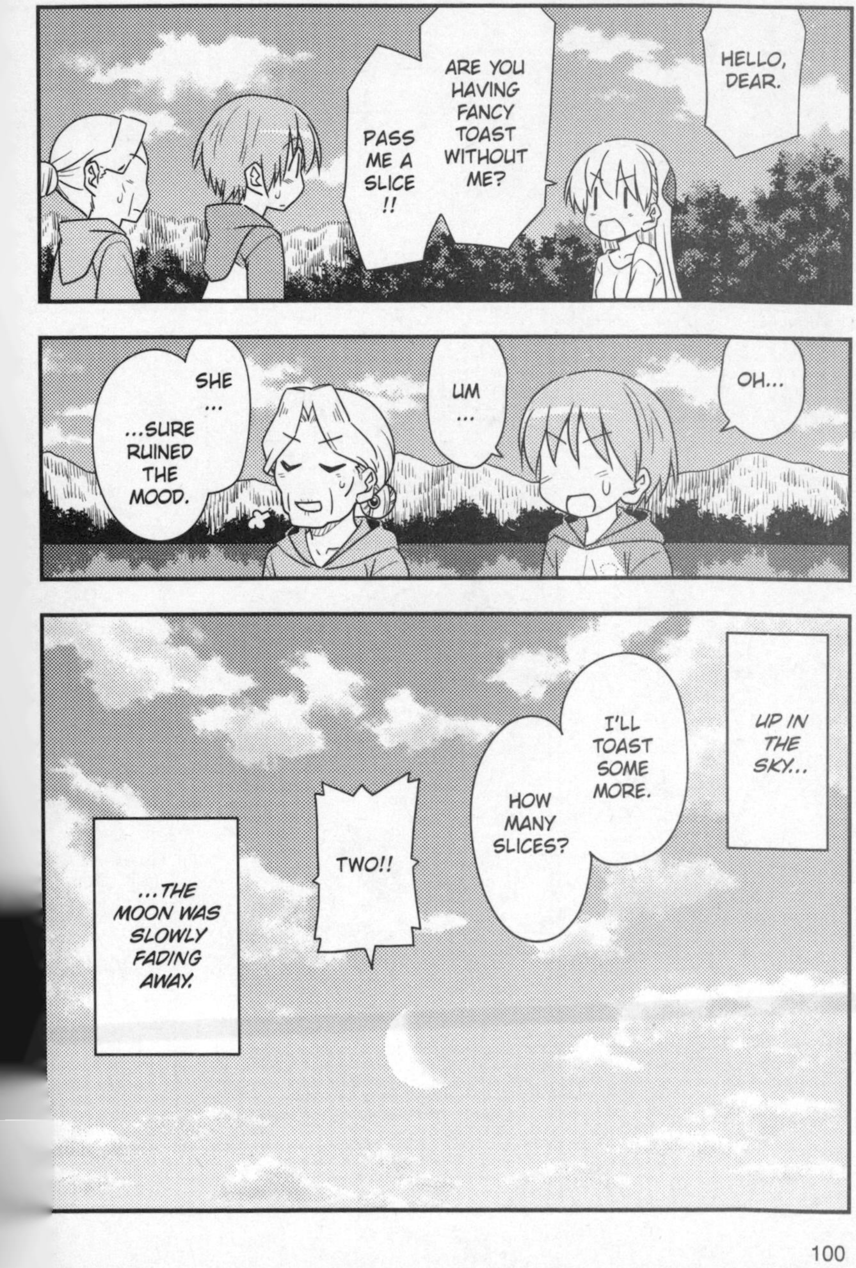
HELLO, DEAR.
ARE YOU HAVING FANCY TOAST WITHOUT ME?
PASS ME A SLICE !!
OH...
UM ...
SHE ...
...SURE RUINED THE MOOD.
UP IN THE SKY...
I'LL TOAST SOME MORE.
HOW MANY SLICES?
TWO!!
...THE MOON WAS SLOWLY FADING AWAY.

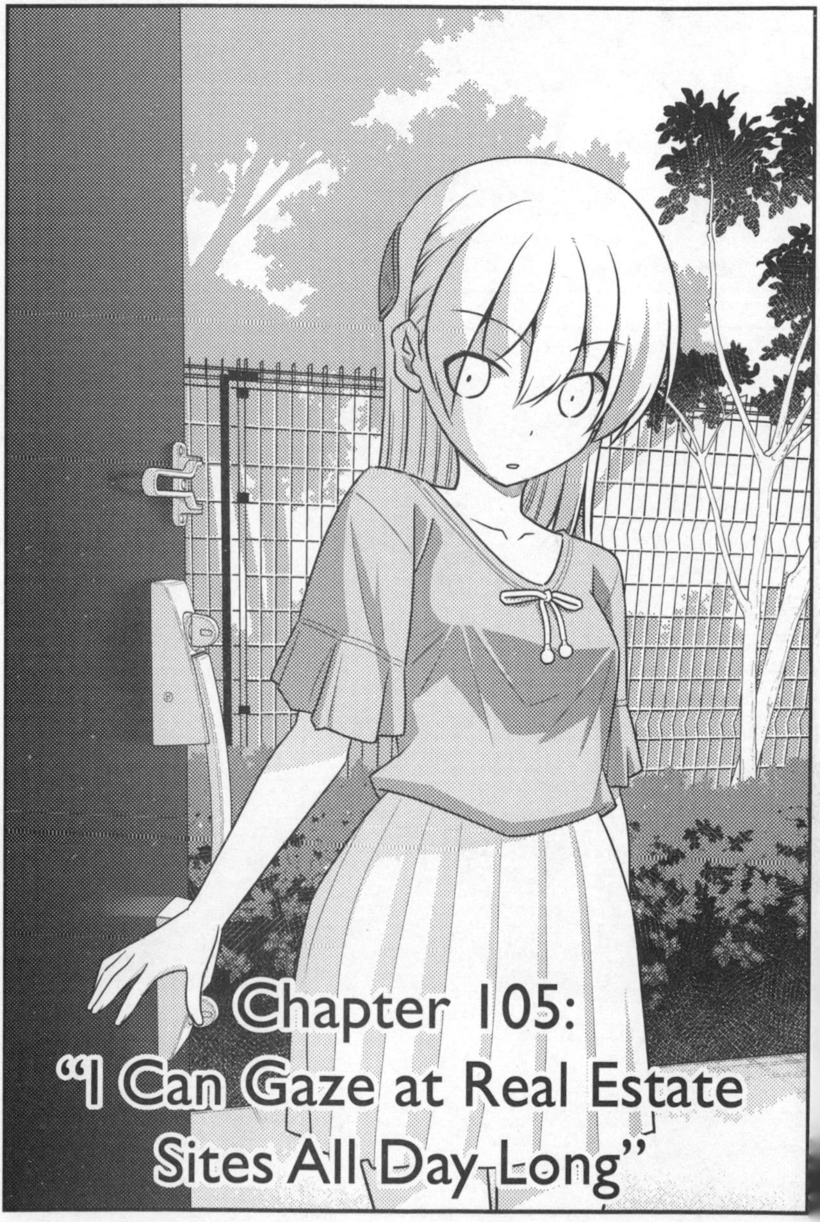
Chapter 105:
"I Can Gaze at Real Estate
Sites All Day Long"

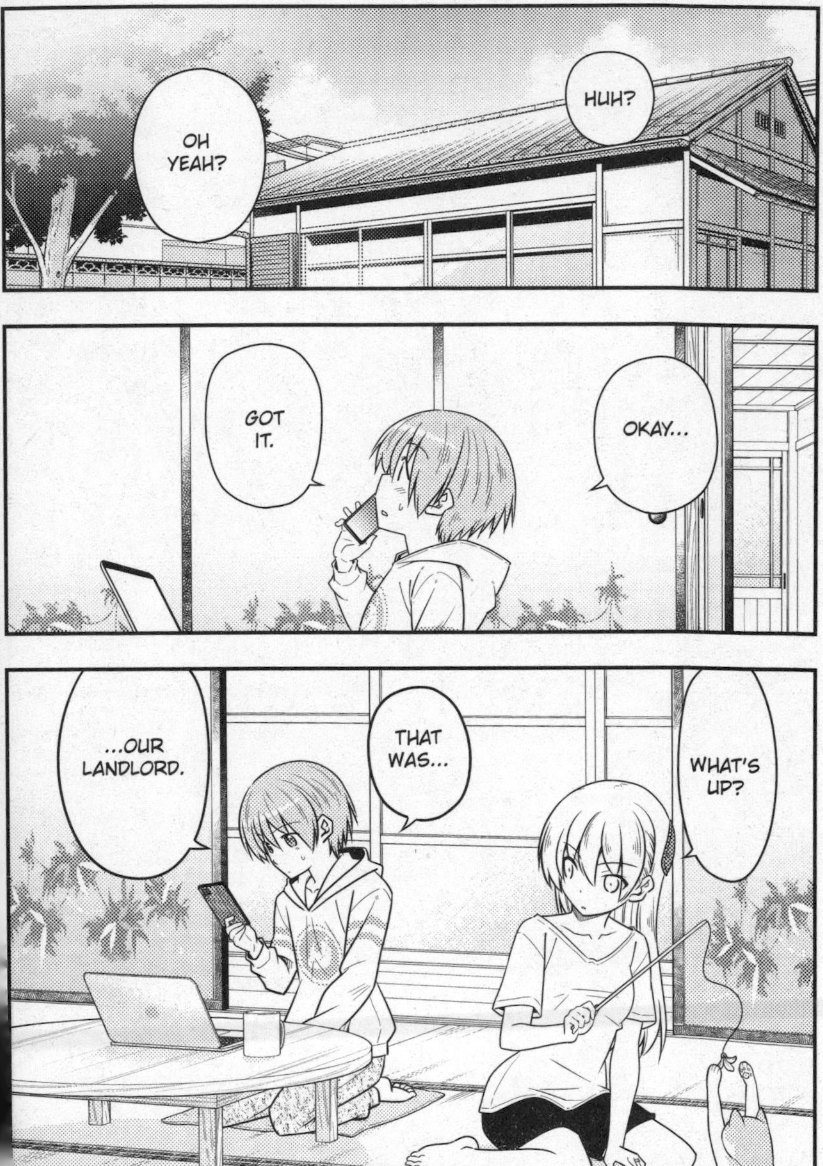
HUH?
OH YEAH?
OKAY...
GOT IT.
WHAT'S UP?
THAT WAS...
...OUR LANDLORD.

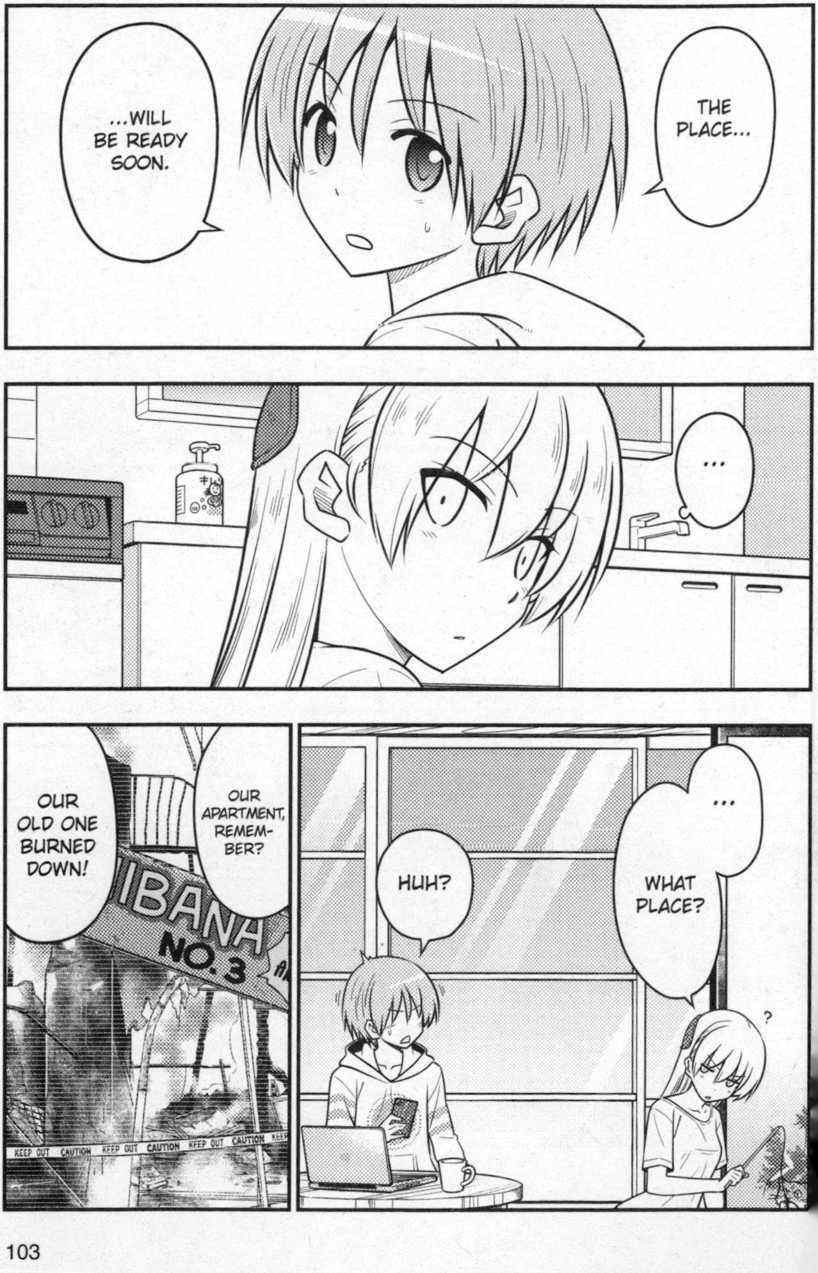
THE PLACE...
...WILL BE READY SOON.
...
...
WHAT PLACE?
?
HUH?
OUR APARTMENT, REMEMBER?
OUR OLD ONE BURNED DOWN!
IBANA
NO. 3
KEEP OUT CAUTION KEEP OUT CAUTION KEEP OUT CAUTION

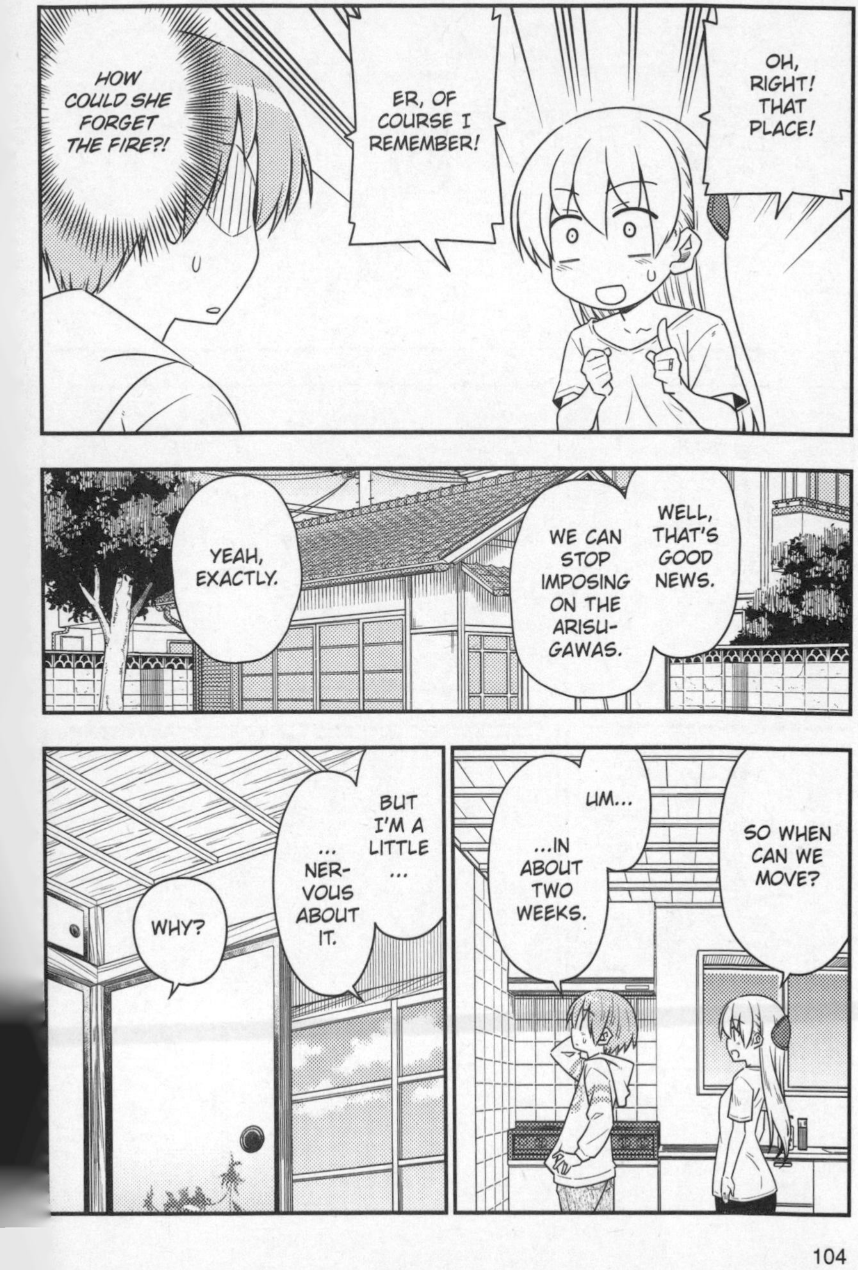
OH, RIGHT! THAT PLACE!
ER, OF COURSE I REMEMBER!
HOW COULD SHE FORGET THE FIRE?!
WELL, THAT'S GOOD NEWS.
WE CAN STOP IMPOSING ON THE ARISU-GAWAS.
YEAH, EXACTLY.
SO WHEN CAN WE MOVE?
UM...
...IN ABOUT TWO WEEKS.
BUT I'M A LITTLE ...
... NER-VOUS ABOUT IT.
WHY?

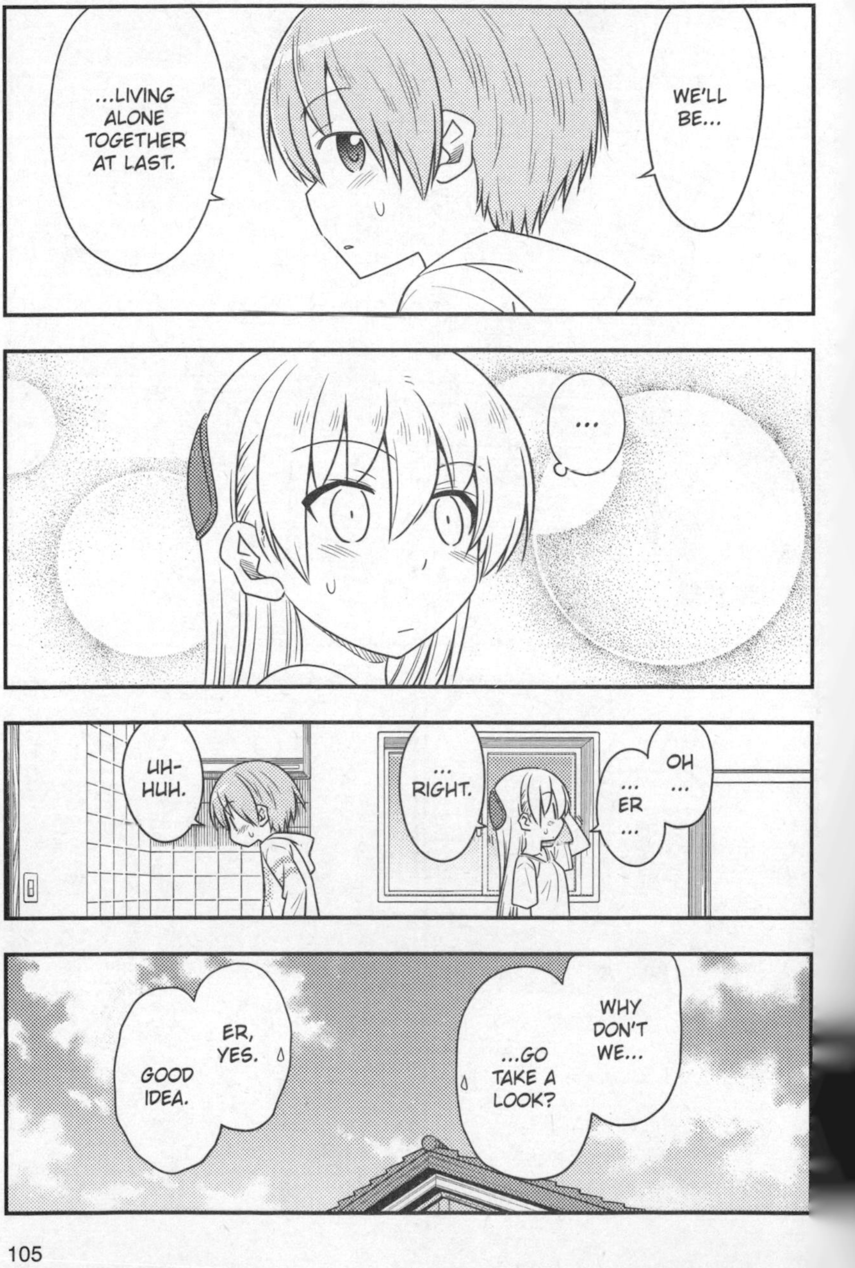
WE'LL BE...
...LIVING ALONE TOGETHER AT LAST.
...
OH ... ... ER ...
... RIGHT.
UH-HUH.
WHY DON'T WE... ...GO TAKE A LOOK?
ER, YES. GOOD IDEA.

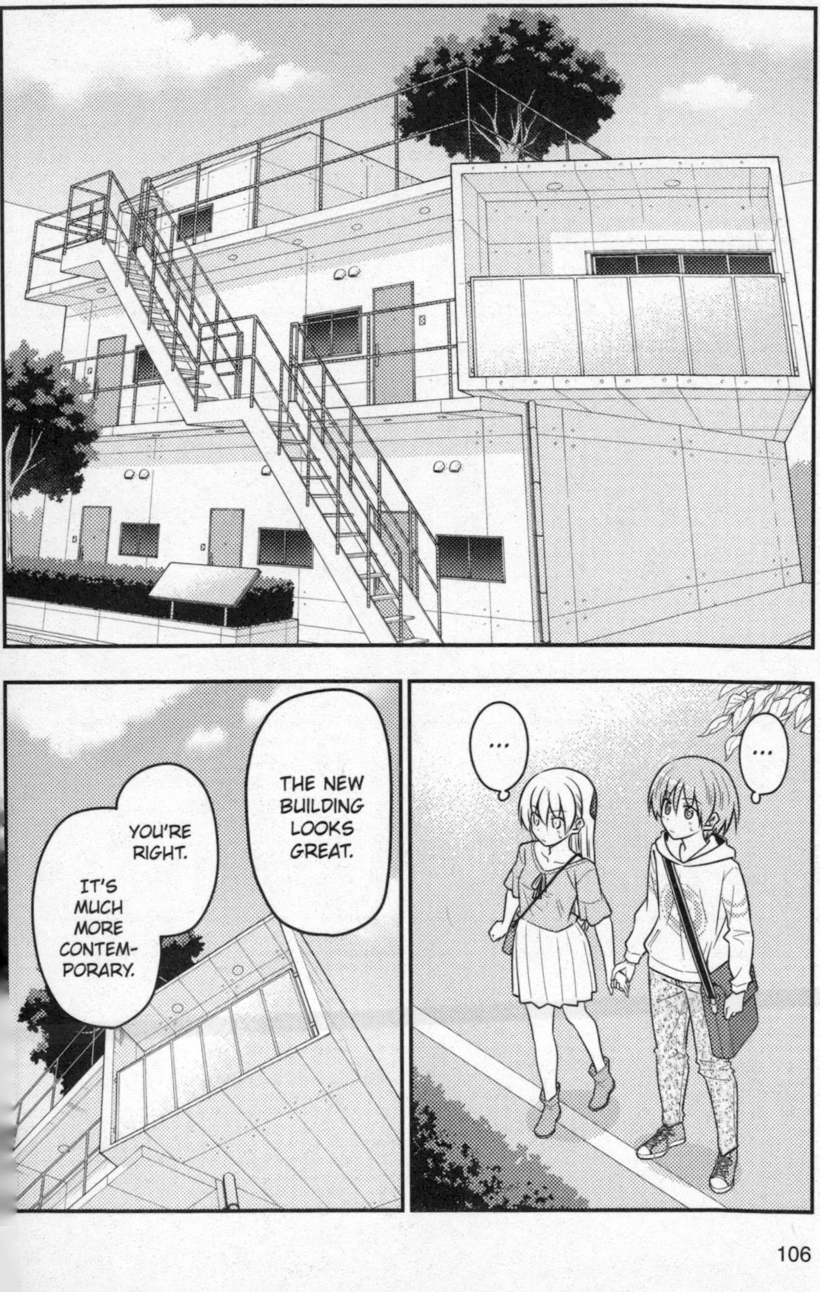
...
...
THE NEW BUILDING LOOKS GREAT.
YOU'RE RIGHT.
IT'S MUCH MORE CONTEM-PORARY.

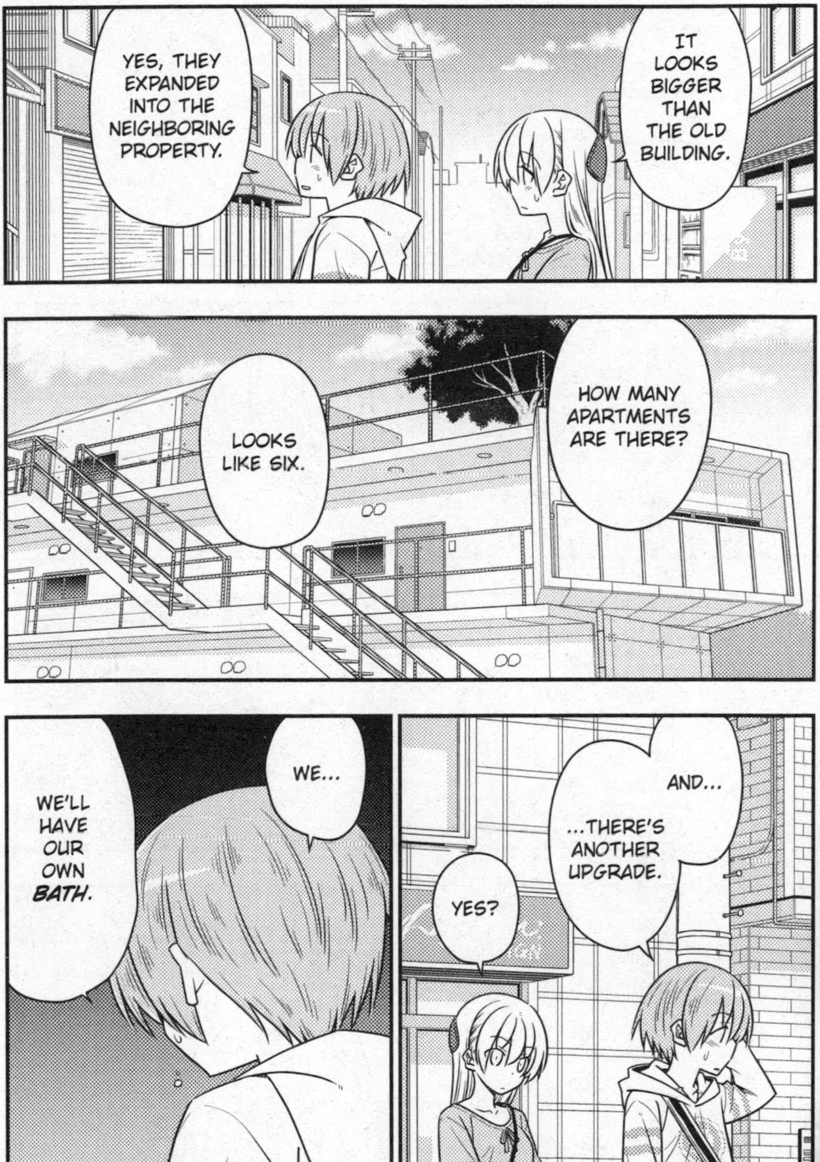
IT LOOKS BIGGER THAN THE OLD BUILDING.
YES, THEY EXPANDED INTO THE NEIGHBORING PROPERTY.
HOW MANY APARTMENTS ARE THERE?
LOOKS LIKE SIX.
AND...
...THERE'S ANOTHER UPGRADE.
YES?
WE...
WE'LL HAVE OUR OWN *BATH*.

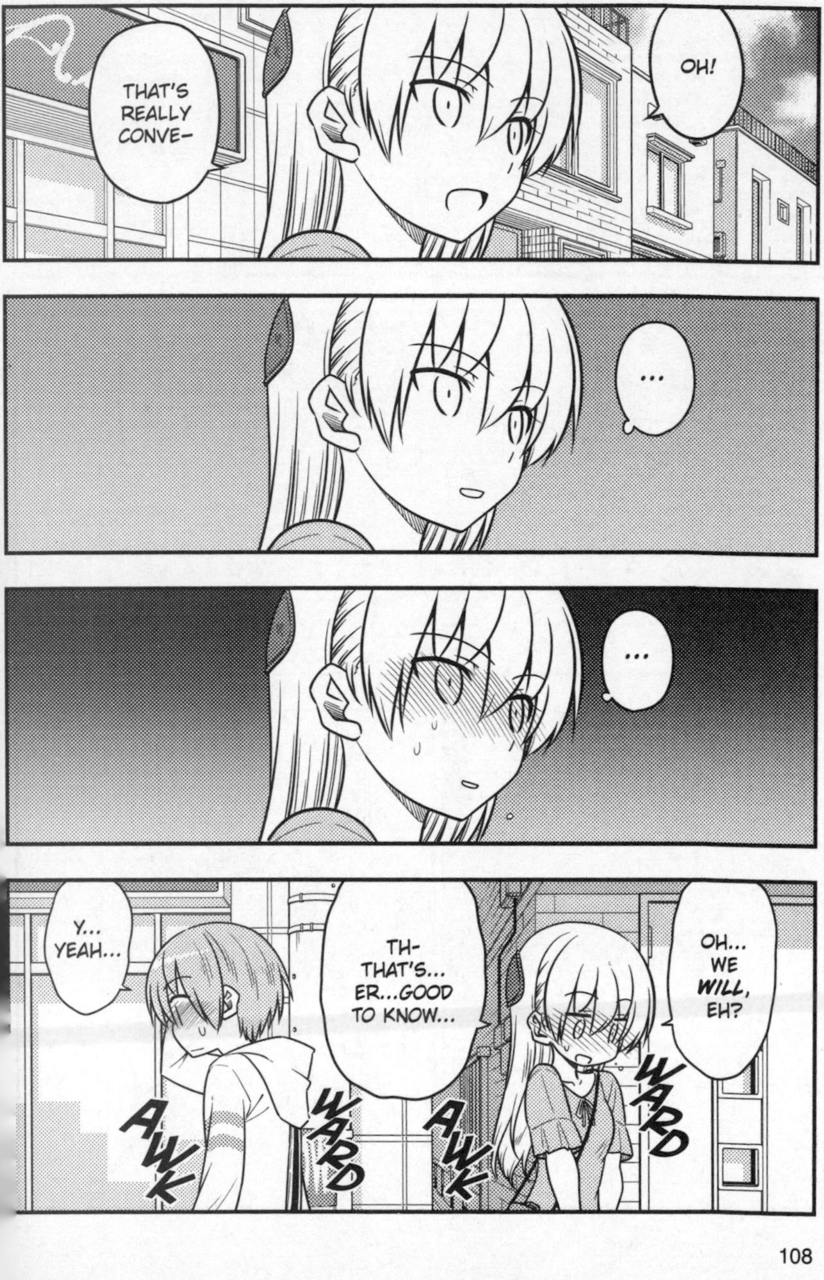
OH!
THAT'S REALLY CONVE-
...
...
OH... WE WILL, EH?
AWKWARD
TH- THAT'S... ER...GOOD TO KNOW...
AWKWARD
Y... YEAH...

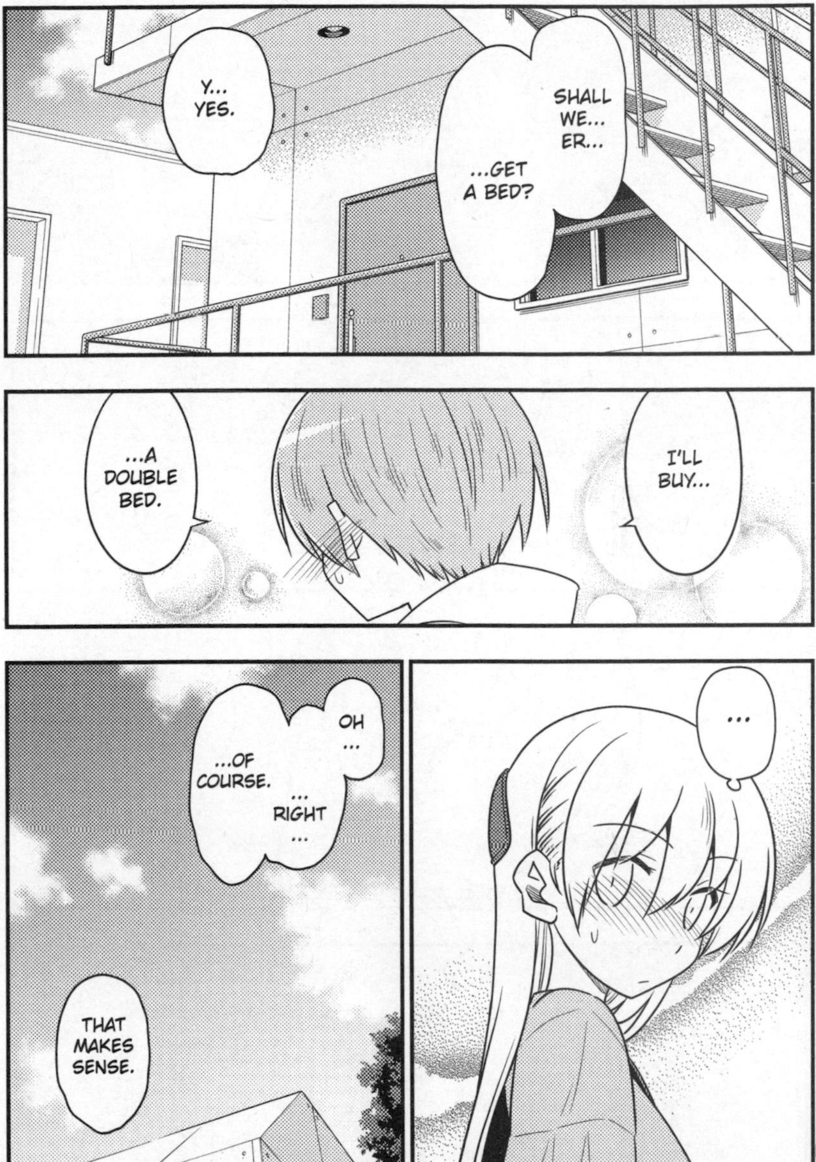
SHALL WE... ER... ...GET A BED?
Y... YES.
I'LL BUY...
...A DOUBLE BED.
...
OH ... ...OF COURSE. ... RIGHT ...
THAT MAKES SENSE.

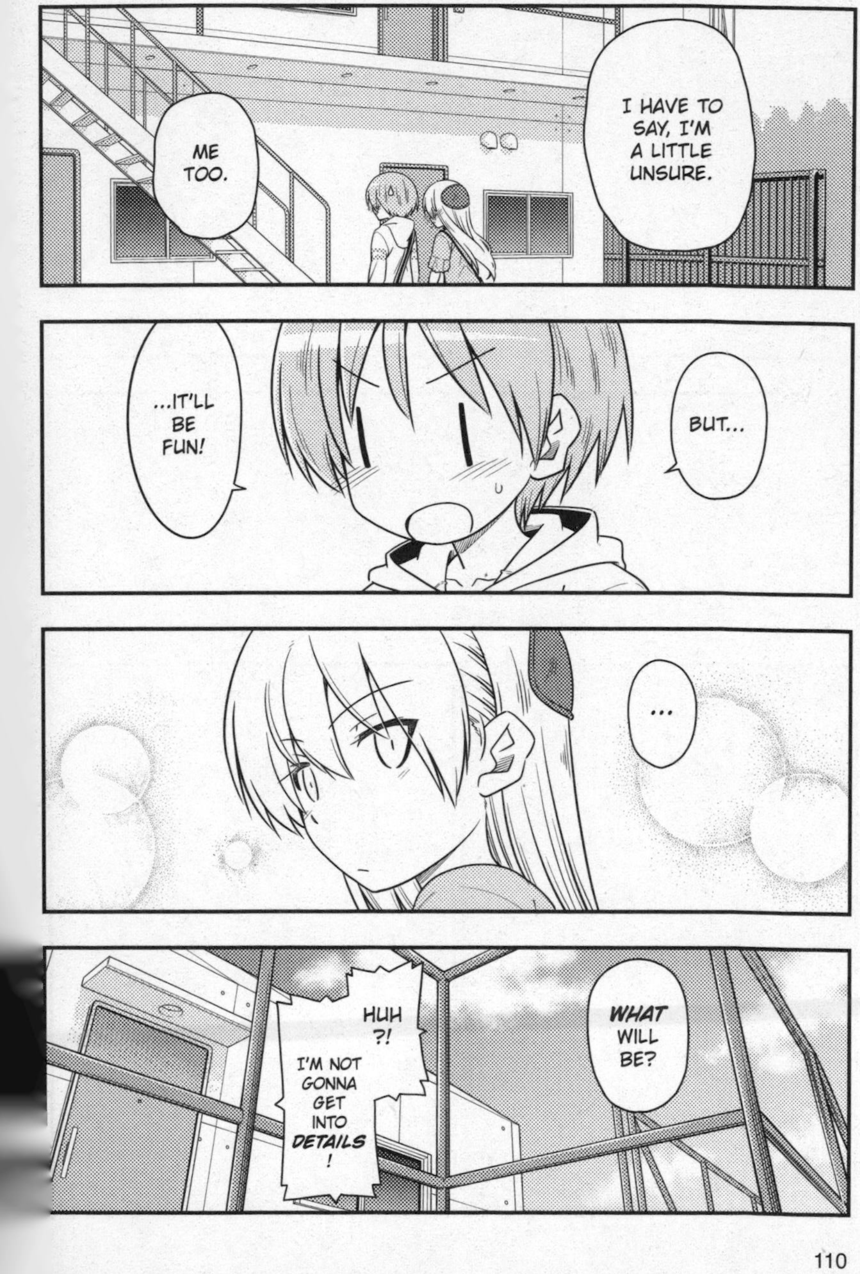

I HAVE TO SAY, I'M A LITTLE UNSURE.
ME TOO.
BUT...
...IT'LL BE FUN!
...
WHAT WILL BE?
HUH?!
I'M NOT GONNA GET INTO DETAILS!

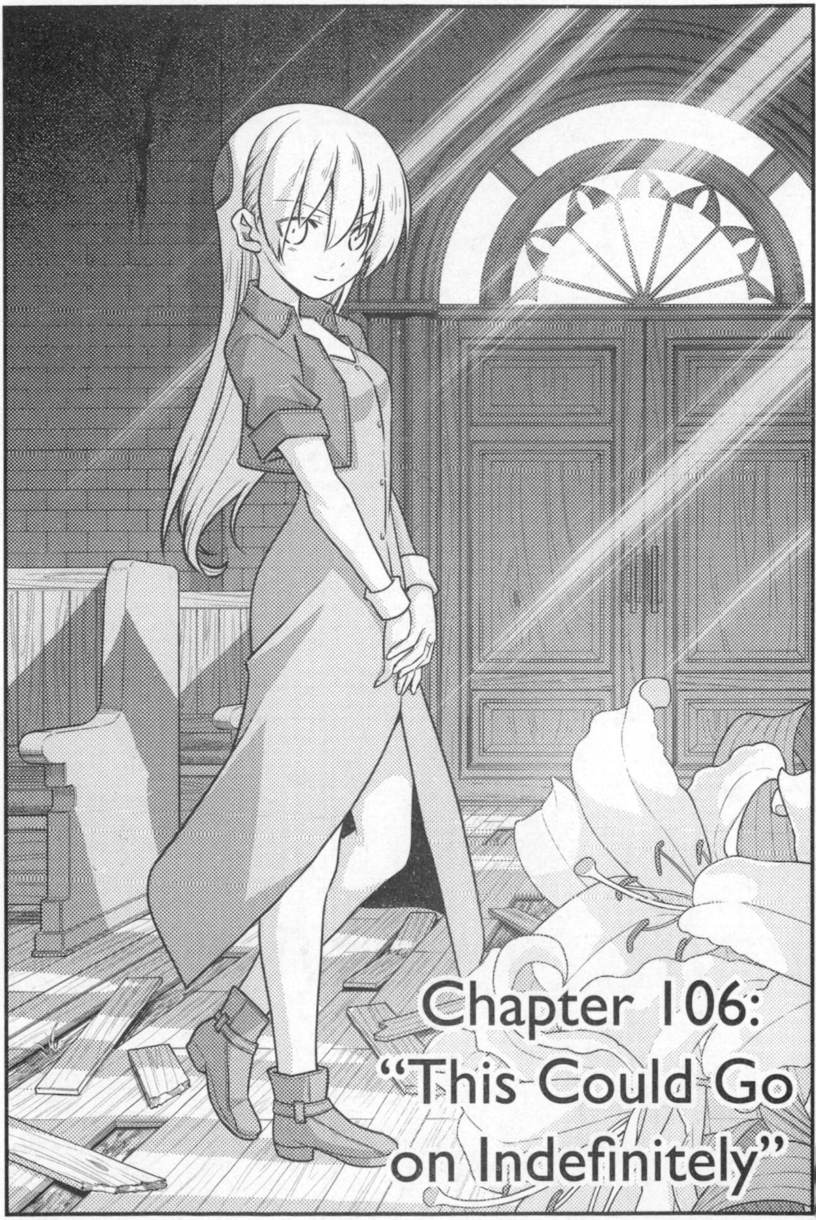
Chapter 106:
"This Could Go on Indefinitely"

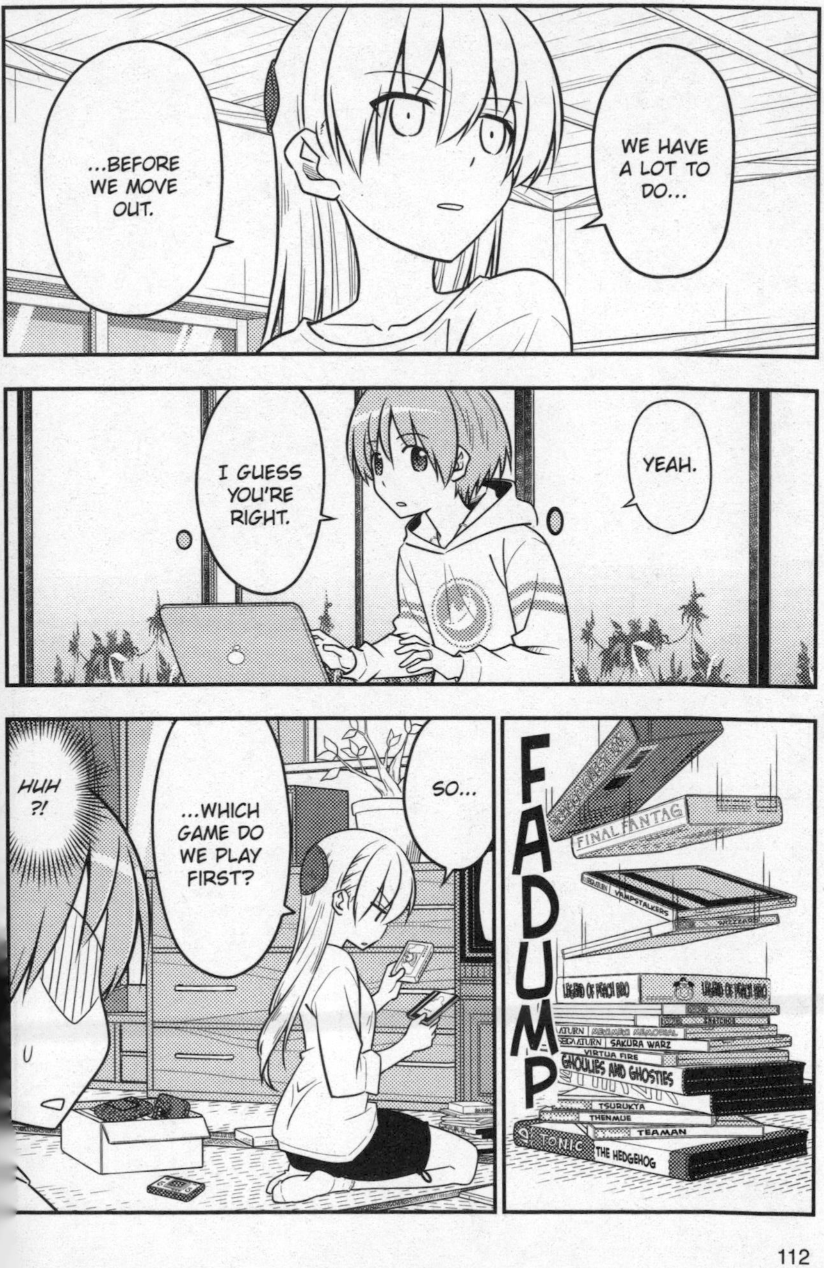
WE HAVE A LOT TO DO...
...BEFORE WE MOVE OUT.
YEAH.
I GUESS YOU'RE RIGHT.
FADUMP
FINAL FANTAG
VAMPSTALKERS
LEGEND OF PEACH BRO
SAKURA WARZ
VIRTUA FIRE
GHOULIES AND GHOSTIES
TSURUKYA
THENMUE
TEAMAN
TONIC THE HEDGEHOG
SO...
...WHICH GAME DO WE PLAY FIRST?
HUH ?!

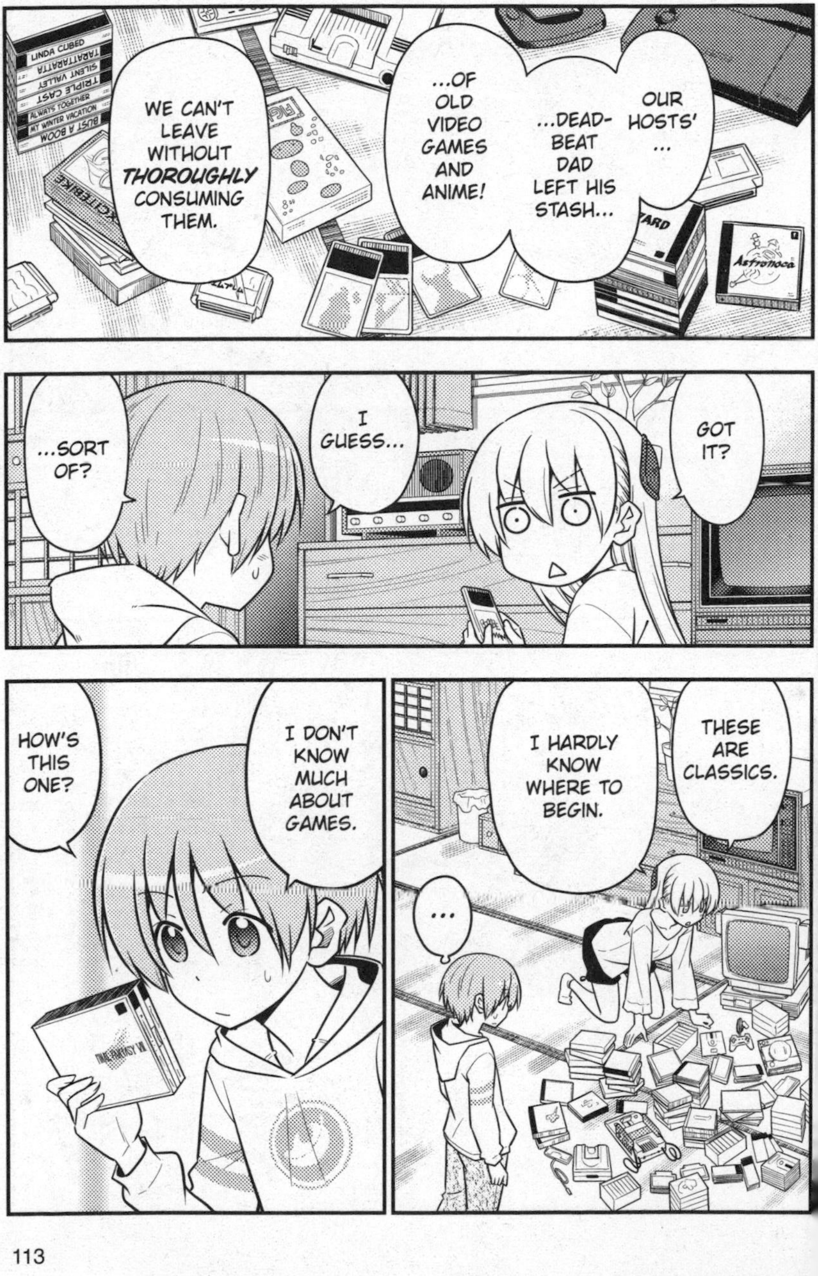
LINDA CUBED
TARATTARATTA
SILENT VALLEY
TRIPLE CAST
ALWAYS TOGETHER
MY WINTER VACATION
BUST A BOOM
Astronoca
OUR HOSTS' ...
...DEAD-BEAT DAD LEFT HIS STASH...
...OF OLD VIDEO GAMES AND ANIME!
WE CAN'T LEAVE WITHOUT ***THOROUGHLY*** CONSUMING THEM.
GOT IT?
I GUESS...
...SORT OF?
THESE ARE CLASSICS.
I HARDLY KNOW WHERE TO BEGIN.
...
I DON'T KNOW MUCH ABOUT GAMES.
HOW'S THIS ONE?
FINAL FANTASY VII

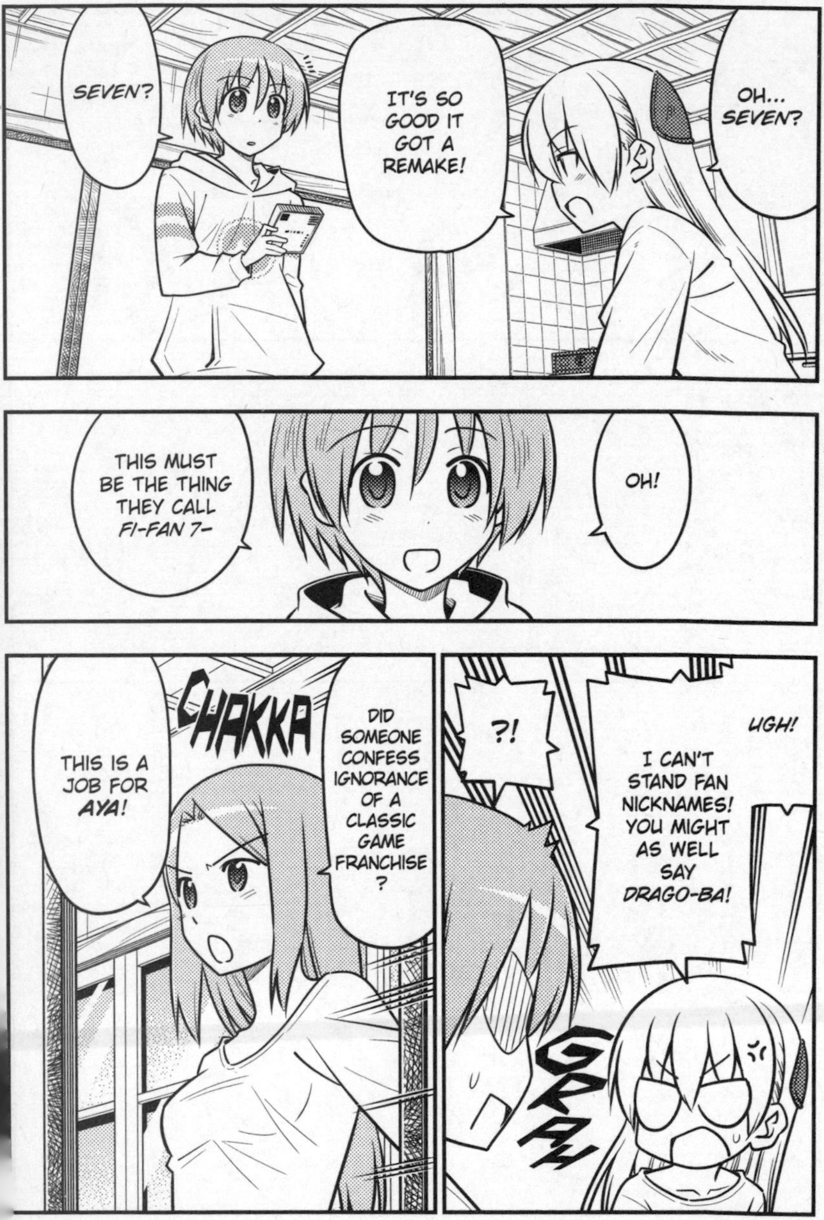
OH... SEVEN?
IT'S SO GOOD IT GOT A REMAKE!
SEVEN?
OH!
THIS MUST BE THE THING THEY CALL FI-FAN 7-
UGH!
I CAN'T STAND FAN NICKNAMES! YOU MIGHT AS WELL SAY DRAGO-BA!
?!
GRAH
DID SOMEONE CONFESS IGNORANCE OF A CLASSIC GAME FRANCHISE ?
CHAKKA
THIS IS A JOB FOR AYA!

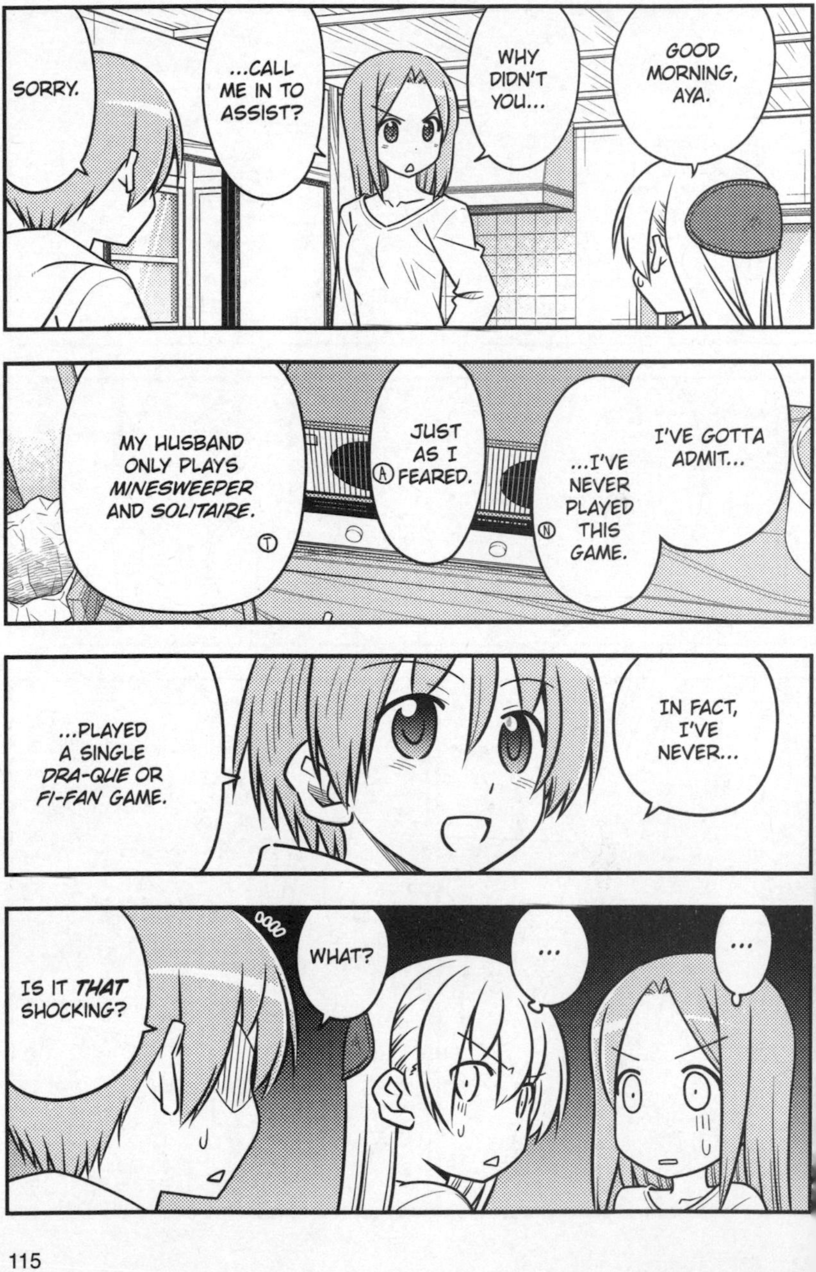
GOOD MORNING, AYA.
WHY DIDN'T YOU...
...CALL ME IN TO ASSIST?
SORRY.
I'VE GOTTA ADMIT...
...I'VE NEVER PLAYED THIS GAME.
JUST AS I FEARED.
MY HUSBAND ONLY PLAYS MINESWEEPER AND SOLITAIRE.
IN FACT, I'VE NEVER...
...PLAYED A SINGLE DRA-QUE OR FI-FAN GAME.
...
...
WHAT?
IS IT THAT SHOCKING?

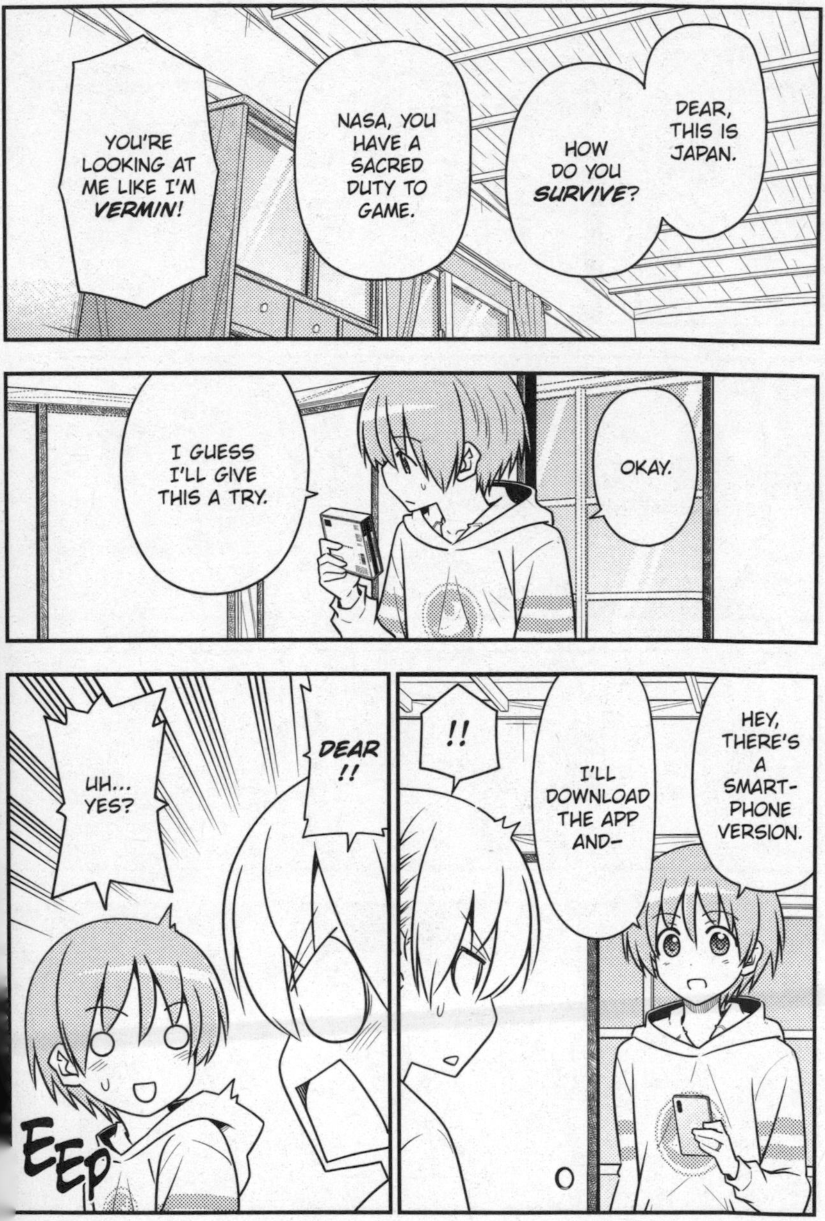
DEAR, THIS IS JAPAN.
HOW DO YOU **SURVIVE**?
NASA, YOU HAVE A SACRED DUTY TO GAME.
YOU'RE LOOKING AT ME LIKE I'M **VERMIN**!
OKAY.
I GUESS I'LL GIVE THIS A TRY.
HEY, THERE'S A SMART-PHONE VERSION.
I'LL DOWNLOAD THE APP AND–
!!
DEAR !!
UH... YES?
EEP

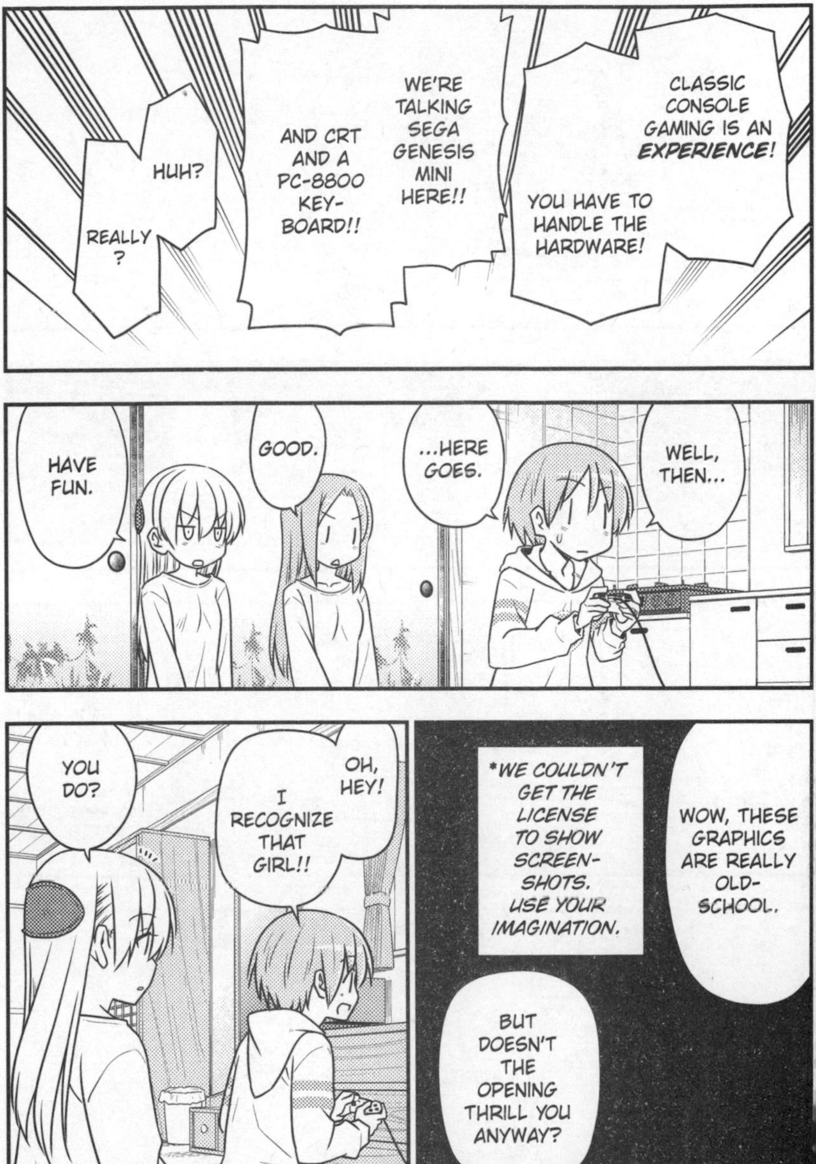
CLASSIC CONSOLE GAMING IS AN EXPERIENCE!
YOU HAVE TO HANDLE THE HARDWARE!
WE'RE TALKING SEGA GENESIS MINI HERE!!
AND CRT AND A PC-8800 KEY-BOARD!!
HUH?
REALLY?
WELL, THEN...
...HERE GOES.
GOOD.
HAVE FUN.
WOW, THESE GRAPHICS ARE REALLY OLD-SCHOOL.
*WE COULDN'T GET THE LICENSE TO SHOW SCREEN-SHOTS. USE YOUR IMAGINATION.
BUT DOESN'T THE OPENING THRILL YOU ANYWAY?
OH, HEY!
I RECOGNIZE THAT GIRL!!
YOU DO?

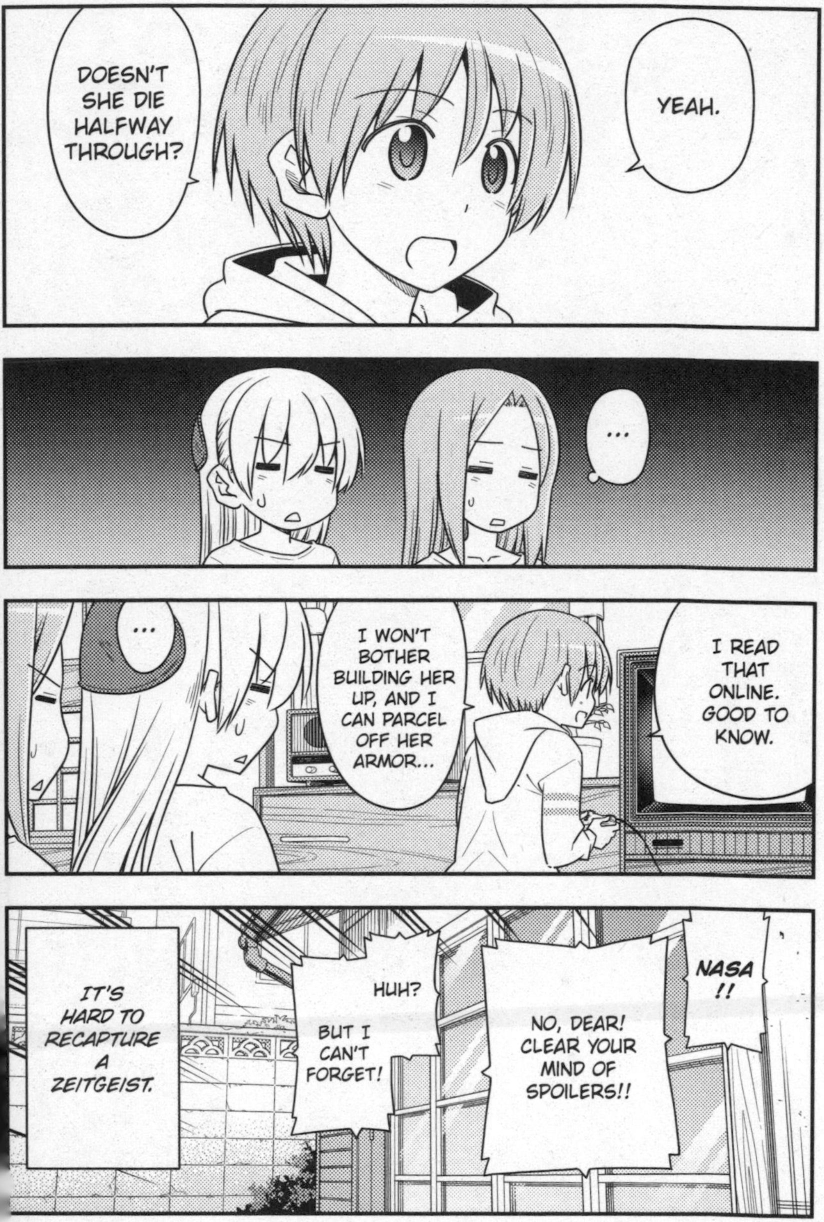
YEAH.
DOESN'T SHE DIE HALFWAY THROUGH?
...
I READ THAT ONLINE. GOOD TO KNOW.
I WON'T BOTHER BUILDING HER UP, AND I CAN PARCEL OFF HER ARMOR...
...
NASA!!
NO, DEAR! CLEAR YOUR MIND OF SPOILERS!!
HUH?
BUT I CAN'T FORGET!
IT'S HARD TO RECAPTURE A ZEITGEIST.

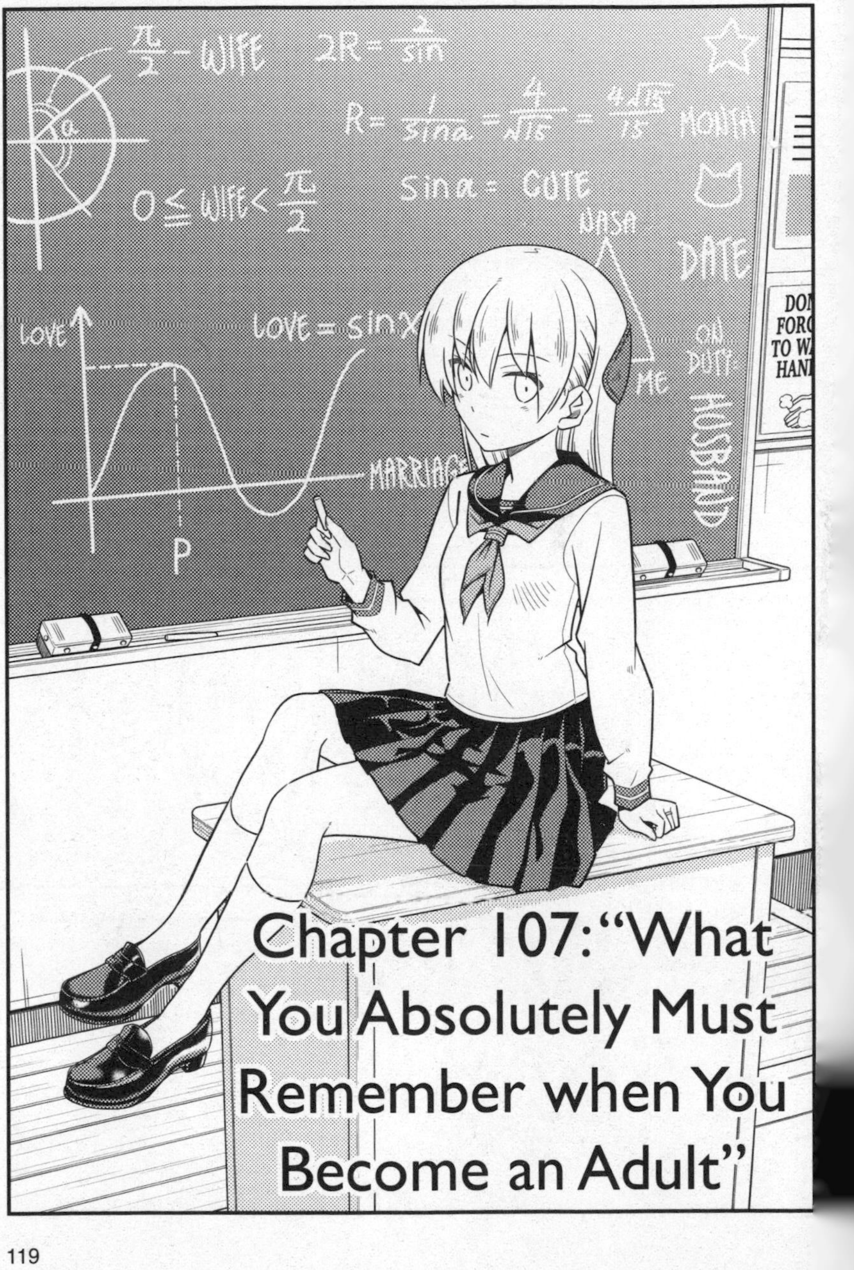
π/2 - WIFE
2R = 2/sin
R = 1/sina = 4/√15 = 4√15/15
MONTH
0 ≤ WIFE < π/2
Sina = CUTE
NASA
DATE
LOVE
LOVE = sinx
ME
ON DUTY:
HUSBAND
MARRIAGE
P
DON
FORG
TO WA
HANI

Chapter 107: "What You Absolutely Must Remember when You Become an Adult"

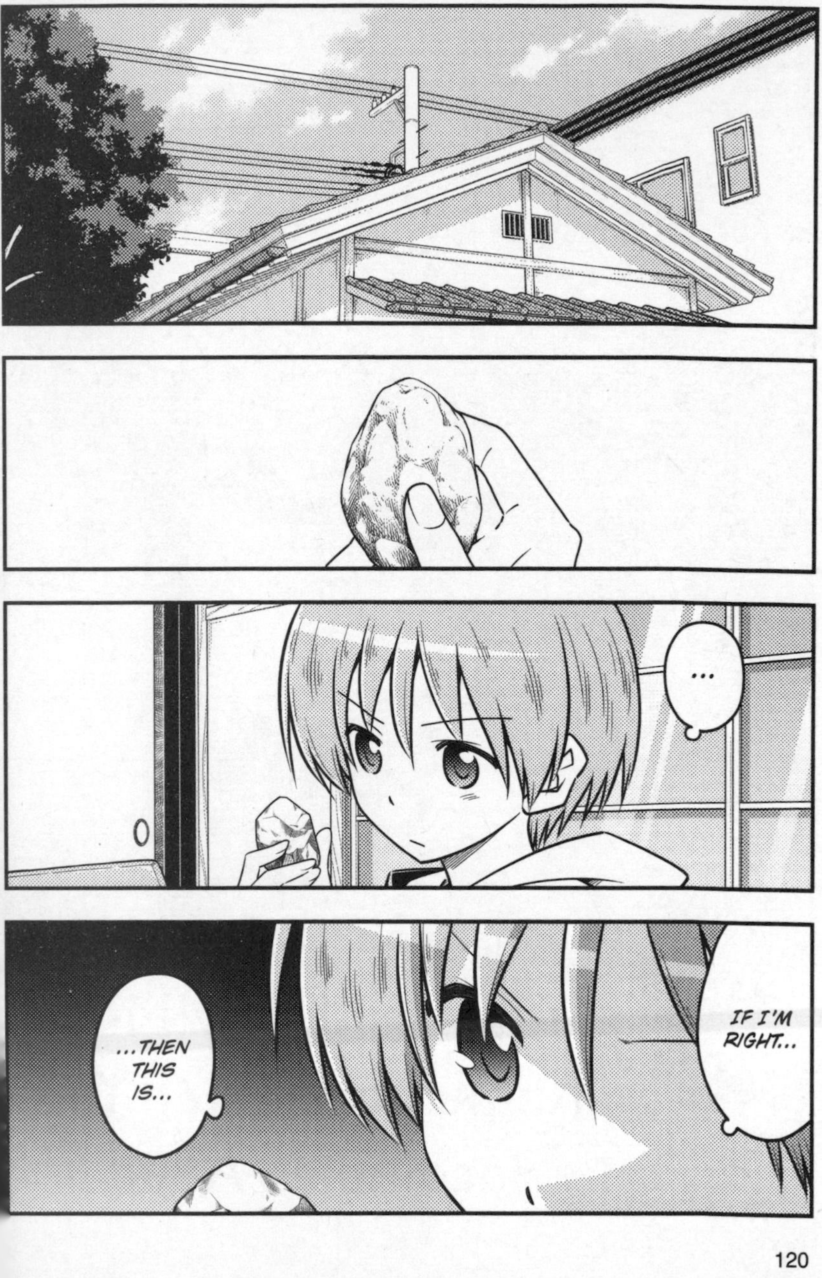
...
IF I'M RIGHT...
...THEN THIS IS...

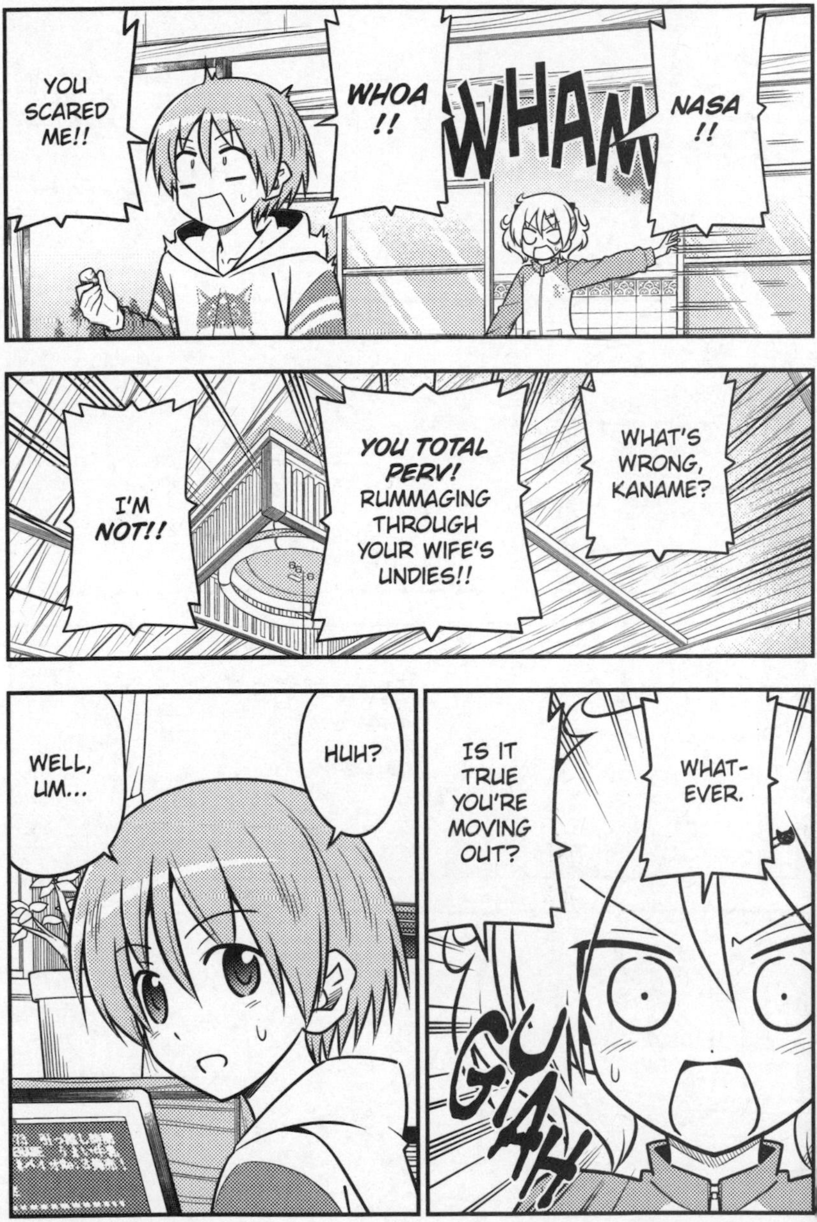
NASA!!
WHAM
WHOA!!
YOU SCARED ME!!
WHAT'S WRONG, KANAME?
YOU TOTAL PERV! RUMMAGING THROUGH YOUR WIFE'S UNDIES!!
I'M NOT!!
WHAT-EVER.
IS IT TRUE YOU'RE MOVING OUT?
GYAAH
HUH?
WELL, UM...

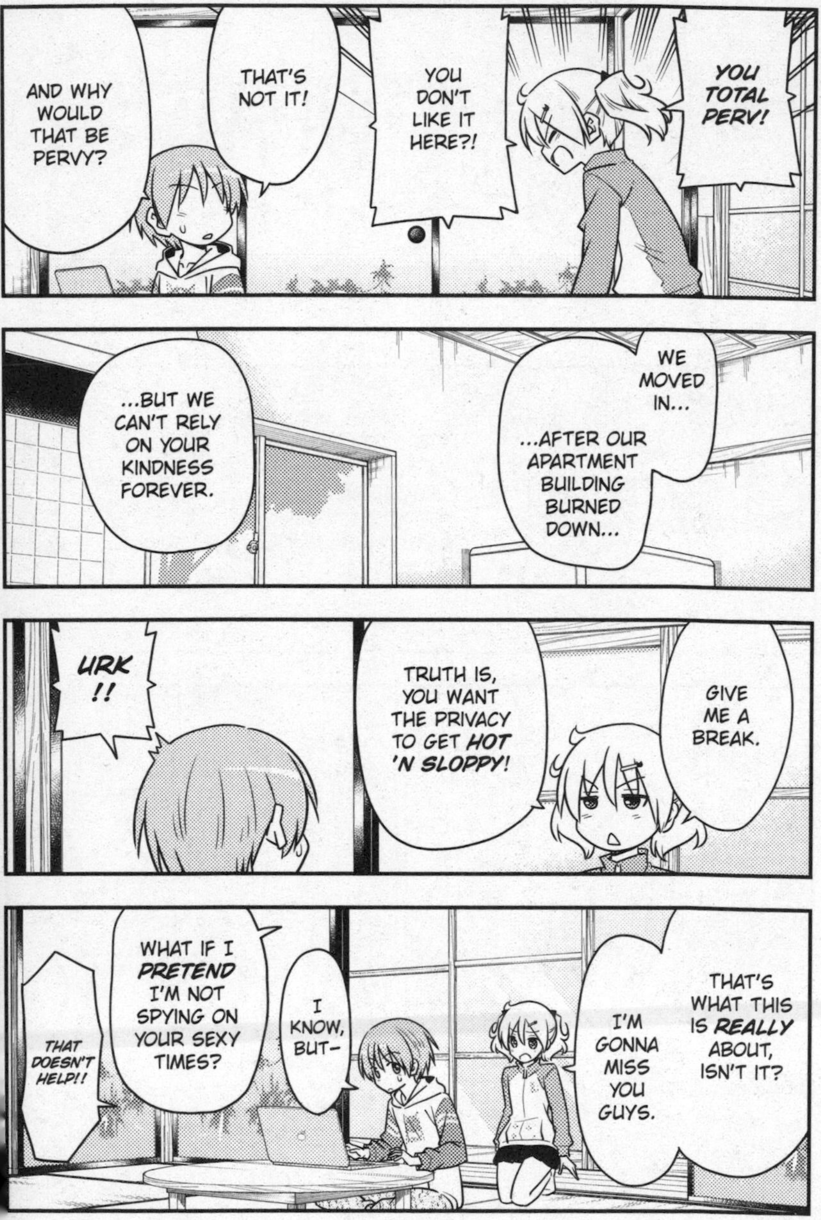
YOU TOTAL PERV!
YOU DON'T LIKE IT HERE?!
THAT'S NOT IT!
AND WHY WOULD THAT BE PERVY?
WE MOVED IN...
...AFTER OUR APARTMENT BUILDING BURNED DOWN...
...BUT WE CAN'T RELY ON YOUR KINDNESS FOREVER.
GIVE ME A BREAK.
TRUTH IS, YOU WANT THE PRIVACY TO GET HOT 'N SLOPPY!
URK!!
THAT'S WHAT THIS IS REALLY ABOUT, ISN'T IT?
I'M GONNA MISS YOU GUYS.
I KNOW, BUT—
WHAT IF I PRETEND I'M NOT SPYING ON YOUR SEXY TIMES?
THAT DOESN'T HELP!!

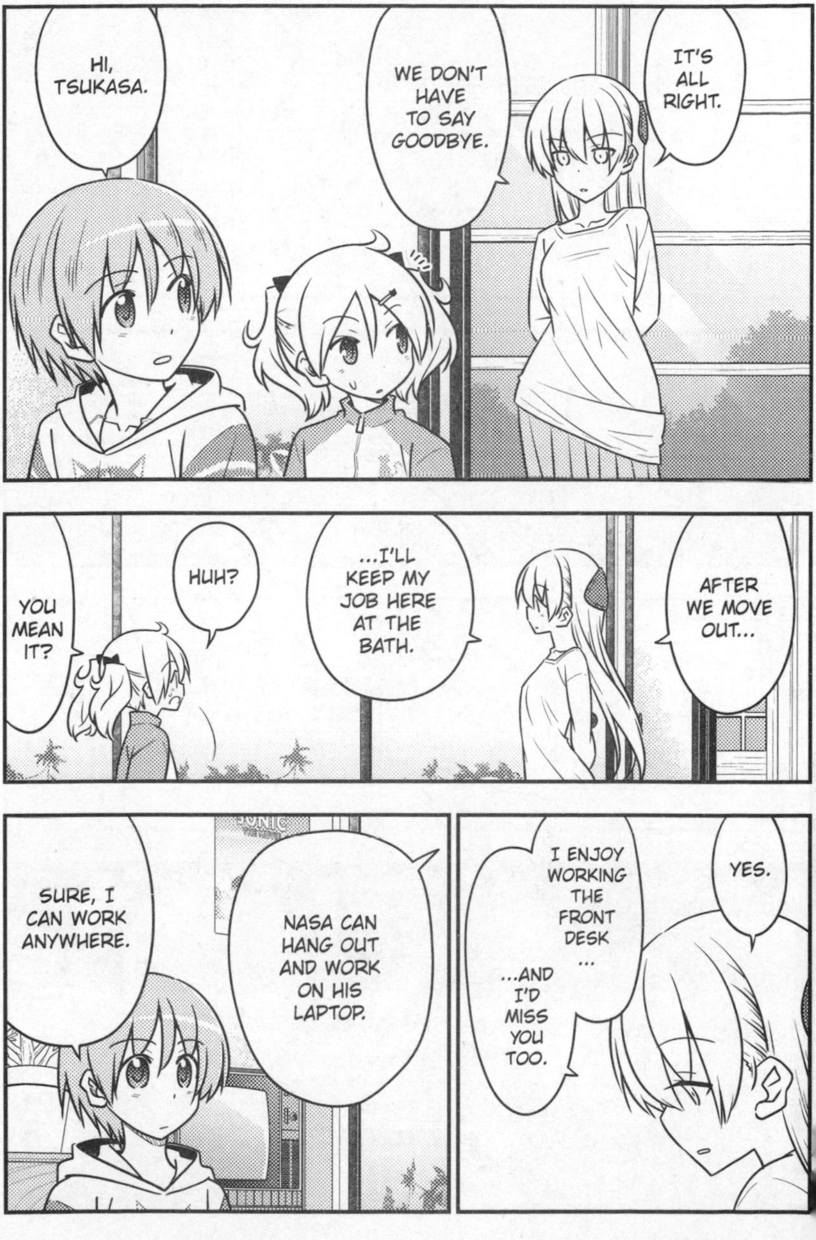
IT'S ALL RIGHT.
WE DON'T HAVE TO SAY GOODBYE.
HI, TSUKASA.
AFTER WE MOVE OUT...
...I'LL KEEP MY JOB HERE AT THE BATH.
HUH?
YOU MEAN IT?
YES.
I ENJOY WORKING THE FRONT DESK ...
...AND I'D MISS YOU TOO.
NASA CAN HANG OUT AND WORK ON HIS LAPTOP.
SURE, I CAN WORK ANYWHERE.

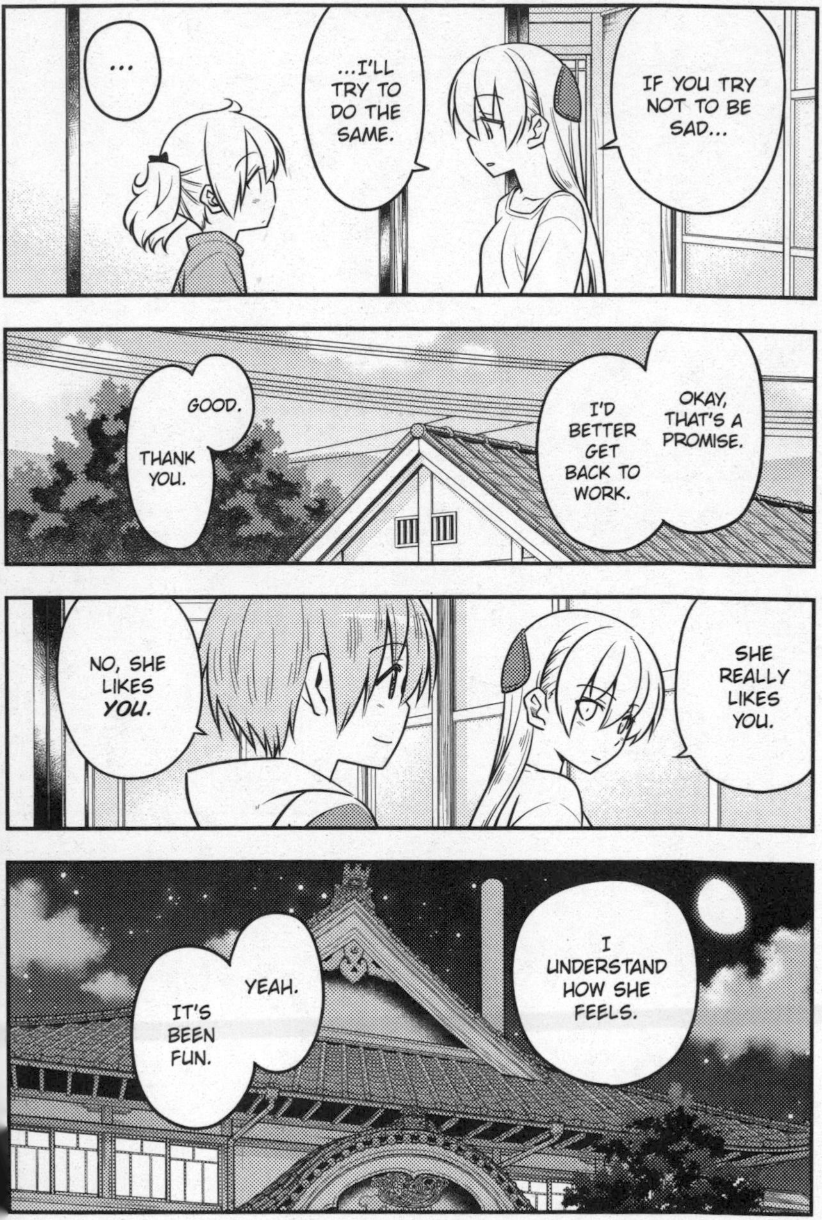
IF YOU TRY NOT TO BE SAD...
...I'LL TRY TO DO THE SAME.
...
OKAY, THAT'S A PROMISE.
I'D BETTER GET BACK TO WORK.
GOOD.
THANK YOU.
SHE REALLY LIKES YOU.
NO, SHE LIKES *YOU*.
I UNDERSTAND HOW SHE FEELS.
YEAH.
IT'S BEEN FUN.

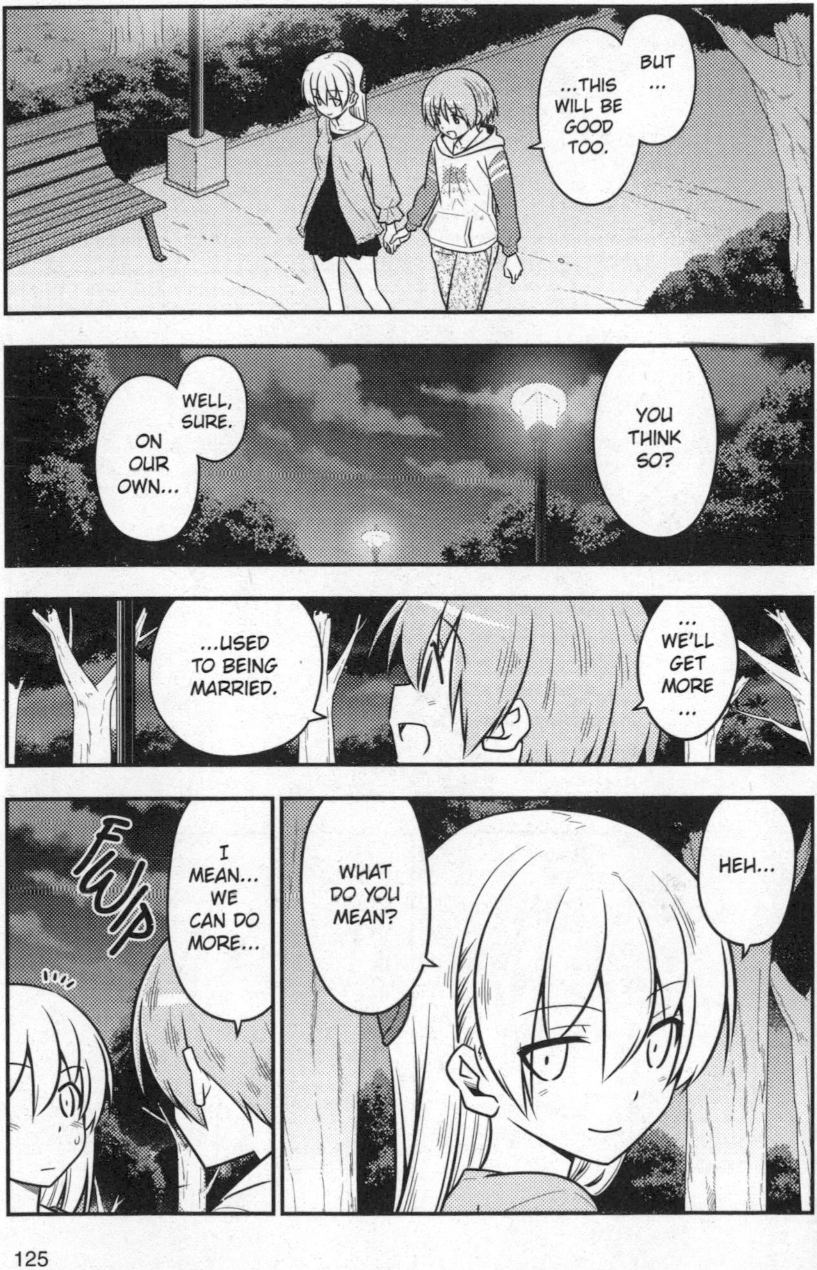
BUT ...
...THIS WILL BE GOOD TOO.
YOU THINK SO?
WELL, SURE.
ON OUR OWN...
... WE'LL GET MORE ...
...USED TO BEING MARRIED.
HEH...
WHAT DO YOU MEAN?
I MEAN... WE CAN DO MORE...
FWIP

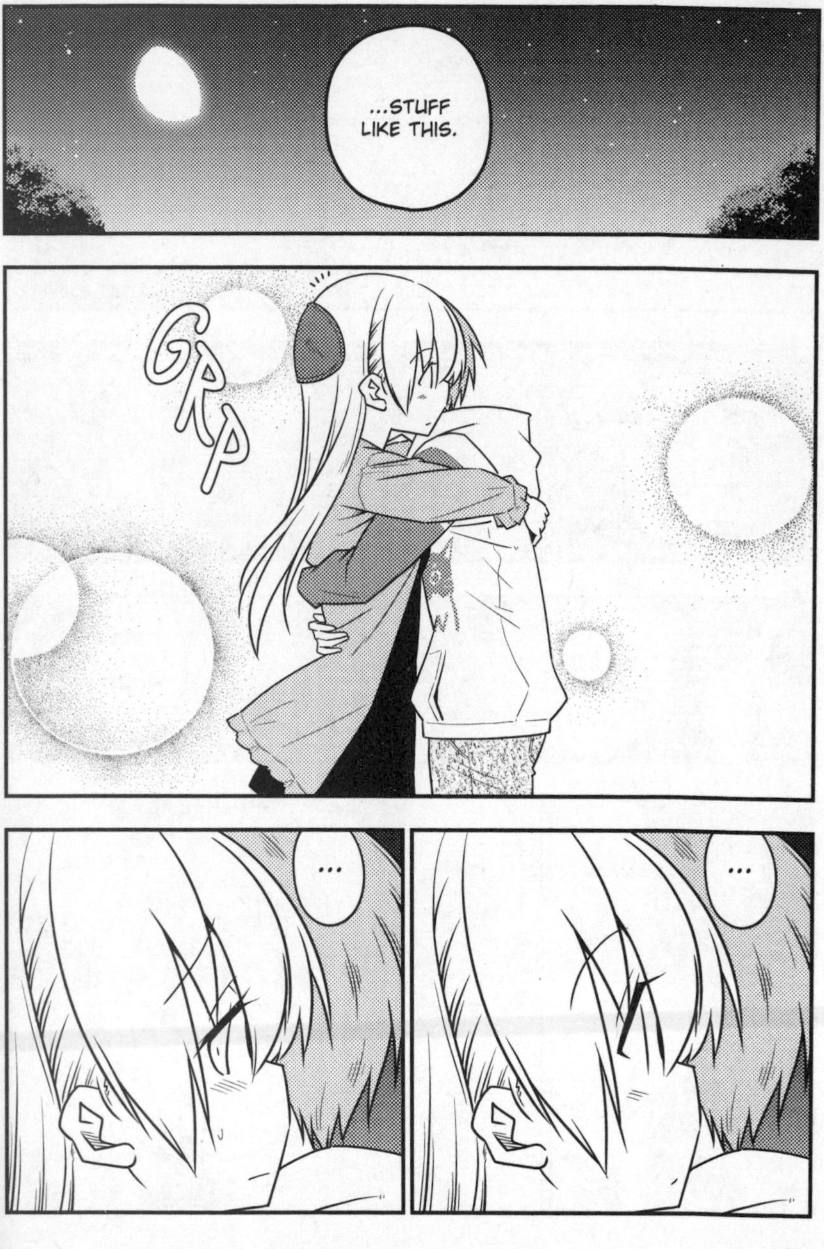
...STUFF LIKE THIS.
GRP
...
...

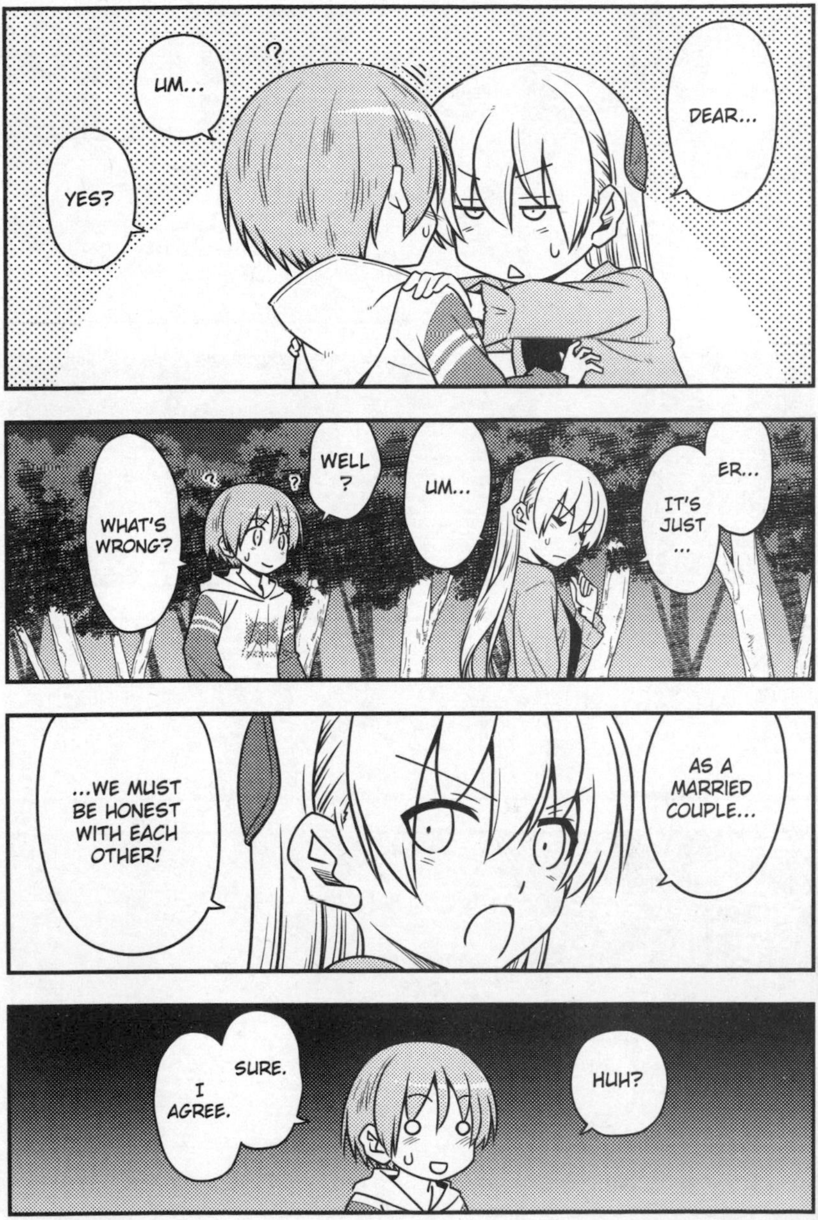
DEAR...
UM...
YES?
ER... IT'S JUST ...
UM...
WELL?
WHAT'S WRONG?
AS A MARRIED COUPLE...
...WE MUST BE HONEST WITH EACH OTHER!
HUH?
SURE. I AGREE.

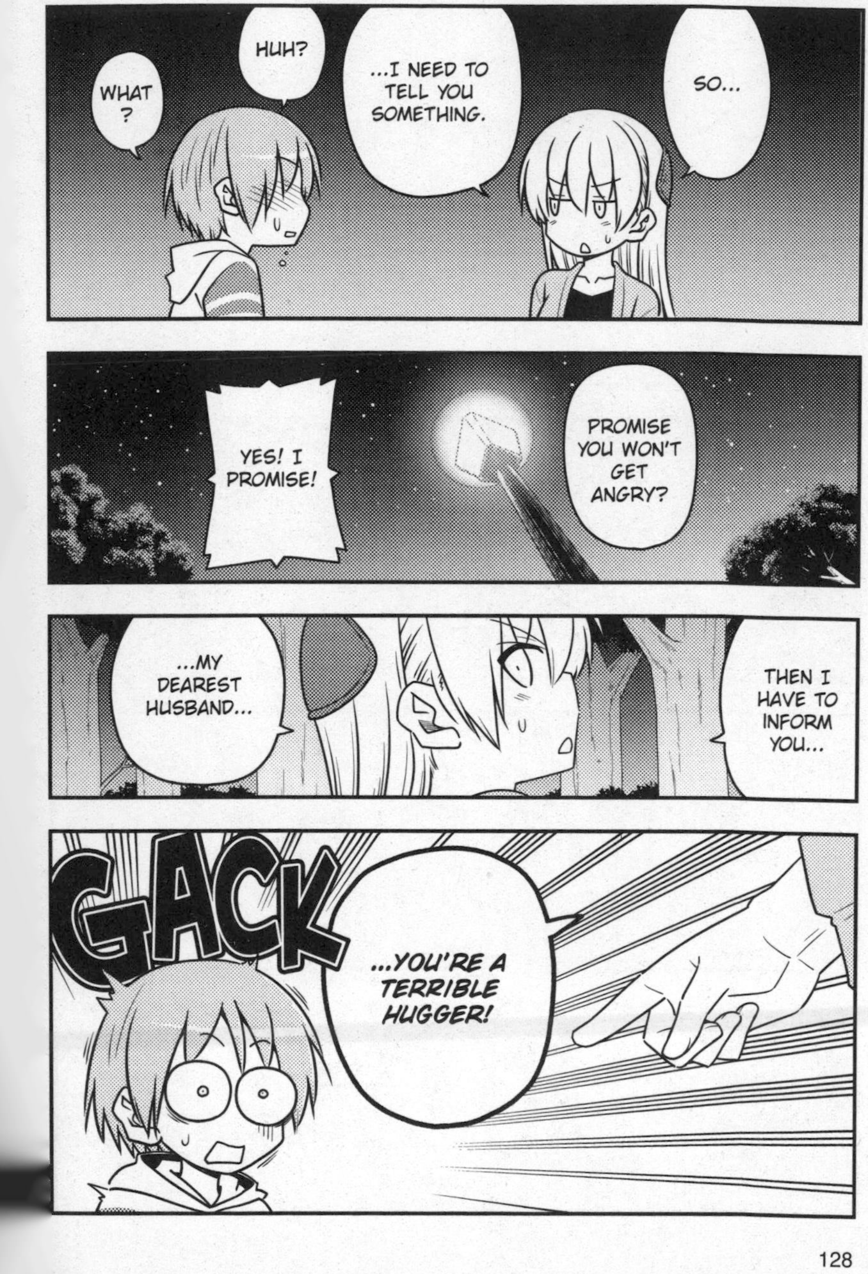
SO...
...I NEED TO TELL YOU SOMETHING.
HUH?
WHAT ?
PROMISE YOU WON'T GET ANGRY?
YES! I PROMISE!
THEN I HAVE TO INFORM YOU...
...MY DEAREST HUSBAND...
...YOU'RE A TERRIBLE HUGGER!
GACK

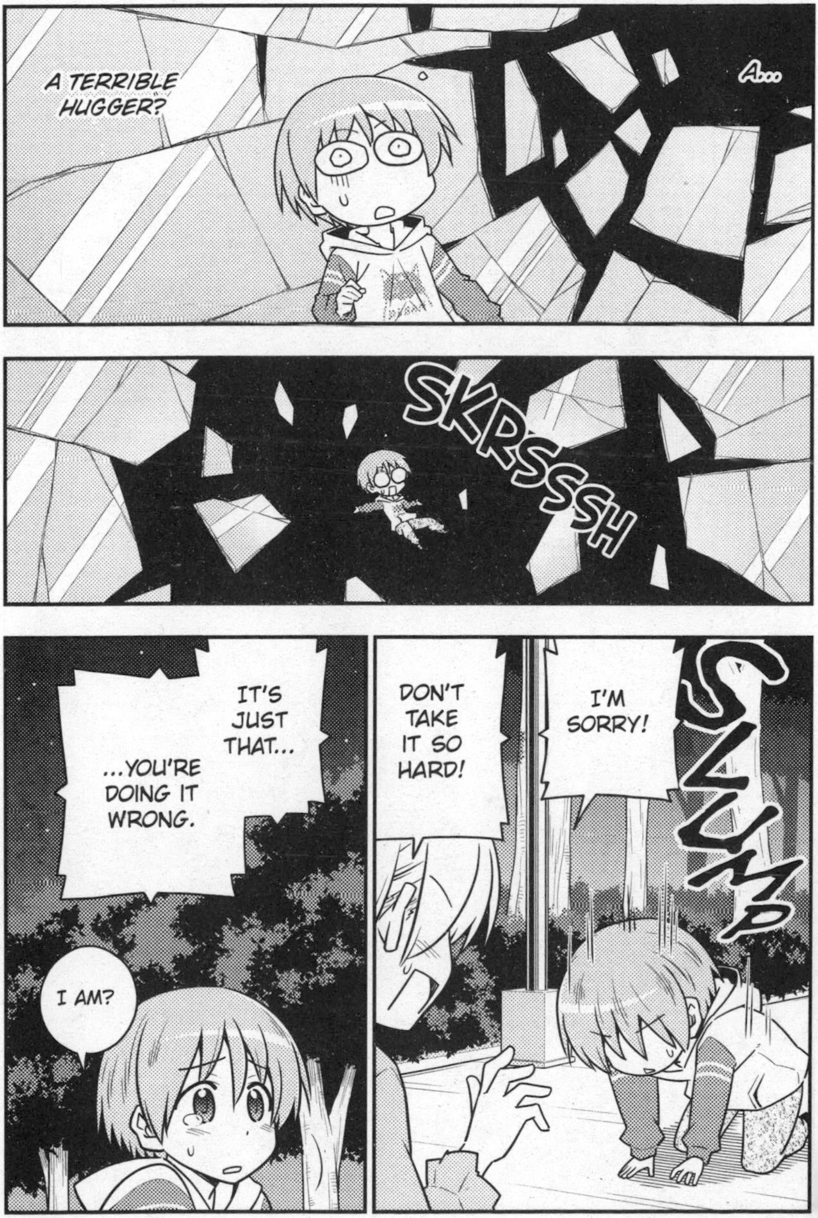
A...
A TERRIBLE HUGGER?
SKRSSSH
SLUMP
I'M SORRY!
DON'T TAKE IT SO HARD!
IT'S JUST THAT...
...YOU'RE DOING IT WRONG.
I AM?

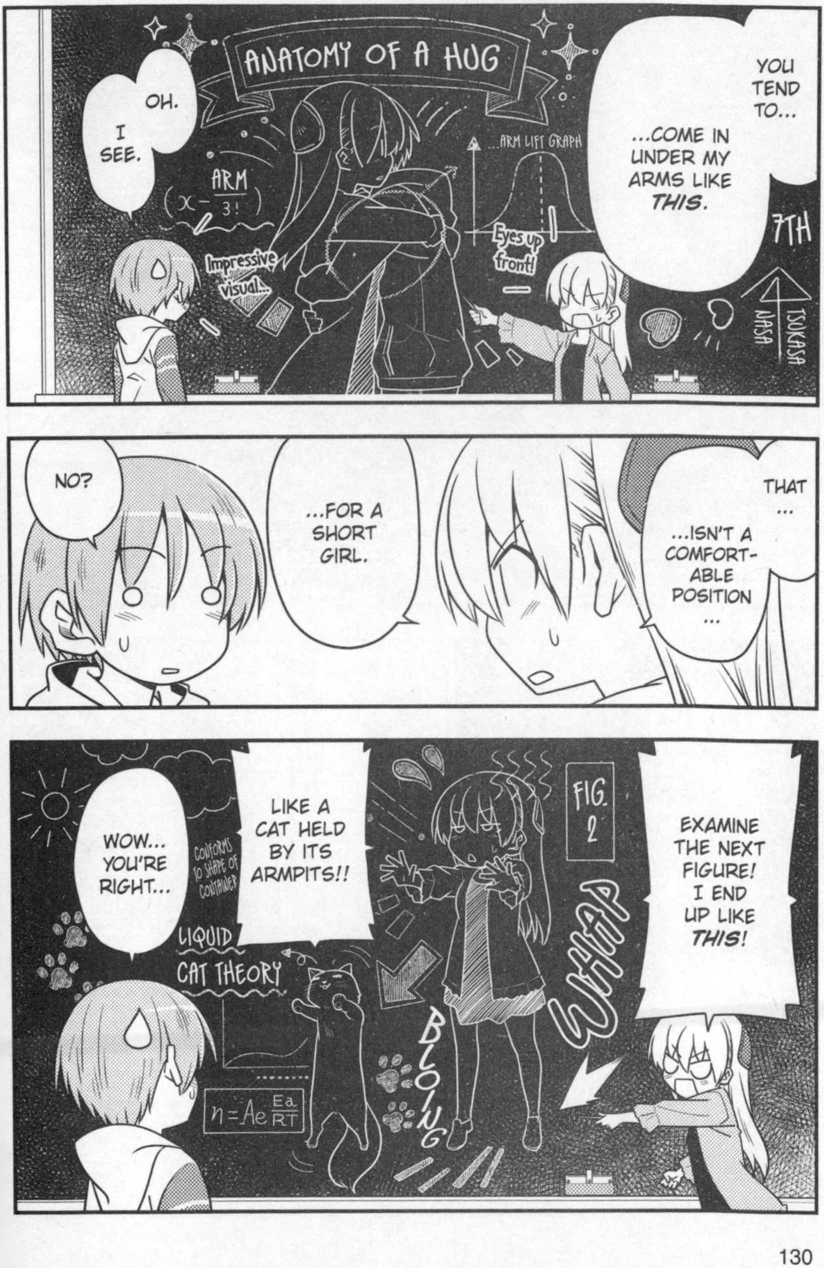
ANATOMY OF A HUG
YOU TEND TO...
...COME IN UNDER MY ARMS LIKE THIS.
7TH
TSUKASA
NASA
Eyes up front!
ARM LIFT GRAPH
Impressive visual...
OH. I SEE.
THAT...
...ISN'T A COMFORT-ABLE POSITION...
...FOR A SHORT GIRL.
NO?
EXAMINE THE NEXT FIGURE! I END UP LIKE THIS!
WHAP
FIG. 2
BLOING
LIKE A CAT HELD BY ITS ARMPITS!!
LIQUID CAT THEORY
CONFORMS TO SHAPE OF CONTAINER
WOW... YOU'RE RIGHT...

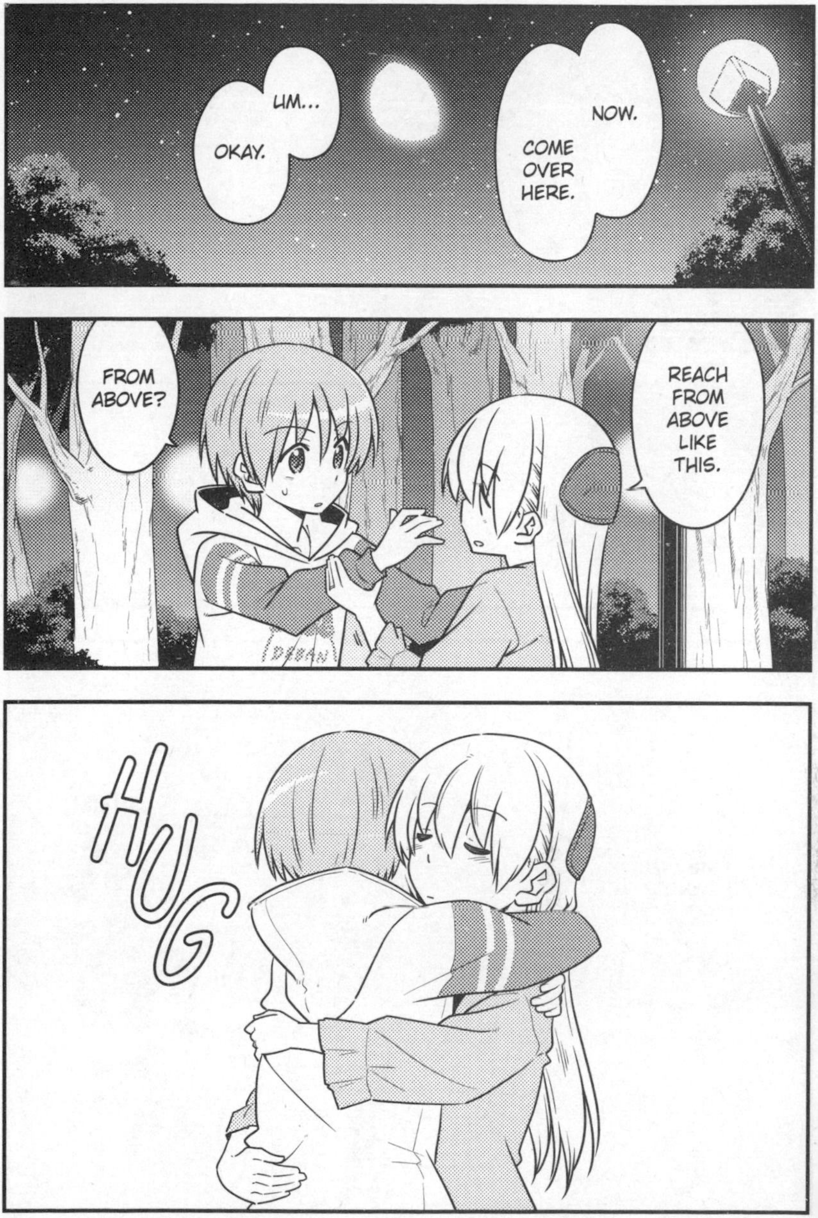
NOW. COME OVER HERE.
UM... OKAY.
REACH FROM ABOVE LIKE THIS.
FROM ABOVE?
HUG

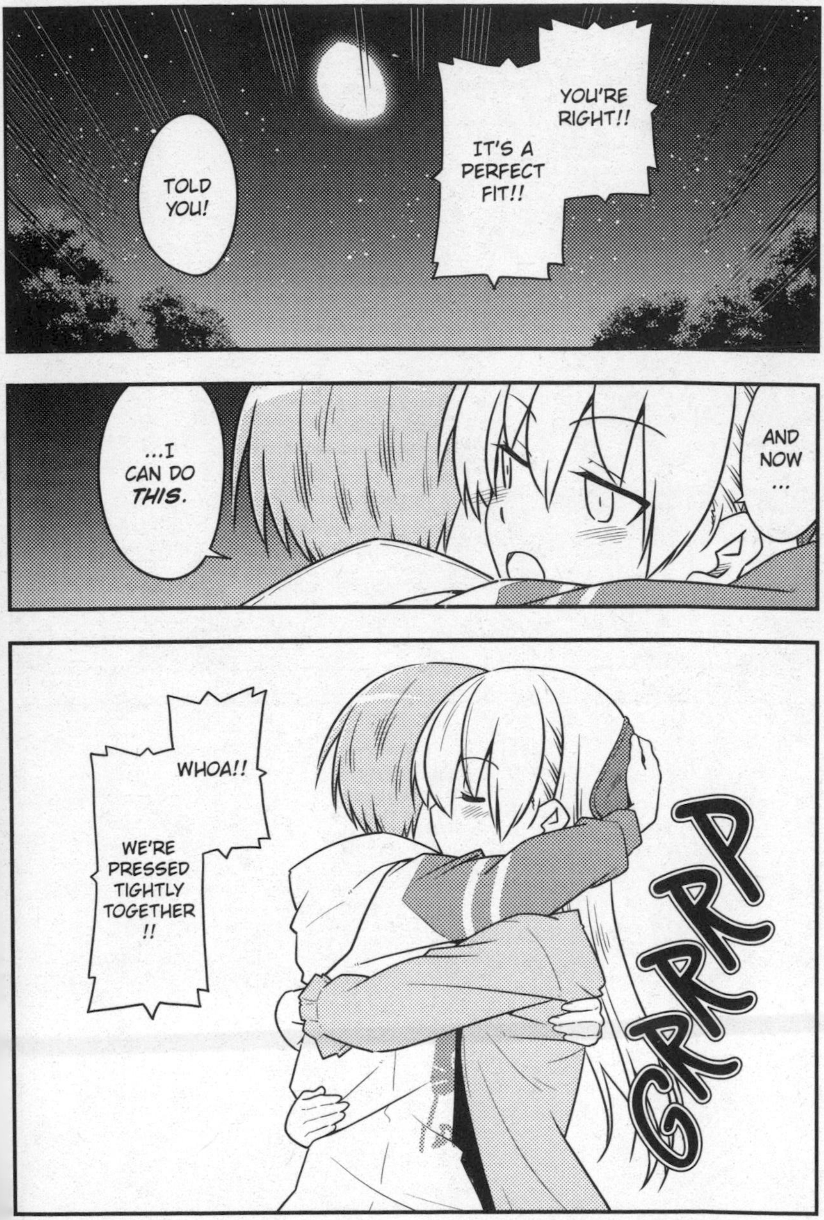
YOU'RE RIGHT!!
IT'S A PERFECT FIT!!
TOLD YOU!
AND NOW ...
...I CAN DO *THIS*.
WHOA!!
WE'RE PRESSED TIGHTLY TOGETHER!!
GRRRP

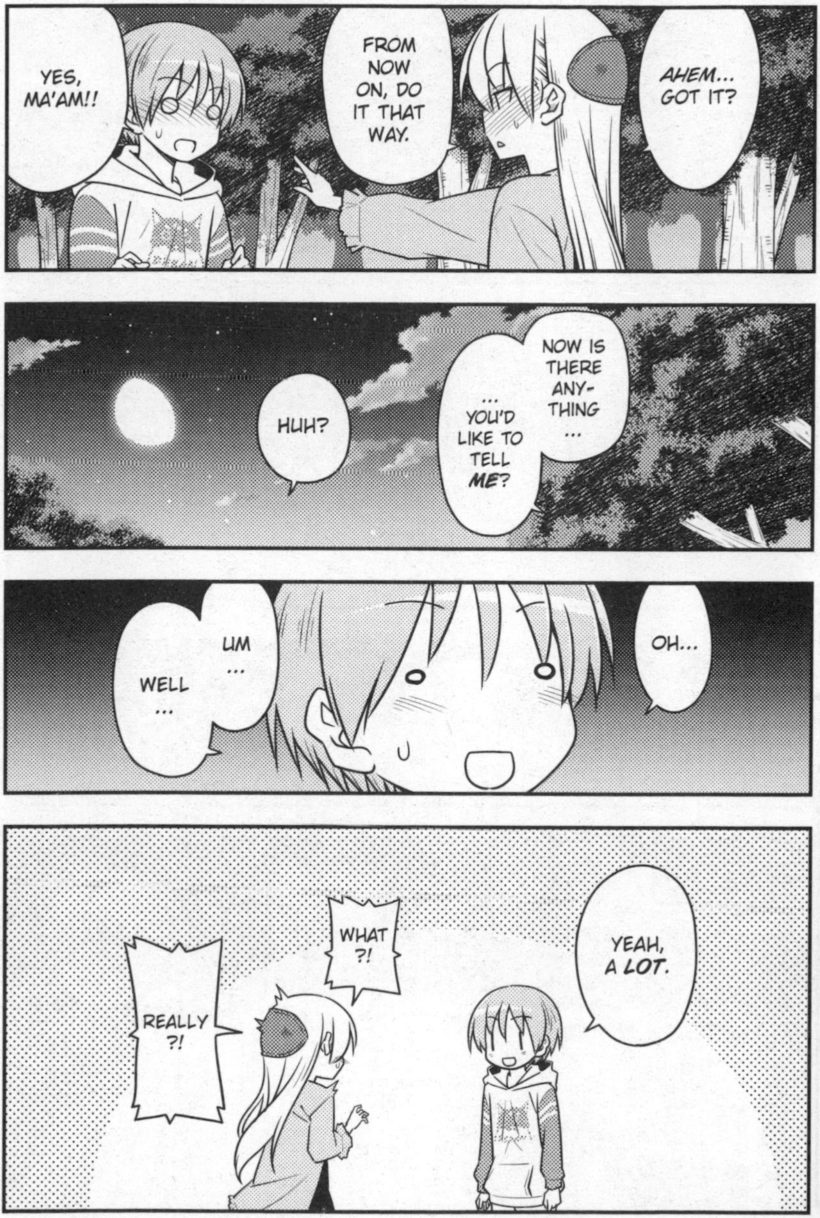
AHEM... GOT IT?
FROM NOW ON, DO IT THAT WAY.
YES, MA'AM!!
NOW IS THERE ANY-THING...
...YOU'D LIKE TO TELL *ME*?
HUH?
OH...
UM...
WELL...
YEAH, A *LOT*.
WHAT?!
REALLY?!

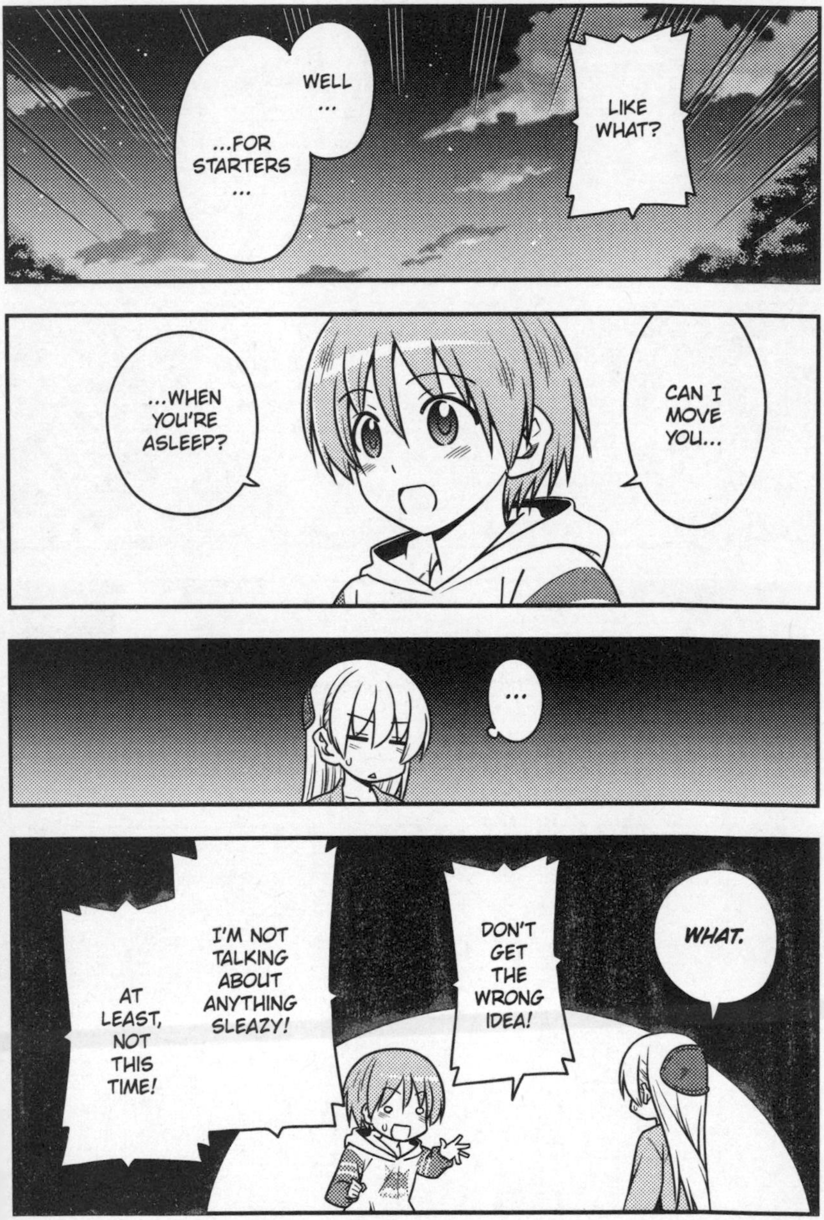
LIKE WHAT?
WELL ... ...FOR STARTERS ...
CAN I MOVE YOU...
...WHEN YOU'RE ASLEEP?
...
WHAT.
DON'T GET THE WRONG IDEA!
I'M NOT TALKING ABOUT ANYTHING SLEAZY!
AT LEAST, NOT THIS TIME!

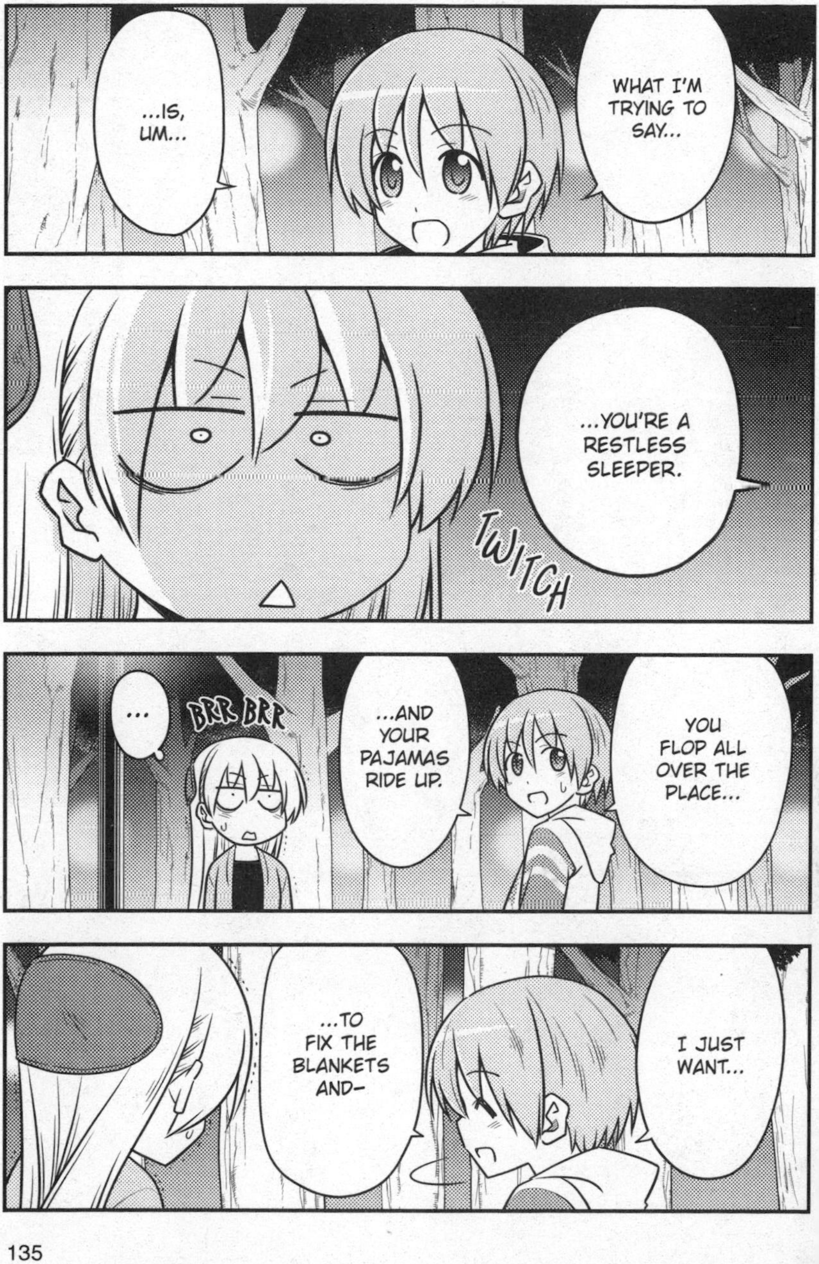
WHAT I'M TRYING TO SAY...
...IS, UM...
...YOU'RE A RESTLESS SLEEPER.
TWITCH
YOU FLOP ALL OVER THE PLACE...
...AND YOUR PAJAMAS RIDE UP.
BRR BRR
...
I JUST WANT...
...TO FIX THE BLANKETS AND-

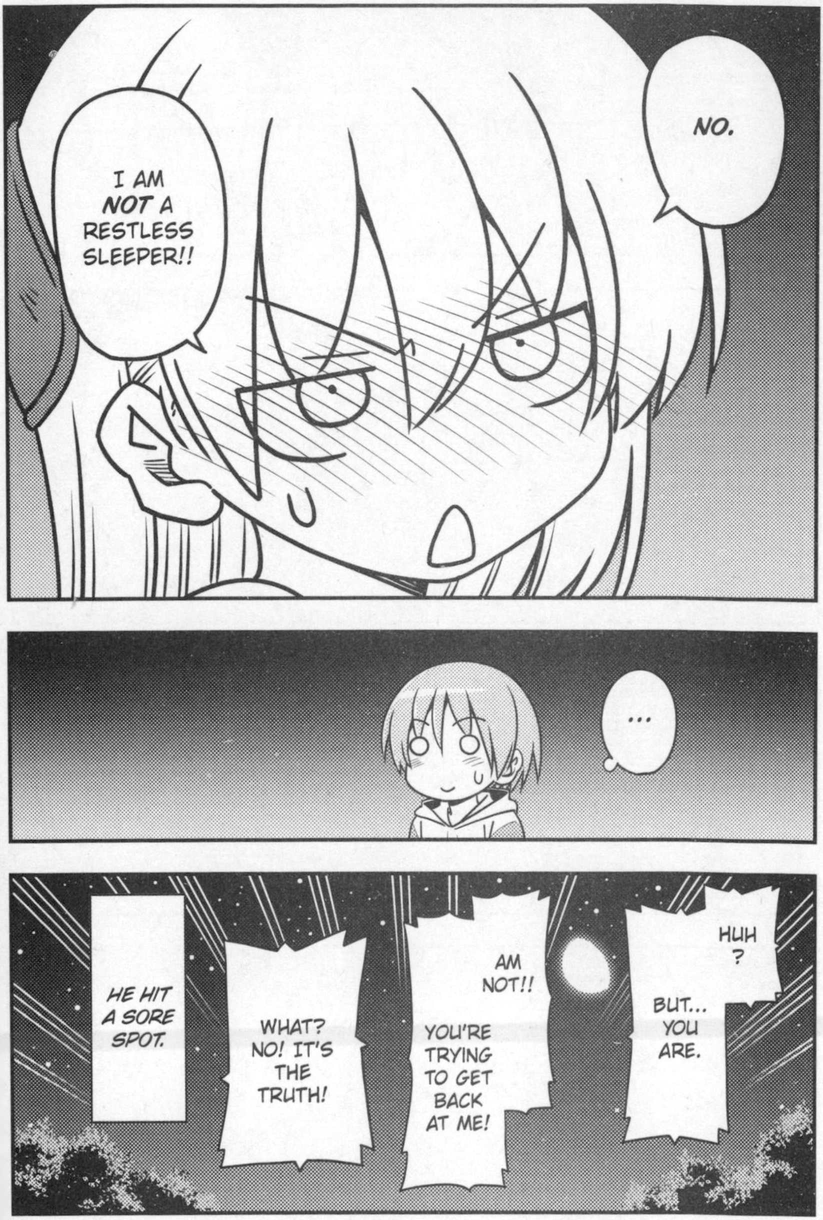
NO.
I AM *NOT* A RESTLESS SLEEPER!!
...
HUH?
BUT... YOU ARE.
AM NOT!!
YOU'RE TRYING TO GET BACK AT ME!
WHAT? NO! IT'S THE TRUTH!
HE HIT A SORE SPOT.

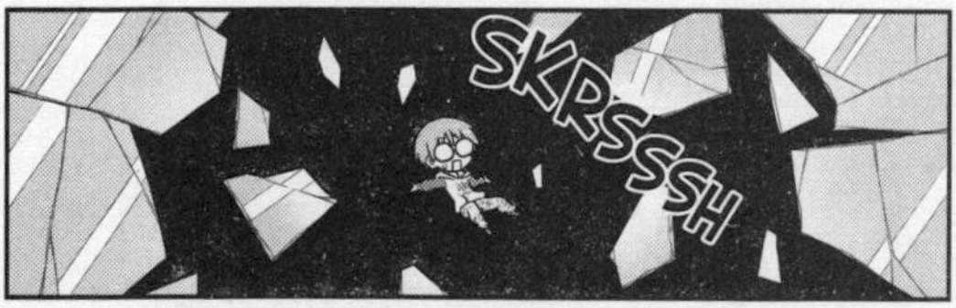
SKRSSSH

FLY ME TO THE MOON

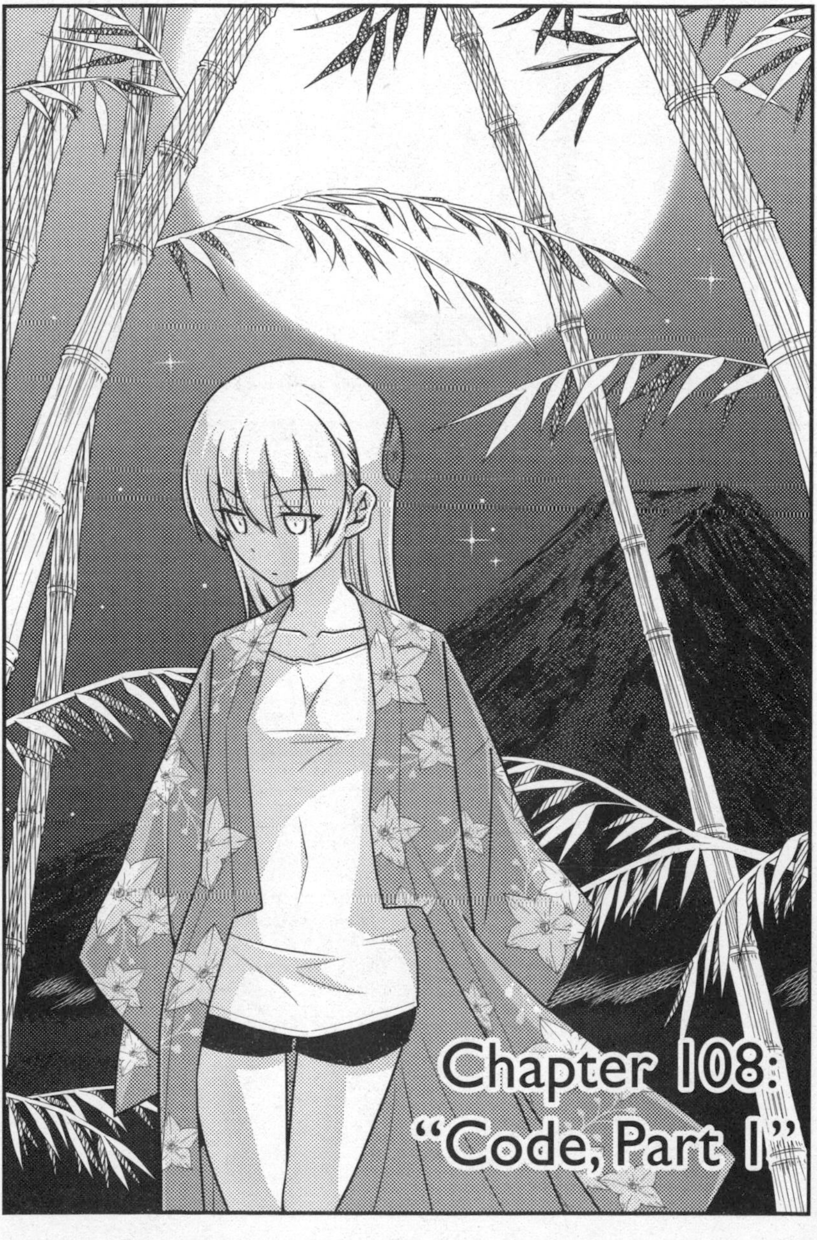
Chapter 108:
"Code, Part 1"

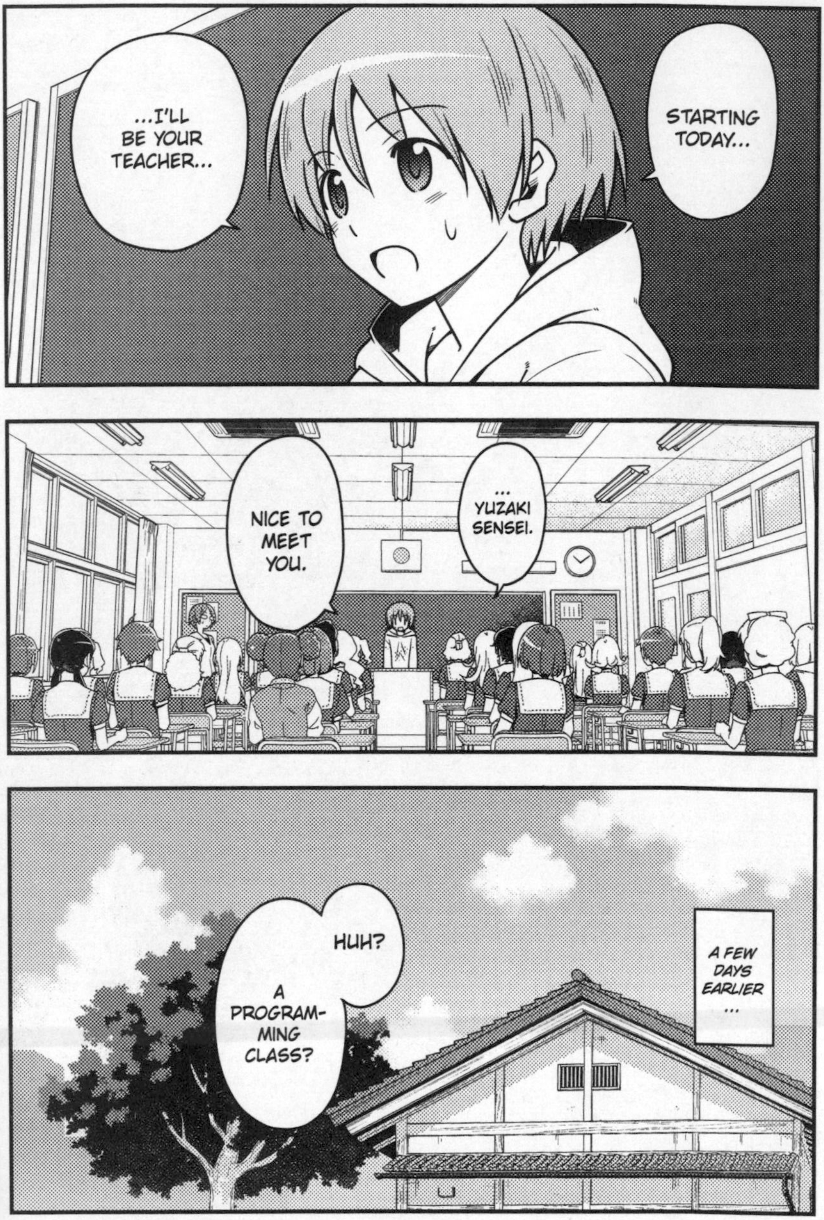
STARTING TODAY...
...I'LL BE YOUR TEACHER...
... YUZAKI SENSEI.
NICE TO MEET YOU.
A FEW DAYS EARLIER ...
HUH?
A PROGRAM-MING CLASS?

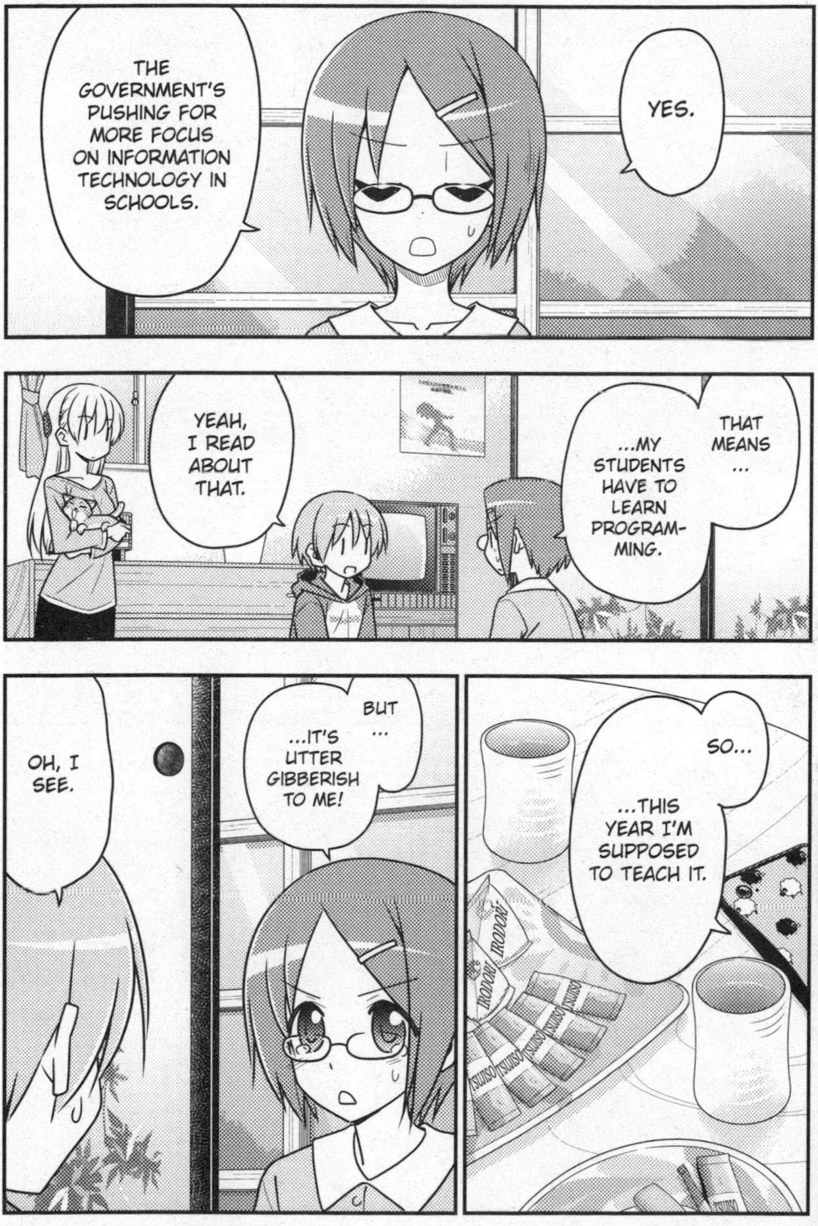
YES.
THE GOVERNMENT'S PUSHING FOR MORE FOCUS ON INFORMATION TECHNOLOGY IN SCHOOLS.
THAT MEANS ...
...MY STUDENTS HAVE TO LEARN PROGRAM-MING.
YEAH, I READ ABOUT THAT.
SO...
...THIS YEAR I'M SUPPOSED TO TEACH IT.
BUT ...
...IT'S UTTER GIBBERISH TO ME!
OH, I SEE.

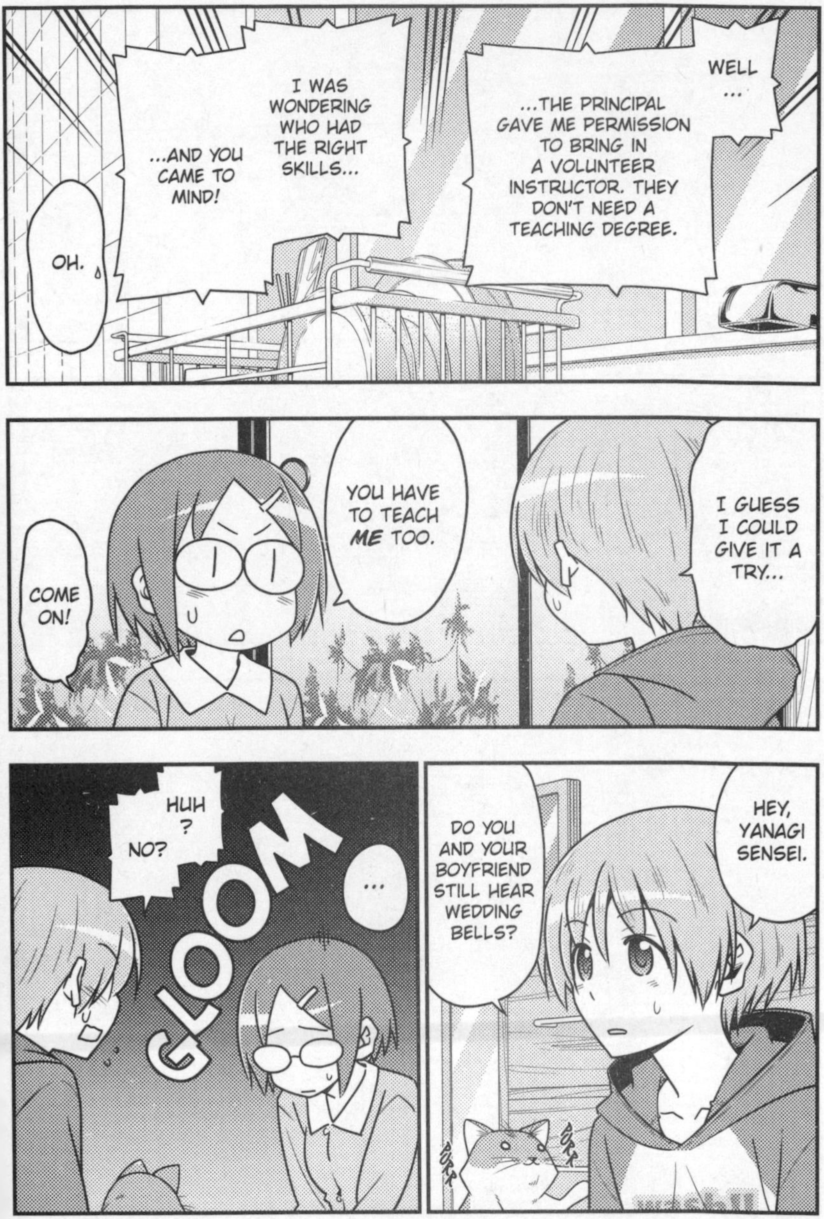
WELL ...
...THE PRINCIPAL GAVE ME PERMISSION TO BRING IN A VOLUNTEER INSTRUCTOR. THEY DON'T NEED A TEACHING DEGREE.
I WAS WONDERING WHO HAD THE RIGHT SKILLS...
...AND YOU CAME TO MIND!
OH.
I GUESS I COULD GIVE IT A TRY...
YOU HAVE TO TEACH *ME* TOO.
COME ON!
HEY, YANAGI SENSEI.
DO YOU AND YOUR BOYFRIEND STILL HEAR WEDDING BELLS?
PURR
PURR
...
HUH? NO?
GLOOM

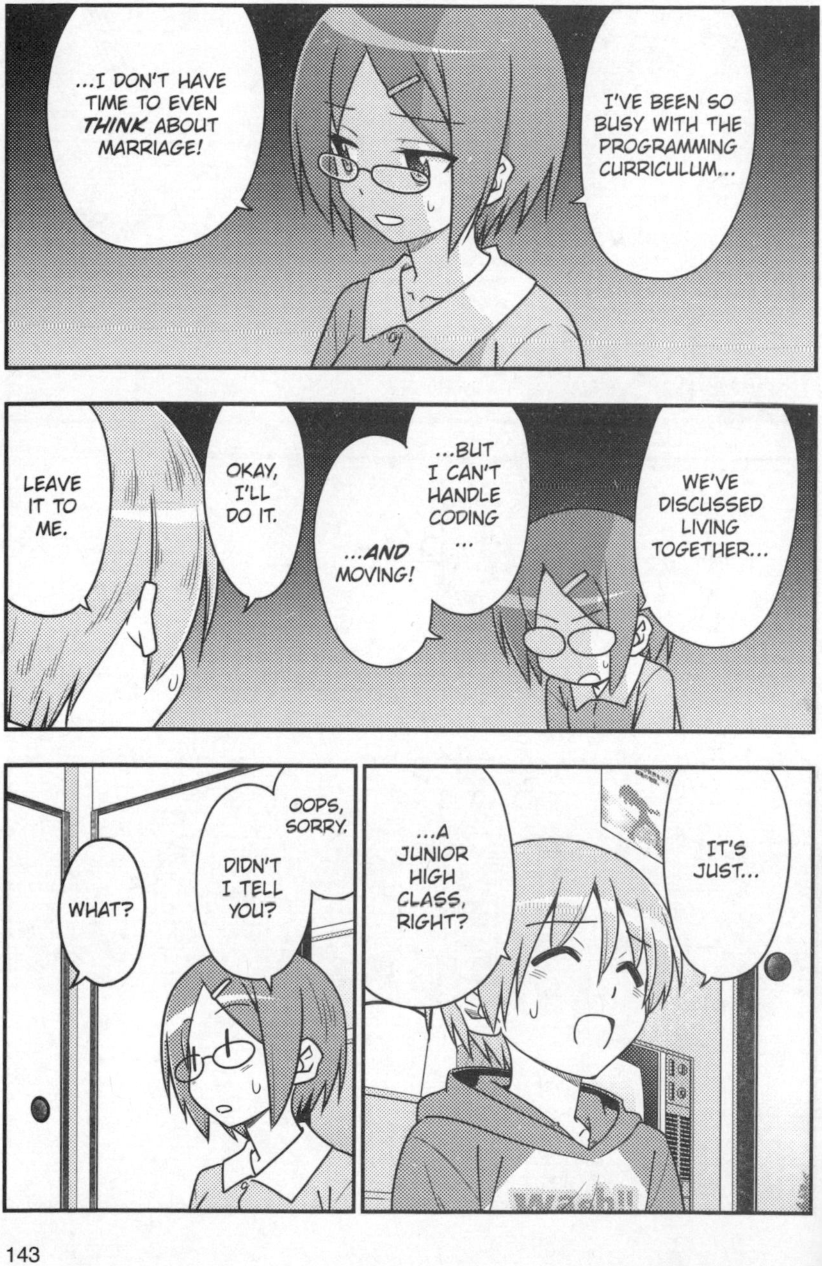
I'VE BEEN SO BUSY WITH THE PROGRAMMING CURRICULUM...
...I DON'T HAVE TIME TO EVEN *THINK* ABOUT MARRIAGE!
WE'VE DISCUSSED LIVING TOGETHER...
...BUT I CAN'T HANDLE CODING ...
...*AND* MOVING!
OKAY, I'LL DO IT.
LEAVE IT TO ME.
IT'S JUST...
...A JUNIOR HIGH CLASS, RIGHT?
OOPS, SORRY.
DIDN'T I TELL YOU?
WHAT?

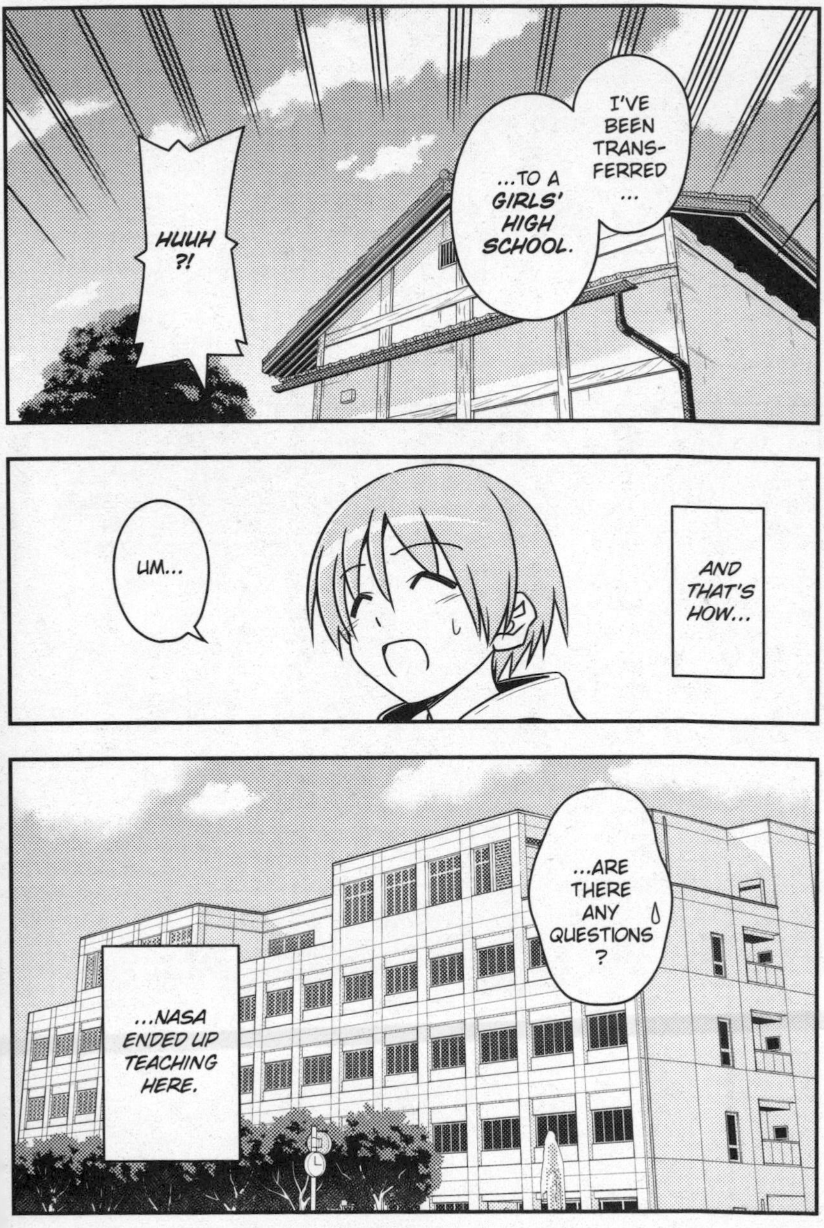
I'VE BEEN TRANS-FERRED...
...TO A GIRLS' HIGH SCHOOL.
HUUH?!
AND THAT'S HOW...
UM...
...ARE THERE ANY QUESTIONS?
...NASA ENDED UP TEACHING HERE.

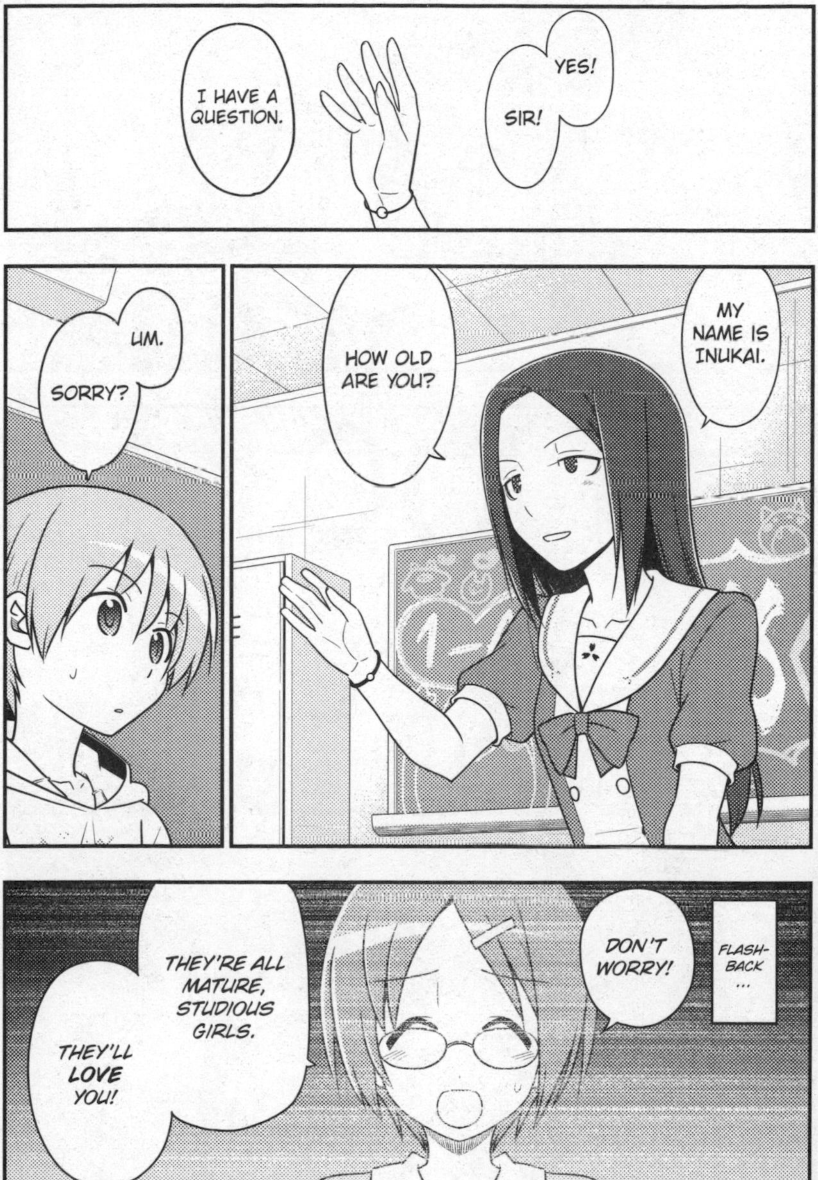
YES! SIR!
I HAVE A QUESTION.
MY NAME IS INUKAI.
HOW OLD ARE YOU?
UM. SORRY?
FLASH-BACK ...
DON'T WORRY!
THEY'RE ALL MATURE, STUDIOUS GIRLS.
THEY'LL LOVE YOU!

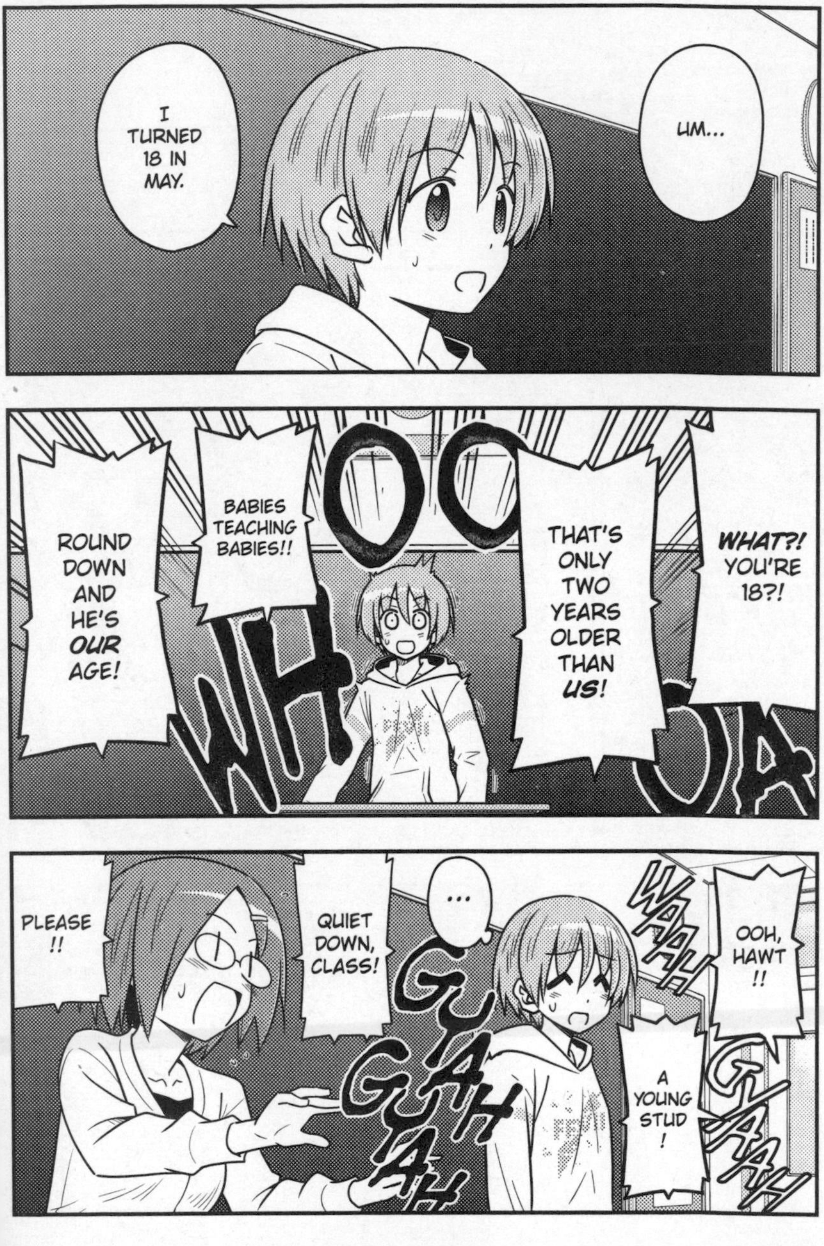
UM...
I TURNED 18 IN MAY.
WHAT?! YOU'RE 18?!
THAT'S ONLY TWO YEARS OLDER THAN US!
BABIES TEACHING BABIES!!
ROUND DOWN AND HE'S OUR AGE!
WHOOOA
OOH, HAWT!!
WAAH
GYAAAH
A YOUNG STUD!
...
GYAH
GYAH
QUIET DOWN, CLASS!
PLEASE!!

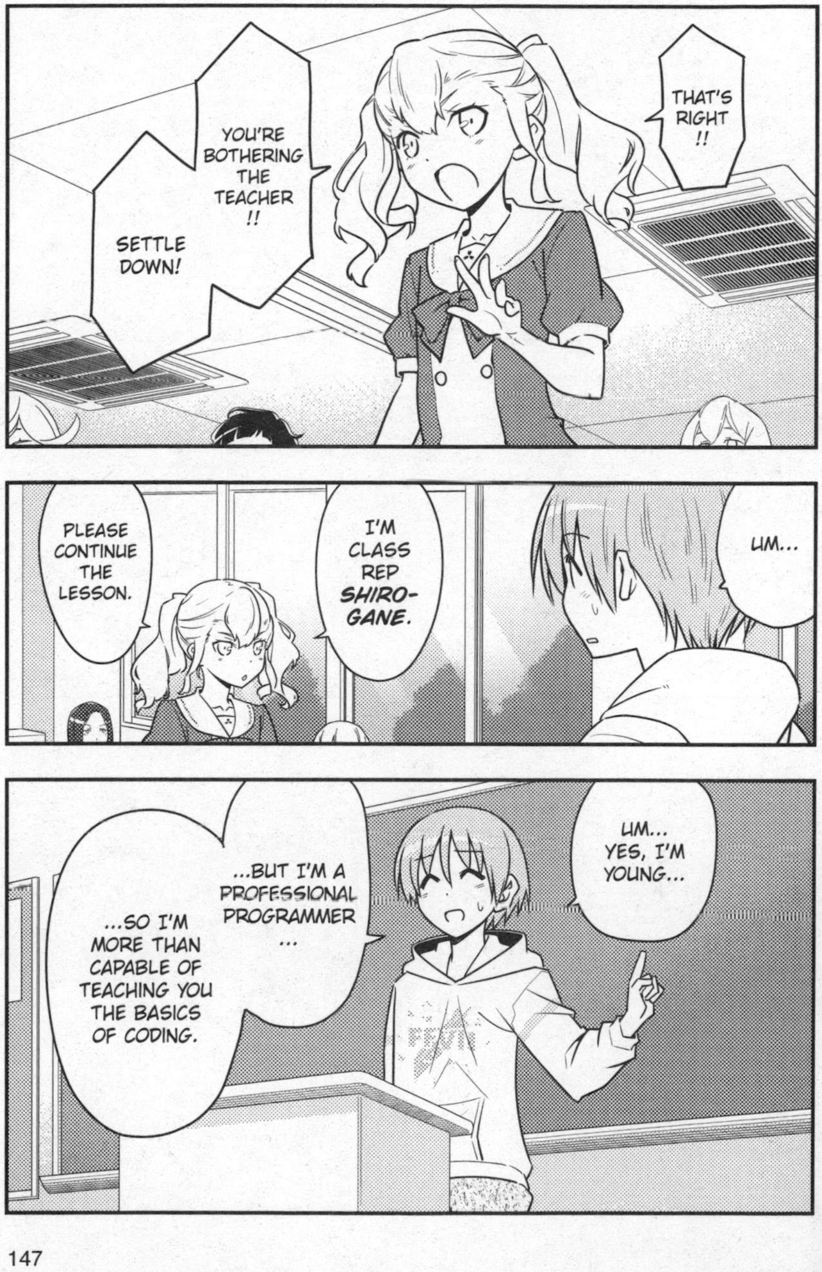
THAT'S RIGHT !!
YOU'RE BOTHERING THE TEACHER !!
SETTLE DOWN!
UM...
I'M CLASS REP SHIROGANE.
PLEASE CONTINUE THE LESSON.
UM... YES, I'M YOUNG...
...BUT I'M A PROFESSIONAL PROGRAMMER ...
...SO I'M MORE THAN CAPABLE OF TEACHING YOU THE BASICS OF CODING.

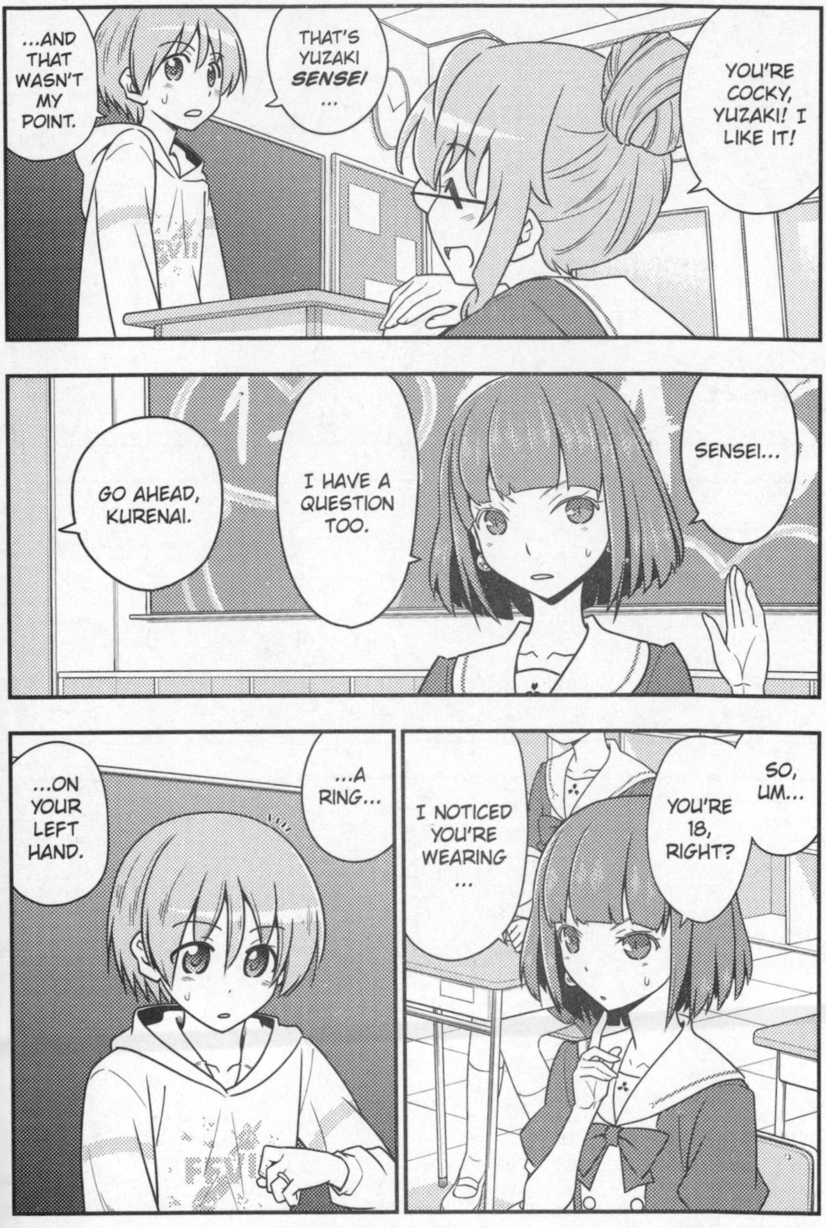
YOU'RE COCKY, YUZAKI! I LIKE IT!
THAT'S YUZAKI *SENSEI* ...
...AND THAT WASN'T MY POINT.
SENSEI...
I HAVE A QUESTION TOO.
GO AHEAD, KURENAI.
SO, UM...
YOU'RE 18, RIGHT?
I NOTICED YOU'RE WEARING ...
...A RING...
...ON YOUR LEFT HAND.

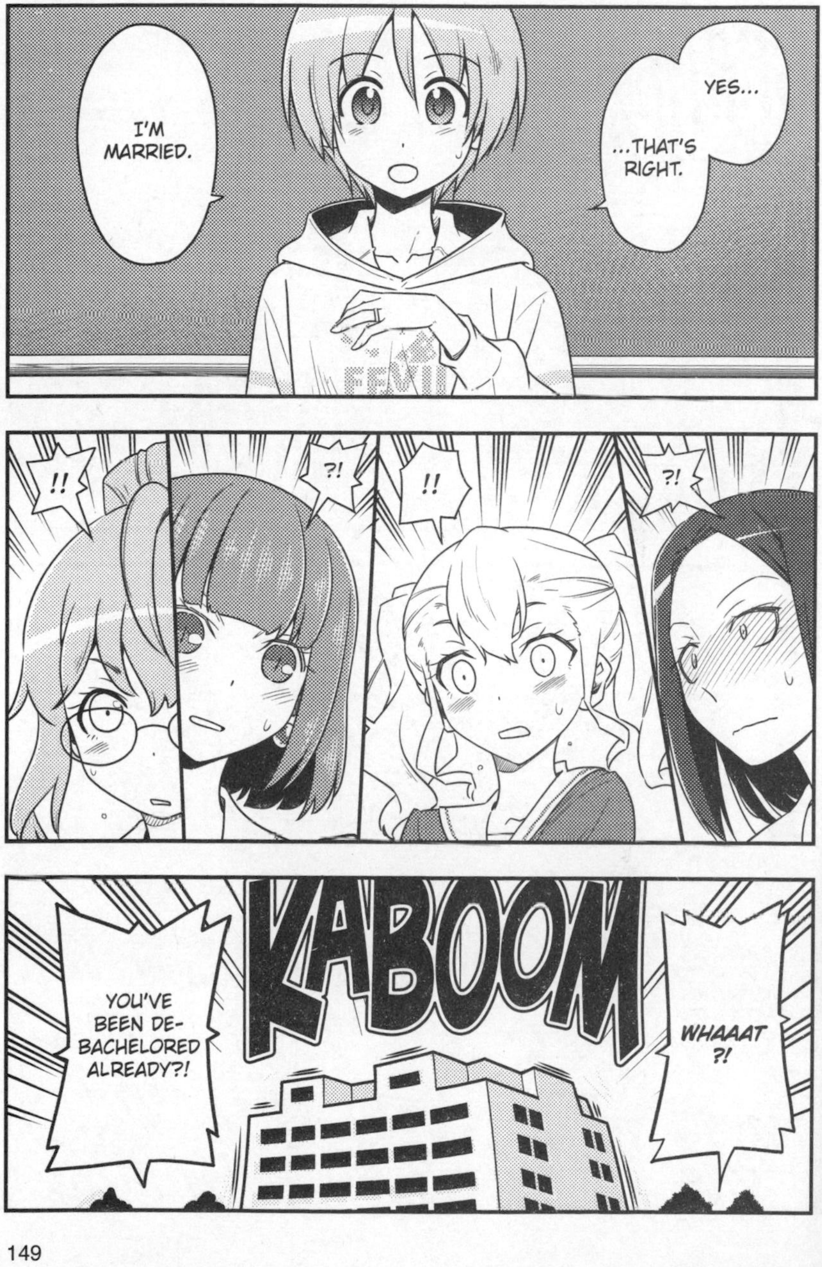

YES... ...THAT'S RIGHT.
I'M MARRIED.
?!
!!
?!
!!
WHAAAT ?!
KABOOM
YOU'VE BEEN DE-BACHELORED ALREADY?!

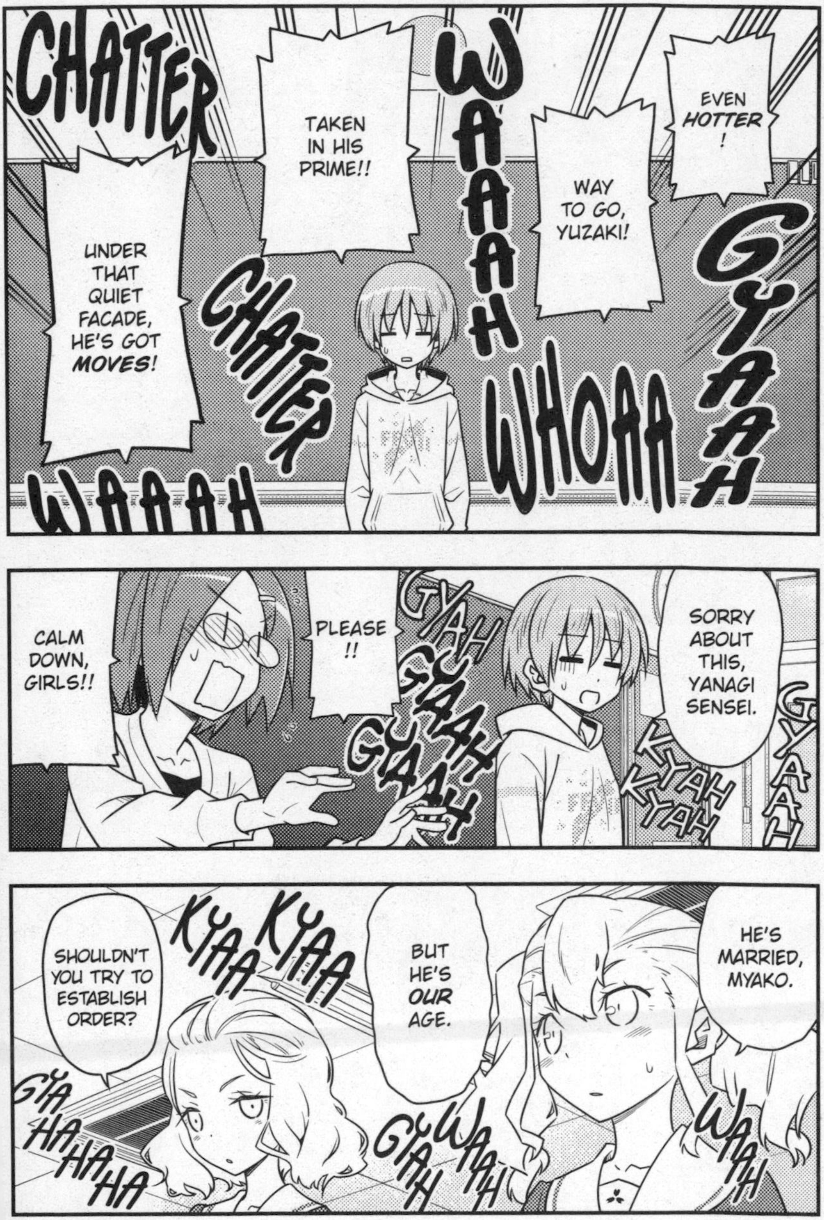
EVEN HOTTER!
WAY TO GO, YUZAKI!
GYAAAH
WAAAAH
WHOAA
TAKEN IN HIS PRIME!!
CHATTER
UNDER THAT QUIET FACADE, HE'S GOT MOVES!
CHATTER
SORRY ABOUT THIS, YANAGI SENSEI.
GYAAAH
KYAH KYAH
GYAH GYAAH GYAAH
PLEASE!!
CALM DOWN, GIRLS!!
HE'S MARRIED, MYAKO.
WAAAH
BUT HE'S OUR AGE.
WAAAH
GYAAH
KYAA KYAA
SHOULDN'T YOU TRY TO ESTABLISH ORDER?
GYAHAHAHA

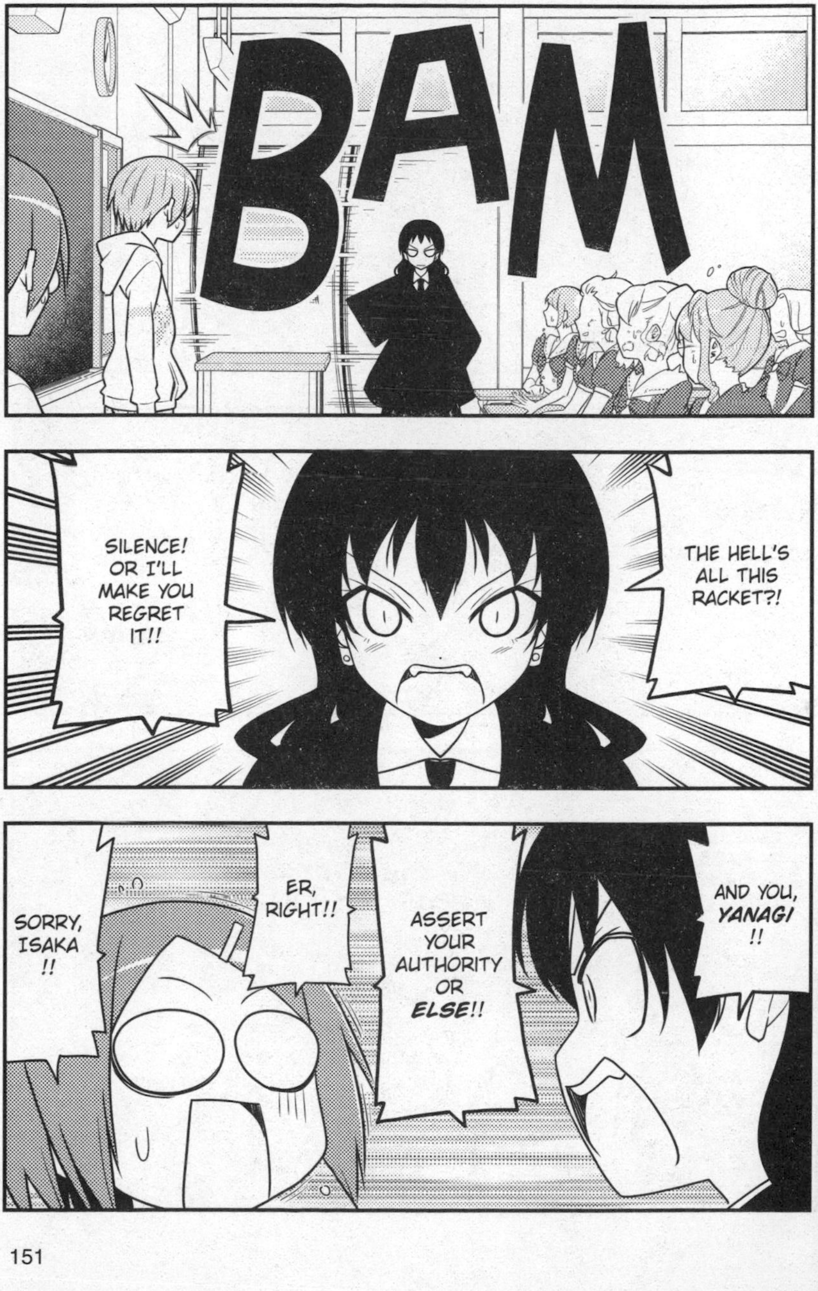
BAM
THE HELL'S ALL THIS RACKET?!
SILENCE! OR I'LL MAKE YOU REGRET IT!!
AND YOU, *YANAGI*!!
ASSERT YOUR AUTHORITY OR *ELSE*!!
ER, RIGHT!!
SORRY, ISAKA!!

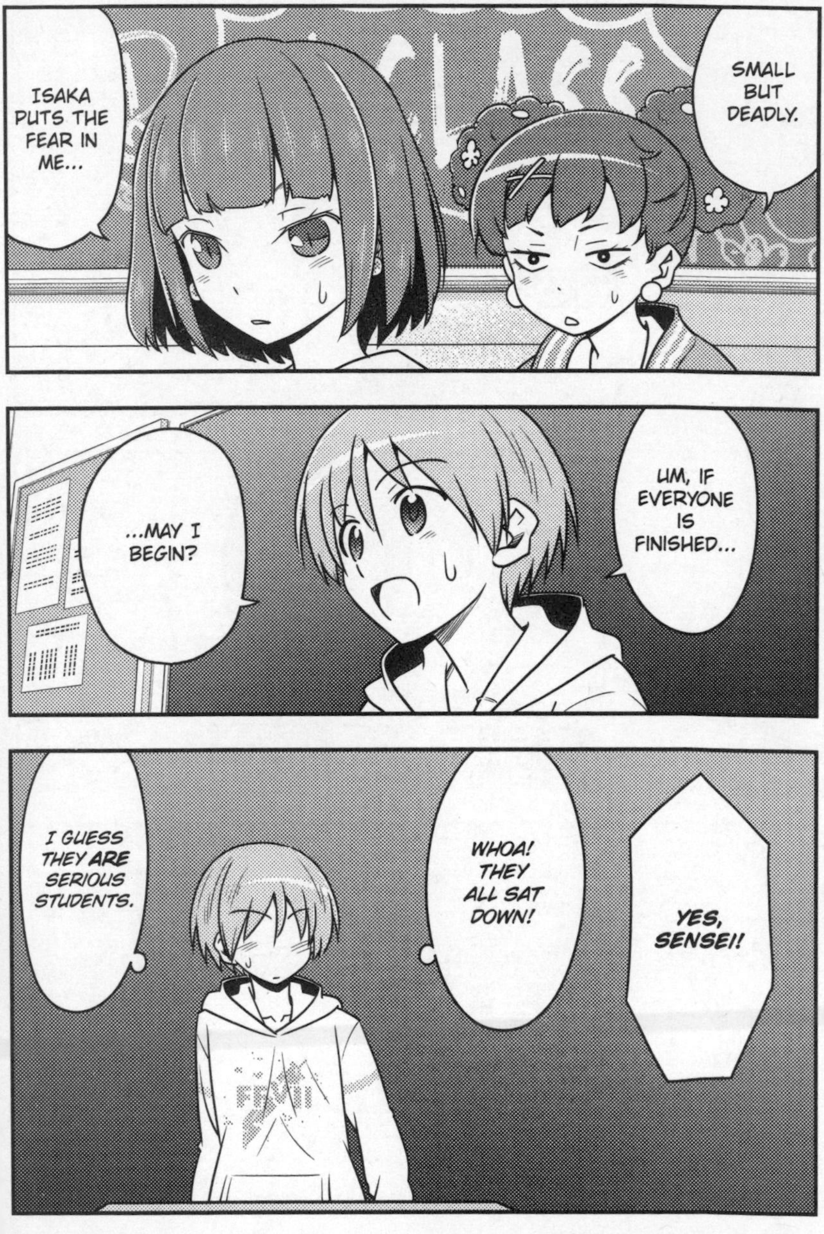
SMALL BUT DEADLY.
ISAKA PUTS THE FEAR IN ME...
UM, IF EVERYONE IS FINISHED...
...MAY I BEGIN?
YES, SENSEI!
WHOA! THEY ALL SAT DOWN!
I GUESS THEY ARE SERIOUS STUDENTS.

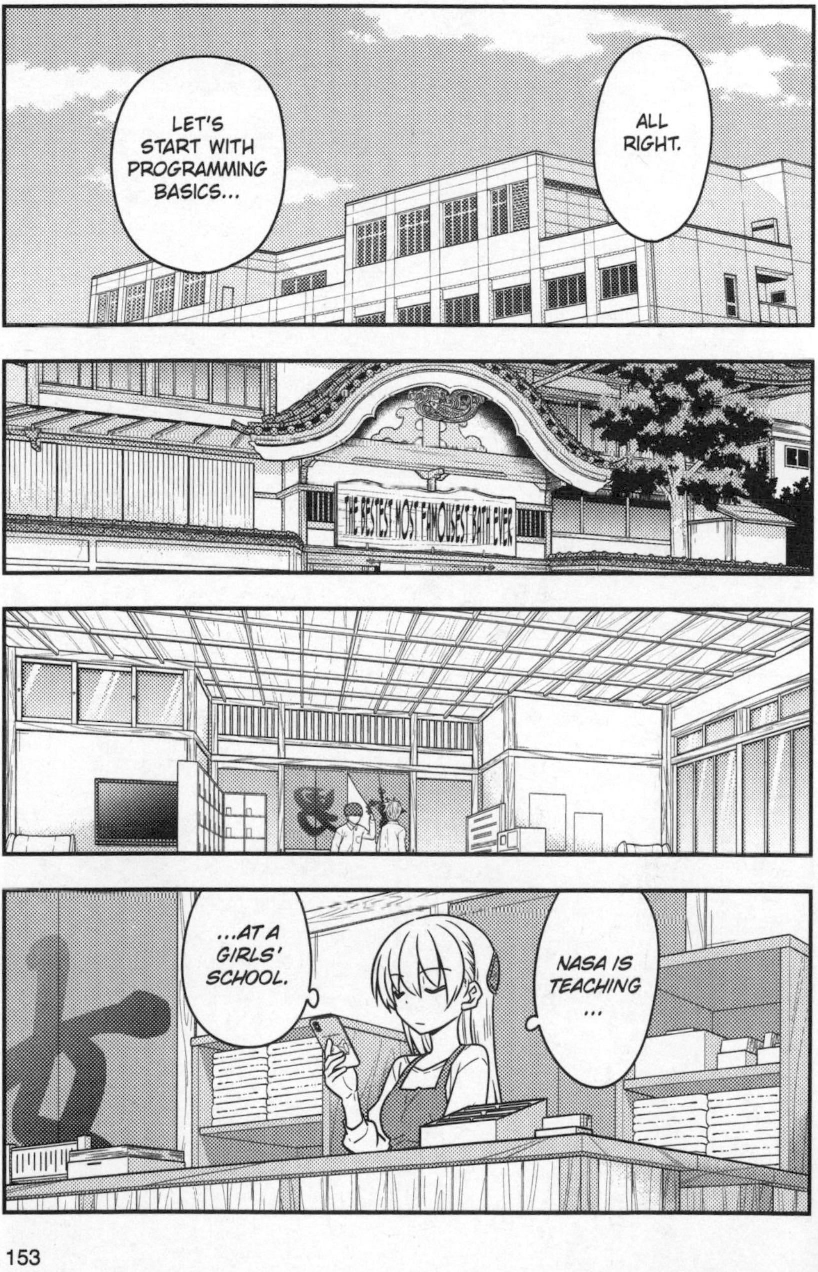
ALL RIGHT.
LET'S START WITH PROGRAMMING BASICS...
THE BESTEST MOST FAMOUSEST BATH EVER
NASA IS TEACHING ...
...AT A GIRLS' SCHOOL.

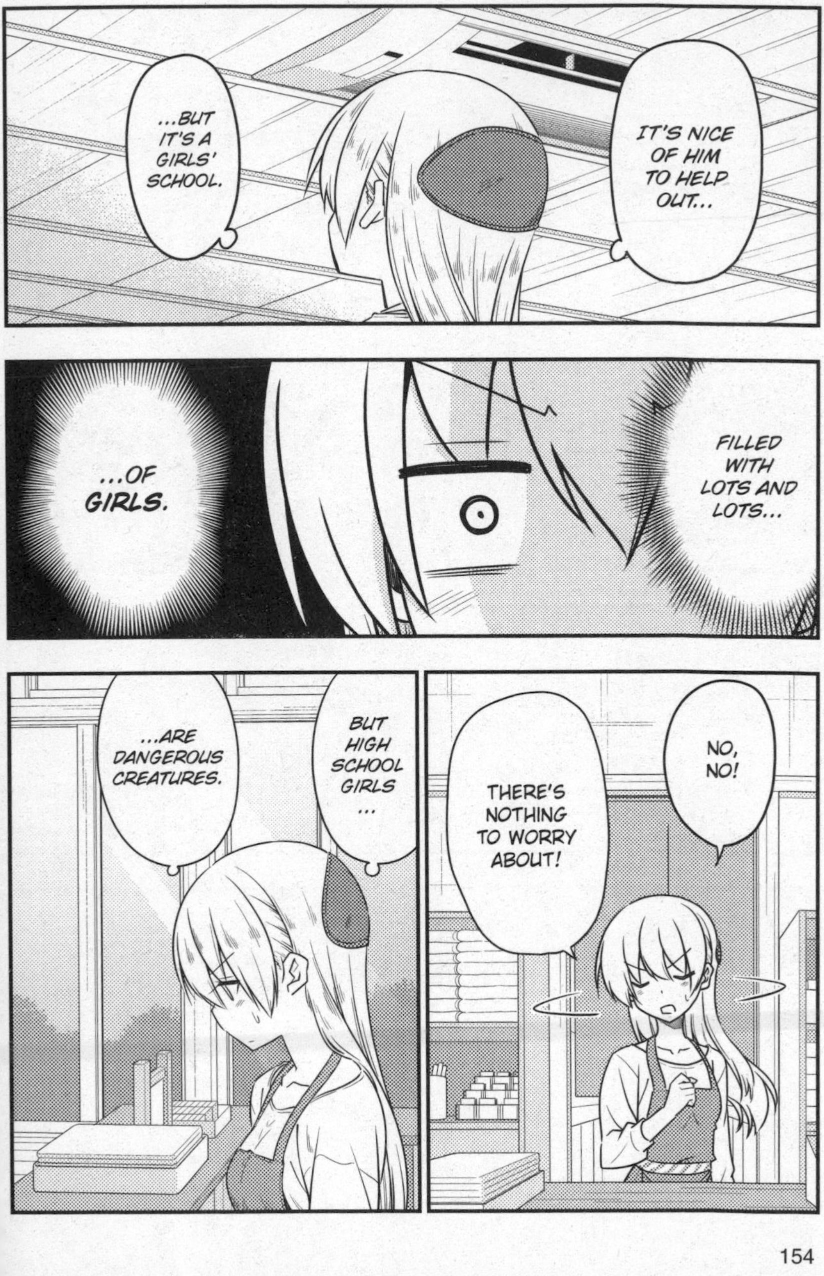
IT'S NICE OF HIM TO HELP OUT...
...BUT IT'S A GIRLS' SCHOOL.
FILLED WITH LOTS AND LOTS...
...OF GIRLS.
NO, NO!
THERE'S NOTHING TO WORRY ABOUT!
BUT HIGH SCHOOL GIRLS ...
...ARE DANGEROUS CREATURES.

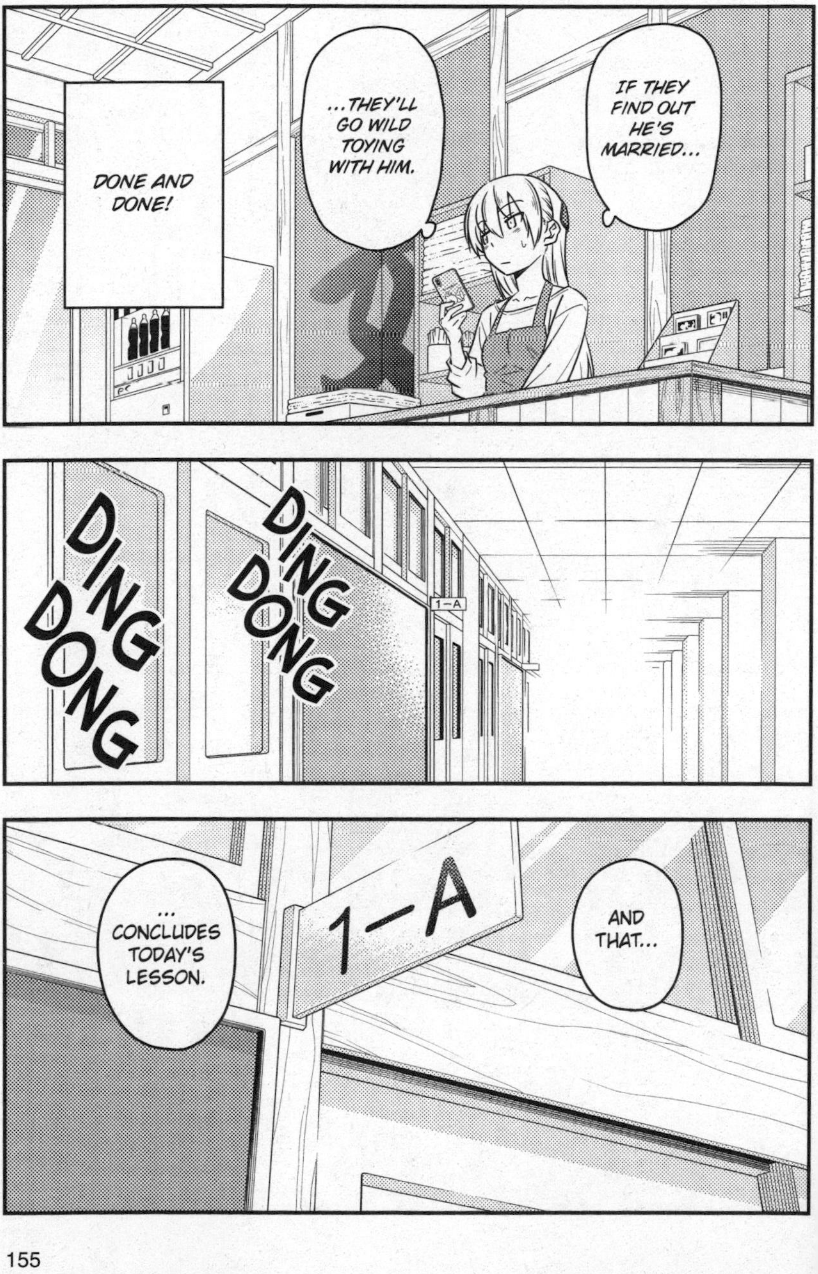
IF THEY FIND OUT HE'S MARRIED...
...THEY'LL GO WILD TOYING WITH HIM.
DONE AND DONE!
DING DONG
DING DONG
1-A
AND THAT...
... CONCLUDES TODAY'S LESSON.
1-A

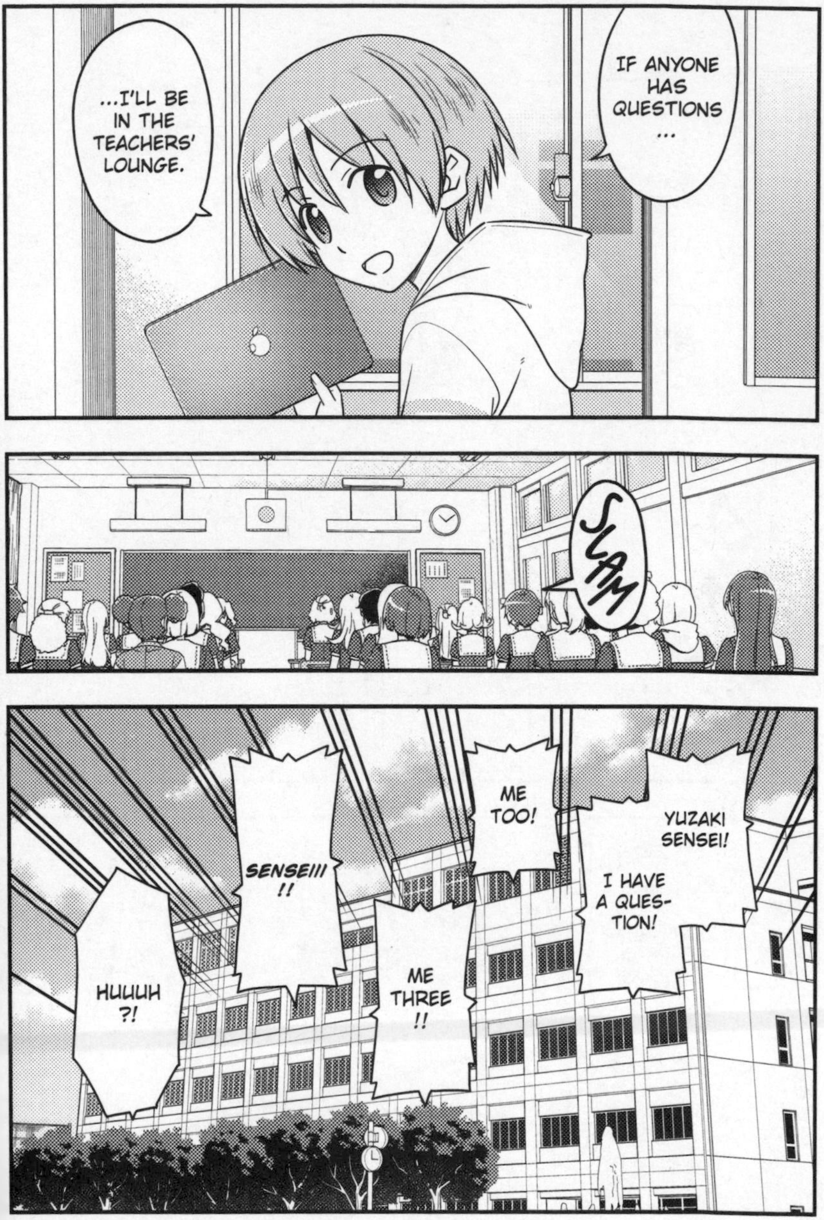
IF ANYONE HAS QUESTIONS ...
...I'LL BE IN THE TEACHERS' LOUNGE.
SLAM
YUZAKI SENSEI!
I HAVE A QUES-TION!
ME TOO!
SENSEI!!! !!
ME THREE !!
HUUUH ?!

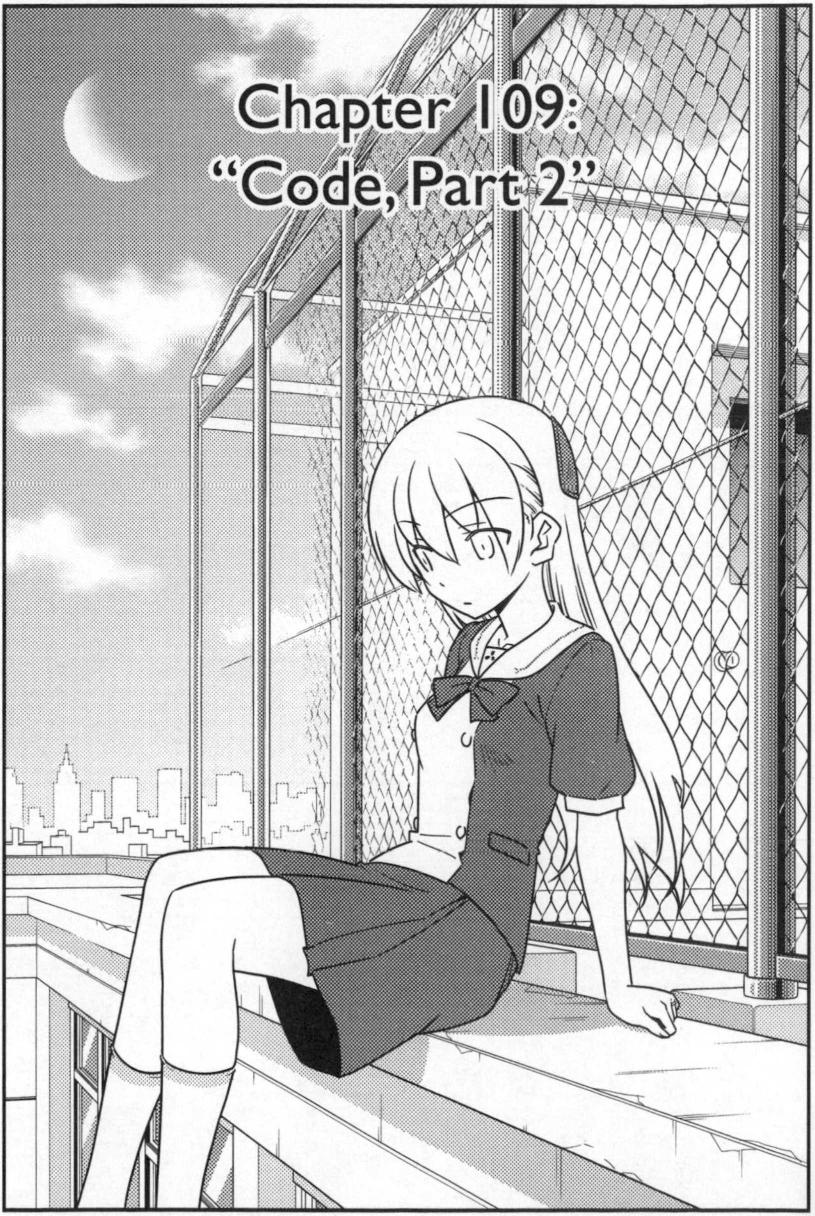
Chapter 109:
"Code, Part 2"

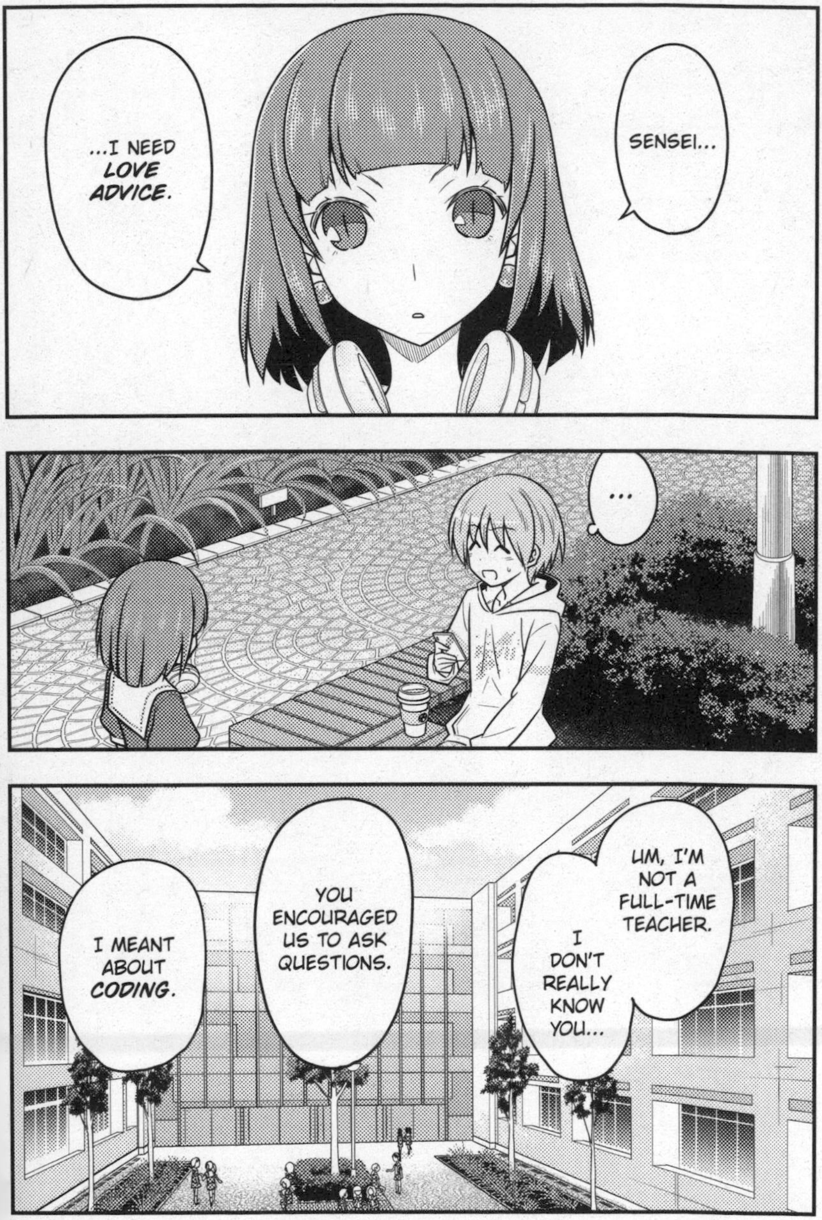
SENSEI...
...I NEED LOVE ADVICE.
...
UM, I'M NOT A FULL-TIME TEACHER.
I DON'T REALLY KNOW YOU...
YOU ENCOURAGED US TO ASK QUESTIONS.
I MEANT ABOUT CODING.

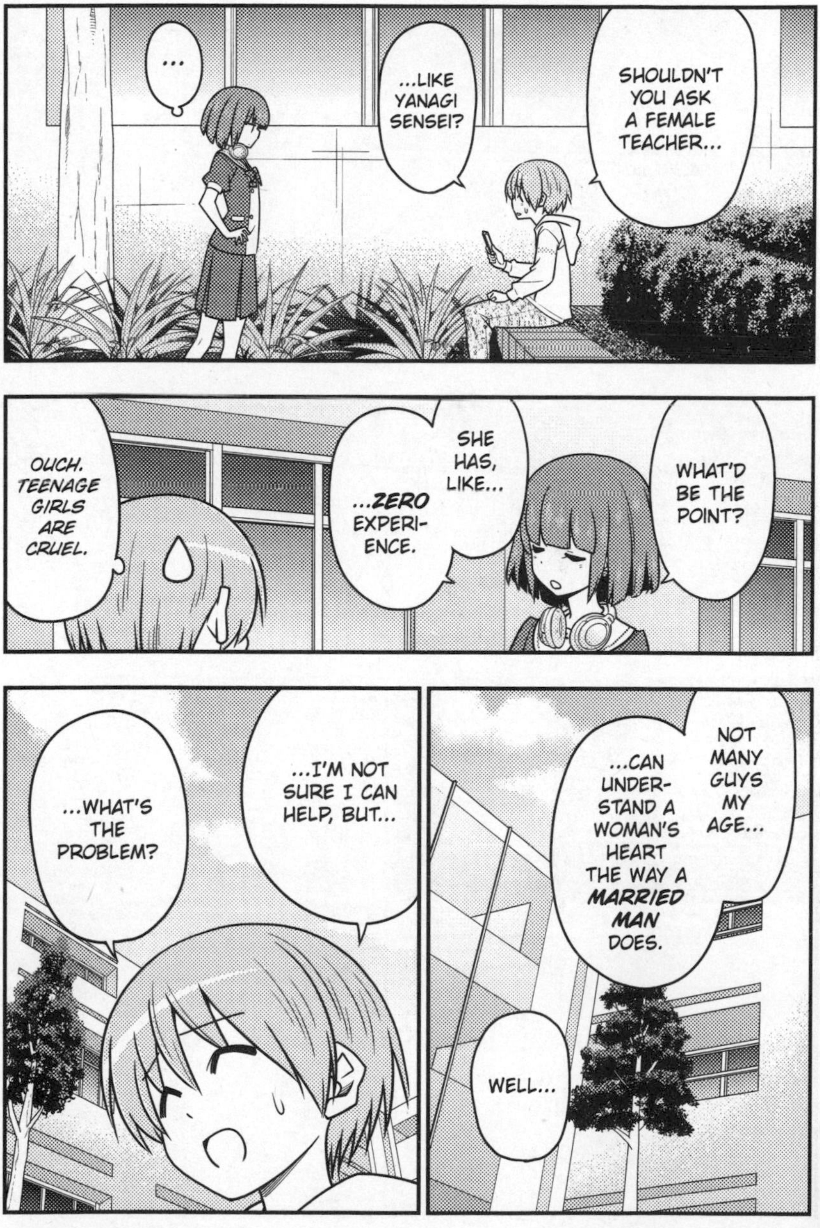
SHOULDN'T YOU ASK A FEMALE TEACHER...
...LIKE YANAGI SENSEI?
...
WHAT'D BE THE POINT?
SHE HAS, LIKE...
...ZERO EXPERIENCE.
OUCH. TEENAGE GIRLS ARE CRUEL.
NOT MANY GUYS MY AGE...
...CAN UNDERSTAND A WOMAN'S HEART THE WAY A MARRIED MAN DOES.
WELL...
...I'M NOT SURE I CAN HELP, BUT...
...WHAT'S THE PROBLEM?

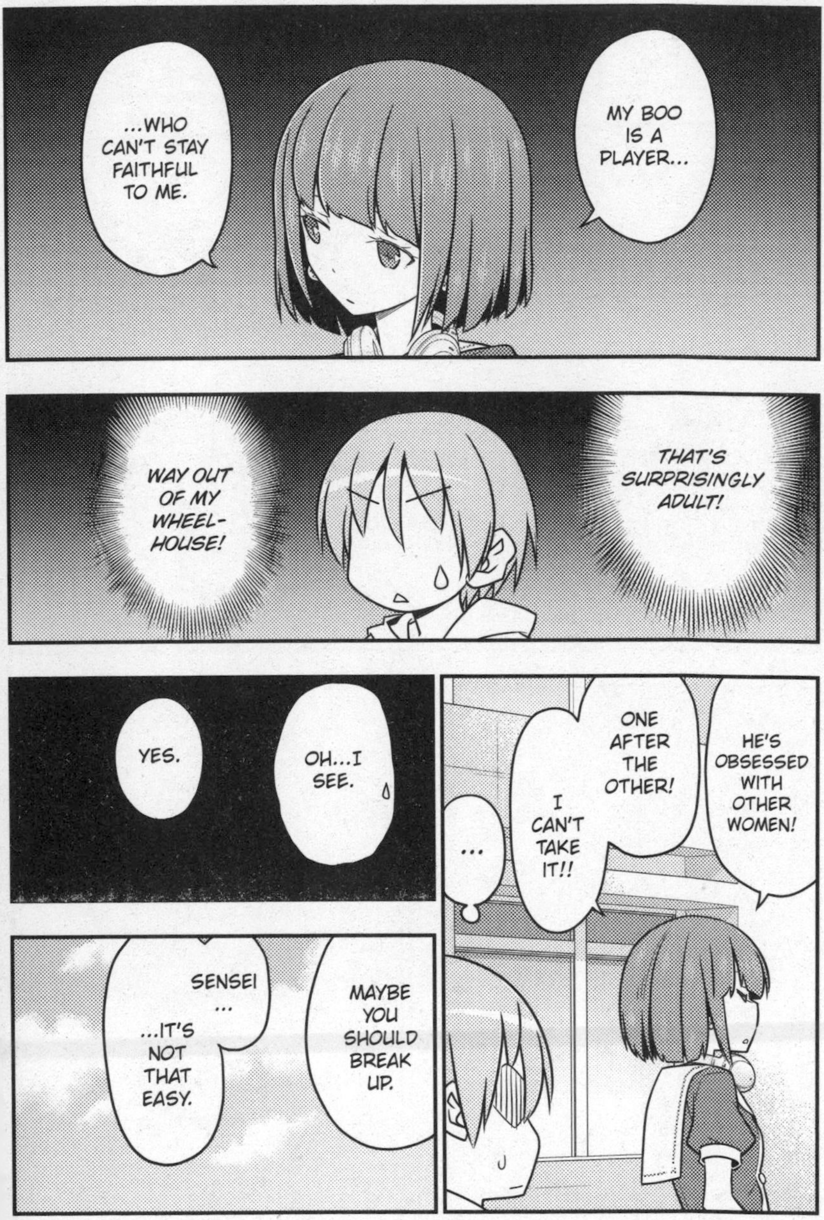
MY BOO IS A PLAYER...
...WHO CAN'T STAY FAITHFUL TO ME.
THAT'S SURPRISINGLY ADULT!
WAY OUT OF MY WHEEL-HOUSE!
HE'S OBSESSED WITH OTHER WOMEN!
ONE AFTER THE OTHER!
I CAN'T TAKE IT!!
...
OH...I SEE.
YES.
MAYBE YOU SHOULD BREAK UP.
SENSEI ...
...IT'S NOT THAT EASY.

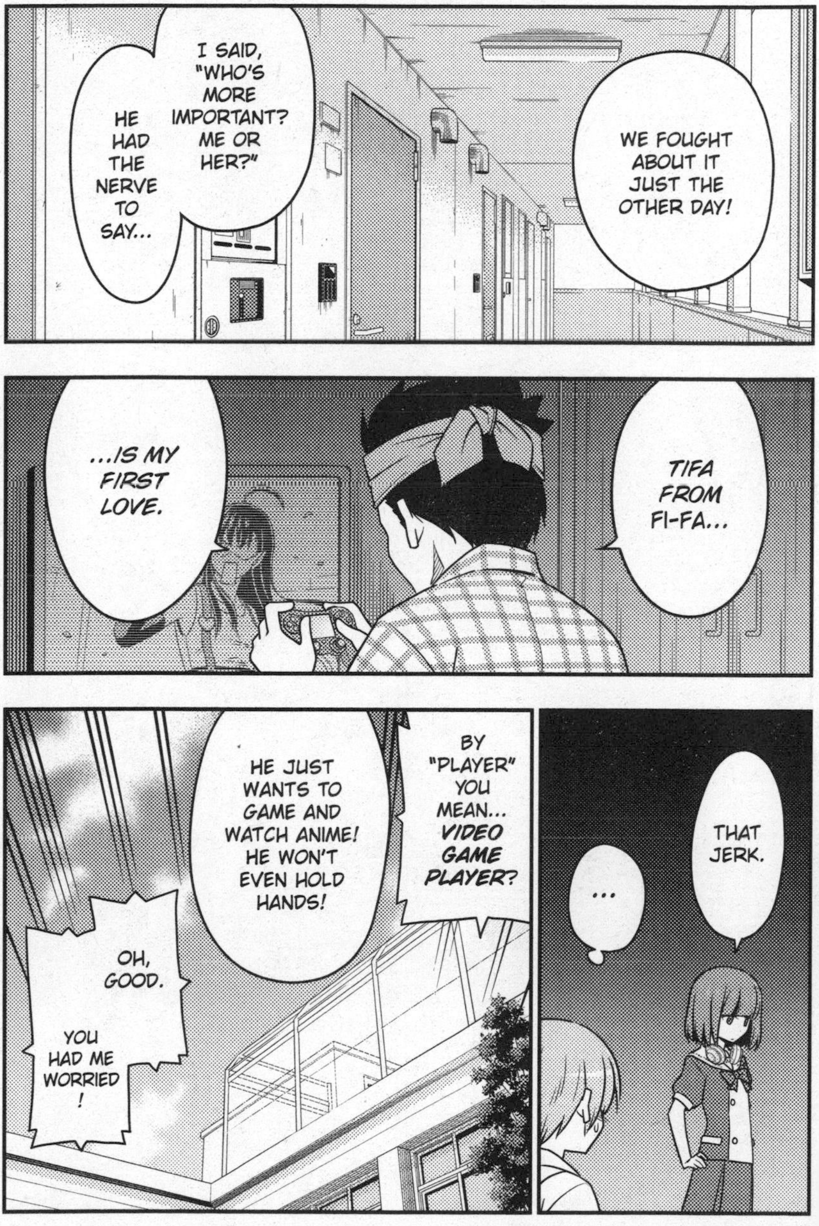
WE FOUGHT ABOUT IT JUST THE OTHER DAY!
I SAID, "WHO'S MORE IMPORTANT? ME OR HER?"
HE HAD THE NERVE TO SAY...
TIFA FROM FI-FA...
...IS MY FIRST LOVE.
THAT JERK.
...
BY "PLAYER" YOU MEAN... VIDEO GAME PLAYER?
HE JUST WANTS TO GAME AND WATCH ANIME! HE WON'T EVEN HOLD HANDS!
OH, GOOD.
YOU HAD ME WORRIED!

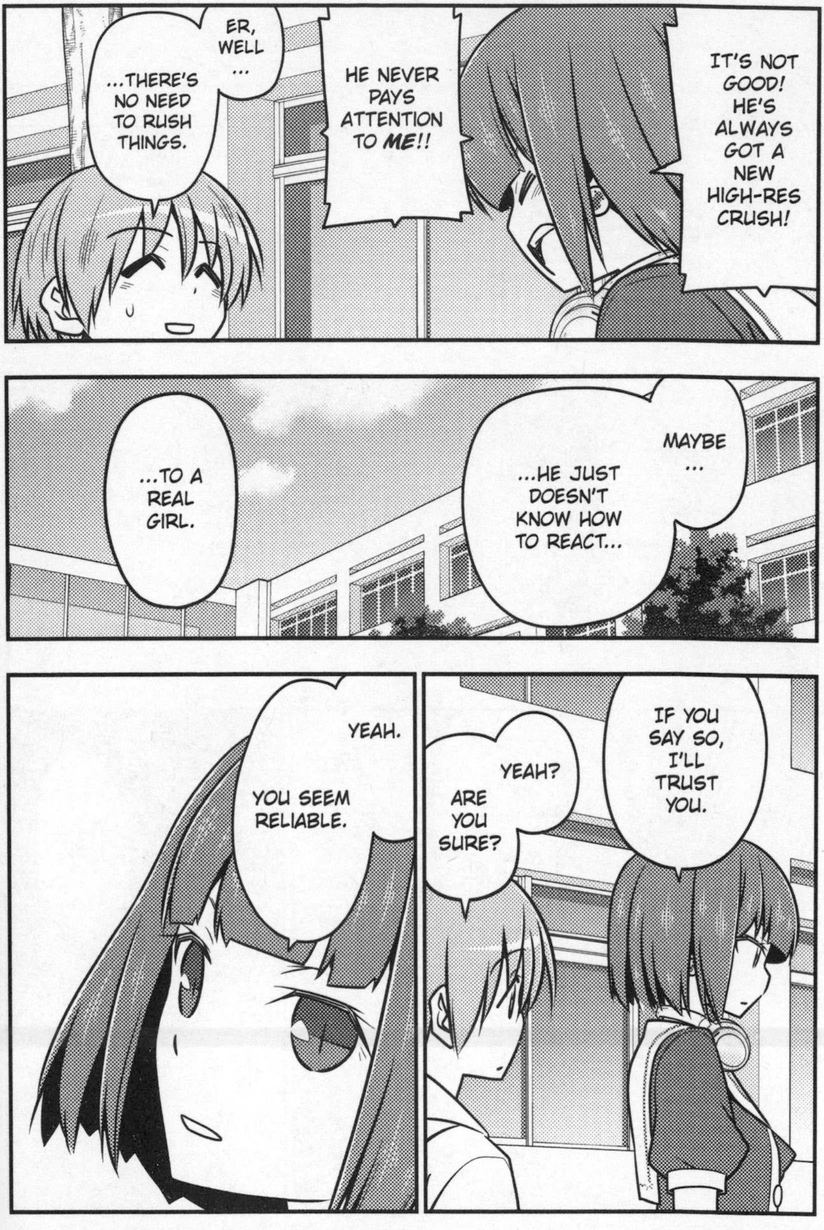
IT'S NOT GOOD! HE'S ALWAYS GOT A NEW HIGH-RES CRUSH!
HE NEVER PAYS ATTENTION TO *ME*!!
ER, WELL ...
...THERE'S NO NEED TO RUSH THINGS.
MAYBE ...
...HE JUST DOESN'T KNOW HOW TO REACT...
...TO A REAL GIRL.
IF YOU SAY SO, I'LL TRUST YOU.
YEAH?
ARE YOU SURE?
YEAH.
YOU SEEM RELIABLE.

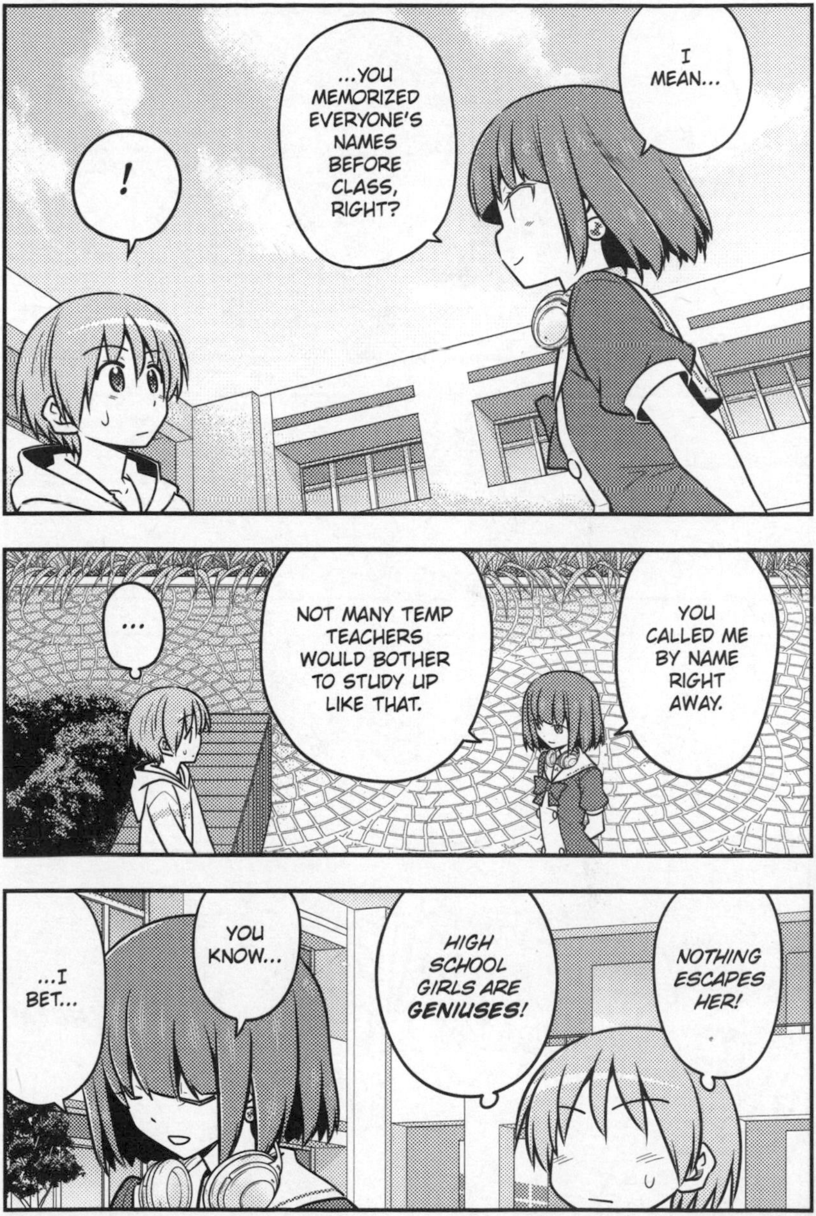
I MEAN...
...YOU MEMORIZED EVERYONE'S NAMES BEFORE CLASS, RIGHT?
!
YOU CALLED ME BY NAME RIGHT AWAY.
NOT MANY TEMP TEACHERS WOULD BOTHER TO STUDY UP LIKE THAT.
...
NOTHING ESCAPES HER!
HIGH SCHOOL GIRLS ARE **GENIUSES!**
YOU KNOW...
...I BET...

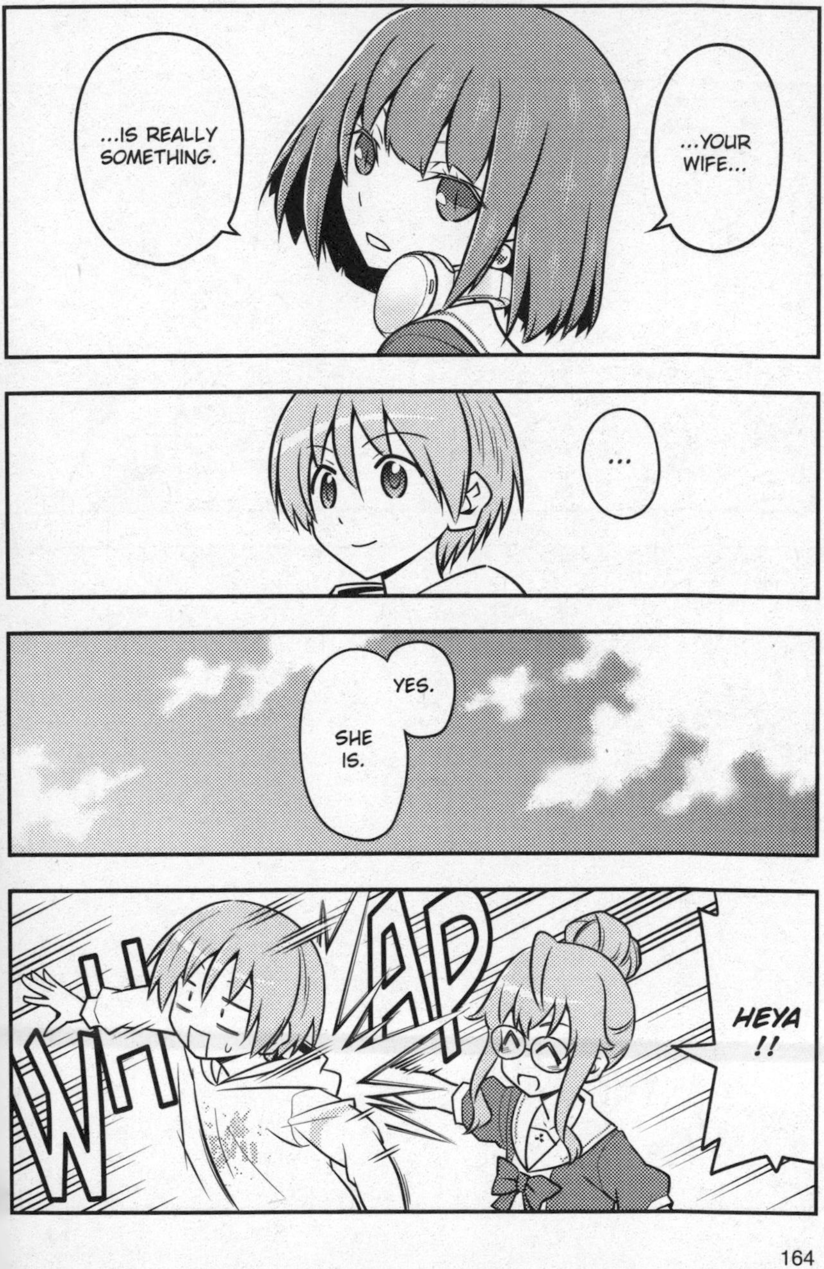
...YOUR WIFE...
...IS REALLY SOMETHING.
...
YES.
SHE IS.
HEYA !!
WHAP

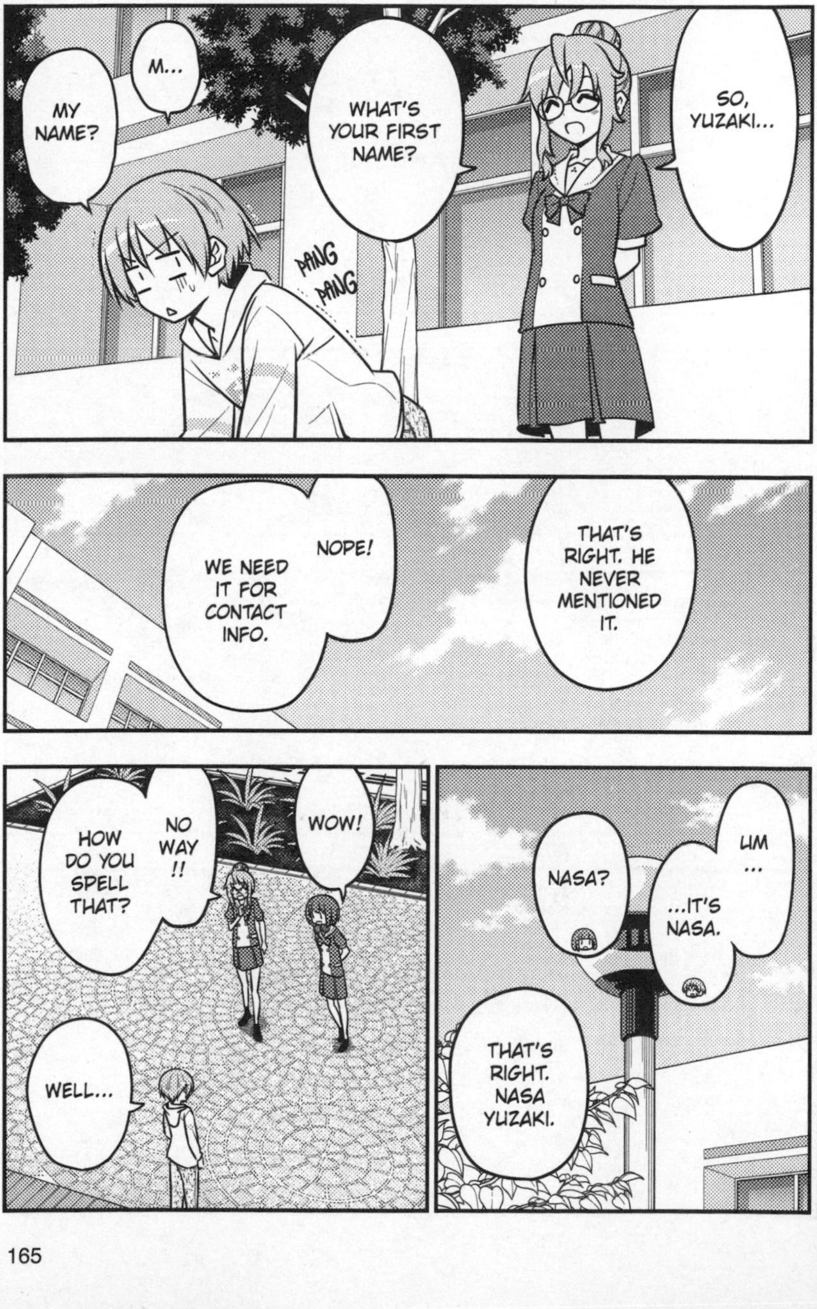
SO, YUZAKI...
WHAT'S YOUR FIRST NAME?
M...
MY NAME?
PANG PANG
THAT'S RIGHT. HE NEVER MENTIONED IT.
NOPE!
WE NEED IT FOR CONTACT INFO.
UM ...
...IT'S NASA.
NASA?
THAT'S RIGHT. NASA YUZAKI.
WOW!
NO WAY !!
HOW DO YOU SPELL THAT?
WELL...

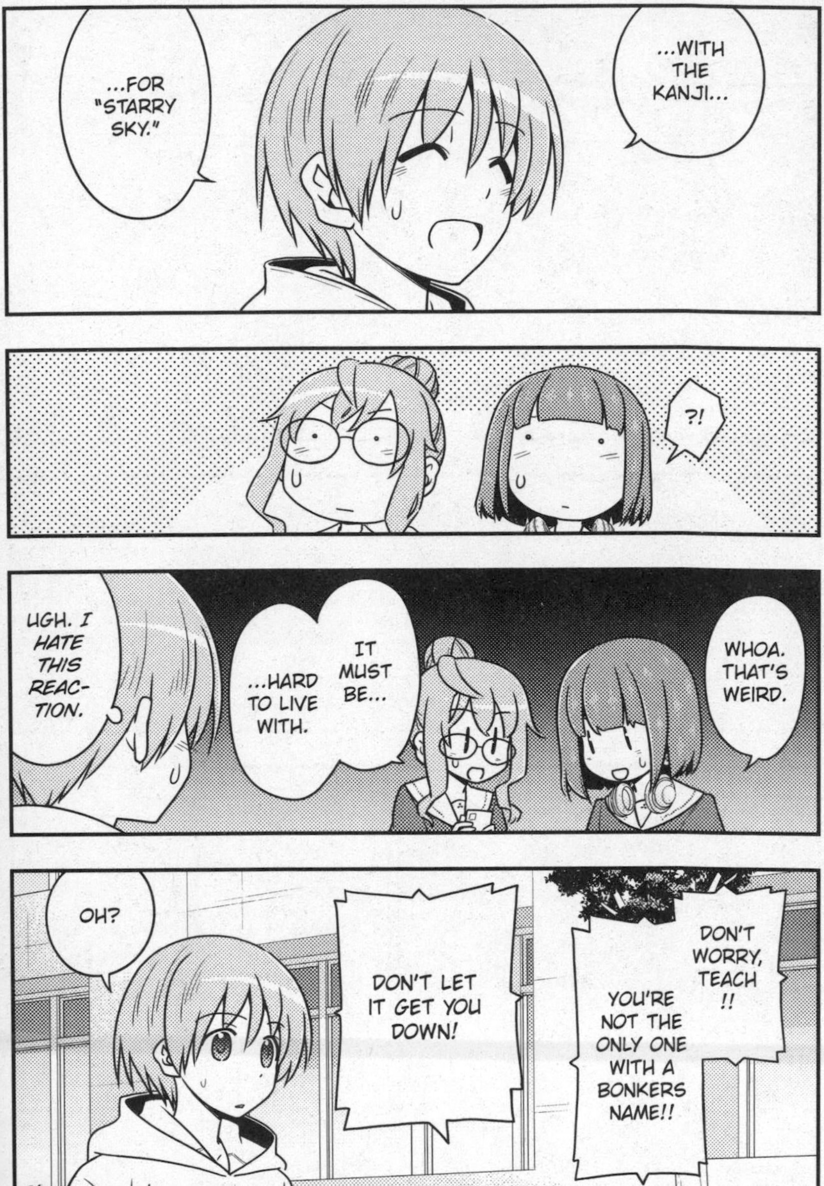
...WITH THE KANJI...
...FOR "STARRY SKY."
?!
WHOA. THAT'S WEIRD.
IT MUST BE...
...HARD TO LIVE WITH.
UGH. I HATE THIS REACTION.
DON'T WORRY, TEACH!!
YOU'RE NOT THE ONLY ONE WITH A BONKERS NAME!!
DON'T LET IT GET YOU DOWN!
OH?

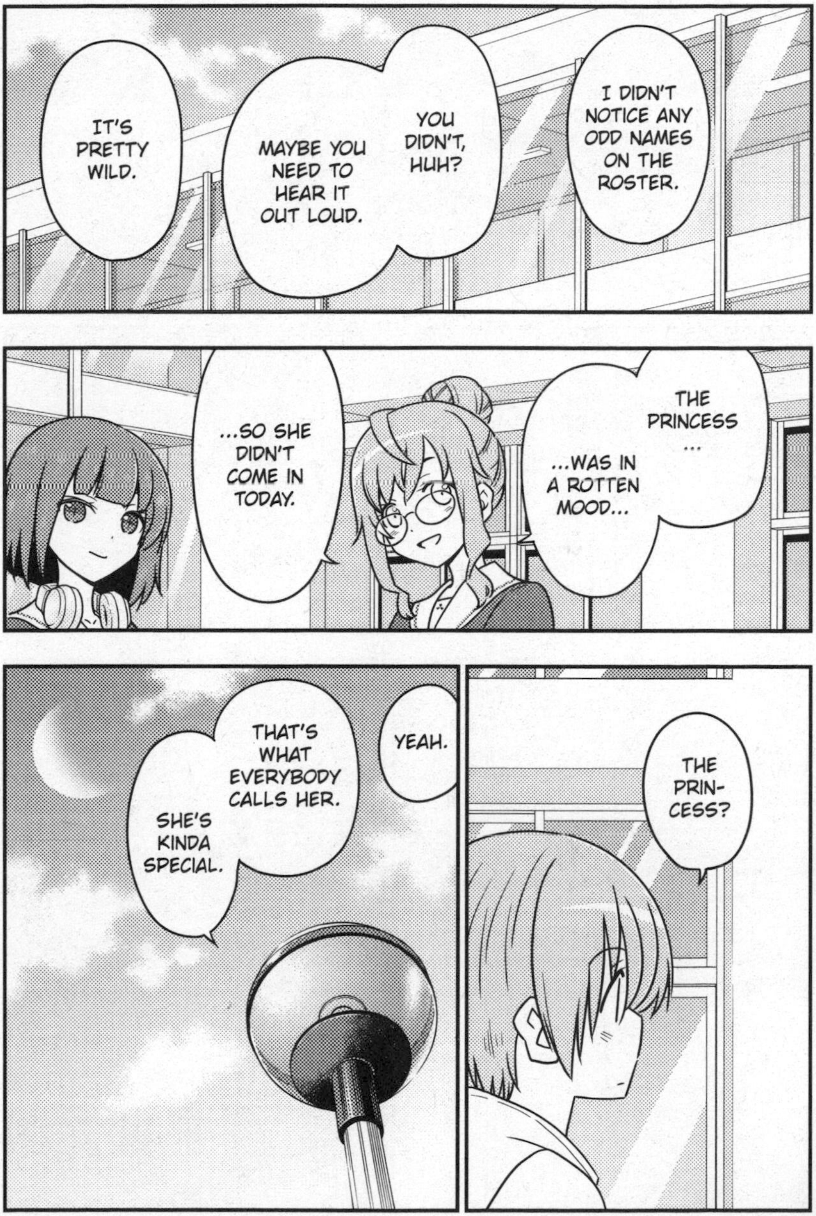
I DIDN'T NOTICE ANY ODD NAMES ON THE ROSTER.
YOU DIDN'T, HUH?
MAYBE YOU NEED TO HEAR IT OUT LOUD.
IT'S PRETTY WILD.
THE PRINCESS ...
...WAS IN A ROTTEN MOOD...
...SO SHE DIDN'T COME IN TODAY.
THE PRIN-CESS?
YEAH.
THAT'S WHAT EVERYBODY CALLS HER.
SHE'S KINDA SPECIAL.

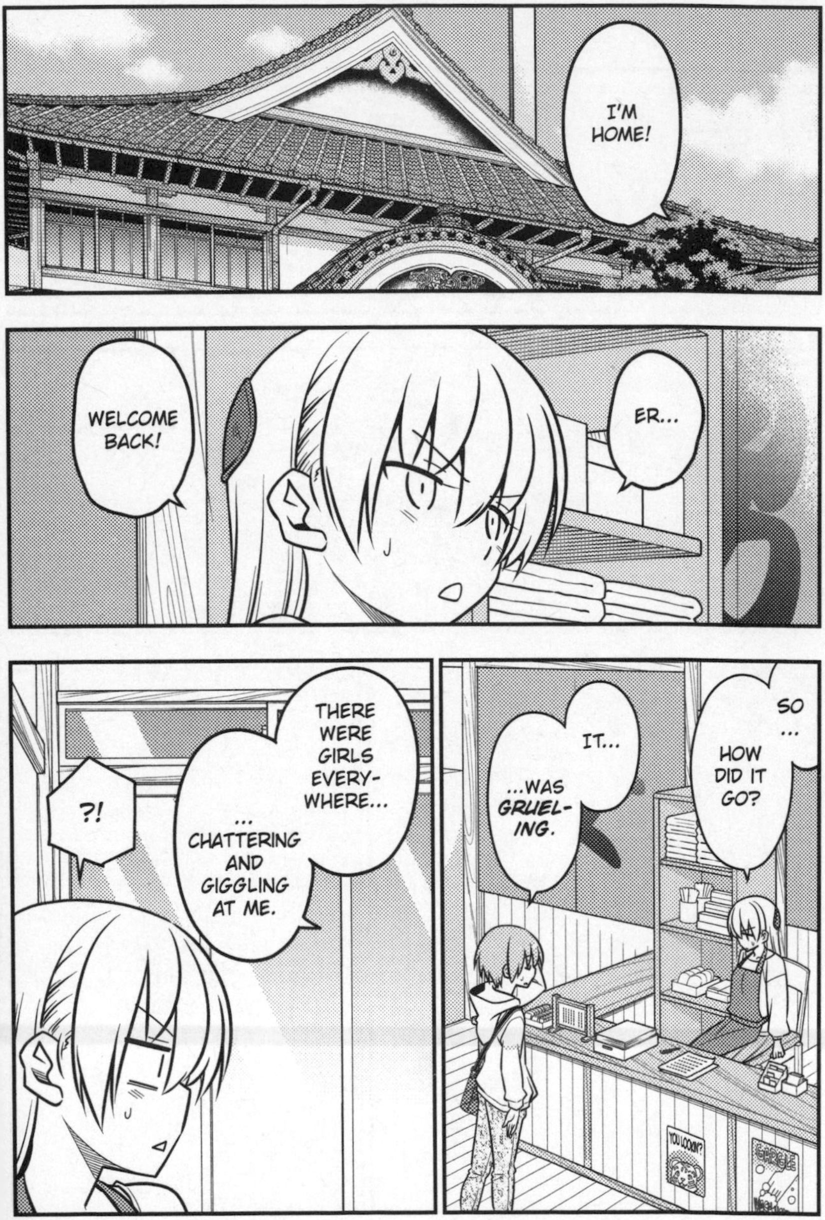
I'M HOME!
ER...
WELCOME BACK!
SO ... HOW DID IT GO?
IT...
...WAS GRUELING.
YOU LOOKIN'?
GARGLE
THERE WERE GIRLS EVERYWHERE...
... CHATTERING AND GIGGLING AT ME.
?!

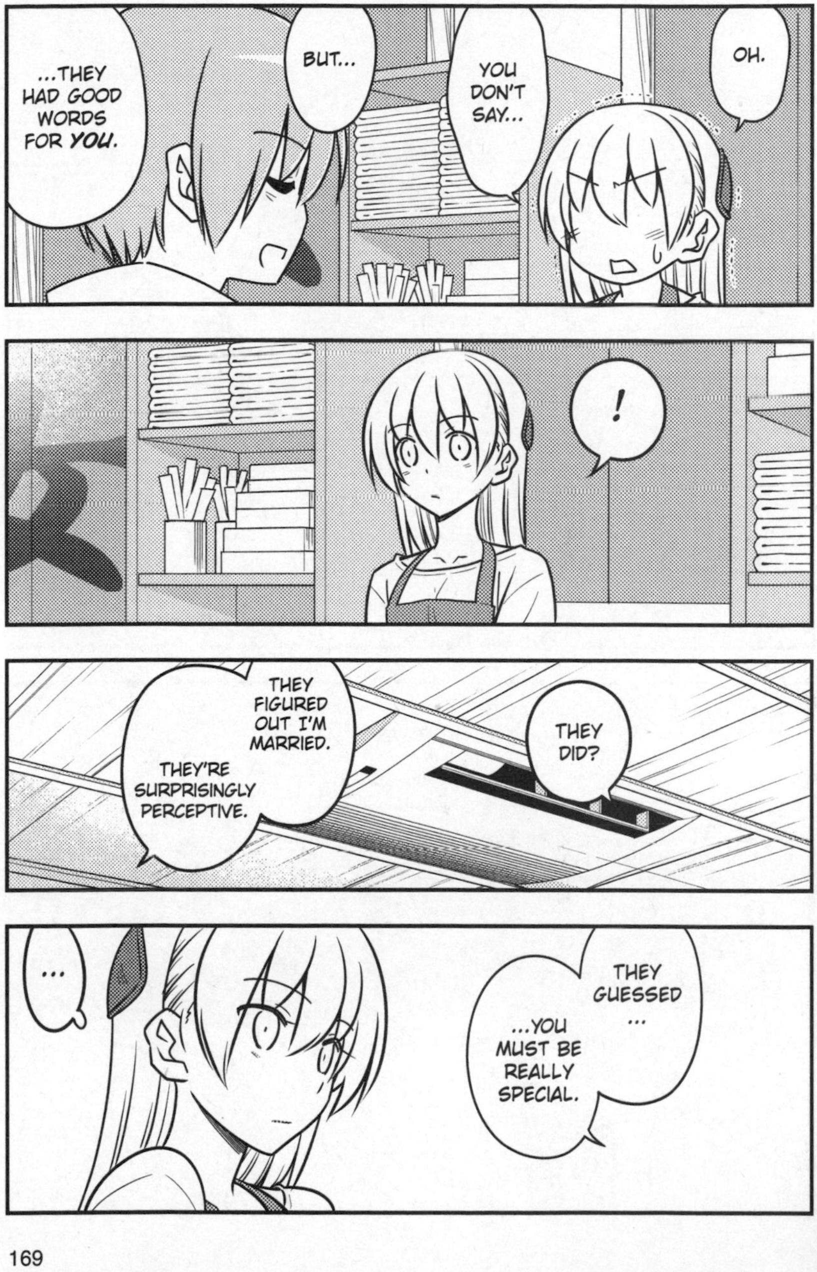
OH.
YOU DON'T SAY...
BUT...
...THEY HAD GOOD WORDS FOR *YOU*.
!
THEY DID?
THEY FIGURED OUT I'M MARRIED.
THEY'RE SURPRISINGLY PERCEPTIVE.
THEY GUESSED...
...YOU MUST BE REALLY SPECIAL.
...

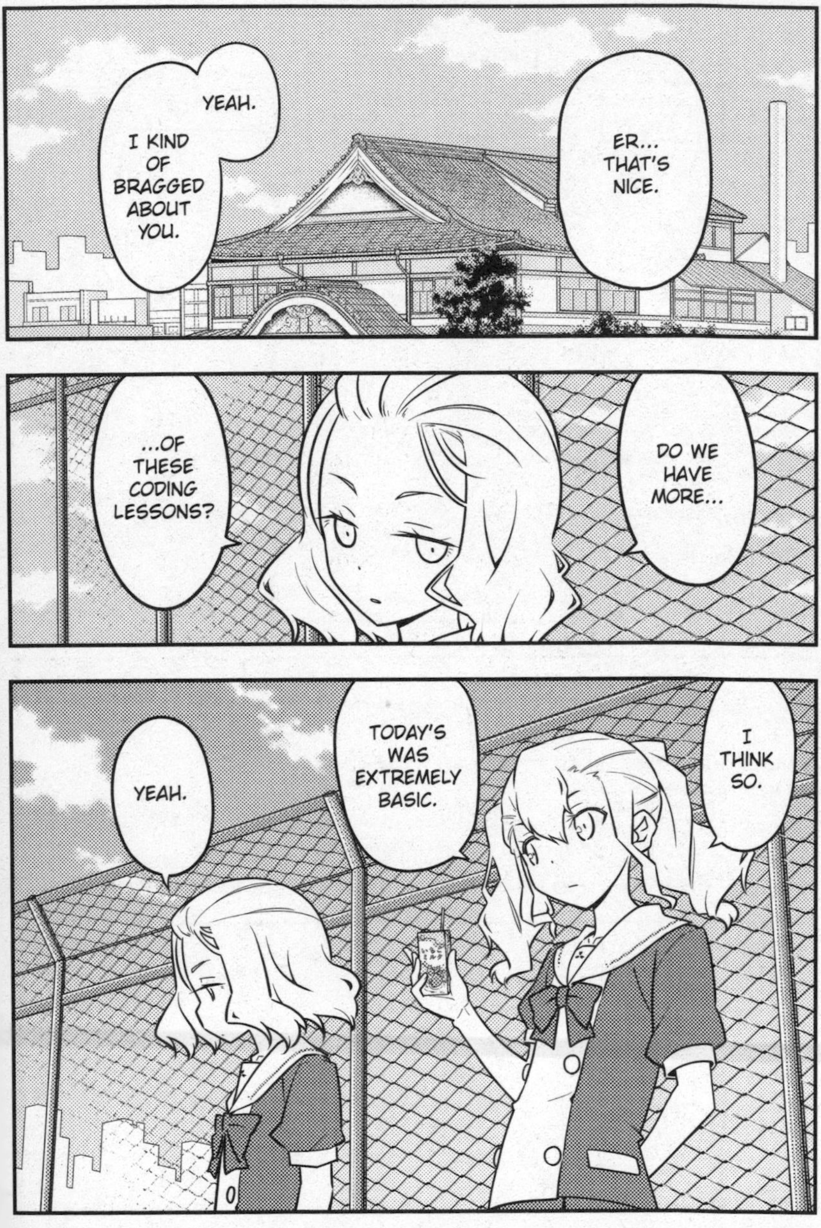
ER... THAT'S NICE.
YEAH.
I KIND OF BRAGGED ABOUT YOU.
DO WE HAVE MORE...
...OF THESE CODING LESSONS?
I THINK SO.
TODAY'S WAS EXTREMELY BASIC.
YEAH.

I WANNA HEAR ABOUT HIS LOVE LIFE!
WHAT'S HIS WIFE LIKE?
HOW'D SUCH A MILD-MANNERED GUY GET HITCHED?
DOES THIS MEAN HE'S **DOIN' IT**?
STOP IT, JESSIE!
WE'LL OVER-HEAT!
IMAGINATION ONLY GOES SO FAR.
I WANNA **SEE** HER.

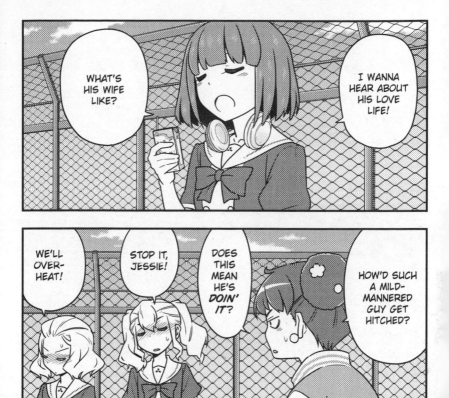

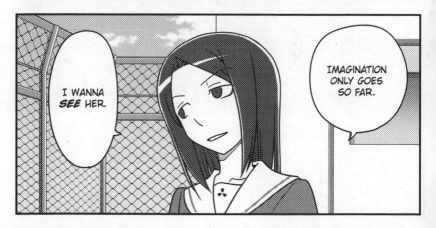

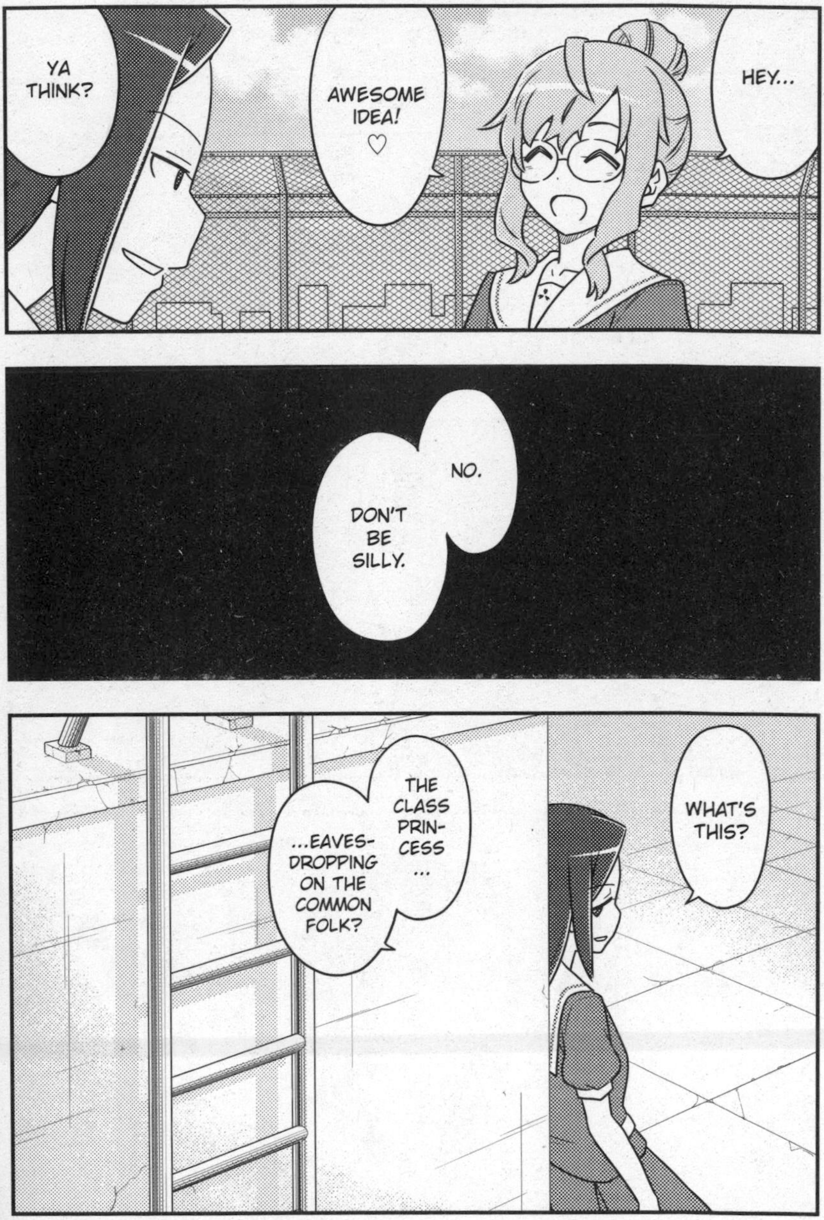
HEY...
AWESOME IDEA! ♡
YA THINK?
NO.
DON'T BE SILLY.
WHAT'S THIS?
THE CLASS PRIN-CESS...
...EAVES-DROPPING ON THE COMMON FOLK?

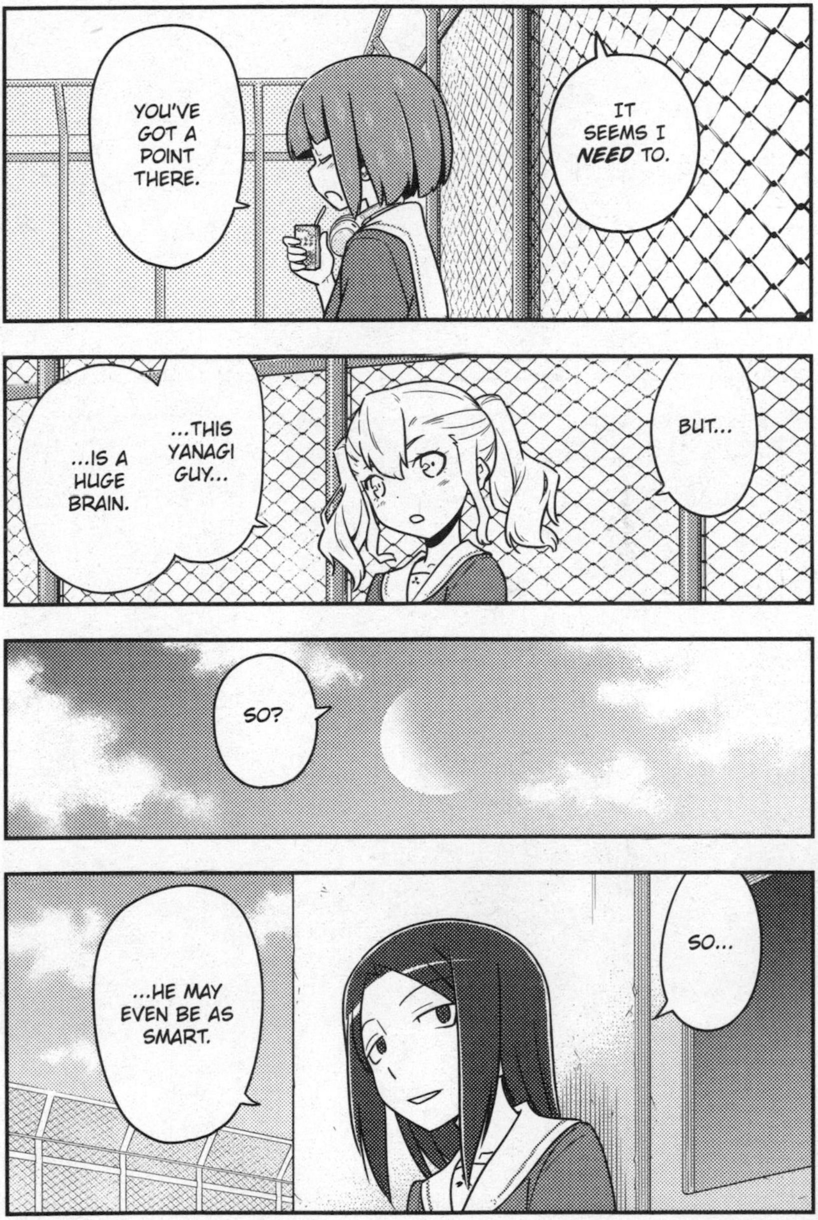
IT SEEMS I NEED TO.
YOU'VE GOT A POINT THERE.
BUT...
...THIS YANAGI GUY...
...IS A HUGE BRAIN.
SO?
SO...
...HE MAY EVEN BE AS SMART.

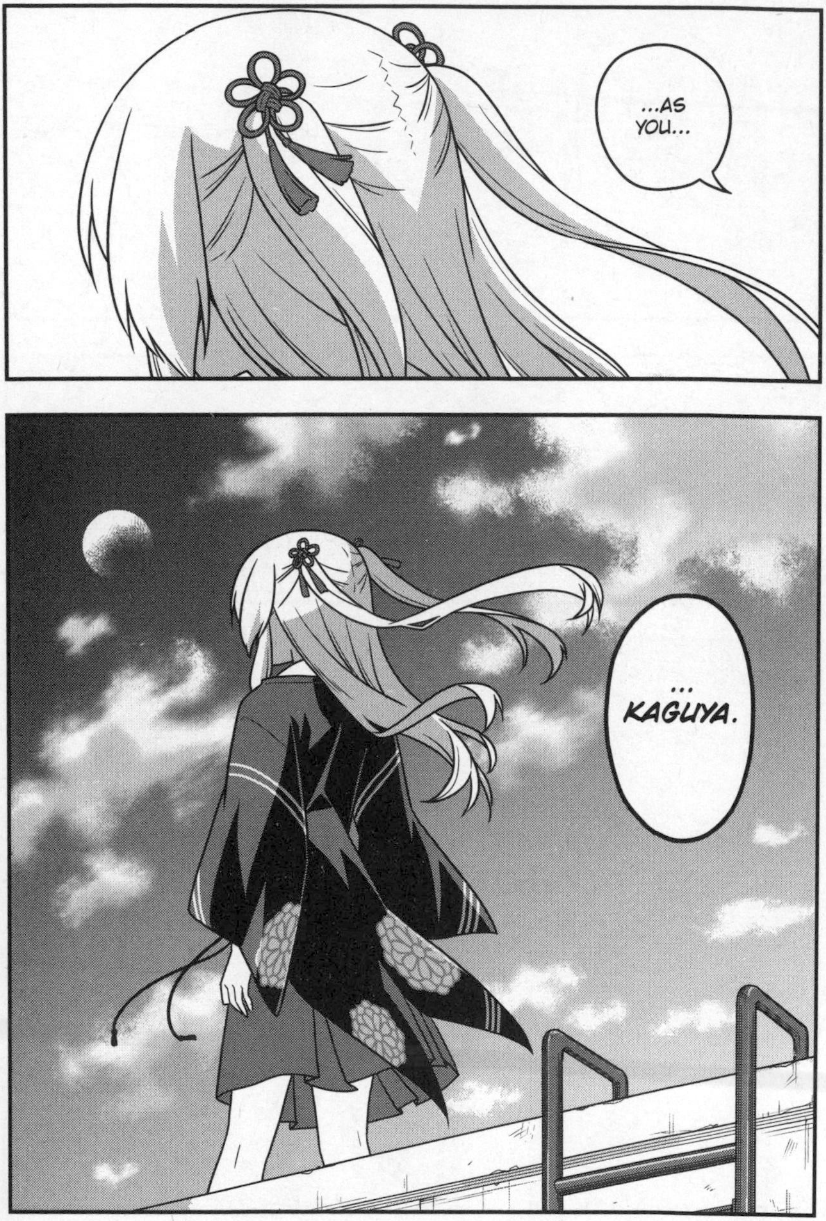
...AS YOU...
... KAGUYA.

—Fly Me to the Moon 11 / End—

Chapter 103 ½: "It's Not Something You Can Show Anyone Else"

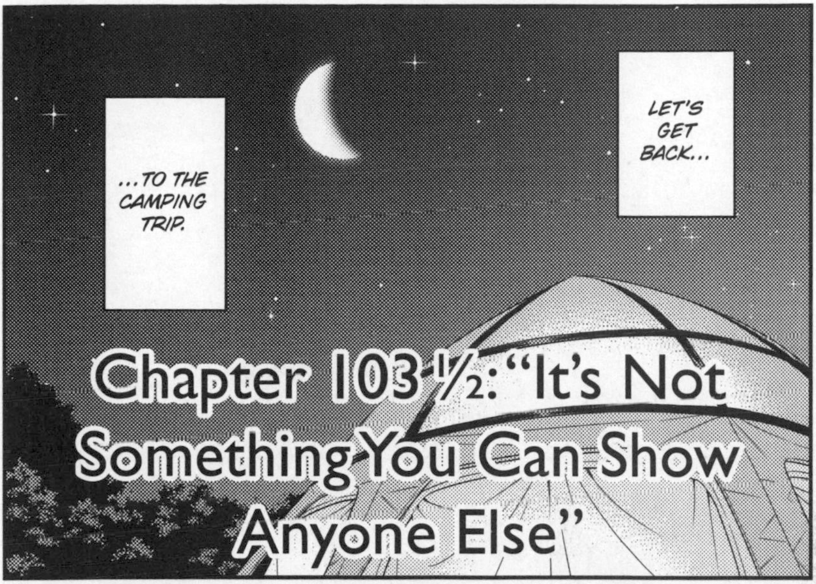
LET'S GET BACK...
...TO THE CAMPING TRIP.

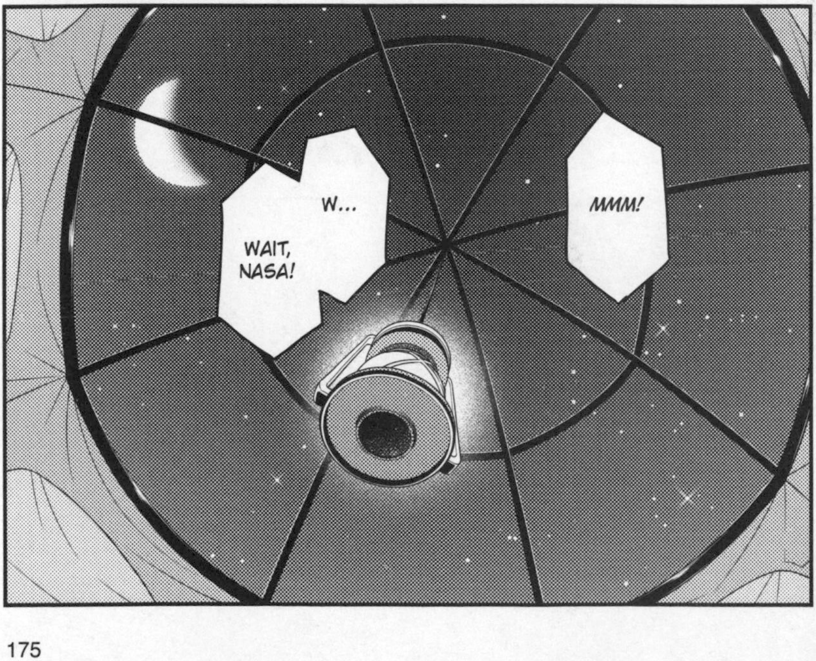
MMM!
W...
WAIT, NASA!

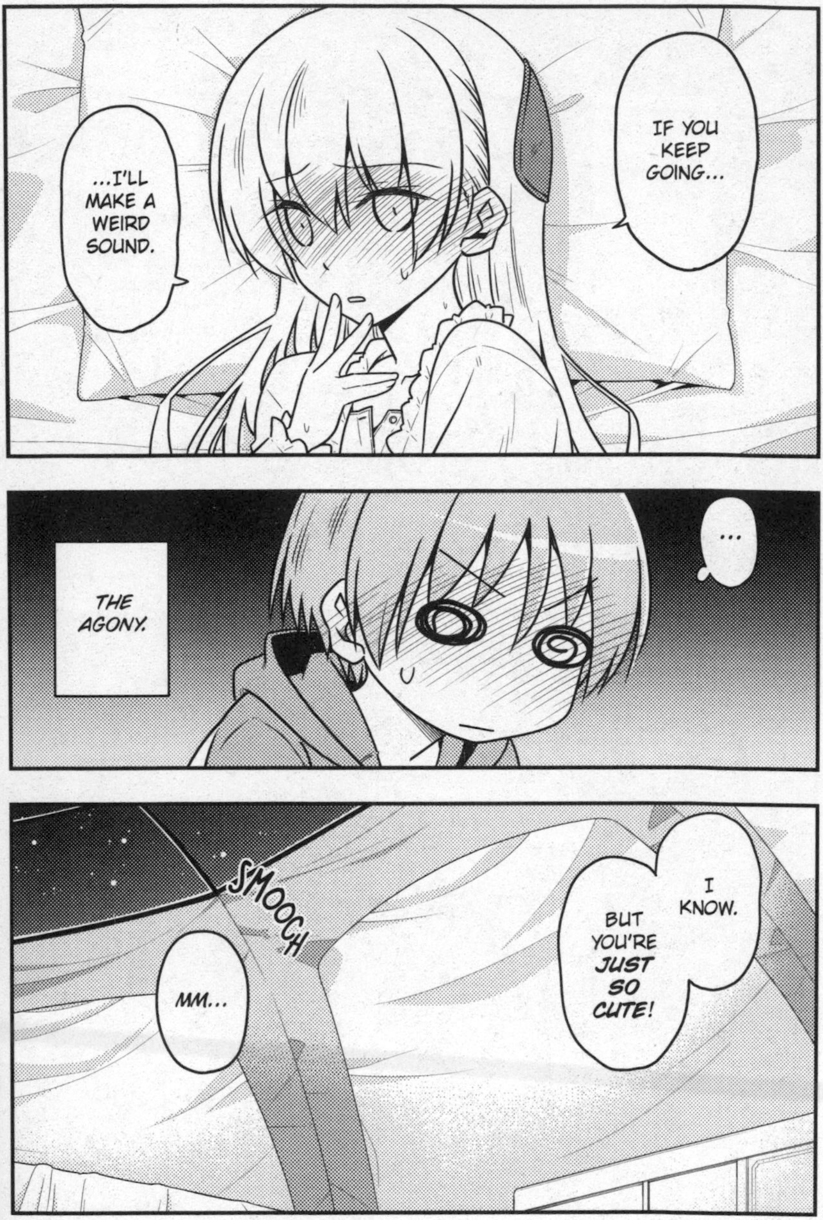
IF YOU KEEP GOING...
...I'LL MAKE A WEIRD SOUND.
...
THE AGONY.
I KNOW. BUT YOU'RE *JUST SO CUTE!*
SMOOCH
MM...

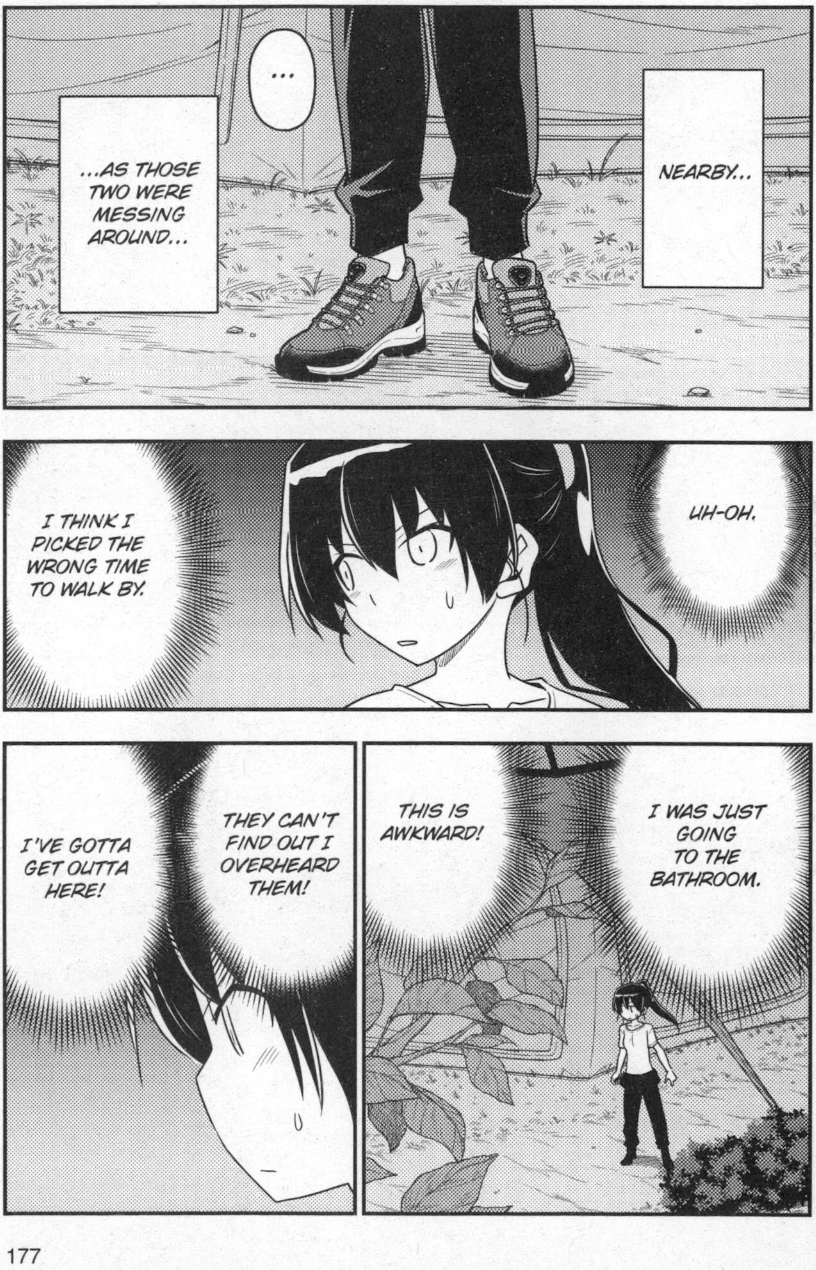
NEARBY...
...AS THOSE TWO WERE MESSING AROUND...
...
UH-OH.
I THINK I PICKED THE WRONG TIME TO WALK BY.
I WAS JUST GOING TO THE BATHROOM.
THIS IS AWKWARD!
THEY CAN'T FIND OUT I OVERHEARD THEM!
I'VE GOTTA GET OUTTA HERE!

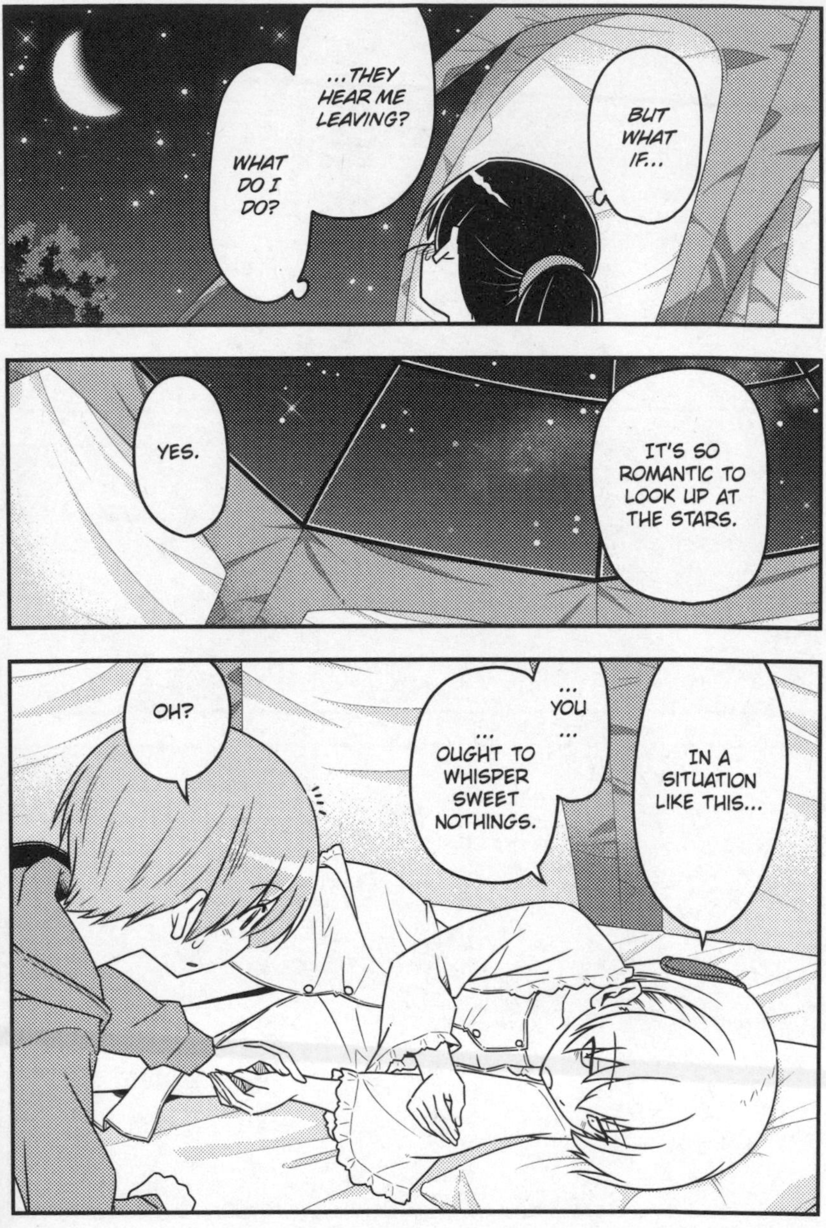
BUT WHAT IF...
...THEY HEAR ME LEAVING? WHAT DO I DO?
IT'S SO ROMANTIC TO LOOK UP AT THE STARS.
YES.
IN A SITUATION LIKE THIS...
... YOU ... ... OUGHT TO WHISPER SWEET NOTHINGS.
OH?

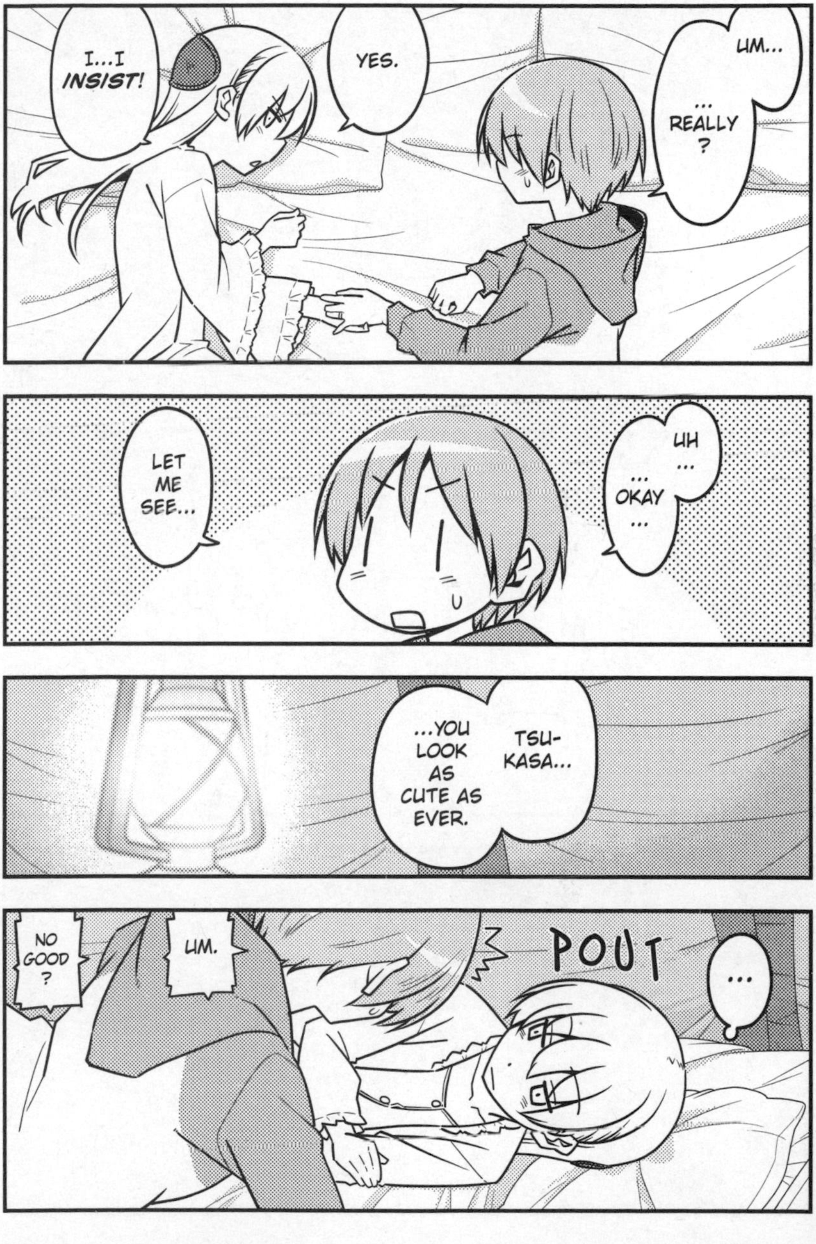
UM... ...REALLY?
YES.
I...I INSIST!
UH... ...OKAY...
LET ME SEE...
TSU-KASA...
...YOU LOOK AS CUTE AS EVER.
...
POUT
UM.
NO GOOD?

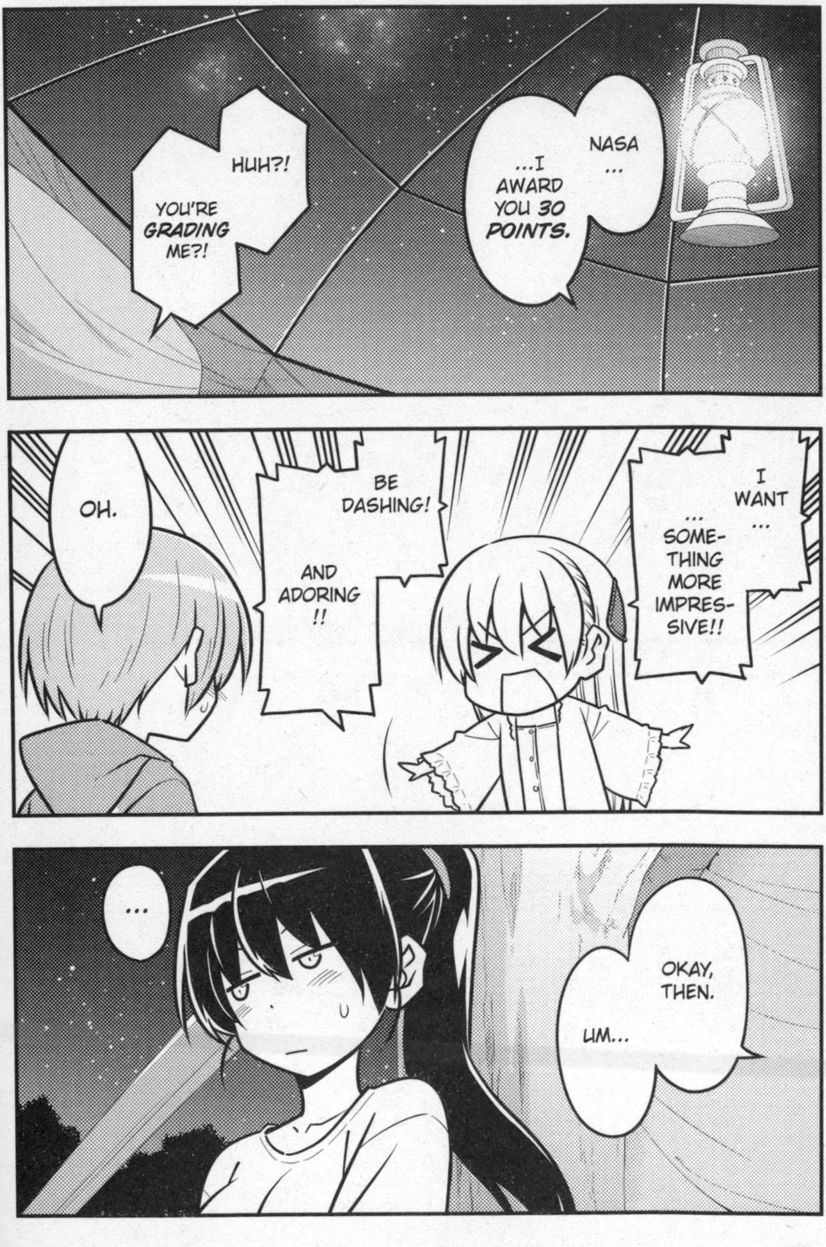
NASA ... ...I AWARD YOU 30 POINTS.
HUH?! YOU'RE GRADING ME?!
I WANT ... ...SOMETHING MORE IMPRESSIVE!!
BE DASHING! AND ADORING!!
OH.
OKAY, THEN. UM...
...

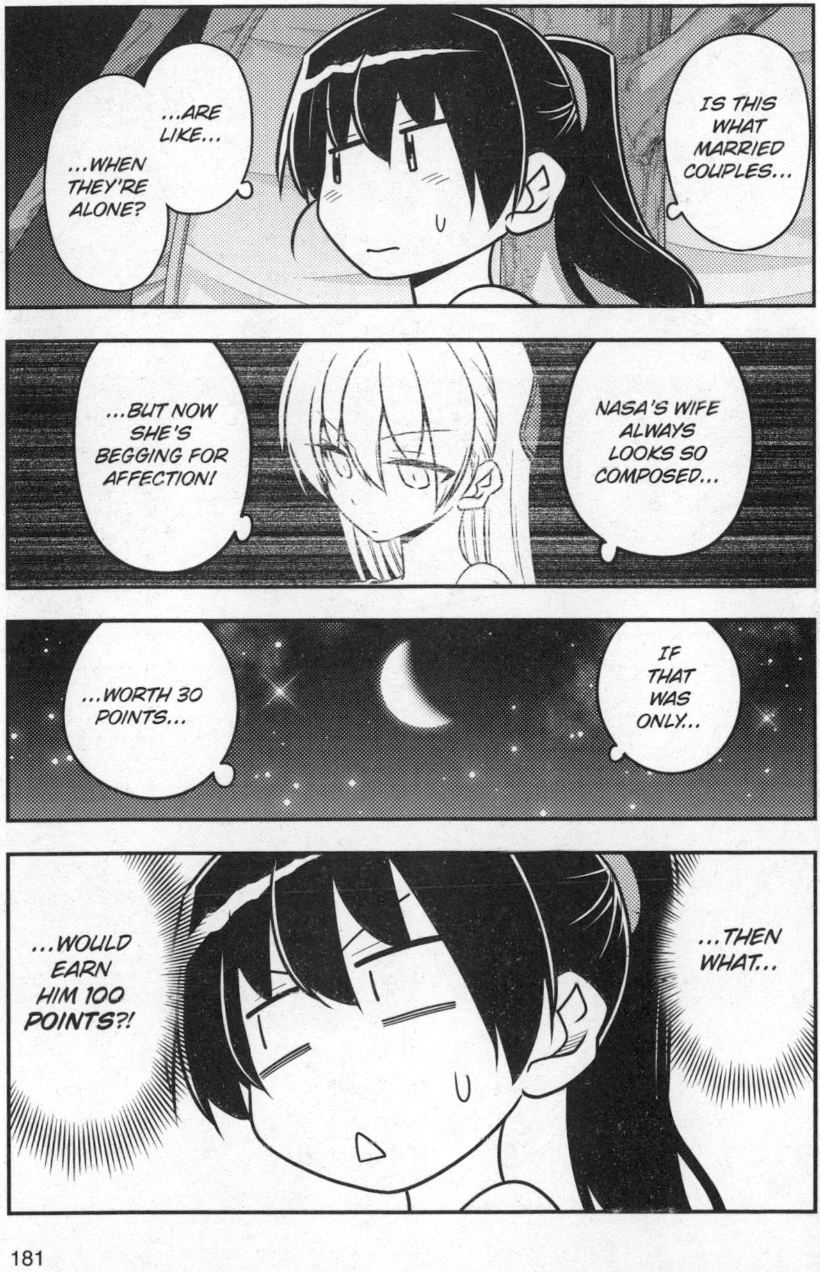
IS THIS WHAT MARRIED COUPLES...
...ARE LIKE...
...WHEN THEY'RE ALONE?
NASA'S WIFE ALWAYS LOOKS SO COMPOSED...
...BUT NOW SHE'S BEGGING FOR AFFECTION!
IF THAT WAS ONLY...
...WORTH 30 POINTS...
...THEN WHAT...
...WOULD EARN HIM 100 POINTS?!

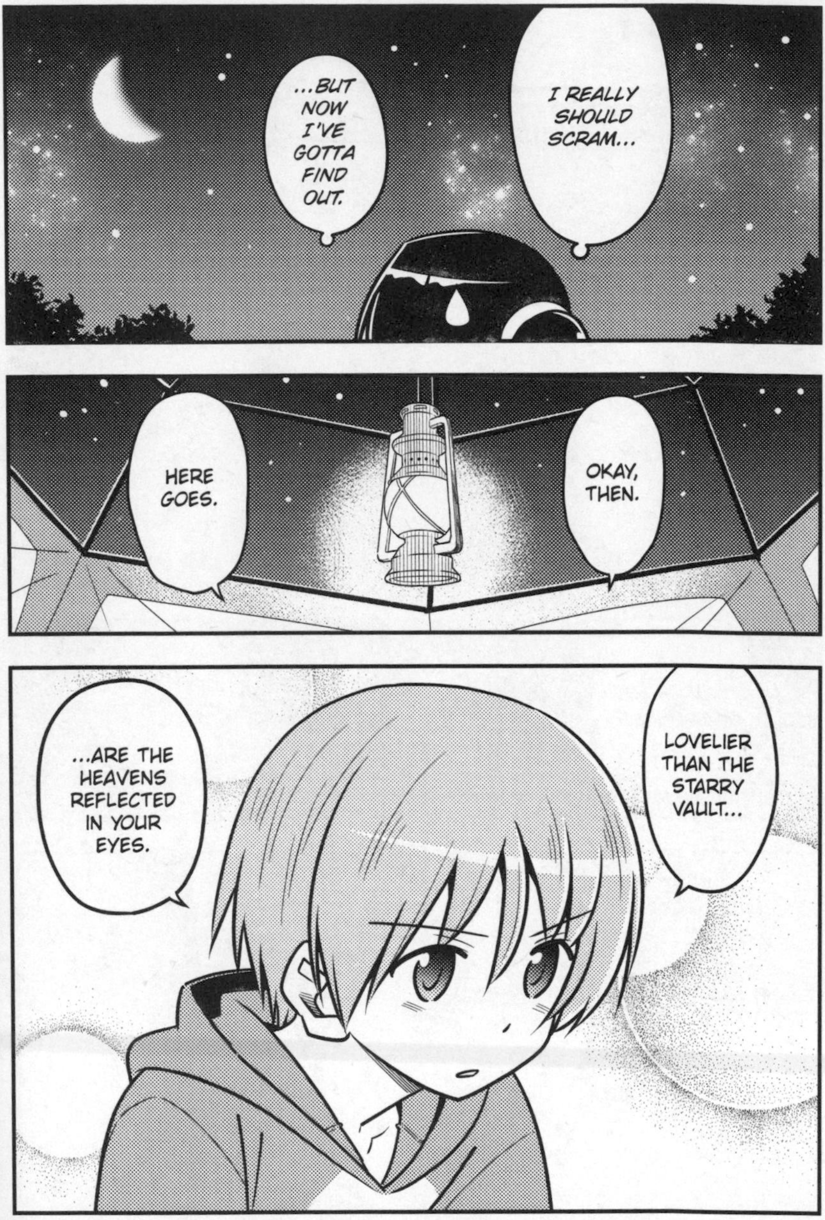
I REALLY SHOULD SCRAM...
...BUT NOW I'VE GOTTA FIND OUT.
OKAY, THEN.
HERE GOES.
LOVELIER THAN THE STARRY VAULT...
...ARE THE HEAVENS REFLECTED IN YOUR EYES.

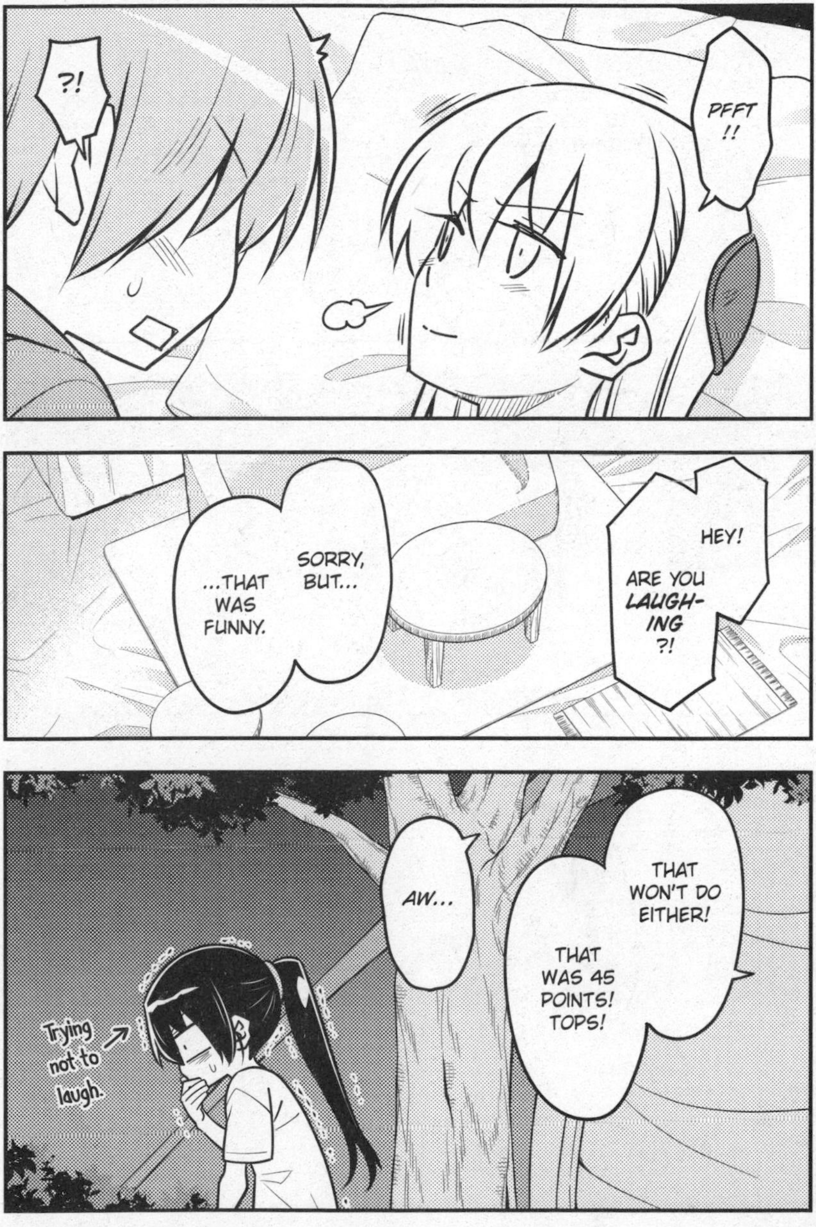
PFFT !!
?!
HEY! ARE YOU LAUGHING ?!
SORRY, BUT... ...THAT WAS FUNNY.
THAT WON'T DO EITHER! THAT WAS 45 POINTS! TOPS!
AW...
Trying not to laugh.

SAY SOME-THING ... ...NATU-RAL.
NATURAL BUT ROMANTIC.
HUH?
OKAY.
I LOVE YOU.
PWIK

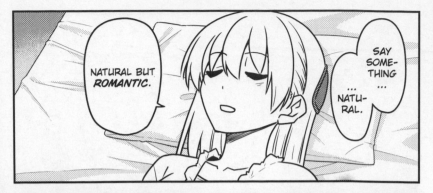

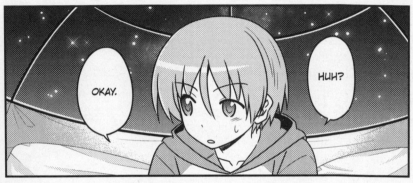

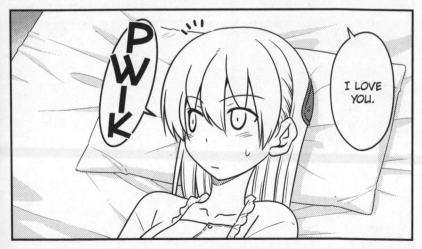

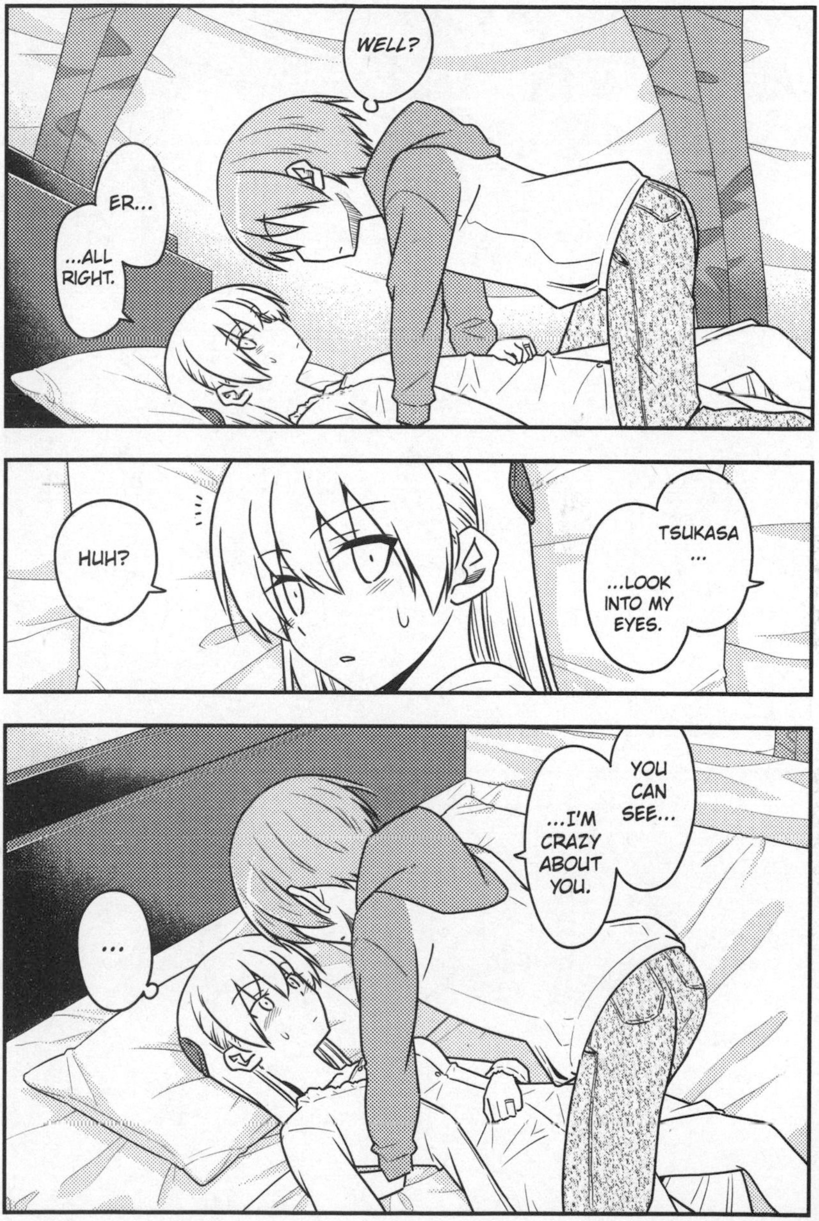
WELL?
ER... ...ALL RIGHT.
TSUKASA... ...LOOK INTO MY EYES.
HUH?
YOU CAN SEE... ...I'M CRAZY ABOUT YOU.
...

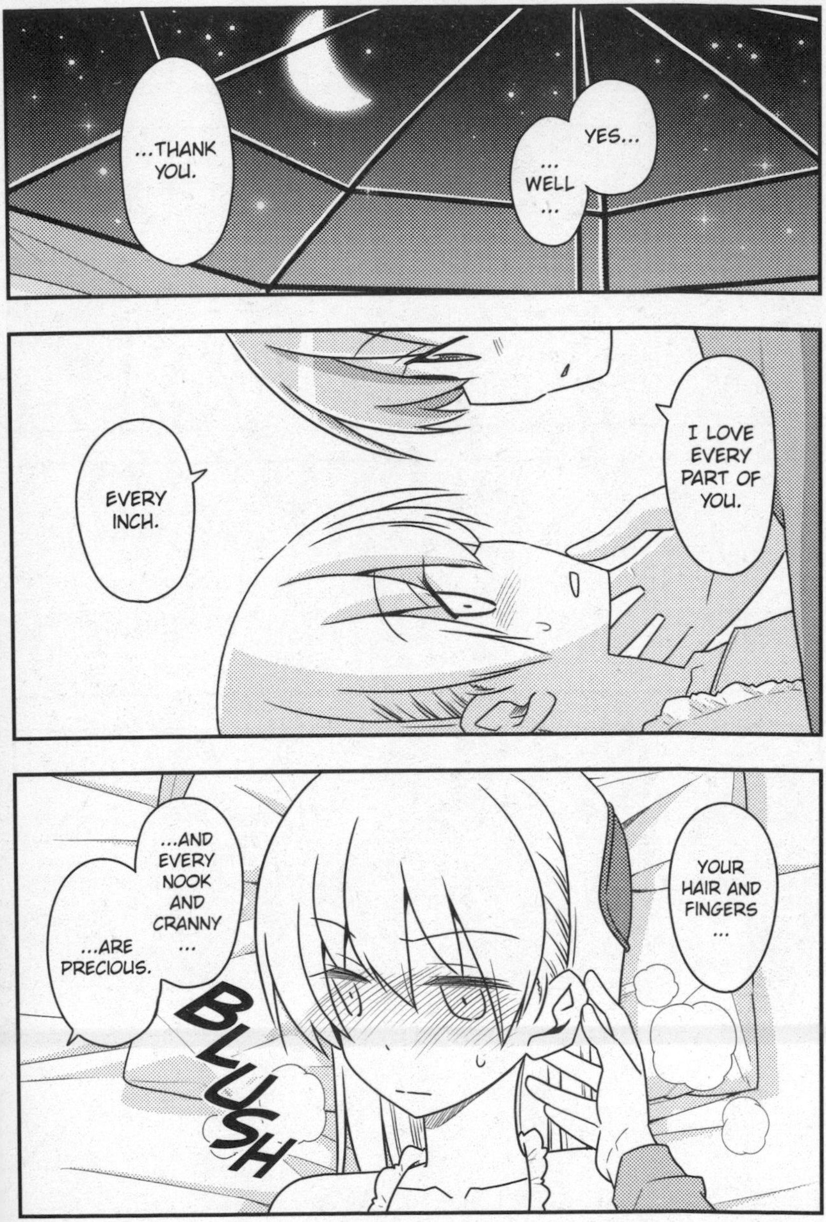
YES...
...
WELL
...
...THANK YOU.
I LOVE EVERY PART OF YOU.
EVERY INCH.
YOUR HAIR AND FINGERS ...
...AND EVERY NOOK AND CRANNY ...
...ARE PRECIOUS.
BLUSH

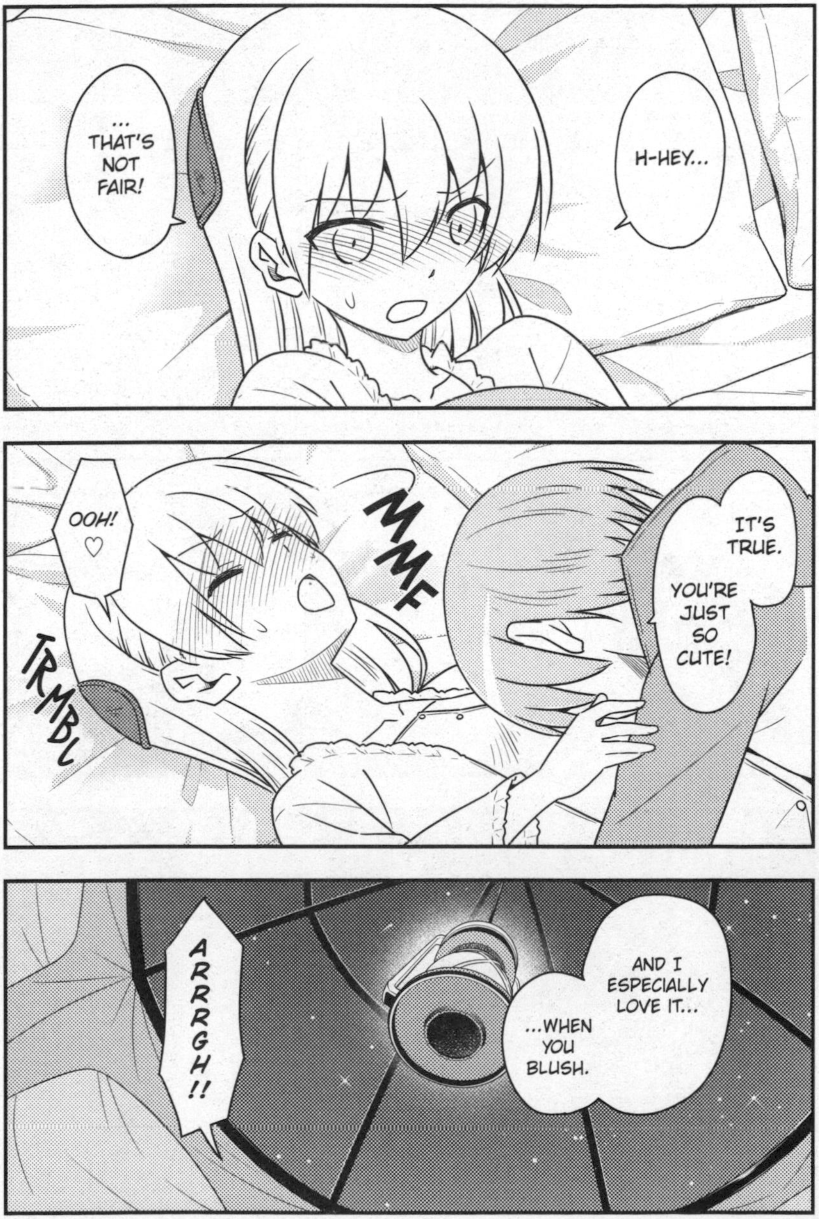
H-HEY...
... THAT'S NOT FAIR!
IT'S TRUE.
YOU'RE JUST SO CUTE!
MMF
OOH! ♡
TRMBL
AND I ESPECIALLY LOVE IT...
...WHEN YOU BLUSH.
ARRRGH!!

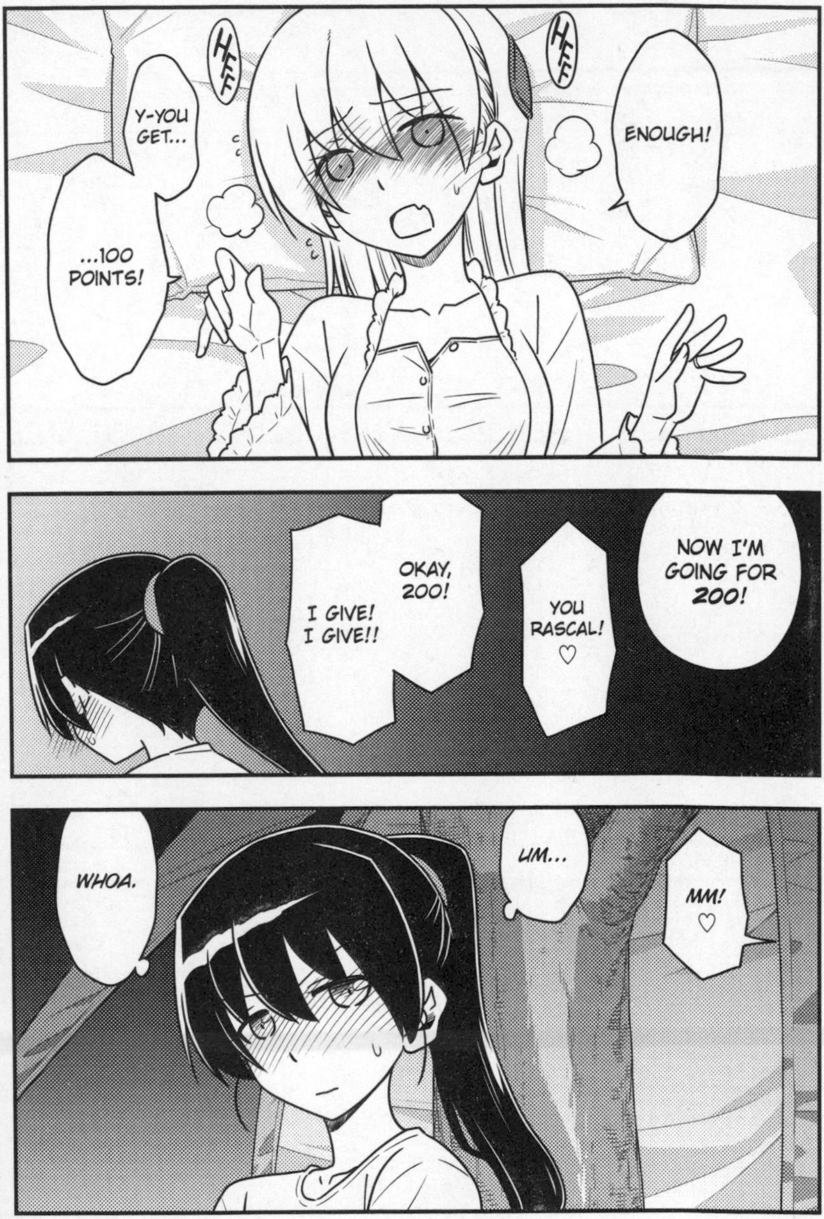
ENOUGH!
HEFF
HEFF
Y-YOU GET...
...100 POINTS!
NOW I'M GOING FOR 200!
YOU RASCAL! ♡
OKAY, 200!
I GIVE! I GIVE!!
MM! ♡
UM...
WHOA.

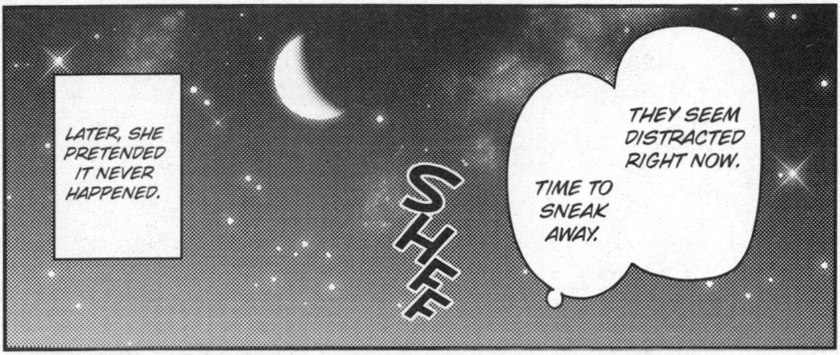
THEY SEEM DISTRACTED RIGHT NOW.
TIME TO SNEAK AWAY.
SHFF
LATER, SHE PRETENDED IT NEVER HAPPENED.

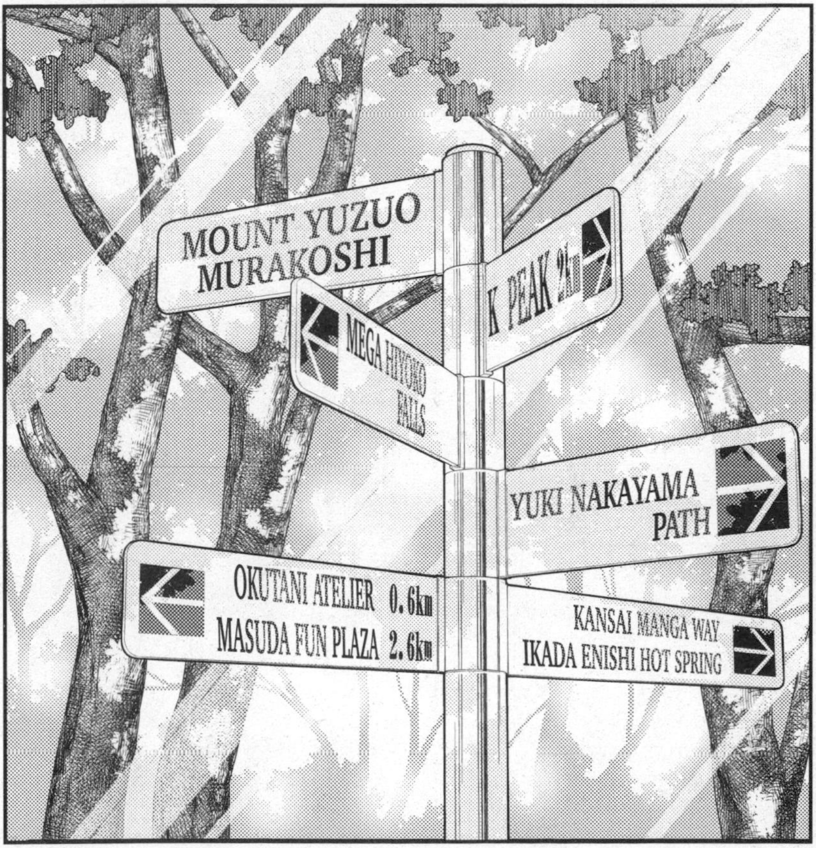
MOUNT YUZUO MURAKOSHI
K PEAK 2km
MEGA HIYOKO FALLS
YUKI NAKAYAMA PATH
OKUTANI ATELIER 0.6km
MASUDA FUN PLAZA 2.6km
KANSAI MANGA WAY
IKADA ENISHI HOT SPRING

Chapter 103 ½ / End

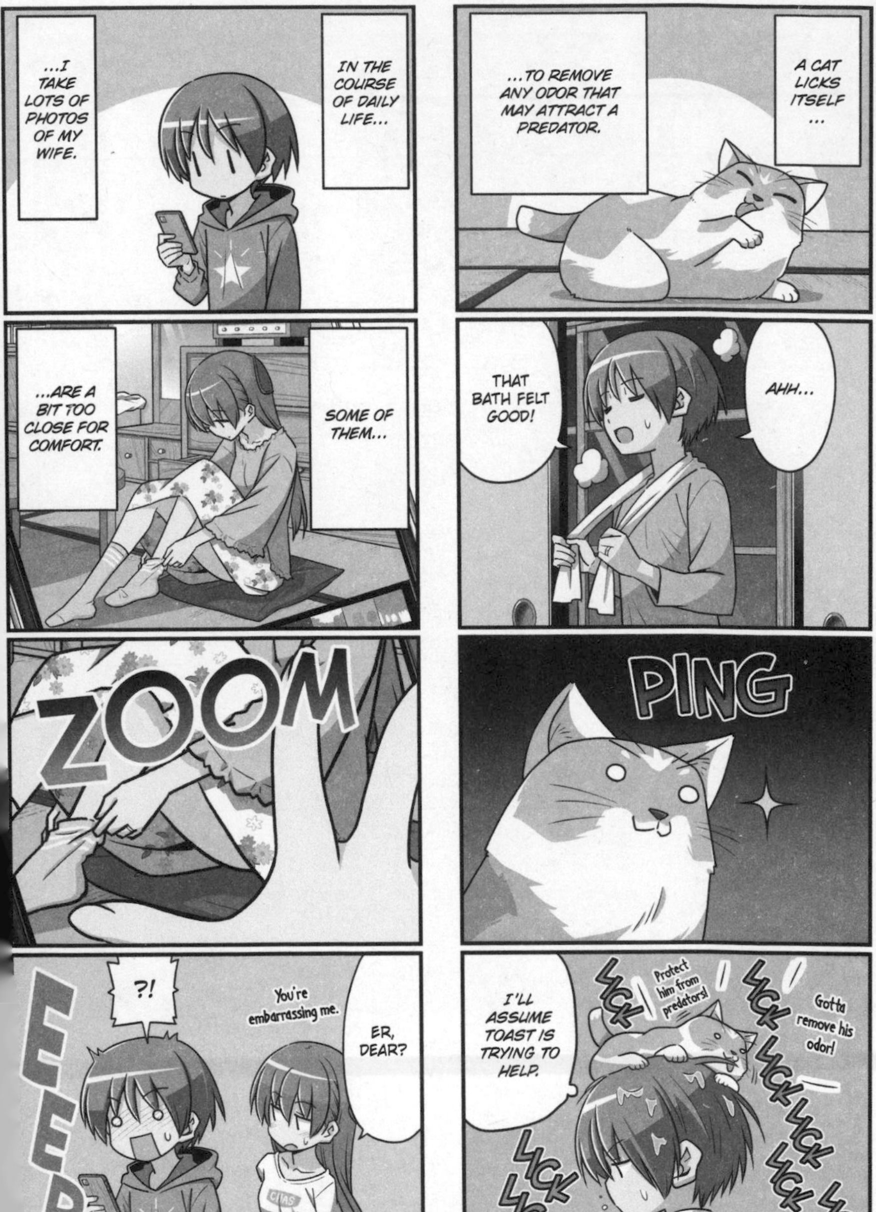
A CAT LICKS ITSELF...
...TO REMOVE ANY ODOR THAT MAY ATTRACT A PREDATOR.
AHH...
THAT BATH FELT GOOD!
PING
Gotta remove his odor!
LICK LICK LICK LICK LICK LICK
Protect him from predators!
LICK
I'LL ASSUME TOAST IS TRYING TO HELP.
LICK LICK LICK
IN THE COURSE OF DAILY LIFE...
...I TAKE LOTS OF PHOTOS OF MY WIFE.
SOME OF THEM...
...ARE A BIT TOO CLOSE FOR COMFORT.
ZOOM
ER, DEAR?
You're embarrassing me.
?!
EEEP

Fly Me to the Moon

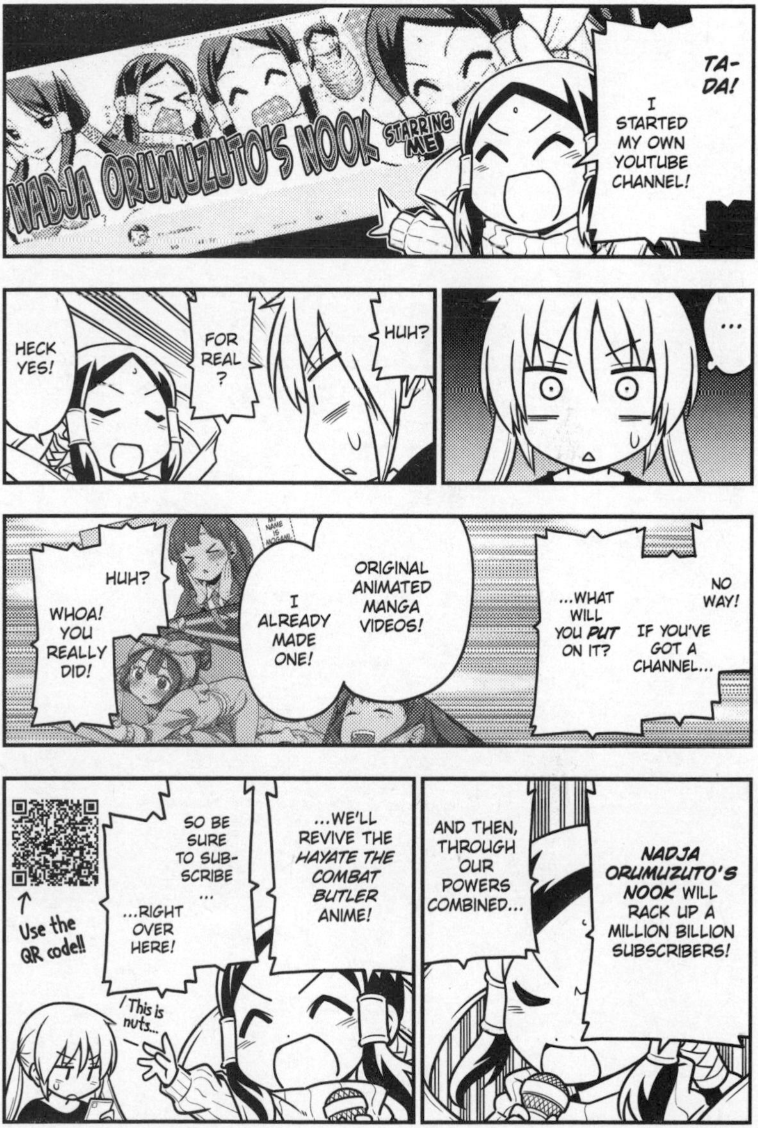
TA-DA!
I STARTED MY OWN YOUTUBE CHANNEL!
STARRING ME
NADJA ORUMUZUTO'S NOOK
…
HUH?
FOR REAL?
HECK YES!
NO WAY! IF YOU'VE GOT A CHANNEL…
…WHAT WILL YOU *PUT* ON IT?
I ALREADY MADE ONE!
ORIGINAL ANIMATED MANGA VIDEOS!
HUH?
WHOA! YOU REALLY DID!
NADJA ORUMUZUTO'S NOOK WILL RACK UP A MILLION BILLION SUBSCRIBERS!
AND THEN, THROUGH OUR POWERS COMBINED…
…WE'LL REVIVE THE *HAYATE THE COMBAT BUTLER* ANIME!
SO BE SURE TO SUBSCRIBE …
…RIGHT OVER HERE!
This is nuts…
Use the QR code!!

Q. What do you do sloppily?

Is there anything I don't do sloppily?

↖ Get yourself together!

Q. 'Tis the season to take vacations! What's your idea of paradise?

Nakano Broadway!

↖ Only Tokyo otaku know about that place.

Q. If you gave yourself a dashing nickname like the Red Comet or the Blue-Eyed Samurai, what would it be?

Princess Bubble!

Outstanding Student!

↑ Not dashing!

↑ Not dashing!

Q. What's your favorite convenience store food?

Dare to try sushi in fried tofu!

↑ Is that really daring?

Q. What's your most vivid travel memory?

Drifting alone across the Pacific.

↖ Say what?!

Q. Who do you think you were in a previous life?

I don't know, but I hope it was Tsubasa Honda.

↖ She's alive now!

I don't know, but probably a horrible sinner.

Q. Heat, cold, super-spicy food... What extreme challenge could you ace?

A sauna!

I rarely lose at anything.

I don't like extreme challenges.

I'm no good at that stuff.

Q. Who's the greatest villain?

Dirk Fact.

↑ Retro ref!

Q. Who's your fave pop idol?

My only idol is my wife.

↖ ...!!!

Q. What do you remember about school exams?

They were too easy to leave much of an impression.

←Are you for real?

Q. What's your culinary specialty?

Black Thunder candy bars!

↑ You just buy those!

Q. What's the farthest you've traveled?

Azteca.

↑ Where's that?

Q. What was your favorite childhood Christmas present?

A Nintendo Switch!

↑ That's too recent!

Q. What hasn't changed over the years?

Video games always rock.

Human life remains fleeting.

My sister's cluelessness.

The Pythagorean theorem.

Q. What was your most memorable gambling experience?

The Lehman shock.

↑ Is that gambling?

Q. What's the best smell in the world?

Yours!

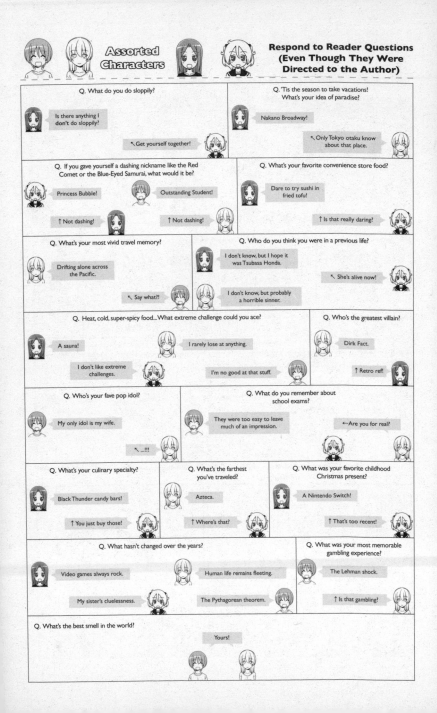

ABOUT THE AUTHOR

Without ever receiving any kind of manga award, Kenjiro Hata's first series, *Umi no Yuusha Lifesavers*, was published in *Shonen Sunday Super*. He followed that up with his smash hit *Hayate the Combat Butler*. *Fly Me to the Moon* began serialization in 2018 in *Weekly Shonen Sunday*.

FLY ME TO THE MOON

VOL. 11

Story and Art by **KENJIRO HATA**

SHONEN SUNDAY EDITION

TONIKAKUKAWAII Vol. 11
by Kenjiro HATA
© 2018 Kenjiro HATA
All rights reserved.
Original Japanese edition published by SHOGAKUKAN.
English translation rights in the United States of America,
Canada, the United Kingdom, Ireland, Australia and New
Zealand arranged with SHOGAKUKAN.

Original Cover Design: Emi Nakano (BANANA GROVE STUDIO)

Translation
John Werry

Touch-Up Art & Lettering
Evan Waldinger

Design
Jimmy Presler

Editor
Shaenon K. Garrity

Printed in the U.S.A.

Published by VIZ Media, LLC
P.O. Box 77010
San Francisco, CA 94107

10 9 8 7 6 5 4 3 2 1
First printing, May 2022

viz.com

shonensunday.com

A hilarious tale of butlers, love and battles!

Hayate the Combat Butler

Story and art by
Kenjiro Hata

Since the tender age of nine, Hayate Ayasaki has busted his behind at various part-time jobs to support his degenerate gambler parents. And how do they repay their son's selfless generosity? By selling his organs to the yakuza to cover their debts! But fate throws Hayate a bone... sort of. Now the butler of a wealthy young lady, Hayate can finally pay back his debts, and it'll only take him 40 years to do it.

SHONEN SUNDAY

Hayate the Combat Butler

Hayate the Combat Butler

Kenjiro Hata

RATED T+ OLDER TEEN

VIZ

HAYATE NO GOTOKU! © 2005 Kenjiro HATA/SHOGAKUKAN

Komi Can't Communicate

Story & Art by Tomohito Oda

The journey to a hundred friends begins with a single conversation.

Socially anxious high school student Shoko Komi's greatest dream is to make some friends, but everyone at school mistakes her crippling social anxiety for cool reserve. With the whole student body keeping its distance and Komi unable to utter a single word, friendship might be forever beyond her reach.

VIZ

Can Detective Conan solve the toughest cases ....while trapped in a kid's body?

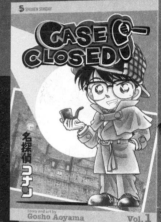

Story and Art by
Gosho Aoyama

High schooler Jimmy Kudo has had many successes in his young detective career. But what will he do when a pair of shady men feed him a poison that turns him into a little kid?

MAO

Exorcise your destiny in an era-spanning supernatural adventure from manga legend Rumiko Takahashi!

Story and Art by
RUMIKO TAKAHASHI

When Nanoka travels back in time to a supernatural early 20th century, she gets recruited by aloof exorcist Mao. What is the thread of fate that connects them? Together, they seek answers...and kick some demon butt along the way!

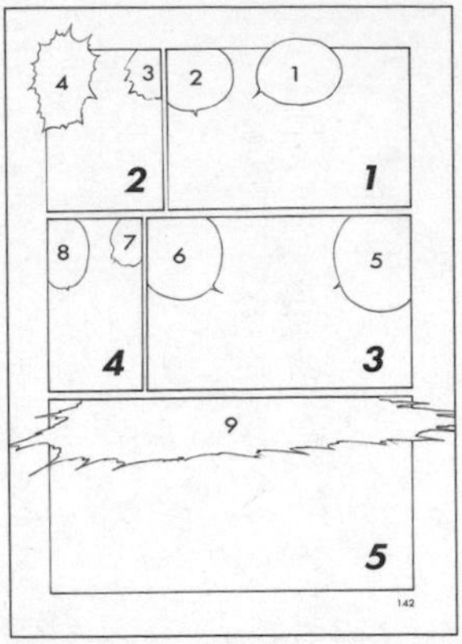

FOLLOW THE ACTION THIS WAY.

Fly Me to the Moon has been printed in the original Japanese format in order to preserve the orientation of the original artwork. Please turn it around and begin reading from right to left.

Unlike English, Japanese is read right to left, so Japanese comics are read in reverse order from the way English comics are typically read. Have fun with it!

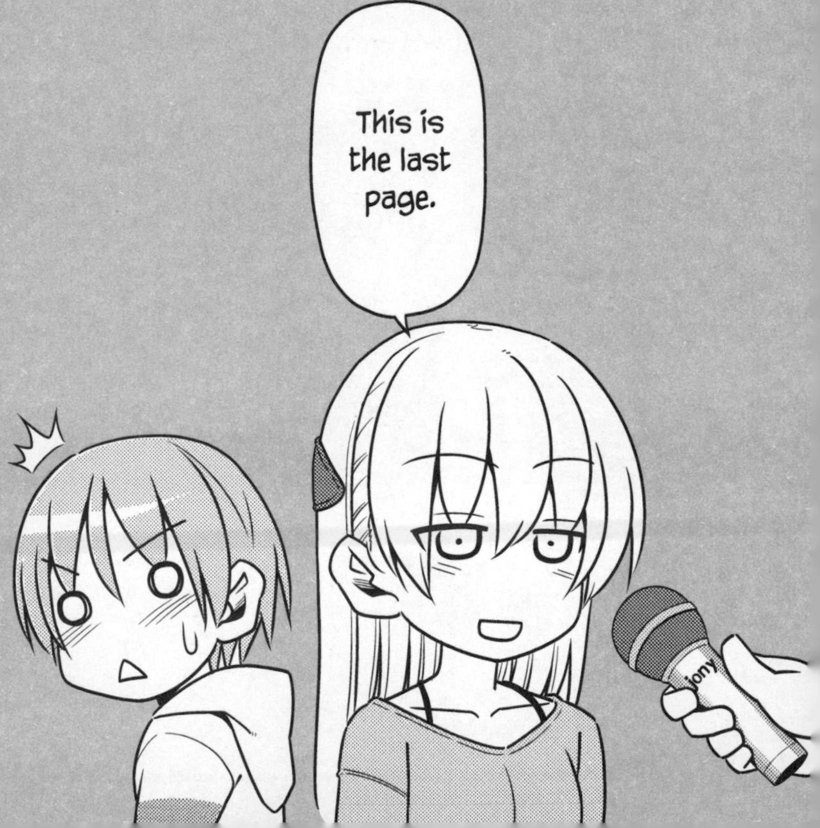

This is the last page.